Subverting Communism in Romania

Subverting Communism in Romania

Law and Private Property, 1945–1965

Mihaela Şerban

LEXINGTON BOOKS
Lanham • Boulder • New York • London

Published by Lexington Books
An imprint of The Rowman & Littlefield Publishing Group, Inc.
4501 Forbes Boulevard, Suite 200, Lanham, Maryland 20706
www.rowman.com

6 Tinworth Street, London SE11 5AL, United Kingdom

British Library Cataloguing in Publication Information Available

Library of Congress Cataloging-in-Publication Data Is Available

ISBN 978-1-4985-9567-4 (cloth)
ISBN 978-1-4985-9568-1 (electronic)

For my mother, Rodica Şerban:
without her love, support, and dedication this
book could not have happened.

Contents

List of Illustrations

Acknowledgments

I have received support and advice throughout the research and writing of this book from institutions, faculty, colleagues, and my family. The book started out as a dissertation project at New York University and was finished while a faculty member at Ramapo College of New Jersey. New York University's Graduate School of Arts and Sciences provided support during the first five years of my doctoral studies and during the writing process of the dissertation through the Dean's Dissertation Fellowship. A National Science Foundation, Law and Social Science Division dissertation improvement grant (#0752404) made possible the lengthy field research. The East European Studies Program of the American Council of Learned Societies awarded me a dissertation writing fellowship that substantially smoothed the writing process. Finally, Ramapo College awarded me faculty development funding in 2012, 2013, and 2015, which allowed me to work on the manuscript.

I am deeply grateful to my dissertation committee for their guidance, patience, and steadfast support. Christine Harrington shaped my sociolegal awareness and steered my interests in questions of power, law, and ideology even before I was sure of them. Her commitment to her advisees and determined focus on critical thinking constitute a model I can only hope to emulate. Sally Merry has been a wonderful mentor and guide into the vagaries of project design and field research. Gently but consistently, she insisted on clarity without sacrificing complexity, a goal I will henceforth always pursue. Frank Upham witnessed my hesitations throughout the years and helped me make crucial decisions regarding my research and professional development. His insightful suggestions over the years spared me many mistakes and wrong turns, and I could not be more grateful that he was always there for me.

Steven Lukes' seminar on power prompted me to start thinking about power and resistance during communism from an interdisciplinary perspective, and to try to unravel the place of law in this dynamic. Katherine Verdery and Gerald Creed graciously allowed me to audit their course on the anthropology of Eastern Europe, which opened up new questions, perspectives, and literatures for my research. Katherine Verdery's work on communism, nationalism, and property in Romania has been enormously influential in shaping my thinking. Mariana Valverde offered valuable suggestions at the very beginning of my research. Her comments shed new light and a new direction for the entire project.

I received constructive comments over the years from many colleagues in different venues, primarily Law and Society Association and other conferences, as well as from journal editors and anonymous reviewers for articles drawn from this book. I am deeply thankful to the community of law and society scholars working on Russia and Central and Eastern Europe, in particular Maria Popova, Alexei Trochev, Matthew Light, Lauren McCarthy, Jaqueline Gehring, Anna Dolidze, Elena Bogdanova, Marley Weiss, Kaja Gadowska, Barbara Havelkova, Marcin Wrobel. I am especially grateful to Peter Solomon, Kathryn Hendley, Kim Lane Scheppele, and my mentor Irena Grudzinska Gross for their feedback, guidance, and support. I have incorporated useful feedback received on articles and conference papers from Nancy Ries, Helen Hartnell, Monica Ciobanu, Liviu Chelcea, Chris Carrigan, Dagmar Soennecken, Austin Sarat, Sangha Padhy, Aaron Lorenz, and Joachim Savelsberg. The anonymous manuscript reviewer of this book also provided very helpful suggestions, which I included in the final version.

This book includes parts from some previously published work, primarily in *Studies in Law, Politics and Society, Special Issue Interdisciplinary Legal Studies: The Next Generation* (2010) (Austin Sarat, editor), *Law & Society Review* (2014), *Europe-Asia Studies* (2015), and *Law & Social Inquiry* (2018). I thank the anonymous reviewers for valuable comments and suggestions.

In Timişoara, I am first and foremost grateful to Mioara Pârvulescu and Marlen Negrescu, who provided invaluable help with my research at the National Archives of Romania. Alexandra Răzvan-Mihalcea, Mihaela Mârşu-Oniţă, and Iulia Nistor helped me become reacquainted with the legal profession and were generous fountains of knowledge regarding property and restitution in the city.

My colleagues in the Law and Society program at NYU—Christine Scott-Hayward, Francesca Laguardia, Umut Turem, Erin Braatz, Gabrielle Clark, as well as Deirdre O'Sullivan, Russell Ferri, Leila Kawar, and Samera Esmeir—read drafts of chapters, gave me detailed and constructive comments, pushed me in new directions and always kept me on my toes. The final result would have been greatly diminished without their help, and their friendship warmed up the long and solitary months of writing at the end.

I owe the greatest debt of gratitude to my family: my mother Rodica Şerban, my sister Camelia Brânzei and her husband Leo Brânzei, my cousin Florian Brata, and in the United States my husband David Rosen and my daughter Sarah. As always, they offered unconditional love and support throughout this very long journey and found my topic almost as fascinating as I did. My mother, to whom I dedicate this book, not only made field research with a three-month old baby possible, but was also willing to relocate during a crucial part of the writing process and help me whenever and however needed. She was an active participant in this project, and I am happy I could share it with her.

Introduction

Law, Power, and Resistance in Early Communist Romania

"Why are so many young voters falling for old socialists?" asked *The New York Times* in June 2017. Part of the answer was that the young generation "came to political consciousness after 1989," so they are not "instinctively freaked out by socialism" (Leonard 2017). It seems that the end of history is finally here, just not quite the way Fukuyama predicted. "Actually living socialism" is elided, a part of history that is simply not relevant to today's youth, captured by promises of socioeconomic justice, such as free education and healthcare.

After half a century of Cold War, this is only somewhat paradoxical. Post-1989, Central and Eastern European countries have been firmly anchored by the triumphalist troika of democracy, neoliberalism, and the rule of law, recent backslides in Hungary or Poland notwithstanding. Communism was an unfortunate, best forgotten detour, or, as the old communist joke went, the longest and the most painful road from capitalism to capitalism. Its legacy had to be corrected and overcome, but the errors of its ways were so obvious, its defeat so complete, that it was best left on the ash heap of history. Academics and nonacademics alike have since focused on understanding and overcoming the challenges of the postcommunist transition (hence the boom of fields such as transitional justice). Historians have benefitted from the opening of the archives across the postcommunist world, but these are still early days for critical histories.

Law is a particularly glaring gap from this perspective. Recent critical legal scholarship from the region notes "the stereotypical picture of Actually existing socialism being merely a 'black hole' or 'blackout' in the legal development in the region," as well as the neglect of the sociolegal study of communist law, albeit for different reasons, in both Eastern European and Western scholarship (Mańko et al. 2016, 12). Sociolegal studies of communist law have been hampered by the hyper positivist legal tradition in the region, the relentless focus on the present and future, and by the implicit belief that they have no value added.

Yet reclaiming the past has valuable lessons to teach us in the here and now, especially in terms of understanding how law can sustain, subvert, or outright resist an authoritarian political system. This is precisely the core of this book: the role of law in everyday life and as a mechanism for social change during early communism, paying special attention to the regime's attempts to extinguish private property and replace it with state property. The key lesson imparted by this empirical sociolegal study of communist law is that law is not there just for the taking. One cannot assume away the history, categories, institutions, and systems of meaning it engendered, and simply use it for whatever purposes the political elite desires. Against American legal realists, law is not just any other tool, and certainly not in the long term. Surprisingly in line with some formalist theories, even communist law enjoyed a certain level of autonomy and consequently was simultaneously a space of state power and resistance to power. Unlike most of the legal scholarship about the region, this study has a solid empirical foundation provided by the newly opened archives in Romania. Also unlike prior studies, the focus is on a mundane, yet crucial part of the human experience everywhere: one's home, and the institution of private property that sustains it.

I grew up in the 1970s and 1980s communist Romania, experiencing the highs of the 1970s—economic prosperity, peace and stability, and the lows of the 1980s—food shortages, cold, and poverty foremost in my memory. All the adults I knew were employed, with one exception: my grandmother. My grandfather worked two, sometimes three jobs so he could afford a stay-at-home wife, and made a point of it: a man's success in life was determined by his ability to keep his wife at home, so she could focus on being a mother and a wife. As a child, this utterly petit bourgeois arrangement somehow did not strike me as unusual. It was only after 1989 that I discovered that my grandfather, a Communist Party official during the 1950s, had used his position to exempt my grandmother from the general work rule. My grandparents bought their house at the end of 1953, a quiet two-bedroom in a shared courtyard that they inhabited for over half a century in downtown Arad. The prior owner, politically astute, apparently decided to sell the house fearing a second wave of housing nationalization. Throughout communism, my grandfather was a diligent and devoted house owner: he built a bathroom from scratch by himself; renovated the kitchen, roof, and attic; painted; and added flooring everywhere.

Understanding actual, lived communism, its lessons, and its relevance for today means acknowledging and understanding these contradictions: on the one hand, my grandfather's sincere Communist Party membership, commitment to equality, the working class, and socialist goals; on the other hand, equally strong held bourgeois values about family structures, private property, the importance of labor, and the family-labor-home nexus. From a *longue durée* perspective, obvious ruptures and discontinuities between pre-communism, communism, and postcommunism seem to obscure deeper continuities of institutions and values, many of them embodied in law, as well as the hybrids created across these regimes. Terminology itself is indicative of these contradictions and a problem not fully resolved a quarter century after the end of the regimes: Is communism, socialism, or "actually living socialism" the correct term? Reaching communism was a work in progress, claimed the Eastern European regimes, and consequently they used "socialist" to describe themselves. "Communism," primarily when referring to the regime writ large, has the advantages of clarity and brevity, yet "socialism" reflects much better the "actually existing" property and legal regimes in the region, including in Romania.

Early postcommunist studies on property hinted at some of these *long durée* continuities. "'It's mine because I worked it' (land) [e al meu că eu l-am slujit]."[1] Upon hearing this comment from an elderly woman, anthropologist Katherine Verdery concluded that Locke was "alive and well in Transylvania" (Verdery 1998, 114). She documented how villagers in Noul Român, in the southern region of Romania, dismantled their collective farm building according to the amount of work each family had put into the farm proportionally, and each family took only the building materials from its section. Labor, ownership, and personhood for them were intimately linked to the physical, material structures of the former collective farm. In Bucharest, anthropologist Liviu Chelcea found that some former owners spoke of their houses as having a soul and personality that died after housing nationalization in 1950 (Chelcea 2004, 14). This conceptualization of houses is suggestive of contemporary theories of property and personhood (e.g., Radin 1996), with roots in Kant's emphasis on the connection between property and agency (Weinrib 2003).

In my hometown, Timişoara, former owners of nationalized houses petitioned the communist regime for the restitution of their homes in the early 1950s using the following language: "please investigate this case and return my house to me . . . return my keys and give me all my rights" (December 8, 1955).[2] This plea reveals a strong property rights consciousness and ideas of rights and justice rooted in an individualistic, "bourgeois," other-than-socialist *nomos* (normative universe) (Cover 1983).

There are hundreds of similar petitions in the archives, but the first time I encountered one, I thought it was a fluke, an unusual occurrence that would not be repeated and that probably did not lead anywhere. I could imagine the official receiving the letter simply throwing it in the garbage and moving on. The well-established story of early communism in Romania, after all, was one of unrelenting power and violence, and resistance to it, such as it was, was physical, armed, and ultimately quashed. Law, and certainly resistance through law, had no place or chance of success. In this narrative, law was simply an instrument of the state, and in particular during the early years, embodied violence and repression. Yet I kept encountering petitions, many of them repeated, some followed up over the years, all of them clearly investigated in significant detail. Some of the petitions were very "legalistic" and typed, while others were hand written in a much simpler style. Who were the lawyers who dared take on such cases in 1950s Romania? Their names did not appear anywhere, but the complaints had an unmistakable lawyerly flavor.

Moreover, the regime amended some of its policies, for example, by trying to clarify the criteria for both takings and restitutions as a result of petitioners' complaints, which was certainly an unexpected outcome. The very existence of the petitions and the official responses to them created a decades-long dialogue between the regime and its citizens about ownership and its role in a socialist system. While clearly unequal, this dialogue cast a different light on the dynamics of law and power in early communism. In the mid-2000s, my interviewees—nationalized former owners, tenants from the communist period, and lawyers—almost without exception and regardless of background, political orientation, or property history, used the terms "mutilated" or "disfigured" when referring to private property during communism.

This suggests continuities of meaning regarding property as labor, personhood, and rights that cut across communist and postcommunist Romania. Locke and Kant are unexpected findings in a country emerging from 50 years of communism, where private property was relentlessly attacked through legal means—expropriation, nationalization, and legal reforms, creating various types of state and collective property. An idea, an institution, a relationship, a right, or an object, property's defining characteristics have been that of "absolute dominion" over physical and immaterial things and as a social, political, and legal institution implemented to resolve particular conflicts in society (Underkuffler 2003, 121; Macpherson 1978, 1). In Eastern Europe, property has been bound up with labor, history, and conceptions of the self in the process of postcommunist redistribution.

The "property question" is one of the two grand narratives of the postcommunist transition to democracy, rule of law, and market economy (the other one is transitional justice; the concept of the "transition" and the subfield of "transitology" itself do not have unblemished records or unquestioned genealogies, as Verdery and Burawoy [1999] point out). Restitution, a component of this grand narrative, aims to reverse processes of expropriation and nationalization undertaken by the former communist governments and restore private property rights or provide compensation for lost property—primarily land and real estate, personal, communal, or religious. Restitution of nationalized or expropriated houses has been particularly acrimonious, as the post-1989 elite has protected tenants' rights against the rights of former owners, contributing to a protracted, painful process (see, for example, Dawidson 2004; *Maria Atanasiu and Others vs. Romania* 2010).

Disputes around restitution and compensation ballooned post-1989: according to the Association of Owners Forcibly Dispossessed by the State (2005), there were around 2 million restitution disputes in courts in 1995. In 2008, the president of the Association estimated that there were 128,000 claims for restitution, and that 1 million former state tenants inhabited the nationalized houses. Of the two, the second estimate seems closer to reality, although they are both very high for a country of approximately 20 million people. Romania made its debut at the European Court of Human Rights (ECHR) with a case on restitution of property (gold coins) in 1998 (Vasilescu vs. Romania),[3] and almost half of all judgments concerning Romania involve property disputes, specifically restitution of private property taken during communism (European Court of Human Rights 2013). Romania lost 435 property restitution cases before the ECHR, and had 3,500 pending cases before the Court in 2013 (Stan 2013; Ponta 2013). By 2017, the number of cases against Romania pending before the Court tripled. Despite the rise of other types of cases involving Romania over time (such as right to a fair trial, and inhuman and degrading treatment), judgments concerning protection of property are still the most numerous (471 out of a total of 1,352 judgments concerning Romania) (European Court of Human Rights 2018).

The centrality of private property post-1989 raises the following question: What impact did 50 years of rejection of private property rights have on property regulation, structure, ideologies, practices, culture, and the legal consciousness of those who lived through communism? How can we explain the hegemony of the concept of private property and private property rights in postcommunism, the "taken for grantedness" of the concept of property as private property post-1989 (Macpherson 1978, 1), exemplified by vicious political and legal struggles around restitution, compensation, and privatization of land and real estate?

This is a book about the survival and remaking of private property in and through law during early communism in Romania, the legal culture of property created during this period, and the kinds of subjectivities engendered. Property law, ideologies, practices, and rights consciousness (how people conceive of and engage with rights) are the sites for examining continuities, changes, and the circulation of ideas about property and property rights during early communism. I focus on the communist regime's attempts to unmake the hegemony of private property, investigate the extent to which law was a mechanism for social change during early communism, and argue that pre-communist ideas of private property survived because of a confluence of factors, including the special nature of houses as homes and assets, the ambiguous role of law as both an instrument of state power and a site of resistance, and the regime's own ambivalence toward houses as objects of private property.

The hybrid nature of communist legality and its plurality, in particular, allowed law to be both an instrument of state oppression and a space for continuity, resistance, and cooptation. I explore the interplay between law as power and law as resistance in the context of private property overall and at its most vulnerable: takings, specifically the taking of homes through nationalization, expropriation, and other legal channels. I thus focus on the property of urban houses during the early transition to communism (1945–1965). I identify the plurality and persistence of some conceptions of property and ownership, the emergence of new ideas about property, how these conceptions were instantiated in everyday practices, related to official laws and policies, offered spaces for resistance to them or simply succumbed, and ultimately the kinds of changes affected in property rights consciousness.

The focus on private property of housing illuminates two broader issues. The first is the nature of communism as a constitutive element of modernity, its emergence, survival, and dynamics, particularly in terms of power and resistance. The second is the role of law in this type of modern society, specifically in terms of constituting hegemonies and counter-hegemonies and understanding these processes in their interaction from the regulatory, institutional level through practices and their operation in everyday life. Law always matters, even under conditions of deep repression, so the more important question addressed here is exactly how does law matter under early communism, and what are the consequences for postcommunism? Obviously, answering this question also contributes to studies of law in other nondemocratic societies.

I find that despite widespread takings, state policies aiming to eradicate "private property over means of production" were nevertheless inconsistent and incoherent, which in turn allowed for the retention of pre-communist ideas of property. My key (surprising) finding was the extent of resistance to takings, urban housing nationalization in particular, during the 1950s and 1960s, primarily through petitions contesting them and asking for restitution. The petitions and the administrative responses to them reveal the extent and type of resistance, the modalities chosen—law, and their impact. They are not easily identified as open attacks on the regime and arguably they are not even resistance to the regime as much as acts of cooptation. Nonetheless, they played a part in keeping alive debates about the role of private property in communism, primarily in a space ostensibly colonized by the state: law. The petitions redefine the nature of power and resistance in early communism and the role of law in sustaining domination and providing spaces for resistance in a system that attempted to redefine the nature of power and law themselves.

From a longer historical perspective, one can trace the hegemonic quality of private property rights in postcommunism back to a plural legal and ideological condition throughout communism, equally informed by the official state socialist legality, pre-communist ("bourgeois") theories of property, the natural law ideology that was at the basis of the dissidents' criticism of the communist system (which also drew from Western theorists), or Western-derived, pre-neoliberal concepts of property (the latter argued by Bockman and Eyal [2002]). This is ultimately an inquiry into what Hann refers to as "the interaction between local models and higher levels of legal and ideological regulation" (2000, 2). I focus on the period between 1945 and 1965 because this was the most active period in terms of efforts to unsettle the hegemony of private property, and because this is the period that shows most clearly continuities with pre-communism. Ultimately, we can see how changing property regimes under communism surprisingly undermined the goals of the system, and the unexpected continuities and synergies between the property stories of pre-communism, communism, and ultimately postcommunism.

MODERNITY AND COMMUNISM IN ROMANIA

An externally imposed economic, political, ideological, social, and cultural system, early Romanian communism can be best understood as an alternative project of modernity that defined itself in contradistinction to capitalist democracy while selectively building on its past. The modern Romania is a composite of three main historical regions—Transylvania, Wallachia, and Moldavia, and a number of smaller regions, such as Banat (the site of this research), Dobrogea, and Bucovina (see Figure 0.1).

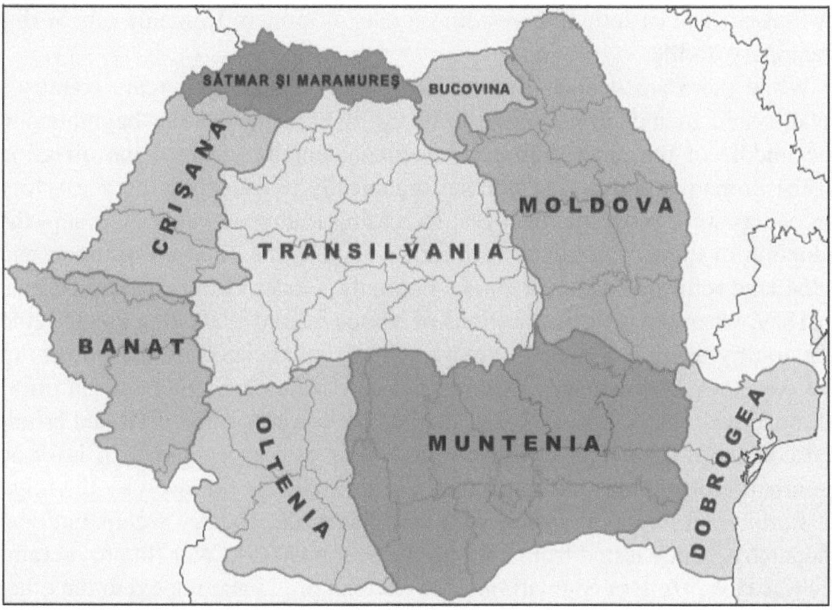

Figure 0.1. Map of Romania. Timişoara Is the Westernmost Largest City, Closer to Budapest, Belgrade, and Vienna than to Bucharest. Courtesy of Andrein (*Source*: https://commons.wikimedia.org/wiki/File:Romania_historic_regions.svg).

Pre-communist Romanian history and its complicated relationship to modernity is therefore also divided among the historical regions of the country, as there were at least two separate histories up to a point—1918. In 1859, Wallachia and Moldavia joined to become Romania (gaining its independence from the Ottoman Empire in 1877), while Transylvania and Banat became part of Romania at the end of the First World War. From a modernization perspective, the latter regions mirror more closely Western developments and perceptions.

Since at least the eighteenth century, the "mental map" of Europe has been constructed and divided between a "civilized" Western Europe and a "backward" Eastern Europe (see Wolff 1994). Studies of Eastern Europe in this vein commonly define it as a transitional zone geographically, culturally, and institutionally, forever caught between Western Europe, Russia, and the Ottoman legacy. Countries like Romania have been "viewed" and have come to internalize a perspective of "backwardness" when compared to Western Europe in political, social, and economic terms (Schöpflin 1990; Chirot 1989). Contemporary developments such as the creation of rule of law monitoring mechanisms just for Romania (and Bulgaria) upon becoming European Union members are simply the latest variation in this narrative, signaling yet again widespread skepticism about Romania's ability to reach modernity. Separately but within the same paradigm, Huntington (1996) used religion to draw the fault line between Eastern and Western civilization in Europe. The eastern and western regions of modern Romania mirror this imaginary divide.

While there are debates among Romanian scholars about the country's relationship to modernity, there is broad agreement that the beginning to the middle of the nineteenth century fundamentally changed the direction of the Romanian provinces, whether organically or following the West. Key propellers were economic changes, increasing European integration, and the adoption of modern political institutions, such as the 1866 constitution and 1864 land reform (Chiribucă 2004). Formally, modern Romania was formed in 1859, when the historical regions of Moldavia and Wallachia entered into a union by using a stratagem not very much appreciated by the powers of the day: they both elected Alexandru Ioan Cuza as their ruler. In an effort to modernize the new state, Cuza adopted the country's first civil and criminal codes (the former in force until 2011), as well as a number of laws on agrarian reform. Short but impactful, Cuza's rule was followed by the reign of Carol I, an import monarch who established the country's constitutional monarchy, which lasted from 1866 to the Second World War (the royal family was Hohenzollern-Sigmaringen, of German origin and related to the other European royal houses).

Politically, despite the adoption of a new, modern constitution in 1866 based on the 1831 Belgian constitution (Banciu 1996, 33–39), which incorporated key aspects of liberal constitutionalism such as separation of powers and individual rights, the reality was rather different. As Chiribucă notes, individual rights and liberties really benefitted the elite, while the majority of the population (rural) could only "contemplate" them. Political participation in particular was limited by a very restrictive electoral system that effectively shut out 80 percent of the population (2004, 86). Political gates for the vast majority of the country (excluding women) opened only in 1918 with the introduction of the universal vote.

More difficult from a modernization perspective was the country's economic underdevelopment. Romania remained overwhelmingly an agrarian-based economy, and not a particularly profitable one, either. The structure of land ownership was decidedly not capitalist—almost half of all land was divided into great estates of over 100 hectares, while small landowners (less than 10 hectares) were about 41 percent of the population (Constantiniu 2002, 236–37). Economically, the transition to modernity capitalized on a feudal agricultural system, a type of "agricultural capitalism" (Chiribucă 2004, 77). Despite a number of land reforms, there were no structural changes and feudal relations persisted well into the twentieth century. In one of the earliest works of Romanian sociology, the socialist thinker Constantin Dobrogeanu-Gherea dubbed this "neo-serfdom" (1910), a variation on themes earlier developed by both Engels (1882) and Lenin (1907).

Although manufacturing and industrialization spiked in the years leading up to the First World War, three-quarters of the country's main exports were agricultural products in the years prior to the war (including lumber, oil, and gas) (Constantiniu 2002, 236–37). At the beginning of the twentieth century, only about 13 percent of Romania's population worked in industrial occupations, three times less than France or Germany at the time, while about 80 percent of the country's population worked in agriculture, the most in Europe at the time (Chiribucă 2004, 76–80).

Opposition to capitalism and modernization came from multiple fronts, converged regarding key aspects, carried over to the interwar period, and originated from both political left and right. This opposition encompassed the creation of the myth of the peasant and rejection of cities and their culture (in movements such as Sămănătorism and Poporanism), deep seated anti-Semitism and xenophobia, and the peculiar "forme fără fond" theory (forms without substance). "Forme fără fond" was a deeply influential intellectual and political critique of Romania's modernization process, in particular of formally and superficially adopting Western-style institutions, such as capitalist liberal constitution and statutes, while maintaining the Romanian "substance," such as a traditional agrarian system (key authors included Mihail Kogălniceanu, Titu Maiorescu, Mihai Eminescu, and the Junimist school).

By contrast, for centuries Transylvania and Banat were part of the Hungarian Kingdom, the Ottoman Empire, and lastly the Habsburg and Austro-Hungarian empires. From a modernization perspective, the turning point for Banat was becoming an autonomous region directly under the administration of the Crown (a province of Austria), following the Turkish loss of Banat and the Treaty of Passarowitz in 1718. In 1778, the Temescher Banat (the Banat of Timişoara) became part of Hungary, but it reverted to being an autonomous region under the direct supervision of the Habsburg crown after the 1848–1849 revolutions. Following the 1867 Austro-Hungarian compromise and the establishment of the dual monarchy, Banat became again part of Hungary until 1918. Unlike Moldavia and Wallachia, Transylvania and especially Banat were pluralistic from an ethnic, linguistic, and religious perspective (and more than either Hungary or Austria) (Neumann 2015). If the population of Romania between 1859 and 1918 was overwhelmingly ethnic Romanian (more than 90 percent based on the 1899 census), the population of Banat was significantly more diverse around the same time: almost 40 percent ethnic Romanians, about a quarter Germans, 12 percent Hungarians, and about 17 percent Serbs and Croats (Gräf 2018, 28).

Modernization processes in both Transylvania and Banat were deeply tied to the industrial, commercial, agricultural, and bureaucratic reforms initiated in the eighteenth century by Empress Maria Theresa and continued by Emperor Joseph II. This state-led development targeted agriculture (introduction of modern methods, crops, forestry, etc.), the mining and metallurgic industries, transportation (including railways), the elimination of serfdom, as well as urban development, particularly visible in the development of Timişoara and other cities (Gräf 2018, 28; Munteanu and Munteanu 2002). Over the course of the nineteenth century Banat became an increasingly industrial and commercial region, benefitting from German and Hungarian capital. By the turn of the century, its main city, Timişoara, had seen the establishment of major industrial and commercial enterprises and banks, coupled with a burgeoning educational and cultural life anchored by a solid middle class (Munteanu and Munteanu 2002).

The First World War slowed down considerably modernization efforts in all regions of Romania. The addition of Transylvania, Banat, Bukovina, and Bessarabia to Romania at the end of the war raised difficult political, economic, and social challenges for the much-enlarged and significantly more diverse country. Post-1918, modernization and nation building became intertwined efforts, and Greater Romania focused on three major reforms:

universal male suffrage, land reform, and integration of its new minorities, with a particular sticking point the emancipation of the Jewish minority (an accomplished task in former Austro-Hungary and therefore its former provinces, but not pre-1918 Romania) (Livezeanu 1995, 12). Formally, the country was a constitutional monarchy, with the monarch retaining significant powers, such as the right to dissolve parliament, yet the various scandals surrounding Carol II and the vacillation of the political parties created political and constitutional instability. The introduction of universal suffrage was a giant step toward democratic modernization, but the combination of high rates of illiteracy (both formal, almost 40 percent of the population in 1930, and functional) and the specificities of the electoral system (the new government organized parliamentary elections, not the other way around) fundamentally undermined the creation and functioning of a true democratic, participatory system (Chiribucă 2004, 85–92).

Power and decision-making resided in reality in the triumvirate monarchy—the two main political parties, which were mostly center and center-right (on a traditional liberal to conservative political scale). The most important ones were the National Liberal Party and the National Peasant Party, and later the Romanian version of fascism, The Iron Guard (Garda de Fier). The Social Democratic Party on the left also had some presence, but the Communist Party was insignificant: the most common estimates are between 800 and 1,100 members by the end of the Second World War (Opriş 2005).

The 1918–1921 land reform redistributed land significantly, arguably eliminating the grand landowners and their estates: small holdings increased from 52 percent to 89 percent of arable land, while large holdings decreased from 47 percent to 10 percent (Constantiniu 2002, 301). However, without other reforms, the land reform achieved little as most land continued to be cultivated manually, using traditional methods. At the beginning of the Second World War, only about 5–6 percent of the land was mechanically cultivated (Chiribucă 2004, 79).

Romania did make tremendous social and economic progress in the interwar period, although it did not catch up with more industrialized countries. Major industries that developed very quickly included oil, gas, and metallurgy. Cities flourished, and the absorption of the modern western regions of Transylvania and Banat certainly helped, although not without creating some resentment as Bucharest's control over local industry and commerce magnified (Munteanu and Munteanu 2002, 265). Nonetheless, Romania remained a predominantly agrarian economy, where only 7 percent of the population worked in industry, and 3 percent in commerce (Constantiniu 2002, 301). The 1930 census indicates that 80 percent of the population was rural, and almost three-quarters worked the land.

Finally, easily one of the most difficult tasks facing the new Romanian state post-1918 was actual unification and the incorporation of large new minorities in the context of nation-state building, long-standing anti-Semitism, and weaker elites post-land reform. According to the 1930 census, there were 71 percent ethnic Romanians, 8 percent Hungarians, 4 percent Germans, 4 percent Jewish, and various other smaller minorities in the country. The bulk of the new minorities lived in the new provinces (Transylvania, Bukovina, Bessarabia, etc.), and were more urban (only 58 percent of the urban population was Romanian, even less in Transylvania, 34 percent), more schooled, and more modern than the Romanians (Livezeanu 1995, 7–12). While Romanians in Moldavia and Wallachia were overwhelmingly Orthodox, 40 percent of Romanians from Transylvania and Banat belonged to the Uniate (Greek Catholic) Church, while the Germans and Hungarians were either Catholic, Lutheran, Reformed, or Unitarian (Livezeanu 1995, 135).

Nation-state building was an intentional, state-led project that centered "the peasant" as the symbol of the new nation, deployed education and culture as key instruments of state building (in large part as a direct response to pre-1918 intensive Magyarization efforts in both Transylvania and Banat), and was defined by struggles between urban and rural, Romanian and foreigner, new and old elites. These categories overlapped with socioeconomic and class statuses that overall distinguished German, Hungarian, and Jewish urban elites from more rural, lower class, historically marginalized Romanians. Nation-state building was further complicated by a fragmented and unstable political landscape, including the continued regionalization of the main political parties themselves and the hegemony of the Liberal Party in the 1920s, which was unpopular in the new provinces (Livezeanu 1995, 11–25).

These endogenous dynamics worked in lockstep with broader European developments, and while the country moved toward the political right, it remained fairly stable. Unsurprisingly, the interwar period therefore witnessed the rise of populist nationalism and extreme nationalism among university students (later giving rise to the Iron Guard), anti-urbanism, anti-Semitism, and general xenophobia (Livezeanu 1996; Clark 2015). Equal rights for minorities, as Irina Livezeanu notes, were seen as "illegitimate, alien grafts" (Livezeanu 1995, 7–8), in part because of the Allies' insistence during the Paris peace negotiations that Romania respected the Minorities Treaties, including the emancipation of its Jewish inhabitants. The latter had been a sore point for Romania since at least the 1878 Berlin Congress, which recognized Romania's independence from the Ottoman Empire but required it to consider all its citizens equal under the law and to fully protect their religious liberty (Woodward 1920; Livezeanu 1995; MacMillan 2002).

Despite (finally!) the recognition of equal rights for all Romanian citizens in the 1923 constitution, widespread anti-Semitism across the political, ideological, and cultural spectrum became the rule, rather than the exception, during the 1920s and 1930s.

In 1938 King Carol II assumed dictatorial control of the country, and Romania regressed from a constitutional monarchy and liberal democratic capitalist system to an absolutist monarchy and fascist-style authoritarianism under a succession of right-wing, anti-Semitic regimes that targeted Romania's Jewish citizens, deprived them of their property and livelihoods, and ultimately their lives. During the Second World War, Romania was a German ally under the leadership of General Antonescu. The transition from authoritarianism to communism began on August 23, 1944, when Romania broke ranks with the Axis Powers and joined the Allies.

This is, very broadly outlined, the situation of Romania at the beginning of the communist transition. Very much a work in progress from a modern nation-state perspective, it was a country of stark contrasts and inequality, struggling to overcome a legacy of uneven development and narratives of "backwardness." As a mostly agrarian society, it lacked key modernization constituencies, such as a strong middle class, and it had a relatively small "bourgeoisie" in the classic sense because it had relatively little commerce and industry (this explains why property takings, such as nationalization and land expropriations, turned predatory toward the working class and poor peasants—there simply weren't enough exploiters available). However, the country did have a relatively large and professional bureaucratic apparatus, soon to be severely disrupted.

August 23, 1944, marks the beginning of the transition from fascist authoritarianism to communism. The political transition, under Soviet control, was relatively gradual, although expropriations started as early as 1945. It began with the capture of three state departments (ministries), including justice, in November 1944, followed by measures of transitional justice and purges (1945–1948 mostly), massively fraudulent elections in 1946 and 1948 that ensured the victory of the Romanian Workers' Party (the predecessor of the Romanian Communist Party), the elimination or absorption of remaining political parties (1945–1948), and finally at the end of 1947 the abdication of King Michael and the proclamation of the Popular Republic of Romania. The 1948 constitution, drafted based on the model of the 1936 Stalinist constitution, sealed the deal (see, generally, Ionescu-Gură 2005; Denize and Mâţă 2005). This political takeover was complemented by the takeover of the economy through massive nationalizations, as well as extensive imprisonment, torture, and executions of those who opposed or were thought to oppose them.

Ideologically, Marxism-Leninism became the official truth of the regime and its principal way of "imagining the real" (Geertz). Its main components were "historical materialism" and "dialectical materialism." Together with political economy and scientific socialism, they constitute the official ideology in Romania during the period studied. A 1962 Romanian high school textbook, for example, described Marxism-Leninism as the "science of the most general laws of development of societies," where class struggle and revolution are at the core of social change, of replacing one mode of production with a more advanced one. "Dialectics" was explained as the philosophical method of looking at the world as a unity where objects and processes influence each other, condition each other, and change as a result of internal struggles between contradictory features (p. 19).

As a political and ideological project, communism laid claim to scientificity and having discovered the "objective laws of history" (Boia 2005; Brunner 1982, 29), and thus promised industrialization, urbanism, equality, objectivism, universalism, and rationality, while rejecting individualism, pluralism, and capitalism (implicitly also feudalism and the agrarian structure that had been integral to Romania up to that point, see generally Verdery and Kligman 2011). The core phenomenon of communism in this understanding is that a group of political actors strives to replace the value system, structures of knowledge, standards of normality, and structural patterns of a society with completely different ones in a relatively short period of time (Patzelt 1998, 243–47). There are three key elements in this reality-reshaping enterprise: ideology, concentrated violence, and mechanisms of impersonal power. The "reality construction" approach to communism underscores both the destructive and the constructive facets of communism in modernity ("power to" and "power over," Lukes 2005), and its essential components, in particular the ones that are usually less emphasized: redefining interests (Lukes 2005), constructing socialist subjects (a type of pastoral state), as well as mechanisms of impersonal power (Foucault 2000).

Institutionally, the communist project relied upon the uneasy relationship between the Communist Party and the state, where the latter was understood to be an instrument in the hands of the working class for constructing socialism. The state, as explained by a leading Romanian theorist of the time, thus had the following functions: to repress exploiter classes, to organize and lead the socialist economy, to undertake cultural-educational work, to defend socialist property, and to defend against imperialist attacks (Ceterchi 1958, 972). The concentration of state power at the top, yet unevenly, and the duplication of the state—party apparatus, however, led to functional breakdowns and internal conflicts (vertically and horizontally, at all levels). As Katherine Verdery observed, there was chronic malfunction in the system, and myriad ways that it was "constantly undermined by internal resistance and hidden forms of sabotage *at all system levels*" (1996, 19–30; 1991, 74–83).[4]

Other failures were primarily the result of ideological breaches—symbols and practices—from prior or alternative visions of modernity. Although Marxism-Leninism had ideological monopoly, it did not become hegemonic. Its partial failure to penetrate popular mentality (Markus 1982, 87) and the relative diversity of interpretations at different times and in various national contexts accentuates both the extent to which the Marxist-Leninist grid managed to organize reality and claim precedence, yet not hegemony, among ideologies, and the spaces for resistance it created. For Eastern European states such as Romania, communism represented an episodic project of modernity, aiming toward a finished product—the complete, self-referential, modern nation-state (Rofel 1999, 11, 29).

Yet other imaginaries of modernity persisted and new ones were constantly created. For Romania, in particular, nationalism was the main alternative discourse, continued from the interwar period and promoted by communism, yet never fully congruent with it (Verdery 1991; Tismăneanu 2003). The half-century of communism, apparently bracketed by the end of the Second World War and 1989, is thus traversed by overlapping projects of modernity, some promoted by the state—nationalism, some advanced from civil society—human rights, yet others persisting from prior times—nationalism and capitalism. The actual, imagined, desired, and assumed modernities define the canvass of directionality and temporality of Eastern European communism, its ideology and actualities, ultimately interfering with its dominant narrative—the communist project. These competing imaginaries of modernity can also be seen as long-term effects of other, prior "third dimensions" of power (Lukes 2005), and are important as resources for resistance against the regime.

One example of successful communist reality construction is equality as a guiding principle of modern life, a value that well outlasted communism. The communist rejection of individualism, pluralism, and tradition, on the other hand, created ideological spaces for resistance. Private property as a traditional symbol of individualism and liberty is a prime example of this failure. In the case of property, communist reality destruction and reconstruction meant, first, denaturalizing ideas about private property as the building block of society and the most desirable lifelong goal for individuals. The second step was to normalize socialist property—both state and cooperative. The first step required eliminating or incapacitating private property owners, hence the massive nationalizations and expropriations of the early 1950s. It also required the elimination of the concept and practices of private property in law, economy, and society, in effect creating a new consciousness and subjectivity of ownership. None of these projects succeeded and none proceeded smoothly and without opposition.

POWER AND RESISTANCE IN COMMUNIST ROMANIA

Totalitarian models of communist power neatly separate the initial capture of power, characterized by terror, from later, more stable and institutional phases, alternatively described as high, post, semi, mature, or late totalitarianism (e.g., Linz 2000; Linz and Stepan 1995; Thompson 1998). Yet terror and normalization were not separate, sequential steps in Romania, but happened in lockstep. Having learned from the Soviet Union, the Romanian regime constructed early systems of surveillance, record-keeping, reward, and punishment for the Party and society (Walder 1994, 299–300).

The late 1940s and early 1950s in Romania were gripped both by terror and the hope that communism was only a temporary state of affairs and the Americans would "come and save us," even though for many workers and peasants, political and economic doors were also opening. Terror, however, served both short-term and long-term purposes. Over time, past uses of active power by political regimes can build up to accumulations of longer-term and quite efficient inactive power (Lukes 2005, 78). Time ensures that self-censorship is internalized, and moreover that victims become contributors to the system. From a path dependent perspective, the passage of time helps us understand how positive feedback processes can lead from open and relatively even conflict (the revolutionary situation and terror), to a system in which power relations become so uneven that anticipated reactions and ideological manipulation make open political conflict almost impossible (Pierson 2000, 77).

Václav Havel once somberly remarked that "[a]ll of us are responsible, each to a different degree, for keeping the totalitarian machine running. None of us is merely a victim of it, because all of us helped to create it together" (1990). The pervasiveness of power in communism and the extent of the collaboration are indicators neither of regime legitimacy, nor of possibilities, types and depth of resistance to it. Understanding the lives of communist regimes and their ultimate downfall, as well as the role of law in this story, depends upon unraveling the intertwining of power, legitimacy, and resistance in communism, where legitimacy both measures and binds power and resistance, and neither power nor legitimacy and resistance are monolithic concepts, even during early, highly repressive communism.

There was no single basis of legitimacy for this system of power, but rather a continuum of legitimacy based on multiple grounds, including ideology, fear, economic performance/goal achievement, paternalism, familiarity, charisma, and nationalism, which varied at different periods throughout the regime's life (Markus 1982; Rigby 1982, 2–12; Wrong 1988, 85–113; Heller 1982; White 1986, 463). The highest level of regime acceptance, not coincidentally, was low on ideology and repression and high on material achievements (late 1960s to early 1970s). In other words, the less obvious the power, the more successful the reshaping of reality and the higher the legitimacy of the regime.

In Romania, this continuum of legitimacy had its peaks—1968 and the refusal to join the Soviet invasion of Czechoslovakia is the most evident—and its valleys—the 1980s, which saw the deterioration of life, the failures of promises of equality and justice, and sporadic revolts, such as the 1987 Braşov workers uprising. The rapid pace of changes, particularly in the 1950s and 1960s, were meant to gain legitimacy by showing the concrete achievements of socialism, to silence critics and resisters, and to make it more difficult to reverse time. Not surprisingly, therefore, news media of the time, including law journals, reproduced and separately underlined the achievements of the regime. The most commonly mentioned were literacy, construction, eliminating exploitation, and truly democratizing the political, social, cultural, and economic systems, for example, by reforming the justice system and through nationalization (e.g., Editor 1952, 452–54).

Communist power was utopian, ideological, voluntaristic, and teleological, yet never quite total, despite its reach. Most times, it was uneven, fragmentary, and inconsistent (Pile 1997, 2). The complex nature of communist power has direct implications for understanding resistance to communism and the relationship between power and resistance in early communism. Resistance is not just an excrescence of power and structure, because then its significance lies only in the success of its collective mobilization and opposition. Rather, openings for resistance derive from the regular exercise of power drawing upon the symbols, practices, statuses, and privileges that have become habitual in social structures (Ewick and Silbey 2003, 1330–34). Resistance is a mode of power wherein power relations are diagnosed, endured, challenged, and sometimes changed (see Pile 1997). While resistance is not necessarily twin to power, "where there is power, there is resistance and yet, or rather consequently, this resistance is never in a position of exteriority in relation to power" (Foucault 1978, 95). In the case of communist regimes, particularly during their first two decades, power needed resistance, power created resistance in order to reaffirm and cement itself (Gough 2008, 18). The categorization and creation of internal enemies that needed to be eliminated, such as housing exploiters, is one example of this strategy.

The spectrum of resistance runs from oppositional action to, arguably, a mere state of being that may not even be recognized as oppositional by either the actors or their intended targets (see Hollander and Einwohner 2004).

Resistance is more often an interactional, complex socially constructed phenomenon that is rarely "pure" or stable and is often contradictory, embodying fragmented identities and interests (Mittelman and Chin 2005). Communist regimes are one of the clearest examples of how individuals may simultaneously resist and sustain structures of domination, how a single activity may be both resistance and accommodation (Hollander and Einwohner 2004, 549–50), and how those who resist are embedded in the system they contest (Leblanc 1999). Armed resistance in the Romanian mountains exemplifies overt, radical, violent resistance against the new regime, aiming to overthrow it, based on a variety of alternative discourses (nationalism, liberalism, fascism, democracy, etc.).

While armed resistance did not succeed, and Romania, unlike other Eastern European countries, did not have a recognizable mass uprising moment, there was enormous variety on the spectrum of resistance to communism, from strikes to peasant revolts to intellectuals' speaking out (Radosav 2006, 82–107). In Timişoara, for example, the main site for this research, newspapers continuously published articles denouncing the communists until they were closed down, and students mobilized and demonstrated throughout 1945 and 1946. Student demonstrations were attacked by red brigades, and students, but not their attackers, were arrested on public disturbance charges. Very common throughout the region and city were the distribution of anti-communist, pro-royal pamphlets: a 1950 handwritten pamphlet, for example, proclaimed that "Communists sold the country to the Russians" (Russian troops occupied the city for 14 years after the end of the Second World War) (Munteanu and Munteanu 2002, 117–20).

The most visible types of resistance against the regime were resistance against collectivization and guerrilla fighting. The latter type was specific to Romania and took place mostly in the mountain areas, drawing inspiration from a long history of guerilla resistance against invaders such as Turks and Tatars. Armed resistance became especially strong after 1947 and persisted until the beginning of the 1960s; apparently, the last partisan was killed in the Banat mountains in 1962 (Deletant in Courtois 1997, 744, French version). These partisan groups, as they were known, belonged to very diverse political orientations and were united only to the extent that they all opposed the new regime. A 1951 Securitate (internal police) document, for example, describes the following distribution of the 800 partisans recently arrested: 88 had been members of the right National Peasant Party, 73 were former Iron Guard members, 79 had been members of the proto-communist Plugari Front (Petru Groza), and 42 had been members of the Communist Party itself (Cioroianu 2005, 309). In Banat and the Timiş-Torontal county, seventeen partisan groups were active, all with different motivations for resistance: economic, political-ideological, religious, and traditional (Radosav 2006, 89–92).

Most of these are clear examples of resistance against the regime, where the actors intended for the oppositional action to be recognized as such by the regime. By the end of the 1960s these types of open resistance disappeared. As the regime tightened its grip, refined its strategies of domination in response to resistance and its legitimacy increased, open defiance became much less of an option. Yet the fast demise of the regime and shifts in its legitimacy cannot be understood if we assume that the lack of open defiance meant lack of resistance (Scott 1985).

Resistance itself shifted and took other shapes, and the petitions and lawsuits against the taking of homes are an example of this different type of resistance. They showcase both resistance to the regime, yet also how individuals accommodated to it, and how strategies of power and resistance are intertwined. The regime responded violently to violent resistance, and peacefully to the petitions. If the petitions are understood as acts of micro-resistance belonging to a broader type of "infra-politics of resistance" (Scott 1990), their value and impact need to be analyzed differently from acts of overt opposition. Micro-resistance, just like impersonal power, adds up over time, especially if legitimacy wavers and core demands are not met. Micro-resistance reinforces divergent ideologies and ambivalence toward the official power regime, while engaging with it and thus accommodating to it.

The focus of this book is precisely these acts of micro-resistance against specific aspects of the regime, intended as such but nonetheless engaging with the regime, recognized as resistance by the regime but not necessarily punished, precisely because they can be simultaneous acts of cooptation as well. The worry from the regime's perspective, as in the case of property and law, is the underlying competing/alternative ideologies motivating the micro-resistance, and the recognition that these acts of micro-resistance are not meaningless or pointless.

From the perspective of the most astute members of the regime, of course, there was no such thing as minor resistance, as they correctly perceived that the success of communism depended upon a single, unitary vision that owed little to alternative interpretations or ideologies. What was at stake was the meaning of ideology itself, the content of Marxism-Leninism in two areas: property and law. Because this was a struggle of meanings and values, it cut across (communist) party lines, and it simultaneously made possible resistance and strained the posited unity of party, state, and people. While many of the agents engaged in it did not necessarily recognize it as resistance, central ideologues did. This explains the recurrent demands, for example, for fighting bourgeois ideas in law, for fighting cosmopolitanism in law, as well as calls for genuinely Marxist legal theories (e.g., Nedelschi 1949, 731).

Neither power nor legitimacy and resistance are monolithic concepts, even during highly repressive periods. As a quintessentially modern form of power, communism aimed to reconstruct reality based on ideology, repression, concentration of power, and reconstructing subjectivities. The exercise of power usually provides openings for resistance, and their co-dependence meant that not only power was "everywhere," but in a sense so was resistance. Law—norms, practices, and ideology—fits in this particular interface between power and resistance.

TIMIŞOARA, ROMANIA

Timişoara is the largest and historically the most prominent city of the Banat region in Romania, at the western tip of the country, bordering Hungary and Serbia. The historical Banat region is larger, and includes the Serbian Banat, which holds a significant Romanian minority population in Serbia (see Figure 0.2). The region was one of the more contentious issues during the

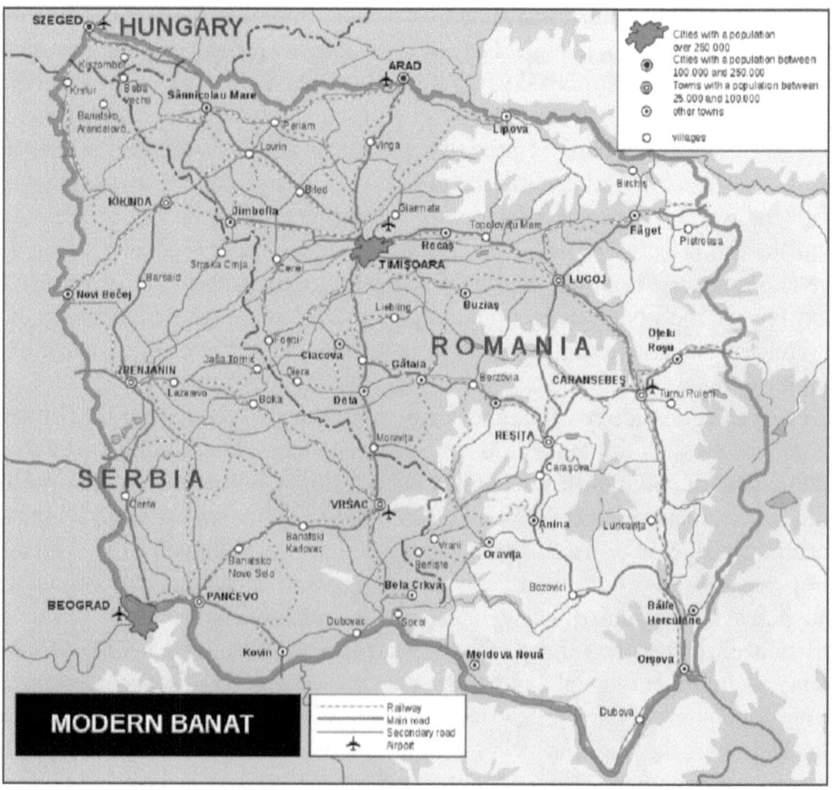

Figure 0.2. Map of the Banat Region. Courtesy of Andrei Nacu (*Source*: https://commons.wikimedia.org/wiki/File:Banat_map.svg).

1919 Paris Peace Conference, and ended up divided between Romania, the Kingdom of Serbia, Croatia and Slovenia, and Hungary in 1919, at the end of the First World War. Banat is sometimes considered part of Transylvania, although the two regions have been distinct historically.

Timişoara's history dates to Roman times. The first record of the city under its current name is from the twelfth century. Throughout medieval times and modernity, the city has been successively ruled by the Hungarian Kingdom (the city was its capital for a while in the fourteenth century), the Ottoman Empire, the Habsburgs (who rebuild it entirely in the eighteenth century and set it on its modern path of development), Hungary (itself part of the Austro-Hungarian empire), and finally Romania after the end of the First World War. Timişoara was also the starting point of the 1989 Revolution against the communist regime.

The composition of Timişoara's population has always been in flux and extremely diverse (between the wars it was nicknamed the "Switzerland of the East"). According to the city's official history, initial settlers included Serbs, Hungarians, and Romanians. The Ottoman Empire brought Muslims who developed its commerce and crafts (although many of them left once the Habsburgs conquered the city). The movement of peoples within the Ottoman Empire brought in other nationalities, such as Bulgarians, Serbs, and Jews. The Austrian conquest opened up massive waves of German colonization in the eighteenth and nineteenth centuries (a first wave had occurred much earlier, during medieval times), with the German population reaching almost half of the city's population in the early nineteenth century. By mid-nineteenth century, the main ethnic groups included Germans and Hungarians (Catholics), Romanians and Serbs (Orthodox), and the Jewish community, living in relatively mixed neighborhoods. The 1930 census noted that Timişoara had 91,866 inhabitants and was the seventh biggest city in Romania. Its population was 26 percent Romanians, 30 percent Hungarians, 30 percent Germans, and 8 percent Jewish. Importantly, these are not necessarily fixed or single identities, but rather a complex ethnic and religious mix "in an area where the whole notion of national identity was as slippery as the Danube eels" (MacMillan 2002, 132).

Timişoara is the seat of the Timiş county, which changed boundaries during the communist regime a number of times. The Timiş-Torontal county (judeţ) was one of two counties of this historical region that was allotted to Romania at the end of the First World War. It formally existed until 1950. The communist project of reconstructing reality also targeted space—thus the new regime introduced in 1950 a new system for the geographical and administrative organization of the country, based on the Soviet model of *raion* as the new links between townships and regions. Before 1950, the country was divided into 58 counties [judeţe], while afterward into 28 regions (until

1968). Below regions there were cities, raions (158 of them), and townships [comune]. In 1952 the number of regions was reduced to 18 (Denize and Mâţă 2005, 60–61). The region was formally called Timişoara and it slowly expanded between 1952 and 1960 to incorporate raions at the south—from Caraş-Severin, and north, from Arad. Its name was changed to Banat region in 1960. In 1968, Romania reverted to its traditional organization of counties (*judeţe*). Most of the matters related to takings happened at three levels: town/city (municipal), regional, and central.

At the beginning of the period studied (1945), the county's population hovered around 600,000, about half of whom were Romanian, a sixth Germans, and an eighth Hungarians (Munteanu and Munteanu 2002, 150). By 1964, the regional administration claimed that its population almost doubled, reaching 1.2 million.[5] Similarly to other Transylvanian cities, Timişoara's ethnic diversity changed for the worst throughout the communist period. The 1999 census noted a population of 320,000, out of which over 80 percent were Romanians, less than 10 percent Hungarians, 4 percent Germans, and negligible numbers of Serbs, Bulgarians, Jews, and Roma.

Architecturally, the oldest surviving buildings in the city date to the beginning of the eighteenth century, giving it the feel of a Baroque city. Most of the medieval castle and buildings prior to 1716 have not survived. The first major growth spurt for the city happened between 1315 and 1323, when King Carol Robert d'Anjou set court here and built a castle. The castle was rebuilt in the sixteenth century, as well as after the 1849 events, in the romantic style. Parts of the castle survive to this day. In the second part of the seventeenth century, houses were built of adobe and covered with wood shingles, and the streets were paved with wood. Governor Claude Fremaut de Mercy fortified the city during that period, as well. The city was almost entirely rebuilt in 1725, when all the buildings were demolished and rebuilt in order to allow for a new, rectangular system of streets and a modern canalization system. By 1733, a significant part of the city walls were made of brick. Union Square also dates from this period (see Figure 0.3).

Most of the construction projects were designed and built locally, and architects were also often trained locally. The city's construction agency dates to 1776 (www.timisoara.ro). Also as early as 1776 the city had an Architectural Office, which supervised all new constructions and renovations. New constructions and renovations had to observe the city's urban planning rules in terms of location, construction materials, destination of buildings, and deadlines. In the eighteenth century, Banat was a border region for the Austro-Hungarian empire and the city one of its prime fortifications. However, as its economic importance grew, the focus on defense slowly changed and entire districts were demolished and rebuilt. The oldest district, Cetate (Citadel), was the administrative center, which included the German and

Figure 0.3. Piaţa Unirii (Union Square)—One of the Oldest Parts of the City. Courtesy of Turbojet (*Source*: https://commons.wikimedia.org/wiki/File:Timisoara,_Piata_Unirii,_flancul_sudic.jpg).

Romanian administration, Catholic and Orthodox churches, schools, hospitals, barracks, and inns. As the city's importance as an industrial center grew during the nineteenth century, the old fortifications became an impediment and were demolished between 1890 and 1910. The city was one of the first in Europe to introduce modern conveniences, as its official website points out: the telegraph in 1855, street lights (gas) in 1857, horse-drawn trams in 1869, telephone in 1881, and in 1884 Timişoara became the first European city to introduce electricity in public spaces. The elimination of the old city walls prompted local architects to propose a new city plan at the beginning of the twentieth century, based on a number of avenues crossing the city from east to west and connecting Cetate with the exterior districts. After Timişoara became part of Romania, new buildings were built in the Byzantine, neo-Romanian, and Cubist styles.

It is not only the ethnic and architectural diversity that sets Timişoara apart from most other Romanian cities. Being subject to successive colonial rulers also brought multiple legal systems: Hungarian, Habsburg, Austro-Hungarian, various influences from the West, primarily through the Napoleonic Code, and much later Soviet laws. The Germans who moved into the city in the past two centuries, for example, obtained their property, and the legal titles accompanying them, under the Habsburg and Hungarian systems, while twentieth-century migrants had to negotiate between the "personal" real estate registration system used in Moldavia and Wallachia and the "real" registration system used in Transylvania (*Cartea Funciară*, also known as the CF). Concepts of property, property rights and legality in the city are consequently to be understood within this background of imperial legacies that define its history, from the Habsburgs to the Soviets.

LAW AND PROPERTY IN PRE-COMMUNIST ROMANIA

Romania broadly belongs to the civil law tradition, although different substrands of it were present in different historical regions (Napoleonic vs. Germanic). A key commonality, however, was an instrumental understanding of law as a tool of modernity and social progress. For the modern rulers of all provinces and Romania overall, Ehrlich's "living law" was an obstacle to be overcome through codification: to codify was fundamentally to become modern.

In 1864, a commission of experts appointed by the first Domnitor (prince) of the United Principalities of Wallachia and Moldavia, Alexandru Ioan Cuza, took 7 weeks to draft the new civil code, the anchor of the Romanian civil law system. They literally translated many of the articles of the Napoleonic Code, occasionally also drawing from the Italian civil code (a more updated version of the French Code), and Belgian law (Hamangiu et al. 2002 ed., Vol I, 22–23).

The authors of the most influential and widely used civil law treatise of the Romanian interwar period (also known as the Hamangiu Treatise)—Hamangiu, Rosetti-Bălănescu, and Băicoianu—thought that the French civil code, and by implication the Romanian one, was fundamentally moderate, "neither revolutionary, nor reactionary, but rather an oeuvre of balance and harmonization" (Hamangiu et al. 2002 ed., Vol I, 24). Hamangiu, the lead author, was at different times a Supreme Court judge and for a brief period the Minister of Justice. All the authors had trained in the French legal system, and two of them had received their doctorates in law in Paris. The treatise itself, published in 1928, reflected the French as much as the Romanian legal doctrine and jurisprudence of the time, and while written for a legal audience, it had primarily a utilitarian, rather than a purely academic purpose (the most recent edition was published in 2002).

Article 480 of the Romanian civil code defined property as "the right of someone to enjoy and dispose of a thing [lucru] exclusively and absolutely, but within the limits set by law." Ownership was the pinnacle of all property rights, since it provided full power over a thing through *usus*, *fructus*, and *abusus*, while all other property rights included only one or two of these attributes, but never all three (they were thus "dismemberments" of ownership, lesser rights) (Hamangiu et al. 2002 ed., Vol. II, 2–3).

Pre-communist Romanian jurists, like their civil and common law counterparts, stressed exclusivity as an essential feature of property and painted the following picture of ownership: the owner was the sole person who could use and dispose of his property and all others had to "respect his power," which included using, disposing of, abandoning, or even destroying the object owned. This is quite an absolute conception of ownership, little domesticated by ideas about social responsibility or property as a web of relationships (however, not unlike Western property theorists of the time, Romanian scholars believed that private property had an increasingly social character). As Hamangiu and his coauthors themselves acknowledged, this was a "purely individualist," even "anti-social" concept of property. Finally, for them private property was perpetual: alienation of property conveyed it without extinguishing it, so the right of property itself was an abstract entity, independent of the title holder. Ultimately, Hamangiu et al. defined property as "the right over a thing that gives the title holder the exclusive and perpetual capacity to use, enjoy and dispose of it" (Vol. II, 3–4).

This was a quintessentially "bourgeois" understanding of property: property was supreme, absolute, and exclusive, and its limitations were exceptional and temporary, amending without fundamentally changing the property paradigm itself. Private property in this form was explicitly linked to its Roman predecessor, praised for its "simple, practical and modern" character, while common forms of property and medieval ones—particularly eminent domain and rights of concession—were portrayed as more primitive. In this narrative of property, the French Revolution had "set free" the cumbersome medieval system of property; private modern property became a simple, absolute, and exclusive right; various privileges and uses were abolished; limitations were accepted only for superior public interest (never private); and its two key features were individualism and exclusivity (Hamangiu et al. 2002 ed., Vol. II, 4–6).

Hamangiu and his colleagues, unlike common-law doctrinaires and in the best positivist sociological tradition, discounted the importance of finding a moral basis or legitimacy for private property. Neither law (Montesquieu) nor possession, time, occupation, or labor provided enough legitimacy. Rather, they argued, private property had always existed, in all times and for all people, it was a natural fact, which proved that its roots were in the organic structure of humanity; it has changed, but never disappeared, and it never would, because it was a civilizing force at the basis of private initiative (Hamangiu et al. 2002, Vol. II, 7–8).

Not surprisingly, the one-time Minister of Justice Hamangiu took a dim view of socialist property, which he considered inferior to private property and comparable to medieval law. He warned against too many changes in the structure of property, against excessive restrictions and takings that would fundamentally change the paradigm, while nonetheless worrying about large inequalities in the distribution of property and issues of social justice.

Legally, ideologically, and institutionally, property in pre-communist Romania was an unexceptional capitalist example, closely resembling its Western European models. It drew inspiration from the Roman conception of property as a unitary notion of ownership and power relationship that was all-embracing as it represented not just the complete form of power over a thing, but also a relationship that absorbed all aspects and interests with respect to the *res* (good) (Samuel 1999, 40–41). As the mother right, it was at the center of pre-communist civil law relationships and obligations, set the standard, defined the civil law universe, and embodied property ideologies of individualism, personhood, and power.

This fairly absolutist conception of property was the context for the communist nationalizations and expropriations. While the takings targeted all forms of property—land, industry, commerce, and so on—housing stands apart. Like land restitutions, postcommunist restitutions have been particularly contentious (but unlike industry and commercial properties). Nationalized and expropriated buildings that served as homes prior to the communist takeover have not only economic value (assets), but also emotional and cultural importance as homes. To the extent that any private ownership was allowed throughout communism, houses and apartments were the main and most prized object. Housing is also exceptional because for the most part, resistance in this field was through law, through former owners' petitions contesting the taking of their homes. This is distinct from most other takings, collectivization, and general resistance to the communist regime.[6] Interestingly, houses have been relatively little studied for the entire region, not just Romania, especially by comparison with land and its collectivization, or the general macro-economy of communism.[7]

Housing nationalization and expropriation had a much narrower scope, covering only approximately 30 percent of all housing in the country (Chelcea 2004, 1, 112; Dawidson 2004, 125), compared to the almost complete takeover of industry, commerce, and land. Unlike these other takings, there was no clear and coherent legal and policy framework for the taking of housing. While slightly more than half of all takings took place under the flagship Decree 92/1950, housing was nationalized or expropriated throughout the communist period under at least ten other statutes and decrees, most of which did not target housing nationalization or expropriation as such (Stan 2006, 184). By comparison, Law 119/1948 was the key legal instrument for the nationalization of all major industry in the country. It left no room for doubt or misunderstanding the regime's policies. The takings of housing lacked finality as some restitutions took place, and some of the housing initially nationalized or expropriated was sold back to the population. Finally, the regime allowed and even encouraged at times the construction of private housing, which was never an option for land, industry, or commerce.

Like collectivization, however, the taking of houses is best understood as a process that lasted at least a decade, encountered significant resistance (Şerban 2010), and was constitutive of the new socialist state at central and local levels (Verdery and Kligman 2011). Similarly to collectivization, the taking of housing illuminates the construction of communist power from the ground up, in particular through the decades-long process of contesting it. Housing nationalization and expropriation are nonetheless profoundly different from other takings precisely in terms of processes and scope, finality of takings and possibilities of restitution, and the creation of new private property in housing, which helped preserve a space for the survival of private property that did not exist or was severely limited vis-à-vis land, industry, and commerce.

Romania stands out within the Eastern European context, although overall there was significant variation among the countries of the region. In the Soviet Union and Yugoslavia, for example, housing was nationalized almost in its entirety (Hegedus et al. 1996, 59), similarly to the Czech Republic, where most private apartment buildings were expropriated by the state (Lux et al. 2009, 251). In Hungary housing fared much better—only apartments in buildings with more than six rooms were nationalized (with no compensation). In Budapest, approximately 200,000 dwellings were thus nationalized. Similarly, in Bulgaria most of the housing sector was nominally private, although about 10,000 residences were confiscated (Mastrapa 2005, 133–34). In East Germany, the majority of housing property was not formally transferred into state property, although it was *de facto* under state control (Köhli and Kintrea 1996, 47).

The research for this book is broadly ethnographic, with some challenges along the way. The bulk of the data at the basis of the book is new—for many of these archival documents, I was the first researcher ever to study them. I spent a significant amount of time at the Timişoara branch of the National Archives of Romania, where I focused predominantly on the activity of the local state bodies—Prefectura Judeţului Timiş-Torontal [County Prefect's Office], Sfatul Popular Banat [County Popular Council], the Bar Association, the Administrative Court in Timişoara, Timişoara City Hall, Sfatul Popular Timişoara [Municipal Council], the Timiş-Torontal Tribunal, and the Authority for the Management and Supervision of Enemy Goods (CASBI). I also used law reviews as primary sources, and I observed restitution disputes at Judecătoria Timişoara. All translations from Romanian (archives, law reviews, newspapers, etc.) throughout this book are mine.

The use of archival data, in particular, raised some questions. The key question has been asked by researchers of communism for a long time and has given rise to various innovative methodologies (such as kremlinology, for example, Conquest 1961), namely how much of this data can be taken at face value? With little access to information and very specific concerns regarding interviews and ethnographic field work prior to 1989 (safety, reliability, etc.), this was not an unreasonable worry. For my post-1989 research, this is much less of a concern: I am using a variety of sources, I focus on local issues, and archival materials over time corroborate each other. There are gaps and silences regarding communication on sensitive topics, but ironically even these are sometimes confirmed in the written materials. Archival materials, and in particular the petitions, reveal directly people's ideas of law, justice, and so on, rather than what they might narrate later in interviews. Petition writers are forceful, straightforward, and as comprehensive as possible since they were pleading their cases (similar to Lovell's [2006] study of letters written by Americans between 1939 and 1941 to the Justice Department's Civil Rights Unit). Court decisions and law review articles are in a sense easier: as public documents, they are politically "clean" and also openly the site of ideological debates regarding law and property in communism, and as such good windows into the construction of a new hegemony.

The six chapters of the book address the hybridity of communist legality and the extent to which communist law was simultaneously, albeit unequally, an instrument of power and a space of resistance; the attempts of the regime to use legal consciousness for the creation of communist subjects, starting from legal institutions and the legal profession; the takings of houses and apartments, and the very legalistic resistance they generated; the resulting responses from within the state apparatus and the courts; and the outcomes of these political, ideological, legal, and cultural struggles for the institution of private property in communist Romania. Overall, they paint a complicated, nonlinear picture, as the regime's efforts failed to knock private property rights off their bourgeois pedestal. Both law and property were sites of contestation characterized by hybridity and plurality, and the construction of communist subjectivities, as it turned out, was similarly infused by multiple conceptions of legality and justice and only partially amenable to communist goals.

NOTES

1. This is Katherine Verdery's translation. The term "slujit" is close to "serve" and has a much stronger connotation, as it implies a relationship of subservience between the land and the peasant, with the latter being in the "service" of the former.

2. National Archives of Romania Timişoara, Collection Sfatul Popular Banat, Inventar 1517, File No 30/1955, page 28.

3. No. 27053/1995, §55, ECHR 1998-III.

4. While I am drawing from both totalitarian theories (e.g., Nolte, Talmon, Arendt, Friedrich, Brzezinski, Bloch, Linz and Stepan, representing different strands of totalitarianism) and modernization theories of communism (Siegel 1998), I found particularly illuminating and useful the works of the sociologist Pavel Câmpeanu in Romania (communism as a syncretic society), philosopher Agnes Heller, anthropologist Katherine Verdery, and economist János Kornai, all of whom were more interested in the internal dynamics of "actually existing socialism," from a perspective that was deeply critical of the regimes yet simultaneously sympathetic to their subjects.

5. National Archives of Romania Timişoara, Collection Sfatul Popular Banat, Secretariat, File 36/1965, page 54.

6. Some former owners of small companies, primarily pharmacies, also contested nationalization, but their numbers are small, and they were uniformly rejected. For example, National Archives of Romania Timişoara, Collection Sfatul Popular Banat, Inventar 1517, File no 30/1953.

7. The most comprehensive study on urban housing nationalization in Romania that I am aware of is the work of Liviu Chelcea (2004), who wrote about state, kinship, and urban transformations during and after urban housing nationalization in Bucharest. I found it particularly valuable for understanding the broader political and historical context of urban housing nationalization, and for thinking about nationalization as a specific urban process.

Chapter 1

The Many Faces of Communist Legality

In 2006, the Presidential Commission for the Analysis of the Communist Dictatorship in Romania, chaired by the political scientist Vladimir Tismăneanu, issued its eagerly awaited final report. The authors of the report include the elite of Romanian scholars, experts, and public intellectuals, primarily historians and writers.[1] Out of 665 pages covering the entirety of the communist period and every aspect of politics, economy, culture, and society, the communist legal system has ten. In these ten pages, the authors underline the features that are "usually lacking in a legal system," such as its repressive, class and ideological character, as well as secrecy, and indicate that these elements ignored fundamental principles of law. They also note the illegitimate character of the regime and some of its strangest manifestations, such as the violation of higher norms by lower norms and the fact that not even the communist regime itself observed its own legality (CADCR Report 2006, 397–407).

The marginalization of law is not surprising, but it is problematic as a gap in knowledge about the full extent of communist legality in theory and practice, and in particular as experienced in everyday life. It also implicitly endorses an understanding of communist legality exclusively from a totalitarian perspective, with an emphasis on its negative, repressive, arbitrary, instrumental, and destructive features (see Podgorecki and Olgiati 1996; also Krygier 1990; Ionescu-Gură 2005, 283–324; Denize and Mâţă 2005, 65–89).[2] Yet the operation of law under repressive political regimes is more complex.

The resistance against housing nationalization and expropriation that is at the heart of this book, for example, raises questions that a negative analysis of law under communism cannot answer. Such an analysis tends to "other" communist regimes and their law in ways that obscure legal continuities and the complexity of any modern legal system, ignores the ordinary at the expense of the dramatic and visible, and paradoxically reinforces the communist regimes' own unitary and instrumental view of law. It also downplays aspects of resistance to communism and cannot readily answer some questions, such as why the regimes ignored their own laws, why nationalized and expropriated owners turned to law in order to fight the taking of their houses, and what they thought they could achieve. The housing nationalization process, undertaken at the height of the repression, nonetheless reveals spaces for resistance in law opened up by legal continuities and through the infrapolitics of resistance during the early transition to communism. Like other types of legalities, socialist legality was simultaneously, albeit unequally, an instrument of power and a space of resistance.

Law is a complex subject in all highly repressive systems, whether communist or not (e.g., Rajah 2012, writing about Singapore). A baseline for communist systems is their duality, the coexistence of law and terror, ordinariness and arbitrariness, normative and prerogative (Hazard 1969), "the paradox of socialist legality" (Ajani 2002, 2) as "the law of political repression and that of ordinary daily life" even at the height of repression (Markovits 2007, 237). Private ownership of houses and the takings of the early 1950s are squarely at the intersection of these two "laws." What are the genealogy and consequences of this legality for property, and how do its internal contradictions and hybrid nature matter (Merryman 1989, 4; Donlan 2011)?

Communist law in Romania was a quintessentially modern, hybrid type of legality dominated by five main discourses: repression, statist-instrumentalism, substantive (class) justice, legal positivism, and subjectification. As a hybrid legality, it draws from multiple normative and discursive sources, primarily modernity, the civil law tradition, the Marxist-Leninist-Stalinist ideology, and the imperatives of the transition to communism. I take as my starting point that socialist law has always belonged to the civil law tradition.[3]

Modernity, both as embodied by Lenin's "high modernism" (Scott 1998)—rationality, industrialization, the promise of emancipation, and as the constantly unfulfilled, deferred desire of "catching up" with the West encouraged a view of law as a purely compliant instrument of social and political engineering. Marxism-Leninism amplified this discourse and posited law as exclusively an instrument of the state, which included law as an instrument of repression and separately subjectification—creating the new socialist man and woman. Yet similarly to other modern legal systems, rationality and its own internal momentum conspired toward creating some "relative autonomy" for law, while continuities with bourgeois (civil) law reinforced habits of legality, legal positivist strands, or simply inertia.

More importantly, these continuities also acted as a web of invisible links still rooted in the pre-communist *nomos* and its narratives of property law and property rights (Cover 1983). Robert Cover argued that "a great legal civilization is marked by the richness of the *nomos* in which it is located and which it helps to constitute. The varied and complex materials of that *nomos* establish paradigms for dedication, acquiescence, contradiction, and resistance. These materials present not only bodies of rules or doctrine to be understood, but also worlds to be inhabited. To inhabit a *nomos* is to know how to *live* in it" (1982, 6). The importance of *nomos* and of the "interpretive commitments" at its heart are especially visible, for example, in the standoff between the petitioners and the nationalization commissions: for the former, their houses embodied labor and their property rights, while for the latter, they were means of exploitation.

The pragmatic goals of the communist regime were also caught between conflicting imperatives: suppression and incorporation of all those who were against it, ordinary management of social life, and the transition to a still hazy communist utopia. The greatest failure of the communist regimes, from this perspective, was to mishandle the fundamental capacity of law to constitute the world we live in.

REPRESSIVE LAW

In the Marxist framework, law is part of the superstructure of society, an expression of the will of the ruling class and thus an ideological tool of oppression of the dominant class. The state comes into existence to maintain the rule of one class over society and law is one of its major instruments. Law both conceals the structures of class domination (later used by Gramsci to develop his theory of the law as a hegemonic tool of the dominant class) and is a site of struggle: "Ideological forms in which men become conscious of this conflict and fight it out" (Marx 1970, 21).

Marx talked about law in three ways: as repression, as ideology, and as the constitution of capitalist relations of production and exchange through contract law (Marx 1992, 88–89) (this would be later developed by Pashukanis). Law, like religion, was rhetoric and illusion with no liberatory capacity: "The ideas of the ruling class are in every epoch the ruling ideas" (Marx 1978, 172). Marx wanted to unmask law and its claims to restrain power, a critique that has since flourished in Western critical studies of law. For Marx, law was an expression of egoism and consequently the rights of man were relevant only for the egoistic individual endemic to capitalist property relations (this resurfaces in the communist denial of any opposition between the rights of the citizens and the state) (Sypnowich 1990, 2–5). However, while law was not seen as central, Marx did not foresee its disappearance any time soon and ascribed to it the role of overseeing the dictatorship of the proletariat and the transition to communism.

In the Soviet Union, particularly during the Stalinist era, this led to efforts to create a useful legal system while avoiding its constraints (Solomon 1996). Eugene Huskey (1991) overall identifies three main discourses of Soviet legality: nihilist (incompatibility of law and socialism), statist (law and socialism are perfectly compatible, and law reaches its highest stage only under socialism), and legalist (law as a universal value and instrument of government). The nihilist discourse was developed in the Soviet Union by Evgeny Pashukanis. Its offshoot, the jurisprudence of terror, jumpstarted the Romanian transition to communism. Romanian officials and jurists, however, never caught the nihilist bug. They had no doubts that law could be a useful assistant of the state, primarily as an instrument of repression and social engineering.

Repression has been the most visible part of communist law, and its excesses have often led to denials that it even is "law." Hannah Arendt distinguished the nature of a totalitarian government from a tyranny in that totalitarianism is not lawless; rather, it goes to the sources of all positive laws: laws of history/nature, which produce mankind as an end product and attempt to dispense with the consensus juris completely (Arendt 1948). This law as repression, as legalized violence/terror (which was Arendt's concern) has at its core "unconstrained political voluntarism and instrumental use of law" (Krygier 1990, 641–42, 648–52).

Violence is at the core of this facet of communist legality, and is most clearly espoused in Lenin's political theory, with his emphasis on the dictatorship of the proletariat that left law out completely, at least in the initial stages of the revolution: "Dictatorship is power, based directly upon force, and unrestricted by any laws. The revolutionary dictatorship of the proletariat is power won and maintained by the violence of the proletariat against the bourgeoisie, power that is unrestricted by any laws" (Lenin 1934, 19). Lenin found law useful only at a later stage, in the Tsarist tradition, as "an instrument for inculcating discipline" (Krygier 1990, 637).

This is no Durkheimian theory of the law, however, since there was no interest in morality, the collective consciousness, or the production of solidarity. Rather, this type of law comes closest to substantive irrationality and remains the most visible and problematic aspect of communist law. Law-as-terror signals the break with the prior regime and sets the date of birth of the new one. It has no claims to legitimacy and no autonomy—it is purely instrumental. It also attempts to distinguish itself from bourgeois law, primarily through its reliance on anti-formalism.

The most significant theoretical attempt to construct a genuine Marxist-Leninist theory of law that privileged law as violence belonged to Evgeny Pashukanis, a Soviet legal scholar executed in 1937 and rehabilitated after Stalin's and Vyshinsky's death in 1956 (Hazard 1979; Beirne and Sharlet

1979; Bowring 2013). Pashukanis contended that it was not possible to construct socialism using the form of bourgeois law, even if the content was new, and that law would wither away, as dictated by the imperative of the historical laws of the advancement of communism (Pashukanis 1929, 61–63; Fuller 1948–1949, 1159). He also placed exchange at the origin of law and of the capitalist system, arguing that the basic concept of law is the legal subject, and that capitalist exploitation takes place indirectly through exchange (Pashukanis 1929, 109–33).

In the Soviet Union, Pashukanis' theory paved the road from contract law to planning directives and legal nihilism, which emphasized general principles and standards and disregarded basic principles such as *nullum crimen sine lege*. The result was the blatant instrumentalism and apparent arbitrariness associated with "the jurisprudence of terror" during the early transitions to communism in Central and Eastern Europe, with vague and over-inclusive law overtly employed for political purposes (Krygier 1990, 656–57). In this sense, communist systems were not simply based on lawless repression, but on repression and domination through law.

The jurisprudence of terror was a first step in the construction of the new communist reality. As noted by totalitarian theorists (Borkenau, Neumann, Arendt), newly installed communist regimes employed "fear as a political weapon" and its organization as "institutionalized terror." At its height, governing through terror fostered isolation and impotence, artificially produced anomie, diffuse, constant anxiety, lack of trust, and destruction of human diversity and spontaneity (Arendt 1948, 55; Pohlmann 1998, 234–35).

Particularly at the very beginning, Soviet-type regimes employed mechanisms of cognitive and emotional manipulation to isolate individuals and prevent them from finding new patterns of orientation that could engender meaning, as well as social support for the old framework of reality. The arbitrariness, secrecy, "confessions," and torture of political detention and show trials were meant to reinforce these goals. Milosz described this process in *The Captive Mind* as reshaping the very basis of (political) judgment so that "dissenting modes of thought or action are no longer understood as 'normal' or to be explained to others as rational or sound" (Patzelt 1988, 248).[4]

Romania was no exception to this pattern. Communist lawmakers amended the criminal code and the code of criminal procedure and introduced new crimes based on the Soviet model, such as counter-revolutionary sabotage and counter-revolutionary propaganda and agitation. They amended the law for the punishment of war criminals, crimes against peace and crimes against humanity, on the basis of which some former political leaders were convicted for "crimes against the working class." Law no 16 from January 1949 introduced the death penalty for crimes against state security and national economy, such as sabotage that undermined the national economy (e.g., destruction of buildings and machinery), as well as for associating in groups that engaged in terrorism and sabotage. Resistance groups from the Carpathian Mountains were sentenced on the basis of this last provision. The death penalty was introduced in the criminal code in 1953. "Economic crimes" in particular were seriously punished, such as refusing to seed or to follow the agricultural plan (Ionescu-Gură 2005, 288–308).[5]

The reconstruction of reality through law also involved isolating individuals and the entire country by closing the borders and restricting freedom of movement within the country. The first measures were taken in 1948, when an amendment to the criminal code punished the fraudulent crossing of the border with detention between 3 and 10 years. The government also introduced special measures controlling the movement of the population within 25 km from the border (incidentally, all of this really concerned only the Western part of the country, bordering Hungary and Yugoslavia, and not the USSR, since no one attempted to escape there) (Ionescu-Gură 2005, 299–301). Most of these statutes and decrees were phrased over-broadly and interpreted accordingly, such as the Decision of the Council of Ministers (HCM) from January 3, 1950, which punished those who "endanger or try to endanger the regime of popular democracy and the construction of socialism." Finally, again on the Soviet model, this period was the peak of show trials, such as those against Pătrăşcanu, Catholic clergy, former political leaders, armed mountain guerillas, and so on. Romanian secret service officers travelled to the Soviet Union as well as to other satellite countries and took notes of how show trials proceeded.

The communist reality construction and the preliminary cleansing of the social and political body in Romania between 1948 and 1955 resulted in hundreds of thousands of deaths and incarcerations. The estimates for the number of people incarcerated during communism vary tremendously and range from 300,000 to 1 million (for a population of approximately 15 million at the end of the Second World War) (Courtois et al. 1999, 419). Dennis Deletant, who wrote extensively on the topic, estimates that approximately 180,000 people were detained in camps by the early 1950s throughout Romania, during the height of its Stalinist repression (Deletant 1995, 24). Other historians calculated 282,000 arrested after 1947, out of which 190,000 died in detention. A larger estimate is 600,000 political detainees for the period 1948–1964, plus around 150,000 Germans deported to the Soviet Union, 200,000 deported to Bărăgan (the Romanian version of Siberia, with equally deadly results), most of whom were from the Banat region, and various random arrests. According to this largest estimate, one in twenty Romanian citizens passed through the prisons, labor camps, and forced domicile centers of the communist regime (Cioroianu 2005, 313). In a single year, 1951, 417,916 people were subject to investigations, and eventually 5,401 were arrested for "hostile activities"

(Deletant 1999, 101). Timişoara had 4 prisons, 1 labor camp, 1 deportation center, 5 special centers for investigations, detentions and internal exile, 1 psychiatric asylum for political prisoners, and 7 (so far identified) common graves and places for executions and assassinations, for a county of 600,000 and a city of 100,000.[6]

Those targeted included, in chronological order and demonstrating the increasingly wide reach of the regime: war criminals; ethnic Germans and Hungarians—many of the Germans deported to reconstruct the USSR were from the Banat region; all Schwab men between the ages of 18 and 45, and women between 16 and 35 were deported, amounting to 6,545 men and 7,330 women from the Timiş-Torontal county (Mioc 2007, 130); leaders and rank members of all political parties, often their family members, and later the young members, primarily college students (detained and executed between 1946 and 1953, leaders of student associations commonly sentenced to 10 to 25 years of hard labor); Catholic priests, nuns, and monks; and the entire Greco-Catholic Church, which was abolished and its property seized. Ultimately, those who endangered or tried to endanger the regime of popular democracy and the construction of socialism (Decision of the Council of Ministers from January 3, 1950) were also detained. This particular Decision served as the main instrument for administrative detention and forced labor at the Danube-Black See Canal, which began in 1949 and where anywhere between 40,000 and 60,000 detainees worked in abysmal conditions at all times (Rusan 2007).

Reasons for political detention in this broader category were extremely varied, such as distributing leaflets against the regime, attempts to run underground newspapers, sabotaging the seeding campaigns in the countryside, hostile religious activity, or simply having owned land or a company before 1944. In addition to arrest, detention, and expropriations, the regime harnessed the power of words to demean and destroy its enemies. Party newspapers and the radio were replete with calls for "eradicating," "crushing," "trampling upon," "weeding out" class enemies, who were variously named "social-democratic lepers," "bourgeois vipers," or "beasts" (CADCR Report 2006, 16). These campaigns overlapped with denazification campaigns. As early as October 1944, for example, the United Syndicates of Timişoara organized a public meeting where speakers called for the "cleansing of the state apparatus and enterprises of all residues of Antonescu and legionnaires [members of the Iron Guard]" (Munteanu and Munteanu 2002, 116).

In prisons and labor camps conditions were notoriously abysmal and mortality high. Investigators, prison, and camp officials were known for their low level of education and extreme brutality; at the highest levels, the NKGB selected precisely such men to head Romania's new security services (Deletant 1995, 18). Savage beatings, assassinations, and torture were common.

The careful cultivation of fear, from nighttime arrests to wiretap listening and secret trials and executions, created an unstable, oppressive atmosphere and a "culture of violence" (Deletant) that marred the early years of communism and whose effects lasted throughout the entire communist period.

Yet despite the explicit use of criminal law as an instrument of repression, despite extensive detentions and the growing network of labor camps throughout the country, the legal discourse of the time was rather coy about it, as it used legal language in "defense of the indefensible" (Orwell 1946). Legal scholars simply did not mention repression, torture, and death other than in code words and phrases, euphemisms, such as "strengthening the dictatorship of the proletariat by using state power to destroy the resistance of exploiters and . . . isolate the bourgeoisie" (Feraru 1951, 268). The justice system was a "strong defense weapon" of the workers against those who try to "halt the construction of socialism and peace" (Niţulescu 1952, 457; the author was the Minister of Justice at the time), with the need for some violence acknowledged as necessary, to the extent that the exploiters resist and only in the beginning (Elian 1965, 13). The latter author, writing in 1965, argued that "the point is not to dominate former exploiters, but to such structure society as to eliminate exploitation per se" (1965, 13).

By the end of the 1950s in Romania, "law as violence" changed: terror was increasingly bureaucratized while remaining widely arbitrary, becoming more rational both in the substantive and the formal sense (including in such paradoxical settings as show trials). To a certain extent this was inevitable, as all rules have certain formal characteristics, canons of interpretation, procedures, and so on that give coherence to the concept of rules of conduct and contain the germ of a concept of legality (Cotterrell 1997, 132).

This type of law resembles Nonet and Selznick's "repressive law" (1978), as well as Foucault's sovereign law. The sovereign Party/state embodied absolute power, truth, and knowledge. Every crime was understood as an attack on the sovereign—the Party, and the right to punish it was an aspect of the sovereign's right to make war on his enemies (Foucault 1975b, 47–48). For Marxism-Leninism, the divine right of the sovereign was replaced by the "iron logicality" of its closed ideological circle, as Marxists rejected "all non-Marxist or different Marxist interpretations and explanations of social and political life as unscientific, and not just as false or heretic" (Heller 2002, 2).

The show trials, like the public executions of earlier times, and despite their indifference to facts and strong irrational elements (Kronman 1983, 81), fulfilled a juridico-political function. Their excesses, arbitrariness, and secrecy had the role of emphasizing the superior power of the sovereign Party: "[t]he public execution did not re-establish justice; it reactivated power" (Foucault 1975b, 49). The audience of this ceremony—both the people and all potential enemies—were thus crucially important, as it was in them and for them that the power of the sovereign was reaffirmed.

STATIST-INSTRUMENTALIST LEGALITY

The repressive role of law in early communism aimed at both social control and to begin the production of a new type of subjectivity and consciousness. Despite similarities, this is a far cry from legal nihilist theories of law of the early Soviet period, as well as from efforts, like Pashukanis', to replace civil law with an entirely new branch of law (economic law) and to reconceptualize and reimagine law. Pashukanis' failure epitomizes the endurance of law as bourgeois law and later developments in communist legal theory will not manage to transcend this concept of law. On the contrary, the increasing production of norms, the move toward judicial review, and the increasing reliance on legality as a mode of legitimation will slowly erode the communist power system.

The Romanian version of what law was supposed to be and do in early communism was directly inspired by Pashukanis' ideological successor, Andrei Vyshinsky, not coincidentally also in charge of supervising the Soviet Union's takeover of Romania. As Stalin decided that the state and the law would not wither away after all, and that there was a need for "stability of laws" (incidentally, a core rule of law requisite as well), Vyshinsky was charged with theorizing, incorporating, and subordinating this new "law." He declared that "formal law is subordinate to the law of the revolution," and consequently that law follows Party policy (Krygier 1990, 638, 657).

Vyshinsky revived classic Marxist positions regarding law, primarily that law was an expression of the will of the dominant classes. Stuchka's views, another major Soviet legal theorist and sometime collaborator of Pashukanis, also regained new currency. Stuchka had argued that "proletarian law" was needed during the transition to socialism because of the practical urgency of finding a system of justice to administer the mandate of economic development. The repressive element was of course also attractive: "Justified by the long-term objective of a socialist utopia, capitalist legal forms were adapted to intensify their coercive potential" (Sypnowich 1990, 18–21). Slowly and reluctantly, a consensus formed that, as Durkheim had argued, violence only leads to violence, force cannot create law, and law must have moral foundations (Cotterrell 1999, 87; Arendt 1970).

By the late 1950s to early 1960s, the "dictatorship of the proletariat" was slowly supplanted by "state of the whole people" and law also became "of the whole people"—an expression of all classes and social sections (through the state), with increased citizens' rights, more inducement, and less compulsion.

The regime's goal was to increase the authority of law and legality, overall indicating a shift from a conflict to a consensus theory of law under communism (concretized through regular waves of release of political prisoners).

The end result of these ideological convulsions was the adaptation of bourgeois law for the purpose of constructing communism (the socialist legal version of "having its cake and eating it too"), based on the assumption that law had no past, it was there for the taking. Post–Second World War communist legal theorists therefore returned to more traditional understandings of law and its role in society: law as a system of social relationships that corresponded to the interests of the dominant class (not unlike the sociological school of jurisprudence in the United States) (Stuchka), but also as a system of norms. Law was seen as social reality, as class law and class justice (Kelsen 1955, 62–66), "the most important means of planning the future, no less than regulating the present," its task one of framing and organizing the new "complex social networks of attachment" (Cotterrell 1999, 63).

In the specific postwar context, the goals of the state, according to Stalin, were to rebuild the country, to develop the national economy and raise the material status of the people, and to increase the military and economic power of the state. In this effort, Vyshinsky argued, echoing American legal realists, jurists were needed as much as engineers, doctors, teachers, and other specialists (Vyshinsky 1948, 303). He further claimed that the correct way to understand the role of law was not in terms of needing legislation, which was not the most important thing, but instead "we need good and cheap administration, intelligent and honest civil servants, good administrators who know how to operate with an administrative norm that is appropriate, opportune, firm and exact" (Vyshinsky 1948, 303). Far from withering away, the state apparatus—in particular for economic and organizational functions—was projected to increase and expand. By 1960, lawyers and legal education became important again, and law schools the breeding ground for state functionaries (Takacs 1960, 595).

The Romanian legal discourse of the time adopted wholesale the statist thesis, starting with Vyshinsky's Marxist-Weberian conceptualization of law as the totality of rules of behavior (norms) laid down or sanctioned by the socialist state, which expressed the will of the dominant class, that is, the working class (Vyshinsky 1948, 303–4). Legal norms were to defend, establish, and develop relationships and rules that were advantageous to the working class and all those who work, eliminate completely and definitively the remains of capitalism in economy and consciousness, and build the communist society (Mancovschi 1949, 1141). Mirroring critiques of bourgeois law, Soviet scholars (translated at length in Romanian legal journals of the early 1950s) argued that law was never passive, as it both consolidated social relations and actively promoted new ones, both reflecting and shaping social relationships

(Alexandrov 1949, 158). Romanian writers picked up the idea: "laws have as their object the regulation of social relations through establishing the rights and duties of persons among themselves and vis-à-vis the state . . . with the goal of establishing a legal order that corresponds to the social and economic necessities of the time" (Raţiu 1948, 1–2).[7]

The chief legal officer in the new Romanian Ministry of Justice in the early 1950s further clarified that law as part of the superstructure was meant to regulate fundamental social relationships, "actively help the base to establish and consolidate itself and to destroy the old base and classes" (Feller 1953, 43). The legal system, based on Stalin's levers theory, got the job of "main lever for all state functions" (Diaconescu 1955, 3). For the courts, this meant defending the popular-democratic regime, the achievements of the workers, the public/common property, personal property obtained through honest labor, popular legality, and the rights of citizens (Boiu et al. 1955, 110). The state, explained a Supreme Tribunal judge, was the instrument through which the dominant class led, while law was the system of legal norms imposed through physical and psychic force. Both had similar roles: to repress as well as to organize society (Elian 1965, 13). Clearly, repression and violence did not aim for destruction for its own sake, but rather to bolster the key function of law as an instrument that constructed communism, which was evident as early as the late 1940s.

The predominant discourse of legality in Romania by the end of the 1950s and beginning of the 1960s was thus a *statist-instrumentalist* one: law embodied the will of the dominant class, confirming, defending, and developing social relationships and rules that were useful to it (Voitinovici 1959, 6). Both law and society were envisioned as putty in the hands of the Party. In 1959, for example, the president of the Supreme Tribunal declared that the legal system ought to solve new legal problems raised by the fortification of socialism and finish the construction of socialism writ large (Voitinovici 1959, 37). As a type of Marxist-Leninist legal instrumentalism, this discourse assumed a perfect identity between the Party, the state, and society on an ideological level. This had two consequences: law was inherently political, and no conflicts of interests could occur, including between an individual and the state.

First, the role of law therefore was not to limit state power, but to strengthen and develop it. Law was clearly subordinated to politics, and could operate only within the bounds established by the political order (Frankowski 1987, 1309; Mancovschi 1949, 1142). Law, in other words, was fundamentally political, embedded in class struggle, and judges and lawyers were political activists. Romanian jurists advised that judges' work was a political activity and thus judges had to be intimately familiar with statutes and decrees—their content as well as their political goals (Bârsan 1955, 209). Specifically, judges were directed to look at the economic positions of the parties and study the resolutions of the Party, as they indicated the new base (in the base/superstructure paradigm) (Auslander 1951, 388).

Romanian socialist legal scholars saw no contradiction between the class spirit of socialist judges and the constitutional requirements regarding judicial independence. Judicial independence in early communism meant judges had to focus on the evidence and search for the truth—the "material," "real" truth, class truth. The principle of judicial independence was not meant to put judges above workers' interests, but just to give them "peace of mind" as a third party outside of the interests of the parties (a jab at impartiality?). However, judicial independence did not mean that the judge was independent of Party policy, or that there were "neutral" interests in the construction of socialism. The socialist judge was thus not supposed to be a passive spectator of clashing interests in court, but an organ of the proletarian state, a political activist, positioning himself on the side of progress and giving solutions to aid the construction of socialism (Lavrov and Tătaru 1959, 7–9).

These legal scholars tried to achieve an uneasy balance: judges and lawyers were political actors, servants of Party policy and Marxist-Leninist ideology, yet by necessity, and especially in a period of transition, they were given a lot of latitude in interpreting the law to conform to this rather abstract theory. They were mandated, in fact, to employ teleological interpretation, which is usually widely feared to open the door to judicial creativity and activism. The Party's solution to this problem post-purges was multipronged. There was strict control over the legal profession through limiting entry to the profession and removing judicial immovability. There were only three law schools in the country, graduating no more than 200 students overall per year. This small pool was consistently socialized through continuous professional and ideological trainings that aimed to ensure unity of interpretation, and also served as ideological supervision (Bârsan 1955, 210–11). Lay judges were also included in the trainings.

Second, there was a presumption against the very existence of conflicts of interests in society. They were tolerated during the transition to communism, until all interests could be properly aligned with the Party's. Consequently, in the construction of socialism, law's job was to serve primarily social interests, not rights, although "private interests are not excluded" (Moldovan 1949, 974). Rights and liberties were inscribed in the communist constitutions, but they could not be used against the socialist society. The starting point was not individual rights, but positive law and the duties that resulted from it, as explained by a trial court judge: "individuals live through society, it is society that gives them the possibility of existence, so the first duty of the individual is to observe the laws of social life" (Moldovan 1949, 973). Rights were not natural and preexistent to the state, but bear the imprint of state origin and could not be opposed to the rights of the workers, to societal interest (Broşteanu 1948, 65; Paul 1949, 570). Duties were at the origin of rights: only fulfilling one's duties led to the creation of material conditions for the guarantees of rights, which in the long term was supposed to lead to the union of rights and duties. The perfect example prefiguring this future, explained a legal scholar in 1953, was the right to work, which was both a right and a duty, as well as "a matter of honor for all those who can" (Feller 1953, 73).

The statist-instrumentalist discourse of legality in communism and the focus on law as a tool of social engineering has some similarities to the American school of sociological jurisprudence. At the beginning of the twentieth century, the American school of sociological jurisprudence issued a critique with long-lasting impact against legal formalism and conceptualism, legal individualism, Hegelian idealism and liberal legalism, eerily similar to communist critiques of "bourgeois law." Both sociological jurisprudence and communist legal scholars had in mind grander ambitions to fulfill the emancipatory promises of the Enlightenment, relying upon law as social engineering.

They both conceived of law as a discrete element in social reality with a historically relative nature, subject to external forces and embodying interests; for both, consequently, legal relations needed to be analyzed in terms of the interests involved (Pound, Engels; Bratus 1949, 359).[8] They also had tremendous faith in the efficacy of human effort, in the case of Marxists bolstered by faith in the objective laws of history. As Pound believed, legal institutions and doctrines were specialized instruments of social control, capable of being improved by conscious, intelligent effort (Pound 1911–1912). Legal instrumentalism in the United States—the view that law should be used as a tool to achieve social purposes and to balance competing societal interests—espoused policy-oriented intervention by the state, favored socioeconomic legislation, as well as judicial review. Law was seen as a means to an end, within specific contexts.[9]

Legal instrumentalism in communism similarly understood law as an instrument of social change, with slight modifications: law was in the service of the Party and the state, and its main goal was to help build communism, specifically by transforming social relationships, changing the old base and superstructure, eliminating exploitation, defending the workers, educating the masses, establishing rules for the working class, and overall serving the social, rather than individual interests. Law's job was not to balance societal interests, as only the interests of the working class mattered, and law was meant to act through statutory intervention, rather than the courts and judicial review. The will and interests of the working class, of course, were rather mystical concepts determined by the objective laws of history and thus wide open for interpretation.

At the beginning of the communist transition, the will of the working class revealed itself through the main reforms undertaken from 1944 through 1950: land reform (distribution of land prior to collectivization), electoral reform, monetary reform, and justice reform (the democratization of justice) (Raţiu 1948, 2). Like functionalists, communist scholars also became somewhat obsessed with an equilibrium model by the early 1970s, when socialism was supposedly achieved and the transition to communism started, and overly preoccupied with stability and order.

ANTI-FORMALISM AND SUBSTANTIVE (CLASS) JUSTICE

Key changes in the justice system and legislation, as well as efforts to update the concept of law and its functions for a brave new world, primarily through its repressive and instrumental functions, were important first steps during the early transition to communism. To build this new world fully, however, this basic, stripped-down law was insufficient. Law needed to deliver more, both for the sake of its own success and legitimacy, and as a constituent element of the new regime: it needed to show that it was capable of constituting the world we live in, in a coherent, meaningful way, and moreover that it could construct legitimacy through legality. This was indeed the main promise of socialist legality—substantive justice as class justice. For socialist legal scholars and practitioners, this was the key distinguishing feature of socialist legality compared to bourgeois legality.

Socialist legal architects constructed socialist law as opposite and superior to bourgeois legality, which was critiqued as ideological (false, untrue), formalist, undemocratic, exploitative, anti-scientific, and reactionary (e.g., Takacs 1960, 596). Oddly underscored were exploitation and private property. While the goals of the new constitutions, for example, included eliminating exploitation, the explicit opposition with bourgeois constitutions was rarely made (e.g., Vasilescu-Albu 1948, 420). By contrast, socialist jurists presented the new socialist regime and its law as truly democratic: the constitution was debated, rights were guaranteed not just declared, and workers shaped the destiny of the country.

Socialism, in other words, was an inherently "good" value-based society because of its progressive justice thrust, illustrated in the writings of the time by the main achievements of the regime: eliminating illiteracy and starting massive new constructions, liquidating the exploiters-bourgeois-land owners (the nationalization of industry is usually mentioned, but only occasionally urban housing nationalization and the creation of state locative space), removing the traditional political parties from power, as they were "corrupt and sold to imperialism," overturning the monarchy, and establishing the Popular Republic of Romania. In this narrative, these successes were based on the alliance between workers and peasants, with workers in the leading role, under the leadership, guidance, and friendship of the Soviet Union. Socialist law, explained legal scholars, was openly ideological, with an explicit class character, which automatically made it better than bourgeois law. The latter pretends to be objective and hides the extent to which it represents only the interests of the ruling class (Auslander 1951, 386–89; Feller 1955, 589; Nedelschi 1949, 732–33; Lavrov and Tătaru 1959, 6). Socialist law was presented as qualitatively different from bourgeois law because it defended the interests of the working class, the superstructure, based on the objective laws of history and social development (Feller 1955, 588), compared to the unscientific, natural law (eternal, unchangeable) claims of bourgeois law.

The most important theoretical point of debate regarding law in communism, however, pertained to formalism, because formalism "as both theory and practice embodies bourgeois legal ideology" (Vasilescu-Albu 1948, 424). At stake was nothing less than the fate of socialist law as a new kind of law that could fulfill its most serious promise—substantive justice, yet remain "scientific" and not become arbitrary. The search was on for socialist legal formalism, as opposed to bourgeois formalism, but distinguishing them was not that easy. Engels himself, in his 1893 letter to Franz Mehring, admitted that he and Marx had neglected the problem of form while stressing that of content in various fields, including law. It was an oversight with lasting impact on the development of socialist legal systems and theory, because the unresolved tension between form, content, function, and structure undermined the goals of the regime and allowed alternative ideas of law and property to persist.

Socialist scholars accused bourgeois legal formalism of privileging proceduralism, legal constructs as abstractions, the separation of form from content, and formal justice. For the most part, these critiques assumed the categories of legal formalism itself, namely the distinction between law making and application of norms, and thus addressed themselves to judges. An example of proceduralism for its own sake was overturning trial court judgments that were missing signatures, such as those of lay judges or court clerks. The solution proposed was a dialectical analysis: if the lack of the signature was an administrative oversight, this should be corrected, rather than overturning the entire judgment; if not, then the reversal would be correct, as it would be both an issue of content and form. Apparently, even the Supreme Tribunal was guilty of formalism on occasion (Gergely 1957, 520–25). Strangely, the end result was a critique of legal formalism that recalled earlier assessments by the American school of sociological jurisprudence, rather than a Marxist critique of law. There were two bows to Marxism: that legal formalism hid the real truth, and that it was anti-Marxist because it denied the class character of law (Vasilescu-Albu 1948, 419–22).

By contrast, Romanian scholars argued, socialist justice would be free, the state was interested in the just application of law, and form had to ease not impede justice. Formal law was thus going to serve material, substantive justice. The judge's role was to discover the truth, and the judge had a very active role in leading the trial (Moldovan 1949, 974–75), which was in line with the civil law, inquisitorial tradition, but was not acknowledged. When the new code of civil procedure was adopted on March 1, 1948, the editorial staff of *New Justice* touted its main improvements, aimed precisely at removing the evils of bourgeois formalism: adaptation, acceleration (such as shorter appeal terms or the right of the court to limit the number of witnesses), simplification (e.g., lack of signature on appeals did not invalidate them automatically), and democratization (e.g., oral lawsuits in rural courts, facilities for those who could not sign) (1948, 46–47).

Separating form from content and decontextualized interpretation were the main formalist culprits in the eyes of Romanian socialist jurists, however. The content of law was the will of the ruling class, as determined by material conditions of existence, while the form was statutes, decrees, and so on. In practice, the separation of form and content led to two types of mistakes: formal justice and arbitrariness (Gergely 1957, 517). The first mistake was to give form its own, independent existence, for example, when judges limited themselves to examining the text of the statute without linking it with the content. Formalism thus made the judge "a slave to the text," ignoring its social-political content, its meaning, and its goals, ignoring the will of the working class: "the essence of formalism is the bureaucratic misrepresentation and distortion of the law," which was a "deathly enemy of socialist development." The second big mistake was the opposite, namely, the judge focused only on the "pure" content of law and attempted to bring to life the will of the working class without law, independently of it or outside of it. This led the judge to rely on his own personal opinion, which was dangerous because it meant that the judge or prosecutor substituted his will to the will of the working class, ultimately "judging without law"/"judecarea fără lege," arbitrariness and abuse (Gergely 1957, 517–19).

In their attempts to explain how a dialectical approach to law differed from bourgeois approaches, socialist authors of the 1950s stressed that law could not be understood without a full analysis of the unitary content-form dialectic. A materialist dialectic analysis of the organic unity of form and content privileged content over form, but allowed that form was active and influenced content. However, form was always behind content, and in transitions new content takes over both old and new forms (Gergely 1957, 516–17).

The content-form discussion existed both within law—content and form of law, and about law—law was understood as the "form" of society.

These may seem to be theoretical issues with little practical importance. Yet at stake in the form-content discussion was the extent to which bourgeois law could be deployed for building socialism while deeper questions about legal meta-structures and narratives could be tabled, all this while professing hatred for bourgeois legality. There was thus no particular concern about inconsistencies in socialist descriptions of bourgeois law or about gaps and silences in discussions of bourgeois versus socialist law. The content of law was described as ideology, as the will of the working class, and the form included sources of law such as statutes and decrees, yet nothing was said about legal constructs and structures, such as the legal geometry of property rights—*usus*, *fructus*, and *abusus*, or the structure of property and its conceptual attachments—easements, liens, and so on. Consequently, these concepts weathered the communist system with barely a ripple.

The form-content debate was meant to ease the use of bourgeois law for new purposes, to justify how the "old civil code, restructured and emptied of its bourgeois content, serves the popular-democratic state in the construction of socialism," as the president of the Supreme Tribunal explained (Voitinovici 1959, 29). It was also meant to portray "good socialist formalism" as opposed to "bad bourgeois formalism" and to rationalize the coexistence of "opportunity" and "legality." This explains why, on the one hand, "bourgeois formalism" turned out to be a broad umbrella for all types of legal sins, from basic incompetence to ideology, while on the other hand, judges and lawyers were magically expected to distinguish between the form of socialist law and formalism.

An example of the former is an embezzlement case where the accused provided new evidence during the appeal phase, namely, evidence that nothing was in fact missing. The appeal court reasoned that if nothing was missing, he could not have embezzled (Gergely 1957, 523). Ideologically, stealing from cooperative property was much worse than stealing from a private owner, so it should have been punished accordingly (equal punishment is guilty of "bourgeois formalism").

Moreover, the fight against bourgeois formalism was unending, since the goal was to eradicate the capitalist legacy in the "social conscience" of the people. A 1955 article in *Popular Legality* noted that while it was clear that legal practitioners knew that bourgeois legal theories were part of the superstructure of a social order based on exploitation, so it could not be used to build popular legality, they paid little attention to this in their work. Practitioners needed to understand that not even isolated, purportedly technical elements of bourgeois law could be used uncritically, without remembering where they came from and without a materialist dialectic analysis (Feller

1955, 585–92). Confusingly, bourgeois statutes were nonetheless still usable if they were given a socialist content benefiting workers' interests or if they were interpreted to conform to the new goals, for example, old criminal statutes used to imprison communist activists could be used for their enemies (Gergely 1957, 518). This was based in part on Lenin's address at the 3rd Komsomol Congress in 1920, where he talked about critically using the past culture of a society to build socialism, a thesis later relied upon by some Soviet theorists to contend that bourgeois legal theories could be similarly employed and still discussed during the early 1950s in Romania (e.g., Feller 1955, 585–86).

Judges and lawyers were also expected to separate the form of socialist law from formalism, and to fight against ignoring or under-appreciating the importance of legal forms: "in practice we have to strictly follow legal form because it also has a function in our socialist society" (Arjanov 1949, 152–53). How was this different from bourgeois forms, however, was never clarified, although there were hints that this was important for legitimacy, for example, revolutionary legality was violated when citizens' rights or "legal forms of relationships between state organs" were not observed (Mancovschi 1949, 1143).

The critique of formalism was at the heart of building up the legitimacy of the new law and its promise of substantive justice, such as the inclusion of social and economic rights in the new constitutions, guaranteeing rights, and eliminating qualifications for political rights, such as the right to vote (Feraru 1951, 265–66, 274–75). The "active role" of the courts also explicitly included substantive justice, as the first vice-president of the Supreme Tribunal explained. The tasks of socialist judges and lawyers, not held back anymore by "formalism and objectivism," were to establish the objective truth, to serve the interests of socialist justice, and overall to ensure that form eased, not impeded, justice (Manoliu 1955, 16; Stănescu-Bellu 1953, 535; Moldovan 1949, 974–75). Judges were asked to apply the law equally, but in cases of factual inequality they had to "equalize" it and only then apply law equally, thus achieving substantive justice (Popovici 1948, 81).

It is this promise of substantive justice that was at the core of reimagining law as socialist law. Yet early 1950s efforts to define socialist law still used "bourgeois law" as the baseline for comparison and the default position for imagining law and its possibilities. There are a couple of striking elements about the socialist construct of "bourgeois law" itself. First, it blended disparate elements from various schools of thought. Second, not much of the critique of bourgeois law was new or particularly Marxist (teleological interpretation, for example, has always been around), and attempts at distinguishing it from "Kelsenian normativism," legal nihilism, or even Soviet-style sociological jurisprudence (Stuchka and Stalghevici) were not particularly successful. More often than not, the critique itself would simply be reiterating that "x is bourgeois," therefore bad, with no further clarification.

Romanian jurists struggled to define this new kind of law by negating bourgeois law, debated whether and how to use bourgeois legal forms to advance the communist cause, and fought bourgeois symptoms—such as formalism—in everyday legal practice. Simultaneously, however, they simply had nothing else to hold on to, therefore the project slowly became less about completely displacing bourgeois law, and more about selectively using it, or, as Inga Markovits described it for East Germany, giving it "socialist respectability" (1968, 5). This leads to the last piece of the socialist legality puzzle: the paradoxical positivism of the system and ultimately the acknowledgment of law's relative autonomy.

SOCIALIST LEGAL POSITIVISM

Repression, instrumentalism, and substantive justice are three key discourses of early communist legality in Romania. Yet the scope of law's action in any society is much vaster, as its non-repressive facets have to fulfill basic tasks of justice and order, as well as technical tasks of coordination necessary to organic solidarity characteristic of any modern complex society (Cotterrell 1997; 1999, 151). For most of these activities, despite massive repeal of legislation and adoption of new statutes and decrees, communist lawmakers, scholars, and practitioners still had at their disposal the bulk of the prior, bourgeois legal system. Yet deploying it without question was not an option.

The central question had not really changed since the Bolsheviks came to power: was it possible to build a radical new world—communism—using old and tainted tools—bourgeois law? The answer from Romania was a qualified and unenthusiastic yes. Drawing from various sources, from Stalin to bourgeois legal theories, Romanian jurists built a type of socialist legal positivism that remained infused with precisely the pre-communist values it attempted to displace. The result was a legal space that showed continuities with the past and provided openings for resistance and difference, in effect for undermining the communist project. As Andras Sajó noted, "totalitarian aspirations are doomed once they allow neutral zones" (1994, 231). This hybrid law was at its heart full of ambiguities and paradoxes, and thus the communist regime never fully trusted it.

While there was general agreement that law was subordinate to politics and specifically to the Party, Romanian jurists also blended the civil law tradition (French) with Marxist-Leninist theories of the symbiosis of party-state-ideology in their attempts to construct a theory of communist law. Oddly enough, the result was a type of neopositivism that was statist, reinforced the subordination of law and judges to the political system, and relied upon formalism as both form of law and a style of judicial reasoning and legislative drafting. This result also strengthened continuities with the prior legal regime, helped with legitimacy building and offered stability, and ultimately, and without intent, some measure of autonomy.

Socialist law in Romania was "positive" on a number of levels: statist and against natural law; as a formal, procedural system; and as defined by continental traditions of positive law, primarily French. First, socialist jurists rejected any notion of natural law and any possibility of law or rights outside the state. Thus, as a Polish scholar succinctly expressed it years later, "only the rule of positive law is the law, and every rule of positive law is the law" (Frankowski 1987, 1311). Second, the legal system was seen as a hierarchical set of authority stages. Romanian authors stressed the supremacy of the statute (Voitinovici 1958, 965–66), that law was a science (Gergely 1957, 515), and emphasized the unity of the legal system. Socialist legislation had a unitary content in all forms, application, and legal effects: "Socialist law is unitary because the will of the working class is consistent and unitary" (Onescu 1958, 1002, 1013). With enough preparation and correct ideological thinking, they argued, one could find the one and only correct answer to legal problems, under the watchful eye of the Supreme Tribunal, which looked to "ensure that courts apply the correct and single/unitary judicial policy" (Voitinovici 1958, 970).

Second, the legal system itself was organized as a pyramid from the constitution downward. The normative acts of each state institution had their strictly specified place within the overall system of normative acts (see later Chkhikvadze 1969, 221). Even at the height of repression, the discourse of socialist legality emphasized the need for administrative bodies to follow the law strictly, specifically their jurisdiction (although lower administrative acts were not just acts of execution, they had to be issued on the basis, within the bounds, and with the goal of executing the statutes only) (Mancovschi 1949, 1143; Feller 1953, 68–69).

Third, socialist law in Romania also clearly continued to draw upon the French tradition that had been its source prior to the communist takeover, and in particular from two classical theorists: Rousseau and Montesquieu. The French tradition stresses the radically democratic character of its political and legal cultures, its distrust of judges, and the separation and subordination of *le droit* to politics (Stone 1992, 24). Particularly valuable for communist legal theory was Rousseau's concept of general will and its consequences regarding sovereignty: it cannot be divided, it cannot be transmitted nor alienated, it is absolutely inviolable, it cannot be represented, except by itself, and it resides in the "body politic," the moral and collective body of the nation (Rousseau 1997, 50). As an imperative consequence, the legislator as the sovereign is by far the most important state institution (Feraru 1951), and the supremacy of the statute the cornerstone of the legal system. The 1948 Romanian constitution thus noted, in Article 3, that state power belonged to the people and issued from the people.

Romanian theorists drew upon Montesquieu to explain the communist system of separation of powers and especially the subordinate place of the judges in this system. Separation of powers, as formulated by Montesquieu, did not imply the division of sovereignty. Montesquieu meant division of functions, of attributions of organs that ultimately have to work in harmony, much like the communist state hoped to implement it (Popovici 1948; Editor 1955). Montesquieu, unlike Locke, listed the judiciary as one of the three powers. He also made it clear that it was not a real power—"of the three powers of which we have spoken, the judicial is, in a sense, null." He did not allow judges any voice in the decision-making process. They were to mechanically follow the law. The ideal was that judges, as civil servants, should not make law, either directly or through interpretation.

This French legacy meshed particularly well with the state-party-law-ideology symbiosis posited by Marxism-Leninism. One of the crucial consequences of this symbiosis was that power in communist states was theoretically undivided. It was organized hierarchically, the government followed the Party line, and there was fusion of legislation, administration, and judiciary. There was no separation of powers, but rather a division of functions, of attributions—the undivided state power was exercised by functionally distinct state organs (Popovici 1948, 79). The job of the legislature was to ratify Party policies, based on the principle of democratic centralism.

A final, crucial aspect of socialist legal positivism as developed in Romania was the "relative autonomy of law" and distance from the state (also breaching the fabled state-party-law symbiosis). Marx had already asked how relations of production develop unevenly as legal relations (*Capital*), while Engels acknowledged that with the increasing complexity of economic life, the direct link between law and economics breaks and law develops its autonomous ideological self-justification in concepts of justice (Cotterrell 1997, 119). Toward the end of his life, Engels highlighted the relative independence of law (Bratus 1949, 365), particularly civil law. Unexpectedly, Stalin also came to rescue law's autonomy. In 1950, he published his famous thesis on linguistics, where he declared that the superstructure played an active role in shaping the base and denied the class structure of language, its indifference to classes. While he did not specifically talk about law, lawyers from the civil law tradition throughout the Soviet bloc were quick to see the hidden potential (see Markovits 1968). The first issue of the *Legal Studies and Research* journal (the legal research arm of the Romanian Academy), for example, started out in 1956 by declaring that law was a science that had its own, objective laws of development, distinct from psychology, economy, or society in general (otherwise it could not be a science). The author was none other than Ion Gheorghe Maurer, a leading Party activist, foreign minister and perhaps the best-known bourgeois-trained lawyer at the top of Romanian communism. In 1964, Rucăreanu and Luchian discussed "the technique of the law" [tehnica dreptului], such as presumptions or establishing the legal age for marriage, and explicitly claimed that they did not have an ideological character: "obviously, such elements being part of any legal system, regardless of the social order, they do not have an ideological character, a class character, and therefore are not part of the legal superstructure" (p. 176).

The relative autonomy thesis became settled post-Stalin. Soviet authors as well as Romanian ones acknowledged the socialist class character of law and that law and state were intimately interconnected in a "dialectical unity," as they both were "a product of the same socio-economic system and political conditions" (Chkhikvadze 1969, 194–96). Law and state would eventually wither away, once "a deeply ingrained sense of collectivism" created under the guidance of the legal system took hold. Law, however, could not "be a voluntaristic product of a socialist state authority" (Chkhikvadze 1969, 198–200), and civil law in particular enjoyed relative independence, since any social formation, once established, becomes somewhat independent. Bratus claimed that civil law must have "internal harmony," and while it was true that the economic factor would break through and change it, there wasn't a one-way relationship between law and the economic base, rather there was reciprocal influence (Bratus 1949, 366).[10]

By the late 1950s to early 1960s in Romania, this was increasingly becoming the predominant legal discourse: socialist law was constructed as a consistent, internally coherent system that was also flexible enough as society changed. Socialist legal positivism was theoretically characterized by the supremacy of the statute, the differentiation of sources due to needs, and strict hierarchy. While there was no distinction between public and private law, the branches of law were still considered necessary, and especially important were constitutional law and administrative law. Socialist legal positivism—the supremacy of statute plus ideology—created the assumption that the legal system was a complete, coherent, internally consistent whole—a happy marriage of formal and substantive legal rationality that did not conflict. Issues of interpretation in the application of rules were solved drawing upon formal rationality: "the formal manifestation of the rule," as well as Savigny's old rules of interpretation (where the traditional historical criterion was replaced with the "functional" or "historico-political" one). As Ajani wryly notes, the old "classics" of bourgeois law enjoyed a kind of immunity from ideological concerns (2002, 4). Extra-legal considerations made their way in through the general clauses, which were supposed to strengthen, rather than bypass, positive-formal law. What might strike an external observer as fundamentally illegal, therefore, such as the violation of statutes by lower administration acts, as was often the case in the urban housing nationalization process, was legible within that system as an expression of substantive (class) justice, or the dynamic implementation of legislation.

Yet this type of legal positivism was also not far from a typical Kelsenian understanding of law as a self-contained system with its own reason and deductive system of rules, separated from morality, politics, psychology, or social reality, a system without internal contradictions that understands judging as the mechanical application of law and whose validity ultimately rests on a hypothetical basic norm situated outside of the law. Kelsen's ideas proved too irresistible for the theory and practice of communist law because they were based on an understanding of law as "scientific" (thus falling squarely within one Marxist requirement); could fill the "basic norm" with any ideology or political value; acknowledged a place for a constitution that could be legally irrelevant (which also conforms to the French tradition of the supremacy of the statute); and, as long as the proper procedures were observed, saw that legality was also prima facie observed.

This was ideal for the communist agenda: while acknowledging that they were separate systems, law and politics nonetheless exerted influence on each other and law was the most important instrument of state politics. Sadurski (1984) commented that positivism dominated Soviet legal culture precisely because a conception of law devoid of moral criteria was functional for the authoritarian regime. Yet Kelsenian positivism has subversive potentialities because it subsumes the state to law (entirely contrary to Marxist-Leninist views on law),[11] and because it attempts to use legality as a mode of legitimation (Priban 1999, 34–35). It also explains how formalism as a style of judicial reasoning and form of law belongs within this broader positivist framework, and consequently how formalist, positive law can be used to first create and then entrench a law and jurisprudence that was in tandem with the overall political developments of the time.

The combination of these various traditions—the Leninist emphasis on the state as the source of law, Kelsen's scientific pure theory, and the classic philosophers explain to a large extent what held "socialist legality" together and why the legal system did not complain of lack of legitimacy. Judges could be considered to be functionally (but not politically) independent and the role of the judiciary was to protect the state from its citizens, rather than the citizens from the state (Frankowski 1987, 325). The actuality of law under communism, however, to a certain extent evaded ideology, particularly with regard to legal positivism and legal formalism, and the interplay between the production of positive law, its formalism, and the legitimation of law.

As a tool of social engineering, this version of a legal positivist system was most clearly useful as a technical means of coordination and management, where the focus became "the administration of things" (Sypnowich 1990, 6), making administrative decision-making more rational and consistent.[12] The imperative of order in law, which "implies consistency, certainty, stability, and, specifically, the maintenance of predictable patterns of action by officials and others" (Cotterrell 1997, 155) thus became a key element in socialist legal positivism. Socialist law as coordination and management was a type of regulatory law with some elements of responsiveness, particularly under late communism, but even in the early stages, as shown by the decrees, instructions and orders dealing with housing nationalization (Chelcea 2004, estimates there were over 250 regulatory acts).[13] It was characterized by the increasing production of positive law, which came to play constitutive and legitimation roles (e.g., with regard to the communist "social contract"). The communist system survived through "organization," yet the unintended consequence was a legal system with increasingly autonomous features and functions, defined by the detailed codification of daily life, the proscriptive nature of statutes, constitutions, and regulation, their often vague and abstract style, and the never-ending morass of unpublished regulations, secret instructions, and administrative orders (Schwarzchild 1986; Reynolds 1994, 805–6).

The continuous production of positive law was not meant merely to provide an appearance of legality, as external observers and dissidents argued (particularly Charter 77). The vast majority of this legal production was essential in order to constitute a new (bureaucratic) social order and did affect the regimes themselves: "Whatever its content, law's rational, systematic character gives it the continuing ability successfully to claim obedience. In modern societies, the relationship between legality and legitimacy is, therefore, one of virtual identity. Law not only provides the technical apparatus for exercise of state power, but also the ideological foundation of authority" (Cotterrell 1997, 137).

"Socialist legality" or "rule of law with a class character" (Krygier 1990, 638, quoting a former president of the Polish Supreme Court) was the troubled outcome of the conflicting imperatives of repression, organization, and transition facing the communist state.[14] "Socialist legality" was also building upon and looking for legitimation in the continental law traditions present in all communist countries, in Romania specifically the French *volonté generale*, which merged with the Soviet doctrine of the unity of state power. Ultimately, however, it represented an uneasy attempt to domesticate bourgeois law for the purposes of the transition to communism, ignoring the fact that many of its assumptions would make that task impossible (as Pashukanis had already pointed out). This is not to signify an eventual softening of communist law, either. After all, it never gave up on its teleological thrust—the creation of socialist man, or on the expediency and instrumentality regarding the use of law and the arbitrariness that came with it (Schwarzschild 1986, 685). At most, this arbitrariness came to be expected.

CONCLUSION

The early years of communism in Romania are defined by repression and violence taking place in the midst of massive legal changes. The period from 1945 to 1965 is mostly associated with repression through law, but it is also the beginning of "socialist legality" as a type of hybrid legality, a space of both repression and resistance, anchored by two key, apparently contradictory ideologies and practices: Marxism-Leninism and legal positivism. Crucially, socialist law failed to imagine itself as a truly novel, revolutionary concept, fundamentally distinguished from what it termed "bourgeois law." Consequently, throughout communism, socialist law was in a permanent existential crisis.

Law (as *Recht*, *Droit*) played a key role in both the construction and undermining of communism. As an instrument of state power, it was deployed to construct, eliminate, and immobilize enemies of the regime, but more importantly, to destroy old meanings, systemic biases, and types of knowledge while creating and helping citizens internalize new ones. In its role as invaluable aid in the construction of socialism, law acquired new powers, foremost among them normalization, education, and constructing communist subjects. The role of law in reifying this new social order and building regime legitimacy cannot be underestimated (as it is essential that it appears nonarbitrary) (Haugaard 2003). Repression through law and the construction of new socialist subjectivities are deeply and purposively linked.

However, law in periods of transition, as Ruti Teitel pointed out (2000), is not just a site of transformation, but also one of continuity. Socialist transitional law thus brought both changes to, and preserved elements of the preexisting legal regime, including property. Law continued to draw from the civil law tradition and prior legal ideologies, which resulted in ideas about legal autonomy and formalism coexisting with the socialist fight against formalism and the Marxist-Leninist ideology of law as a pure instrument of the state. Law in communist regimes never became a self-sufficient, self-centered system. The "paradoxical double structure of the communist system," based on widespread and arbitrary abuse of power, yet also declaring its acceptance of the principle of legality (Priban 1999, 32–33), is grounded in the distinction between "ideology" and "actuality" and mirrored in law. Law cannot be expected to serve as a counterweight to "the system" or a restraint on power, certainly not within the "public transcript" of law and power. Yet its paradoxes and duality have meaning for both the exercise of power and spaces of resistance (without, as Sally Merry warned, romanticizing resistance).

The tension between "ideology" and "actuality," and the symbiosis between Party and state directly play out in the legal arena: law's arbitrariness and instrumentalism, and the legitimacy of law itself in this paradigm, derive from orthodox Marxist-Leninist views on law, and are connected to the Party, while its attempts to autonomy and legality are connected to the state and notions of popular sovereignty and general will. The legitimacy of law itself—as a trustworthy mechanism mediating between state and society—thus depends on its ability to distinguish itself from the Party.

Spaces for resistance in and through law were opened by submerged legalities, continuities, inconsistencies, gaps, and silences—the most striking is the "taken for grantedness" of implementation, as there is no gap problem, no law in books and law in action dichotomy, no questions of law's effectiveness, impact or unintended consequences. Resistance in and through law was possible because of the multiplicity of power centers (central and local), because law provided a cultural space and consciousness for resistance for people who refused to fit into social categories that defined their lives, such as nationalized owners (Merry 1995, 18, 23). Ultimately, it was a failure of imagination in reconceptualizing law and what law does. Law was also a site for resistance because it is inherently backward looking, a feature acknowledged by socialist legal scholars as well: "Stability conferred by permanence has a strong, diffuse and clear force. Law tends towards conservatism, towards closing inward in its experienced forms" (Vasilescu 1976, 6). If, as Ewick and Silbey (2003, 1335) point out, counter-hegemony is bred by current hegemonies, any legality is inevitably both a site of power and resistance.

A better description here might be socialist law's duplicity in creating and tolerating spaces for resistance. The implications are critical: the lack of coherence of socialist legality theoretically and practically contained unresolved tensions and opened up spaces of autonomy that offered possibilities of resistance through law, such as petitions against nationalization and expropriation as a type of micro-resistance through law. Although not directly a restraint on state power, the failure to reimagine law during communism inherently was about defining limits, power, and resistance. The hegemony of private property was not fundamentally unsettled during this period. Finally, to the extent that this hybrid legality was not fully "theirs," the regime's bureaucrats abused it and never fully trusted it.

For property in particular, the legal ideology of property rights embodied mixed messages about the role and meaning of private property in socialism, as the concept of private property itself was circumscribed by both old conceptions of property and ownership (primarily connected to labor), as well as new ideas about property (inclusive of equality). Legal formalism, itself a bourgeois legacy, mediated interactions between nationalized owners, local administrative bodies, and central Party/state organs, resulting in feedback from the regime and eventually halting nationalization. Meanwhile, past ideas of property, particularly based on labor, continued to inform people's self-understanding, yet also helped them recreate themselves as ambiguous communist subjects.

NOTES

1. Sorin Alexandrescu, Mihnea Berindei, Constantin Ticu Dumitrescu, Radu Filipescu, Virgil Ierunca, Sorin Ilieşiu, Gail Kligman, Monica Lovinescu, Nicolae Manolescu, Marius Oprea, H.-R. Patapievici, Dragoş Petrescu, Andrei Pippidi, Romulus Rusan, Levente Salat, Stelian Tănase, Cristian Vasile, Alexandru Zub, Ruxandra Cesereanu, and Smaranda Vultur. The report is publicly available at www.presidency.ro.

2. In their 1996 Preface to the collective volume *Totalitarian and Post-Totalitarian Law*, for example, Adam Podgorecki and Vittorio Olgiati define totalitarian law from a socio-legal perspective in the following manner: "[T]otalitarian law" is not only a formal centralized device instrumentally used by totalitarian regimes to create, implement, and tighten comprehensive social and institutional control over any field of social activity. It is also a specific body of binding rules whose meaning fluctuates according to arbitrary political decisions; whose technicality functions as a façade to mask the arbitrary exercise of power; whose social acceptance is based on both false consciousness and human degradation; whose sanctions imply the disintegration of social ties and the promotion of an atmosphere of diffuse social nihilism; and whose end is an institutional legitimacy, irrespective of its degree of popular acceptance (1996, ix).

3. Pre-1989, there were two main schools of thought on this issue: the first included scholars who claimed that changes to socialist law were so significant that it was a different family of legal systems. This group included some of the key names in the fields of comparative and socialist law, such as René David, John Hazard, and John Merryman. The second group, which included scholars such as Friedmann and Lawson, questioned the depth of the changes and argued that socialist law was a subgroup of civil law. The outlines of the debate are neatly summarized by John Quigley (1989) in an article on socialist law and the civil law tradition.

4. At the most extreme, as Arendt argued, the aim of totalitarian education has never been to instill convictions, but destroy the capacity to form any (1948, 468).

5. Other statutes included Law no. 183/1949 on economic crimes, Law no. 351/1945 against illegal commerce, Decree no. 58/1948 establishing a special repressive regime (punishing nationalization-related crimes), Decree no. 199/1950 for crimes against state security, the army and national economy. I do not aim here to

present all of these numerous statutes and decree, but simply to introduce the major changes of the period.

6. Available at http://www.memorialsighet.ro/ro/recensamant.asp.

7. Versions of this definition of law appear in Nedelschi (1949), Mancovschi (1949), Auslander (1951), Manoliu (1955), Onescu (1958), and Elian (1965).

8. Pound assumed that social resources are scarce like economic resources, did not define clearly interests (objective mixed with subjective), assumed society vocalized its demands, implied law as value neutral, and did not specify which claims should be recognized and protected (he added "reasonable" claims later).

9. Llewellyn described the dual function of law: conflict resolution and conduct guidance/channeling. He developed the law-jobs theory (functions of law: needs that need to be fulfilled in society), and later the law-government theory (because law and governmental functions are inseparably intertwined) (1962).

10. Bratus, one of the most prominent Soviet jurists post–Second World War, defined civil law as the totality of the most abstract and general legal principles, one of the forms of expressing and consolidating the general conditions of production. It follows that the same civil law norms can serve the relations of other social formations in which these conditions repeat themselves (Bratus 1949, 361). This is merely a reformulation of Renner's theory on legal continuity.

11. "The primacy of law over the state and vice versa is a problem that does not exist in the Marxist science of law, because it regards them as a dialectical unity" (Chkhikvadze 1969, 195).

12. Later, law was compared to computers, and new rights or judicial review of administrative action were seen through their potential of keeping the bureaucracy on its toes (Markovits 1989, 418–20).

13. Cotterrell (1999, 71) adds regulatory law to Durkheim's categories, because it has strong restitutive aspects.

14. Socialist legality "is a condition in the life of the state when the law regulates all issues on the functioning of the state organs and the legal situation of the individual; the existing legal regulations are being observed by the organs, agencies and institutions applying this law; and sufficient guarantees enable the individual to defend his rights and liberties if the law is broken in any way" (Garlicki 1987, 1285). This late 1980s definition is on its face indistinguishable from a "rule of law" understanding.

Chapter 2

Law, Subjectivity, and Legal Consciousness

The stories told by law and of law during early communism are necessarily incomplete if they are only about repression, instrumentalism, substantive justice, and positivism. Whether overlapping or conflicting, these four discourses of socialist legality all shared one important goal: changing society all the way down to the individual level and producing a new kind of socialist subject. Coercion and terror on a societal scale are effective within certain limits, but they are expensive and only partially useful for any constructive efforts. A key element for the regime's long-term success was legitimacy, which ultimately depended on willing socialist subjects. Power, as Steven Lukes (2005) observed, is at its most effective when it is least observable. Like other regimes, communist states became interested in power as the imposition of internal constraints: the creation of the communist man/woman through the shaping and naturalization of new beliefs and desires. The interplay of all four discourses of socialist legality are essential in this process.

Imagining the "ideal" communist subjects was relatively simple: they would have an internally consistent, coherent philosophy of their own life and situation, positing them as relatively autonomous, rational agents within an ideological grid that collapses preferences and interests into "true," "objective" interests, as defined by the grand narrative of communism. However, it was not sufficient for this to happen through external, nonautonomous factors such as lack of alternatives, habituation, and resignation (Lukes 2005, 122, 134–35). Some level of cognitive precommitment was necessary, and this was the special challenge of communism: achieving the hegemony of a new system of values (e.g., equality, socialist property), with people accepting, adopting, and finally taking it for granted (Patzelt 1998, 243).

A major feature of communist power was its intentional, constant strive toward both objectification and subjectification. The focus was on each and every individual, at all times, on mind and body, toward the creation of the "perfect communist." Hannah Arendt (1973) saw in this a system of domination from within, while later Foucault stressed mechanisms of impersonal power that suffuse everyday life and construct individual subjects. Foucault wrote about Western subjectivity, yet the more immediate application is communist subjectivity: "There are two meanings of the word 'subject': subject to someone else by control and dependence, and tied to his own identity by a conscience or self-knowledge. Both meanings suggest a form of power that subjugates and makes subject to" (2000, 331).

Particularly in the early days of communism, the attention to the individual was taken to remarkable extremes. The attempt to achieve the atomization and massification of society (Arato 2002, 475), and the incorporation of the individual were undertaken in distinct stages: division, discipline, and normalization. The first step was the initial weeding out of the bourgeois, "the enemy of the people," "the reactionaries," "the saboteurs," "the parasites," through two main mechanisms: law (rationality) and psychiatry (social prophylactics). The former mechanism ensured the stabilization of the new social order and created an arbitrary and bureaucratic network of power that produced two new categories of subjects: the communist inquisitor versus "the enemy of the people," the latter defined by real or more often imaginary guilt (based on intentions or supposed intentions). Arbitrariness as a technique of power further ensured that the communist could always become the accused, one particularly prone to self-denunciation (Lefort 2002, 450, 457–59; Lubonja 2001, 239).

Purges, mass imprisonment, terror, and violence were an initial step in the construction of the new communist reality, but also the most blatant one. More subtly from a subjectification perspective, core Party members and their Soviet counselors in Romania, like elsewhere, also relied upon sessions of ideological training and propaganda, such as the onslaught of housing-related newspaper publications preceding the 1950 housing nationalization in Romania; the closing off of avenues of escape, internally and externally (such as borders); and destroying all evidence of contrary reality, thus the use of censorship, use of standard words and phrases, and so on (Patzelt 1998, 254–59). For those who did not obey or critiqued, mechanisms of discipline included stigmatization, isolation, and ultimately conversion or liquidation. Methods of isolating troublemakers included communicative deprivation (e.g., show trials), strategic context formation (constructing the troublemaker as an outsider, for example, through denunciation, slander, media campaigns), degradation (treating him/her not as an individual, but as the personification of a "type," such as "bourgeois," followed by show trials, or ceremonies of criticism and self-criticism), and as a last resort liquidation (exile, killing, or the labeling of the troublemaker as mentally ill) (Patzelt 1998, 262–67).

Criminal law was from the very beginning infused with a repressive as well as an educational-ideological role. Show trials, parasite laws, labor camps, and also sessions of "ideological education" were mechanisms that produced the new communist solidarity, the new collective consciousness (against Durkheim). As a means of determining the content of socialist justice, law's educational-ideological function was particularly important (Cotterrell 1997, 155). Law was supposed to influence the consciousness and behavior of men: "In epochs of great social change . . . law becomes an important means of social transformation, demonstrating new models of social relations" (Chkhikvadze 1969, 197). Legal norms aimed to regulate behavior, not directly relations of production (Onescu 1958, 1008). This is essentially a constructive-repressive role of law, which purposely and explicitly worked to construct the new communist subject.

Law becomes even more important as outright repression recedes, since law is central to creating new second-class citizens through disciplinary practices and normalization, from social and economic discrimination to regimentation and collectivism. After the initial communist cleansing of the social body, communist states created new "second-class" citizens through disciplinary practices that ranged from mass surveillance, spying, internal exile, to discrimination and persecution through social and economic sanctions (Priban 1999, 31). Former owners of nationalized houses, for example, did not have access to social services or pensions. Practices of normalization included collectivization (in the sense of forced collective life) (Lubonja 2001, 239), a system "of centrally defined and guaranteed life strategies for the individual" (Fehér 1982, 74), where major decisions regarding work or place of living were to a large extent independent of individual choices and spontaneity was rarely possible (Lefort 2002, 454).

At their "best" and from the very beginning, communist systems such as Romania's implemented policies already adapted from the Soviet experience, and thus aimed to fully implement panopticism: they constantly and exhaustively surveyed, classified, punished, and rewarded, in a system of full regimentation that was coherent internally to a degree unknown in liberal societies. One of the most important mechanisms in this respect was the system of widespread mass surveillance. The extent of the collaboration with and surveillance by the communist regimes varied from country to country, with East Germany apparently leading the pack with 1 in 8 citizens as collaborators of Stasi (the secret police), as revealed by the 1990 Sauer report. In Romania, there were 150,000 registered active collaborators with the Securitate in December 1989—a negligible percentage by comparison (Oprea 2002). Yet the illusory goal of the ideal communist subject, in line with socialist morality and legality, utterly selfless, defending state and public property above all else and always at the beck and call of the Party never came to be, since without overt surveillance they were not aligned with the goals of the system and its practices of governing. Not surprisingly, the Czech and Polish dissidents were hoping for an existential, not a political, revolution, based on the universality, inviolability, and independence of human rights from any political power structure (Priban 1999, 35–36). Thus, the defining feature of communist regimes from the very beginning was not terror, but the conscious effort to create the most useful subjects.

The result for these subjects was a combination of consent, resentment, and rationalization, the peculiar splitting between the public and private selves (Milosz's *ketman*, or the Romanian *dedublare*),[1] as well as inertia, internal resistance (internal exile), and acts of micro-resistance, conscious and unconscious. There is a difference however between late communism, where cynicism and the performance of double consciousness reached remarkable levels of sophistication and citizens both took the regime for granted and simultaneously ignored it as much as possible (e.g., Sajó 1994), and the early communist period.

Yet the ultimate failure of the communist project lies precisely here: it is the failure to create the ideal communist subject, fully aligned to socialist ideology, itself morphed into a new brand of morality. This failure is intimately linked to the failure to reimagine law and its capacity to remake reality, and the internal contradictions of socialist legality. This is ultimately a type of failure at the level of legal consciousness and subjectivity.

LEGAL CONSCIOUSNESS AND THE NEW SOCIALIST SUBJECT

Subjectivity, the creation of a new socialist "man" and "woman" was at the core of successfully building communism. Both the power of the new regime and resistance to it are filtered through subjectivity. Coercion and surveillance are necessary, but not sufficient methods for constructing the new communist subject. They happen in and through law; however, long term they are less important than the production of a new collective consciousness, new social solidarity and morality through both disciplinary and normalizing measures, and through "cultural-educational" aspects—law as Party ideology. The creation of socialist legal consciousness was thus essential for the long-term creation of communist subjects, and even more so for property, emphasizing legal instrumentalism and the centrality of state property to the detriment of private property.

Legal consciousness holds different meanings in contemporary studies of law and society, compared to the Eastern Block literature. Both start from a similar baseline of law as part of the superstructure, as ideology (thus broadly

Marxist, although there is a strong cultural turn in the West). In the US-centric sociolegal world, understanding legal consciousness leads to explaining legal hegemony, that is, how the law sustains its institutional power despite the gap between the law in books and law in action (why do people acquiesce to a system that promises equal treatment, yet systematically reproduces inequality?). Law is powerful because it is invisible, because "its constructions are uncontroversial and have become normalized and habitual," "sedimented" (Silbe 2005, 323–31). American legal consciousness studies embrace empirical research and assume a progressive political position (Garcia-Villegas 2003, 139). Yet this concept of legal consciousness leaves a lot to be desired: it is not entirely clear what the relationship is between ideology and consciousness (instrumental, constitutive, etc.), whether legal consciousness implies action, participation, or just attitudes, how exactly does one distinguish between consciousness in general, and legal consciousness, whether legal consciousness is individual or collective, what exactly is the relationship between self and legal consciousness, and what is the content of legal consciousness—attitudes, ideas, practices, processes?[2]

Legal consciousness has come to encompass a dynamic, constitutive process, a type of social practice embracing individuals' recursive engagement with the law in all its manifestations—institutions, norms, processes, meanings, categories, boundaries, and so on (Şerban 2014). The value added of the concept of legal consciousness, despite its relative vagueness, has been to open up very productive areas of inquiry into how people engage with and mobilize the law, how they relate to it (resist, subvert, accept), and how these complex relationships with the formal legal system, broadly understood, help create meanings, identities, and subjectivities. The legal consciousness literature responds to the challenge posed by Scheingold that the willingness to turn to law in the United States is significantly shaped by the "myth of rights," which includes faith in the nexus of rights-litigation-social change and in the symbolic power of rights (Scheingold 2004). Rights and (state, formal) law, in this framework, are thus inextricably linked, and the struggles to understand whether and how rights deliver on their promises have until recently been approached within a liberal legal tradition.

Western studies of legal consciousness overall have focused on three broad areas: engagement with the law (attitudes, use, mobilization, variations in legal consciousness); relationship with power (resistance, hegemonic legality); and the creation of meanings, identities, and subjectivities (e.g., Engel 1998; Silbey 2005; Tyler 1990, 2002; Merry 1990; Engel and Munger 2003; Bumiller 1988; Engel 1984; Hull 2003; Marshall 2003, 2005; McCann 1994). One of the most perplexing issues in this literature, however, is the extent to which studies of legal consciousness struggle with the problem of hegemony. Contemporary as well as historical studies, going back to Thompson (1975), point to both law's development as an ideological tool of repression, but also as a space for resistance: "It began to seem as if the law was constituted by both domination and resistance, consensus and conflict" (Silbey 2005, 341). This particular dynamic is very much at work in understanding law in a socialist context.

There exists a fine distinction between European and American understandings of legal consciousness. The latter focuses on people's experiences with official law, while the former is closer to Ehrlich's concept of legal consciousness as people's own idea of law and right (Hertogh 2004, 459). European studies consider law a dependent variable (the definition of law is not provided by the researcher, but is part of the empirical enquiry itself), and legal consciousness includes "people's sense of law and right."

There are some intersections with Soviet and Eastern European understandings of legal consciousness. There were two different approaches to legal consciousness in Soviet legal studies, legal philosophy, criminology, and legal psychology. Legal theoreticians viewed legal consciousness as a part of law (law could "materialize," for example, in legislation, and these "materialized" forms of law reflected legal consciousness). Legal psychologists defined consciousness as a general term and viewed legal consciousness as a subfield of consciousness, a "collection of ideas, views, feelings and traditions which reflect people's attitudes toward legal issues in society" (Kaugia 1996). This is somewhat close to earlier American understandings of legal consciousness as aptitude, competence, awareness of law (vs. perceptions and images of law) (Engel 1998, 111–20), and has a normative thrust that has "mutated" and been picked up in recent talk about "legal consciousness" in transitional countries (i.e., there is no "legal consciousness"). It is also close to "legal consciousness" as construed in early communist Romania.

The Romanian communist regime saw legal consciousness as a key part of the general category of consciousness, and assumed it could be shaped at will to help create the ideal communist subject, which in turn was essential for its legitimacy, longevity, and hegemony. The creation of socialist legal consciousness, with deep roots in the early repression of the 1950s, was therefore the linchpin for a new type of communist subject. Because truth was understood to be the correct reflection of objects and phenomena existing outside of human consciousness (Gergely 1957, 516), it followed that the latter could be shaped and changed, puttylike, with enough effort and direction. Consciousness within the Marxist framework lies behind material changes, so it was the state's job (per Lenin) to build the new consciousness, even for the workers (Ceterchi 1958, 977). The development of the new communist subject, of "homo socialis" (as opposed to Adam Smith's "homo economicus") (Mayo 1948, 78) included the development of a new socialist awareness of law, of "socialist legal consciousness," and the explicit linking of socialist morality and legality.

Romanian scholars such as Anita Naschitz, who published a book in 1964 on socialist legal consciousness and wrote widely on the subject, considered legal consciousness a key element in the construction of socialist legality and subjectivity. Naschitz, a researcher at the Institute for Legal Research of the Romanian Academy, defined legal consciousness as class legal consciousness and as part of ethical and political consciousness, the link between the other elements of the legal superstructure (legal relationships), and between law and material conditions of existence. Legal consciousness, according to Naschitz, is a complex social and psychological phenomenon, composed of rational, affective, and volitional elements. Legal ideology is the core of legal consciousness. The affective and volitional elements are important for establishing meaning for subjects, as well as for guiding human conduct.

Naschitz ascribed three functions to legal consciousness: cognitive (knowing/seeing reality through the legal lens), axiological (meaning, value judgments, including attitudes vis-à-vis positive law), and normative (guiding human conduct in accordance with the interests of the dominant class). The content of legal consciousness is ideas, feelings, and preferences regarding current or future law, as well as one's own attitude and others' attitudes regarding the law and those who violate it. Law reflects legal consciousness, while legal consciousness is a transmitting mechanism of forces and pressures from material life to law, thus contributing to the creation of law. Finally, Naschitz saw the social role of socialist legal consciousness as overcoming bourgeois law and developing socialist law, implementing socialist law, defending the socialist legal order, and creating the basis for the future withering away of law (quoted in Rucăreanu and Luchian 1965, 175–81).

For Naschitz, legal consciousness was thus a "thing," distinct from practice, which followed it. Legal consciousness could be measured and compared, it could grow or diminish—Naschitz noted that creating a socialist legal consciousness was one of the most difficult tasks in the construction of socialism (making people learn that socialist law was fundamentally different from any kind of exploitative law, that it defended their interests, etc.). Legal consciousness determined the attitude of classes toward the law, and its importance was supposed to increase with social progress. Socialist legal consciousness was "constantly revolutionary," allowing for the discovery of reality and objective truth, and was "clearly qualitatively superior" to bourgeois legal consciousness (Rucăreanu and Luchian 1965, 177–81).

Creating a socialist legal consciousness was therefore a conscious process, and moreover one that was never too far from repression. It entailed educating the masses regarding work discipline and observance of laws (Mihalca 1949, 300; Feller 1953, 72), and reeducating them regarding their interests, specifically explaining to them that their interests were identical to the state's, or that care for socialist property was a duty and a vital interest that was also personal (Manoliu 1955, 16). The job of the legal system, from this perspective, was to protect social interests over individual rights, to help denaturalize individual rights and remove their legal protection, while constructing the new *homo socialis* whose own subjective preferences simply blend into the wider, objective social good. In essence, this was an attempt to collapse subjective and objective interests (Lukes 2005). It also entailed solidifying class consciousness and efforts to "humanize and democratize justice" (Schreiber 1948, 4–5).

In this process, key legal actors—judges, prosecutors, lawyers, notaries public, scholars—themselves needed to be reformed and reeducated. "If we want changes in socialist consciousness," observed a law professor in 1957, "courts must themselves be a prime example of legality, otherwise citizens lose respect and trust" (Gergely 1957, 526). The legal consciousness of judges, defined as "the totality of opinions, conceptions and representations about what is right and not right, legal and illegal," was thus a prime target for reform, because judges' opinions "always have a class character" (Lavrov and Tătaru 1959, 8–9). Yet reforming the judges' consciousness, even after the purges and reforms, was clearly no simple task, particularly since there seemed to be somewhat of a chicken and egg problem regarding socialist legality and socialist legal consciousness: if justice-making itself contributed to the creation of socialist legal consciousness, as the president of the Supreme Tribunal claimed in 1959, but judges did not have yet a socialist legal consciousness, where was it supposed to come from?

Lawyers were considered an even more reactionary group in need of reform (judges, after all, had always been state functionaries in the Romanian civil law system). This is why the deep reorganization of the profession aimed directly at eliminating the individualism of the profession and retraining lawyers not to privilege the interests of their clients above all, but rather to "help the popular justice system establish the objective truth." The president of the Presidium of the Central Council of Lawyers' Collectives directly instructed lawyers to be careful not to interpret the law subjectively, outside or contrary to the will of the working class, and in criminal cases, to defend the defendant, not the crime per se, because the role of socialist justice was also to educate, and lawyers were a key part of this process (Dimitriu 1955, 233–34).

It is this continuum—from brutal repression through disciplinary mechanisms, normalization and the focus on recreating subjectivity that anchors the project of reimagining the law, because it aimed not just to reorganize and reform the justice system, but also to instill new values and norms of conduct in line with communist precepts. The relationship between repression and legal consciousness was thus envisioned as an inversely proportional one—as socialist legal consciousness developed, there would presumably be less and less need for repressive norms (Elian 1965, 14–17).

Law is integral to the story of building communism: law's job was to provide it with legitimacy, to help build socialist subjects, first inside key systems, such as justice, then at a societal level. It was not meant to restrain power but to be a nimble and faithful aid to state power. However, "law," as shown in chapter 1, was not itself reimagined, reconceptualized. Its possibilities, limitations, histories, inconsistencies, gaps were ignored by the new masters. Insiders to the law, whether consciously or not, rarely took up the challenge, and eventually retreated within familiar territory: law as coercion, law as a tool of the state, law as an instrument of (substantive) justice, and finally some version of formal rationality. The beginnings, however, were auspicious for the communist project, as the regime introduced massive changes to the court system, bar and legal education, hoping to transform the bourgeois justice system to a socialist one institutionally, as well as at the individual level.

TRANSFORMING THE JUSTICE SYSTEM

The inexorable march toward communism required the wholesale change of the state, society, and economy directed by the vanguard Party. This entailed the destruction of the previous system, its law included. Yet the construction of communism also needed rules, as well as a new cadre to implement them. The success of these changes depended on three factors: eliminating the enemies of the regime, replacing them relatively quickly with at least minimally qualified judges and lawyers, and changing the content of law and what law was supposed to do and be—in essence, reimagining law. Yet despite major purges and the abolition of chunks of pre-communist legislation, the communist regime was overwhelmed by the depth and speed of the changes needed, which led to privileging criminal and public law, the neglect of civil law, and the reliance on bourgeois law for building communism.

The modern structure of the Romanian judicial system originated with the unification of Moldavia and Wallachia in 1859, and was based on the French model. The first High Court for Cassation and Justice (i.e., Supreme Court) was established in 1862. The most recent pre-communist statutes regulating the High Court and court system were adopted in 1924 and 1925. The basic structure was trial court → tribunal → court of appeal → High Court (organized in sections). Similarly to the French system, judicial review of administrative acts and administrative law were distinct, well-established areas of law, but unlike the French model, the High Court had jurisdiction over judicial review of legislation as well (and considered it a mark of progress) (Albu 2001).

The Ministry of Justice was one of the first state apparatuses captured by the communist Party in 1944. Lucreţiu Pătrăşcanu, a lawyer who had earned his PhD in political economy at the University of Leipzig in 1925, was the Minister of Justice of Romania between 1944 and 1948 (when he himself was purged) (Betea 2001, 14). In 1947, he reported to the Political Bureau of the Party that he had faced three major tasks when he took over the justice system: purges, changes in legislation, and the democratization of justice. His goal here was twofold: to eliminate traces of right-wing authoritarianism (after 5 years in the Axis camp and 6 years of assorted dictatorships—royal, fascist, and military), and to prepare the transition to communism.

Of the 2,600 magistrates Pătrăşcanu found when he took over, he removed 600, while 250 were temporarily suspended. This was really the minimum, from his perspective, as he found all lawyers, judges, and so on in the justice system to be "reactionary," and thought that the fundamental purging of the justice system would have required removing 80 percent of magistrates, and not just the 20 percent that actually happened. The Ministry of Justice itself had only 1 communist Party member in 1944, but by 1947 their number had increased to 140 (Ionescu-Gură 2005, 283–84).

More purges, particularly at the top, happened with the reform of the court system and the bar. The number of trial courts [judecătorii mixte şi rurale] tripled in 1948, the year of the major reforms, from 376 to 1,087. The idea behind this, explained Pătrăşcanu, was to bring justice and the judge to the villager for lawsuits that concern rural life. Accordingly, new courts were situated to minimize travel time—no court was more than 10 km (6.2 miles) away from anyone who needed it (Ionescu-Gură 2005, 285). This increase in the number of lower courts, however, came with a 50 percent decrease in the number of higher courts, as well as reshuffling of staff (both judges and court clerks) that resulted in a 12 percent decrease in the overall number of magistrates (from 2,802 to 2,453).

Purges (retirements and forced resignations) were deepest at the highest levels: 16 out of the 55 judges at the Court of Cassation (the equivalent of the Supreme Court) were fired, also 194 appeal court judges out of a total of 332, as well as 149 of the 864 tribunal judges. Those who had been politically active prior to or countered the new regime did not receive any pension regardless of age or time in office (Ionescu-Gură 2005, 286). In 1948, the Court of Cassation was renamed Supreme Court and after 1952, Supreme Tribunal. The Court had a high of 64 judges and 4 sections in 1939, but it gradually lost judges and jurisdiction through the judicial organization reforms of 1947, 1949, 1952, and 1968 (Albu 2001). Candidates for the Supreme Court were vetted by the Secretariat of the Central Committee of the Party; officially, they were proposed by the government with the recommendation of the Minister of Justice and appointed by the Presidium of the Great

National Assembly (MAN). Starting in 1950, the job title became part of the Party's formal job classification system [nomenclatura], so all appointments, resignations, and firings had to be approved by the Secretariat (Ionescu-Gură 2005, 285).

The 1948 judicial reform also introduced lay judges [asesori populari] as part of "the democratization of justice." Lay judges participated on equal footing with career judges in both civil and criminal trials and outnumbered them (1 judge and 2 lay judges at trial courts and tribunals, 2 judges and 3 lay judges for appeal courts) (Schreiber 1948, 4–5). The 14 courts of appeals had 235 judges and 544 lay judges, the 60 tribunals had 874 judges and 4,176 lay judges, and trial courts had 1,274 judges and 35,488 lay judges (Ionescu-Gură 2005, 293). Their function was to "judge based on class affiliation," according to General Party Secretary Gheorghiu-Dej, and they were accordingly selected from among workers, peasants, and more rarely clerks or intellectuals. Lay judges were carefully vetted by the Party, and percentages of workers and Party members were determined in advance. For elections for lay judges in March 1957, for example, 55–65 percent had to be workers and 70 percent Party members or candidates (Ionescu-Gură 2005, 295–96).

The legal profession—"a reactionary institution" organized on an "individualized" basis and dominated by "bourgeois legal mentalities" (Mayo 1950, 950)—was also a target. Minister of Justice Pătrăşcanu believed that the number of lawyers pre-1945 was too big compared to the real needs of the population (quoted in Chichinaş 2009, 2). The bar was radically reformed in 1948: the bar association was abolished and replaced by lawyers' collectives organized by county/region and the entire profession was set to become simply an auxiliary in the justice process, subordinated to the Ministry of Justice. Public notaries, prosecutors, and military justice were similarly reformed to bring them fully within the control of the Party.

The criteria for joining the new lawyers' collectives included the effective exercise of the profession of lawyer as the primary source of income, and not having manifested "antidemocratic attitudes in their public or professional lives." The Minister of Justice who replaced Pătrăşcanu after his arrest in 1948, Avram Bunaciu, reported to the Political Bureau of the Central Committee of the Party on October 7, 1948, that as a result of the reforms only 4,500 lawyers remained active, out of 18,000 in the entire country (Ionescu-Gură 2005, 286–87). This meant that 75 percent of the entire bar had been purged. By 1959, however, the membership of the national jurists' association had shot back up to 12,000 (Editor 1959, 82–83).

In 1950, Decree 39 explicitly banned from the profession as "unworthy" [nedemni] former landowners, manufacturers, and businessmen, all those who exploited or exploit salaried labor, as well as those with a criminal record for crimes against the "political, social and economic basis" of the country, or any other crime deemed by the collective to cause incompatibility with the profession. Not coincidentally, these reasons are similar to the ones employed during the housing nationalization process. Reasons for the purging thus included other sources of income, inherited wealth, owning land or real estate, as well as real or imagined links with fascists or antidemocratic groups and activities (Chicinaş 2009, 12). The number of lawyers for each collective was now set by the Ministry of Justice (which by 1954 would gain full and official control of the legal profession, formerly independent).

For the Timişoara region, this number was set at 150 lawyers and 30 provisional lawyers (trainees). In total, 412 lawyers, 50 provisional lawyers, and 7 defenders applied for admission to the new collective in 1948. The Ministry of Justice further assigned 70 lawyers and 17 trainees throughout the Timiş-Torontal region, leaving for the city of Timişoara 50 lawyers, 28 legal consultants for companies, 2 lawyers who were incompatible, and 13 trainees, as reported by the local newspaper, *Luptătorul Bănăţean*, on April 28, 1948. Thus only 38 percent of those who applied were allowed to continue as lawyers, but those who applied for admission were only half of the total number of lawyers (in 1940, the Timişoara bar had a little over 850 lawyers).[3]

By comparison with the bar and the court system, law schools escaped relatively unscathed, although law professors associated with other political parties or movements were of course purged, and many of them ended their lives in prison or spent significant time in detention. Illustrative is the case of Istrate Micescu, a civil law professor at the Faculty of Law, University of Bucharest, member of the liberal party, Minister of Foreign Affairs (1937–1938), and later Minister of Justice (1939–1940), responsible for the creation and implementation of anti-Semitic legislation in Romania during that period. He was sentenced to 20 years in prison and died there in 1951.[4]

The main goal in reforming law schools, explained Ludovic Takacs (council member in the Ministry of Education and Culture), was to "get them closer to life," to connect theory and practice better (1960, 598). Law school graduates also had to fit the new class profile, for example, from the over 1,000 students enrolled during the 1959–1960 academic year, 55 percent were sons of workers and 17 percent of peasants. Overall between 1948 and 1959, there were 5,891 graduates from all 3 law schools in the country (Bucharest, Iaşi and Cluj, corresponding to the 3 historical regions of Romania). Their quality was lacking a bit, however, noted Party officials, as they showed poor class attendance and poor exam results. Only 57 percent of students from the Bucharest law school passed all their exams, and only 42 percent first year students passed their exams (Takacs 1960, 595–99). Only 35 percent of trainees who took their first exam for becoming full lawyers in October 1954 passed, and they generally had a poorer knowledge of civil law than criminal law (Dimitriu 1955, 241).

Civil law was clearly a particular area of neglect and in order to rectify the situation, a new law review—*Legalitatea Populară* [*Popular Legality*]—was created in 1955 to help lawyers and legal consultants in their practice. The Minister of Justice Gheorghe Diaconescu declared that the law review was to pay special attention to civil law, since civil law issues were the ones most frequently brought before the courts, but courts usually underestimated them, did not pay enough attention to them, and did not know enough civil law (1955, 3–5). *New Justice*, which had started publication in 1948, heavily favored criminal law and procedure.

Legislation was the final main target of Party reformers. Early on, Minister of Justice Pătrăşcanu set out to abolish the anti-Semitic legislation of the Second World War, draft legislation punishing war criminals, new electoral legislation, and revise most of the major codes—criminal code, codes of criminal and civil procedure, and code of military justice (Ionescu-Gură 2005, 283–90). The first vice-president of the Supreme Tribunal claimed that over 2,800 statutes and decrees from the pre-communist era were abolished between 1944 and 1952 (Manoliu 1955, 13), some of them in block, in an effort to "eliminate the bourgeois superstructure" (Deniza and Mâţă 2005, 72). Other key structural changes during this period included removing an entire layer of the court system—the appeal courts, removing the immovability of judges, transforming the bourgeois prosecutorial and police systems into the Soviet-style *procuratură* and *miliţie* and increasing their roles significantly, and eliminating judicial review of legislation.

The Party's main goal during this early period, under direct Soviet supervision and having learned from the early Soviet mistakes, was to bring the legal system strictly within its control in two significant ways: first, by replacing career personnel, particularly at the top, and adding lay judges—workers and peasants who were supposed to offset the "reactionary" and "bourgeois" tendencies of the career judiciary; second, by replacing legislation or, if that was not possible for all statutes and decrees, infuse it with class character (through interpretation, the participation of lay judges, etc.). Even when old statutes and codes remained in force, they were to be interpreted to fulfill the new ideological goals (Elian 1965, 16). In this process, criminal law and public law became privileged fields, while civil law, less of a threat, was mainly neglected.

These were important changes, but the transformation of law, its metamorphosis from a bourgeois to a communist mode of organizing and controlling society also depended on changing the idea of law itself. The battle for reimagining law took place not only at the level of reforming institutions and practices but also at the level of discourses and subjectivity. The endgame was to colonize law, construct it as a mechanism of social control and social engineering that would, in turn, remake humanity in a socialist image.

Despite the initial institutional changes and the regime's tight grip of the law, this colonization did not proceed smoothly.

LAW AND SPACES FOR RESISTANCE

The construction of a new type of power regime vertically and horizontally—the communist regime in Romania during the first 2 decades of communism—was a colossal undertaking. Yet communist regimes are quintessentially modern forms of power, and their legalities are also modern, drawing from familiar sources. This complex genealogy and the presence of multiple legal discourses, from repression to legal consciousness, position law during the transition to communism as simultaneously, albeit unequally, an instrument of power and a space of resistance. The question for communist legality is not whether law constrained state power, but the extent to which fractures in the state—law relationship and law's hybridity, its peculiar belonging to both the capitalist and the communist *nomos* opened up alternative spaces of resistance or simply difference.

These spaces for resistance arise out of continuities—of people, theories, methods of interpretation, and even content of statutes and decrees. Continuities with bourgeois law, for example, reinforced old habits of legality or simply inertia, while legal positivism and formalism were strategically adapted for carving out not only some autonomy for the least powerful branch of the government but also spaces of resistance for the citizenry (e.g., through petitions against nationalization and expropriations). I limit the discussion here to the "infrapolitics of resistance"—micro-resistance during the reform of the justice system, as well as spaces of resistance opened up by efforts to redefine formalism and positivism. I focus primarily on overall discourses and practices, rather than those specific to property, which are the focus of the remaining chapters.

The project of building socialist legality, of reimagining law, ran into serious problems at the level of the entire justice system, specifically in terms of finding enough new individuals willing to actively help rebuild it. Legal reality constructors operated at two levels: practice and scholarship/ideological leadership. The problem with the vast majority of practitioners was that they had been trained under bourgeois law, and even those who managed to escape the purges were less than enthusiastic supporters of the new regime. In 1955, for example, the human resources and education director in the Ministry of Justice discussed improving the ideological and professional training of judges, both young (poorly prepared) and old. The older judges knew law very well but "failed to keep pace with the times, have not internalized the new socialist principles, and do not know the new legislation" (Bârsan 1955, 216).

In the midst of purges and rapid policy changes, moreover, courts struggled to keep up. The main problems were less about following the Party's leadership and more about basic competence. Many courts were disorganized, inefficient, ambivalent and made lots of "political mistakes." Ion Ionescu, for example, a judge who led various tribunals in 4 districts in the southern part of Romania, was singled out for criticism in 1955. He apparently did not know what was going on in his courts and took no measures to improve their work. It seems that in 40 cases, the parties missed appeal deadlines because the files were archived before the decisions were final. The judge held only formal meetings, with no criticism or self-criticism sessions. He "could not care less" about procedures, the judges under his supervision played no active role in court proceedings, showed a poor understanding of legislation, and decided punishment without any attention to proportionality. His trials took too long and he did not study the case files beforehand (e.g., he approved formal charges in a case in which the defendant was ultimately acquitted because no crime had been committed). In some of his civil decisions the holding contradicted the facts established during the trial or court record, some decisions were issued with no legal basis, and overall he was passive, uninvolved in judicial politics, a poor manager, and, most importantly, completely neglected the political and ideological training of his judges and did not ask for help from the local Party organs (Boiu et al. 1955, 114–16). The new president of the Cluj tribunal (major city in Transylvania), by contrast, was presented as a model of leadership: he reorganized the tribunal; exercised supervision; established new work plans; organized the collective study of new legislation, instructions of the Minister of Justice, and decisions of the Supreme Tribunal; and paid special attention to educating lay judges. His own case files took no longer than 4 months from start to finish (Boiu et al. 1955, 110–12).

In 1955, the education director in the Ministry of Justice publicly criticized courts and judges that did not take seriously the new continuing professional and ideological trainings for judges. The new system established by the Ministry was based on individual study and outlines, monthly sessions, and wrap-up sessions. The individual study was done on the basis of syllabi established by the Ministry. If judges or court clerks had any questions, they raised them during the monthly training sessions, while the wrap-up sessions took place at the regional tribunals. Judges also had to study the decisions of the appeal tribunals. Many judges, however, did not do their own outlines, or they did them superficially, or simply copied them from other judges. Other courts, such as the Timişoara and Oradea tribunals, were more creative: they worked in study groups who wrote outlines that were then distributed to the rest of the judges in the county. This was also not deemed acceptable. Judges did make helpful suggestions to help improve their work, however. They asked to receive the decisions of the Supreme Tribunal, and asked for help in establishing personal libraries (Bârsan 1955, 210–16).

Stănescu-Bellu, a Timişoara lawyer who had been previously detained, noted in a 1953 *New Justice* article that the great majority of jurists had "a lazy attitude, waiting for others to reform legal science." In this article, which is a multifaceted example of cooptation, official contrition, as well as perverse resistance, he further pointed out that the legal profession was obstinate, as shown by the irregular publication of *New Justice* itself, that there was a significant scholarly void in the work of the Romanian Academy (*Legal Studies and Research* would only start publication in 1956), and that there was little discussion and publication of case law that illustrated changes in law. He concluded that jurists were lazy, practitioners not interested, all refused to combine professional and ideological training, and thus all refused to "contribute to the creation of a legal consciousness in the interest of the workers" (Stănescu-Bellu 1953, 534–35).

As far as creating a socialist legal consciousness that privileged state property, by 1955 judges still made "mistakes" when dealing with crimes against public property by punishing them too leniently (Bârsan 1955, 218; Lavrov and Tătaru 1949, 3). Judges did not protect socialist property strongly (Gergely 1955, 312–13), which only encouraged the persistence of "petit bourgeois" attitudes regarding socialist property (Manoliu 1955, 15–16). Regularly, law reviews published extensive articles discussing the protection of socialist property (e.g., Niţulescu 1960), yet the message clearly had a hard time getting through. This is of course not surprising, as upsetting the hegemony of bourgeois private property depended upon fundamental changes in the legal and ideological regime of property, which did not happen. In particular, the appropriation of the concept of private property for communist purposes significantly undermined efforts to denaturalize it.

Lay judges, a key element in the democratization of justice, were also less than enthusiastic participants: many of them refused to serve because they were paid less than in their regular jobs, which prompted various sets of policy changes establishing financial incentives for them (Ionescu-Gură 2005, 296). In June 1949, 40,954 lay judges were elected in the entire country—15,020 workers, 23,818 peasants, and 2,116 clerks. They needed to be trained, so the Ministry of Justice established 3 one-year law schools in Bucharest, Iaşi, and Cluj, as well as in smaller legal training centers affiliated with tribunals, offering 3-month sessions that were supposed to ground lay judges in a new legal culture and new class consciousness, according to Pătrăşcanu. Bunaciu, his successor as Minister of Justice, claimed there was a need to renew the justice system because "99 percent of the career judges are, if not against us, surely not with us" (in 1949).

Lay judges were officially on an equal footing with professional judges and were supposed to be a political pressure device, yet their enthusiasm and training never really improved. In 1955, the human resources and education director in the Ministry of Justice mentioned that various methods had been tried to train them, with limited success. Some courts took the training classes seriously but others did not, while in other places lay judges did not even bother to show up for classes. Over time, their participation in training lessened significantly, probably because the lessons were "too theoretical and abstruse" (Bârsan 1955, 223).

This failure is not entirely surprising. Law schools were the breeding ground for the new type of communist legal professional, whose task was to revamp basic legal concepts as well as entire branches of law in the midst of rapid and not necessarily coherent policy changes. Courses for lay judges included criminal law, constitutional and administrative law, political economy, general theory of law and state, dialectical and historic materialism, organization of the judicial system, workers' law, and the law of cooperatives (Ionescu-Gură 2005, 296–97). The emphasis, continuous throughout communism, was on public law, criminal law, and cooperatives' law. Conspicuously missing were civil law and other private law subjects. Their neglect meant that much of it would be left alone, but also that lay judges, already at a disadvantage educationally, received only very truncated and superficial versions of legal education.

Lawyers, like judges and legal scholars, adapted to changes but also resisted them, both openly and surreptitiously. Limiting the number of lawyers, for one, was met with resistance. The president of the Cluj collective, for example, objected to the limits set for the Cluj region—130 lawyers and 40 trainees. He asked the Minister of Justice to reconsider this low number and give them 200 lawyers, arguing that the city of Cluj had a military tribunal with the largest jurisdiction in Transylvania, a criminal court specially charged with judging war criminals, and two law schools. After assigning lawyers throughout the county, he continued, the city would be left with only 38 lawyers, a number much too small even when compared to similar jurisdictions in terms of number of lawyers per inhabitants (Bucharest was allowed 2,100 lawyers for 1 million inhabitants, while Cluj had 130,000 inhabitants and 40 lawyers). Cluj had a special situation, too, since Northern Transylvania had been incorporated into Hungary for part of the war: "The majority of lawyers from the Cluj collective were either deported by the fascist regime, or were refugees from Northern Transylvania, also because of this regime. As such, they lost everything they had. . . . Not allowing them to become part of the collective would lead to the miserable situation wherein they and their families . . . would have no livelihood [să fie lipsiţi . . . de bucăţica de pâine necesară]" (quoted in Chicinaş 2009, 3–4).

Some of the lawyers purged in 1948 were allowed to return after 1950, but mostly as in-house counsel for companies [jurisconsult], not attorneys, and they were banned from the lawyers' collectives. By 1959, the number of jurists in the Timişoara region was up to 738, almost to its pre-1948 level. The local association boasted that they had held over 700 presentations throughout the region to popularize legislation, had a library with over 450 titles, and wrote articles and notes for both *New Justice* and *Popular Legality* (137 decisions, 40 notes, 15 papers) (Editor 1959, 82–83). Panait Stănescu-Bellu, for example, a lawyer from Timişoara active during pre-communism, communism, and after 1989, was detained between 1950 and 1952, and upon his release and rehabilitation was allowed to practice as a legal consultant and later was readmitted in the lawyers' collective (Stănescu-Bellu 2006).

There is also evidence that some of the lawyers continued to practice, illegally, after they were disbarred. In 1955, the president of the Presidium of the Central Council of Lawyers' Collectives noted the "widely practiced" phenomenon of "clandestine lawyers" (they found 148 such cases in the city of Oradea, north of Timişoara) and talked about the need to eradicate it (Dimitriu 1955, 235–36).[5] Even lawyers accepted by the new regime, however, were problematic: many of them continued to identify with the interests of their clients, as opposed to the interests of socialist justice (Stănescu-Bellu 1953, 534–35), and were guilty of formalist and bourgeois tendencies. These included asking for too many delays in court, not studying the case files, excessively long closing statements, excessively performative pleadings, quoting bourgeois legal theories in court, and commuting to work (Dimitriu 1955, 237–38). Lawyers were seen as undemocratic because they served only the interests of the exploiters, charged very high legal fees so workers did not have easy access to lawyers, and manipulated the truth in order to obtain victory for their clients (Dimitriu 1955, 232–33).

The situation was even direr in terms of ideological leadership, particularly at the very beginning of the transition to communism, when entire issues of *New Justice*, for example, included only Soviet authors in translation, in large part because there were so few Romanian jurists on the communist bandwagon. *Justiţia Nouă* [*New Justice*] and *Legalitatea Populară* [*Popular Legality*], the former having a more doctrinal and ideological bent, the latter a more practical one, were the two main legal reviews of the time. The third one was *Studii şi Cercetări Juridice* [*Legal Studies and Research*], published by the Romanian Academy starting in 1956. Court decisions were not widely available (the decisions of the Supreme Tribunal only started to be published in annual collections in the 1950s), so the decisions and law review articles published in these law reviews performed important functions for practitioners throughout the country: informing them about the kinds of cases that came up more frequently before courts, troublesome legal issues, as well as signaling the Party policy and ideologically "correct" and "incorrect" decisions and doctrinal approaches.

The importance of legal scholars in Romania, similarly to other civil law systems, should not be underestimated. Treatises, commentaries, and even law journal articles aimed to systematize the law,

> formulate general theories about basic codes and legislation, in relation to the evolution of the legal system as a whole. . . . In the civil law, doctrine is an inherent part of the system and is indispensable to a systematic and analytical understanding of it. The doctrine is not a recognized source of law, but it has exercised a great influence in the development of law. It molds the minds of students, it gives direction to the work of the practitioners and to the deliberations of judges, and it guides the legislators towards consistency and systemization. (Dainow 1966–1967, 428)

Despite the fact that some of these discussions seem dogmatic, conceptualistic, formalistic, and overtly scholastic, as Inga Markovits noted for East Germany, their importance should not be dismissed:

> Communist legal debates . . . have to be looked at not so much as causes but as symptoms of social and political change. Even where theoretical tenets seem to have no practical consequences, they are highly indicative of the underlying political situation. . . . The intensity with which even the most esoteric theoretical issues are debated in communist jurisprudence reflects the political significance attributed to them: for the participants, these are not nice points of legal aestheticism, but essential questions regarding society's progress towards communism. (1968, 2–3)

One-time authors who published in the *New Justice* and *Popular Legality* were a mixture of Party and state officials (such as various Ministry of Justice representatives), practitioners trying to expunge old sins and gain some acceptance with the new regime (such as Stănescu-Bellu, the Timişoara lawyer mentioned earlier), newly minted lay judges, and eager young scholars trying to make their mark. Repeat authors (other than Soviet jurists in translation) included, on the one hand, jurists concerned with promoting the ideological goals of the communist regime, and on the other hand scholars focused on doctrinal analysis.

Authors in the former category were ideologically strident, such as Mihail Mayo and Emil Feraru. Both of them wrote articles on the virtues of Soviet justice and on the reforms of the justice system. Mayo was also an attorney working for the new regime as an *ex officio* defense attorney in a number of highly charged show trials against leaders of the Catholic Church, including the ones from the Banat region. He had a long career, publishing law review articles as late as 1979. Emil Feraru was also a show trial defense lawyer for Catholic priests charged with high treason and spying for the Vatican. In his memoires, one of his clients remembered that Feraru's argument, as a defense attorney (!), claimed that the Vatican had always been involved in espionage and every Catholic priest, bishop, and so on was an agent for the Vatican. His closing argument as a defense attorney was: "My clients are nothing but a link in the long chain of millenary espionage that has to end now. It is true that the real culprits are in Rome now, headed by the Pope. He should be judged and sentenced. Those here only execute the orders received from Rome and Washington. In the name of the working class I ask for the maximum punishment."[6]

Authors in the latter category, however, focused on doctrinal analysis, and illustrate well the quiet persistence of bourgeois law ideology and doctrine, particularly in the civil law field. Authors such as Salvator Brădeanu, Traian Ionaşcu, and Mihail Eliescu had been trained during the interwar period in the continental legal tradition and continued to write in that tradition. Their work can be best described as adapting the Napoleonic tradition to socialist restrictions while preserving as much of it as possible. Transylvanian jurists such as Brădeanu, an expert on land law and later the law of cooperatives, had been primarily concerned with the project of legal unification of Romania post-1918 (when Transylvania and Banat became part of Romania) (Mâţă 2008). Both Ionaşcu and Eliescu were among the best-known civilians of the twentieth century in Romania, the former as a general civil law specialist, the latter as perhaps the most important scholar of inheritance throughout communism. For this group of scholars, their technical expertise partially insulated them from communist politics (especially compared to criminal or public law branches).

Their strategy did not go unnoticed. The president of the Bucharest tribunal, for example, in an article against legal cosmopolitanism, attacked judges and lawyers as "prisoners of old methods and preoccupations," "vegetating in an idealist dogmatism" that was anti-scientific, reactionary, and a product of the imperialist bourgeois influence. The "sterility" of these efforts, the tendency toward "pure law" (clearly an attack on Kelsen) resulted in "law articles published mostly in foreign—preferably French—journals, while those written in Romanian were in a language far removed from the masses and their problems." He further bemoaned that "there are still around jurists who venerate bourgeois legal theorists and are not critical of them and do not contribute to the creation of a national legal science" (Nedelschi 1949, 730).

The president of the Bucharest tribunal reviewed a number of widely used treatises published between 1946 and 1948—civil law by Manolescu, criminal law by Dongoroz, inheritance by Eliescu—and criticized them for indulgent over-quotation of bourgeois theorists, not discussing Soviet ones, and ignoring the class character of law (Nedelschi 1949, 731–35). The authors were indeed guilty as charged. The civil law author, Manolescu, praised the French civil code as a great legal synthesis of a new, more democratic society, which swept aside feudalism; to him, law became democratic through the civil code, through it "law knew man," it became humanistic as differences between people were erased and the code attempted a synthesis around the notion of individual, of human. His definition of law was thoroughly bourgeois: "Law is general and uniform, promises abstract justice for all. The norm that cannot be formulated [neformulabilă] is individual and particular, and realizes concrete justice for all." Eliescu, who worked on inheritance, wrote in 1948 that inheritance was based on "individual property, family and social solidarity, and the principle of free will."

As late as 1976, legal scholars noted the intractability of civil law in particular (e.g., Vasilescu 1976). Civil law was singled out as a bastion of bourgeois ideas where formalism continued to predominate (Arjanov 1949, 154), and which enjoyed relative independence from the economic base and the state (Bratus 1949, 366). This was not only a theoretical issue, as the concern was that the "formalism and objectivity" of law professors, scholars, judges, and lawyers trained under the previous regime and operating in apparently technical fields (like civil law) in fact covered their "attachment to the former regime and hate for the workers" (Mihalca 1949, 299).

There was concern that judges in particular needed to be careful about adopting the wrong method of investigation—formalist and metaphysical, failing to pay sufficient attention to the realities of each case. An example of a case that was singled out as egregiously formalist was that of a postman who had defrauded the state. The local court sentenced him to 2 years, the prosecutor appealed, the Supreme Tribunal ruled that the sentence was not proportional (too small), and on remand the local tribunal resentenced the postman to 2 years and 1 month in prison (Gergely 1955, 307, 312). In this case, the local court appears to have used formalism as a tool of resistance—whether on an ideological or hierarchical basis.

Legal consciousness, it seems, is not quite as easily controlled as the regime imagined, and consequently neither is the construction of new socialist subjectivities. The justice system was a very qualified success, achieved initially through massive institutional reorganization. Insiders to the law and their legal consciousness were never fully transformed, and lawyers never really ceased to be bourgeois lawyers, particularly those specializing in civil law.

Outsiders to the law, whether enemies of the regime or friends, negotiated their own journey. The takings of the late 1940s and early 1950s are the quintessential political, legal, social, and cultural process at the heart of building communism. They are therefore an ideal case study that illuminates the construction of both socialist subjectivities through law, as well as of socialist legality itself. The newly marginalized, as former owners in the early socialist period were, lost their privileged status (owners protected by capitalist law) and became "strangers to the law" who had to try to reassert their rights to inclusion (Abrego 2011), outsiders to formal law looking in (Kirkland 2008). Meanwhile, state bureaucrats, which included both those with legal training and without, gained access to the levers of power and implicitly its instrument, law. The construction of socialist legality itself took place through the interactions between the former owners and the officials throughout the nationalization and expropriation processes, through the meanings and cultural practices at the intersection of these interactions (Ewick and Silbey 1998, 22).

NOTES

1. For a broader discussion about how this influenced the anthropology of Eastern Europe, see Friedman (2003).

2. There is by now a vast literature on legal consciousness in the United States and other Western countries. Key authors include Susan Silbey (1998, 2005), Patricia Ewick (1998, with Silbey), Jean and John Comaroff (1991, 1992), David Engel (1998), Frank Munger (2003, with Engel), Sally Merry (1985, 1990), and Michael McCann (1994).

3. National Archives of Romania Timişoara, Collection Barou, Baroul Avocaţilor Definitivi.

4. Other examples from the Bucharest law school are George Strat and Hanibal Teodorescu (Stănescu-Bellu 2006, 33). There is a vast literature on the communist repression and its victims, including memoirs, testimonials, and biographies (e.g., Ioanid 1999; Nicodim 2003; Buteanu 2004; Stănescu-Bellu 2006; Sipoş 1999; Popescu 2000), memoirs and testimonies of former investigators (e.g., Jela 1999), and historical analysis (e.g., Cesereanu 2005, 2006; Deletant 2001; Marineasa and Vighi 1994; Bălan 2000). Comprehensive websites include www.procesulcomunismului.com (which has a database listing most of those detained), The National Institute for the Study of Totalitarianism (www.totalitarism.ro), and The Romanian Institute for Recent History (www.irir.ro).

5. The legal profession was again reorganized in 1954, under Decree no. 281, published in the Official Bulletin no. 34/July 21, 1954.

6. Mons. Ieronim Menges, in Ciobanu (2003), and http://www.vladimirghika.ro.

Chapter 3

Property in Extremis

The Taking of Homes

The Romanian communist regime's goal, following the policy of the new colonial master, the Soviet Union, was the elimination of private property over means of production, and more fundamentally, dismantling the hegemony of private property. Private property exists in and through law, so the success of denaturalizing the institution and concept of private property depends upon the reliability of this medium. Law itself, however, was in transition and deeply contradictory, simultaneously backward and forward looking, an instrument of repression and a space of relative autonomy, inertia, and resistance, particularly in the area of civil law. The communist regime, in other words, used a relatively unreliable and untrustworthy tool—bourgeois law, hastily amended, inherited from the prior regime—to undertake a paradigm shift.

Takings (nationalizations and expropriations) were the primary means of achieving the goal of dismantling private property, and March 6, 1945, is the "official" start date for the new regime, when the first communist government, under the leadership of Dr. Petru Groza, took oath. Yet the reconfiguration of property relations, albeit within a capitalist framework, started taking place during the Second World War, with the passage of anti-Semitic laws depriving the Jewish population of its urban and rural property (Federation of Jewish Communities of Romania 1993), and of wartime requisition laws (e.g., Law 139/1940). The expropriation of Romania's Jewish population was a hallmark of the wartime fascist regime of Ion Antonescu (1940–1944) that spearheaded the Holocaust in Romania. Jewish owners experienced multiple waves of expropriation: during the war, followed by formal but delayed and incomplete reparatory measures post-1945, then distinct immigration waves to Israel that also entailed loss of property, as well as nationalization and expropriation connected to the transition to communism (see Friling, Ioanid, and Ionescu 2004;

Rotman 2004, 61–65). The fascist regime did not attempt to dismantle private property as an institution and system of values, and focused on property theft from Jews as well as other groups (e.g., Roma), but there are important continuities from a legal and property rights consciousness.

Requisition laws were extended after the war for a significantly longer period during the 1950s and were often used as a default measure for takings. Archival documents show both the penchant of local administrative bodies to rely upon requisition for seizing desired private property, real and mobile, as well as resistance from private individuals, who complained and petitioned for restitution as late as the 1960s.

These measures are significant because even though they were not part of the communist agenda of fundamentally unsettling private property, they constituted the field of postwar transition to communism, and already signaled the confusion of the new regime vis-à-vis property. Anti-Semitic laws were repealed after the war (even though the implementation of restitution was delayed and incomplete, and restitutive measures were only temporary [see, for example, Friling, Ioanid, and Ionescu 2004; Rotman 2004, 61–65]). This was mirrored during the next ten years in the expropriation and restitution of German and Hungarian property.

The communist reshaping of property took place in five short years, between 1945 and 1950, primarily through legal avenues basing their legitimacy on three distinct ideologies: postwar transition of punishment (expropriation of ethnic Germans, Hungarians, of abandoned property, and all those considered to have collaborated with the Nazi regime; "abandoned property" often times belonged to those who fled immediately after the end of the war, or those sent to labor camps in Siberia and elsewhere); land reform—initially expropriating all estates over 50 ha and giving land up to 5 ha to poor peasants (1945), later expropriating everything that had not been expropriated in 1945 (1949); and the elimination of property as exploitation ("the great nationalization"). The height of the transformation is 1948–1950, with the passage of the new constitution of the Popular Republic of Romania, the nationalization of industrial and commercial enterprises of all kinds, including houses, and the finalization of land reforms. Houses and apartments were lost through every one of these avenues. By 1950, the state had become the official or de facto owner of most industry, commerce, and land in the country.

The 1948 constitution of Romania, based on the 1936 Stalinist constitution, secured the constitutional basis for the nationalization laws to come and espoused for the first time the socialist state's ideology regarding property. The constitution acknowledged only three types of property: state, cooperative, and private (in that order of importance) (Article 5). The constitution directly nationalized certain assets (e.g., mines, forests, telegraph, telephone, post, radio) (Article 6), and established that, when necessary for the general interest, all means of production, banks, and insurance companies become state property (Article 11). Article 15 established the principle of the planned economy.[1]

The most visible attack on housing was Decree 92/1950 for the nationalization of the most valuable housing stock in the country. Overall, the regime used at least ten legal mechanisms to seize houses and apartments, and processes of nationalization and expropriation continued throughout communism (unlike the situation of land or industry), and were partially overlapping. Approximately 30–40 percent of houses were nationalized or expropriated, but the overall policy regarding houses and apartments was much more ambivalent than this number would indicate. There was, in fact, no unitary, coherent policy regarding housing. The taking of housing was partial and arbitrary, the regime justified the takings in a variety of ways—punitive, redistributive, utilitarian, and was inconsistent in how it treated the seized property afterward. The state took houses away and then gave them up, as if it couldn't quite make up its mind.

There are three, not necessarily mutually exclusive, categories of legal mechanisms for the taking of housing: nationalization (direct and indirect), expropriation, and covert expropriation. Direct nationalization targeted explicitly urban housing, while indirect nationalization and expropriations targeted urban and rural housing equally. The variety, scope, unevenness, distinct justifications, and haphazard implementation of these mechanisms are one indication that the regime did not have a coherent policy regarding housing. The lack of a coherent policy regarding private property in housing is due to multiple factors: conflicting policy imperatives, the multiple meanings of houses, and most importantly, the ambition of the entire project. After all, the communist regime confronted an institution that had been central to Romanian law, politics, economy, society, and culture for almost a century, and had been instrumental to its modernization efforts.

JUSTIFYING THE TAKINGS: EXPLOITATION AND THE HOUSING CRISIS

The nationalization of urban housing in 1950 took place at the depth of Stalinist repression and was the last major strike of the new regime against private property and housing inequalities in Romania. Aside from the land problem, it was the most difficult part of the restructuring of private property for the communist regime. As painful as the nationalization of industry and commerce was for those involved, the bulk of the population was only indirectly affected, as many of the now state-owned enterprises continued to function, albeit with significant changes in management, reorganization, and so forth. Houses were an entirely different matter, however, as a much larger swath of the population would be directly affected. Yet this was also the last important class battle, "the site where the enemy has been hiding," as described in a meeting of the Ministry of Interior (Chelcea 2004, 111).

For the communist regime, houses and apartments were primarily about exploitation, they were "means of production," that is, rental property, and their nationalization was justified in the context of poor urban living conditions, superficially similar to nineteenth-century critiques made by Proudhon and Engels in *The Housing Question*. Private property of housing was inherently exploitative, as private property was the appropriation of someone else's labor, it was power. As a power relationship over persons and things (Macpherson 1978, 4; Gray and Gray 1999, 13; Alexander 1991, 276–77), private property embodied the coercion or exercise of power by the propertied (housing owners) against the property-less (tenants and those who could not afford to own).

In the classical Lockean ideal, private property is a "moral space within which an individual has control over his own affairs" (Reeve 1986, 142–43), it delineates a clear separation between the individual and society, and is fundamentally a guarantee of freedom. Marx criticized the separation of the individual from society, of public and private, and the liberal focus on autonomy and protection, and thought private property was antithetical to freedom (in *On the Jewish Question*). This is not the same freedom Locke was talking about, however. For Marx, freedom was associated not with privacy, but with rationality and community—the conscious planning of one's life, and freedom from external, irrational, uncontrollable forces. Private property needed to be destroyed because by necessity it divided people, opposing the divergent interests of the propertied and property-less (Brenkert 1979, 123–28).

More pragmatically, however, from the regime's perspective, was the extent to which post–Second World War Romania, and in particular big cities, had a housing problem. Historically, the average size of the families and number of inhabitants living in a house in Timişoara was not significantly different from other European cities.

Table 3.1 indicates that while the average size of the family in the city decreased in size, housing conditions tightened over time, and the average number of inhabitants per house grew consistently throughout the years, so much so that despite a housing boom in the interwar period, when 4,643 private homes were built, totaling 5,786 apartments (1920–1936), by the beginning of the Second World War the average number of inhabitants per house was almost 11 (Munteanu and Munteanu 2002, 139–40).

In 1936, the total number of private houses in the city was 6,992, representing 82 percent of the total number of buildings in the city. Out of these, 87 percent were single-floor houses and only 13 percent had two or more levels;

Table 3.1. Average Size of Family and Number of Individuals/House

Indicators/Year	*1787*	*1870*	*1918*	*1936*	*1966*	*1977*	*1992*
Average no. of inhabitants per family	4.4	4.8	4.5	3.8	3	3.1	2.9
Average no. of inhabitants per house	7.6	12.7	15.9	10.9	11.5	13.9	15.1

Source: Munteanu and Munteanu (2002, 139).

Figure 3.1. One of the Main Boulevards in the City, circa 1950, Depicting Large, Multi-family Homes. *Source*: Primăria Manicipiului Timişoara, www.primariatm.ro.

the multilevel houses were spacious, modern (over 70 percent of homes had electricity), located in the prominent neighborhoods of the city and usually had gardens or significant backyards (see Figure 3.1). Ethnically, ownership of houses was unequally divided (Munteanu and Munteanu 2002, 210) (see Table 3.2).

Particularly at the high end, the housing market was dominated by Jewish and German owners, who were thus disproportionately impacted by urban housing nationalization. In terms of number of rooms, the vast majority of houses had only one or two rooms (Munteanu and Munteanu 2002, 211).

Table 3.3 shows that in Timişoara, 80 percent of housing was one and two-room apartments, which indicates that the vast majority of the people living in the city at the time had limited income. They were primarily workers, civil servants, small craftsmen, and so on. A 1937 "social investigation" by City

Table 3.2. Ownership of Houses by Ethnicity (Percentages)

Number of Floors/House	*Public*	*Romanians*	*Germans*	*Hungarians*	*Jewish*	*Others*
One floor	1.54	25.82	23.95	19.55	20.17	8.97
Two floors	6.26	18.50	20.41	6.39	42.72	5.72
Three floors	16.66	7.82	16.32	8.50	44.25	6.45
Four floors	21.57	11.76	17.65	7.84	39.22	1.96
Five to six floors	18.18	9.09	27.27	9.09	36.37	-
Average	2.46	24.65	23.43	18.17	22.68	8.61

Source: Munteanu and Munteanu (2002, 210).

Table 3.3. Dwellings by Number of Rooms in 1936

No. of Rooms	*No. of Total Dwellings*	*Percentage*
1	15,081	57.24
2	6,470	24.56
3	2,797	10.61
4	1,250	4.74
Over 4	750	2.85
Total	26,348	100

Source: Munteanu and Munteanu (2002, 211–2).

Hall revealed that in four out of the five boroughs of the city, over 50 percent of the population lived in studios (Munteanu and Munteanu 2002, 212), primarily because of income disparities and lack of sufficient housing, despite significant progress during the interwar period.

Once the Second World War began, the pace of new construction dropped dramatically, and by the end of the war hundreds of buildings had been destroyed. The uncertainty and severe poverty of the immediate postwar period was not conducive to new construction, either. The last pre-nationalization census noted a total number of 14,471 buildings (including annexes such as garages, sheds, summer kitchens, etc.) (Munteanu and Munteanu 2002, 218). Resolving the housing crisis was therefore a key point of legitimation for the new regime, which considered nationalization and expropriation of housing necessary both ideologically and pragmatically.

HOUSES AS HOMES AND ASSETS

Ordinary citizens, meanwhile, saw their housing equally as homes and income-generating assets. In other big European cities a more prototypically capitalist housing model prevailed, dominated by rational, profit-pursuing landlords. In major Romanian cities, by contrast, small, private, "patriarchal" landlords (i.e., no specialization and delegation) were the main providers of housing before nationalization (Chelcea 2004, 12). Romanian citizens built and acquired houses with two purposes in mind: to provide shelter for the extended family and as a "retirement fund" (Chelcea 2004, 84). Houses and apartments were distinctive in so far as they belonged equally to two social spheres: they were both family homes and income-generating assets, particularly for old age and the extended family (Chelcea 2004, 93). Houses in the pre-communist era were primarily used as homes throughout Romania, fostering an understanding of private property as important not just in an instrumental sense, but also emotionally and psychologically.

Moreover, the rental market in prewar Timişoara was quite small, since the vast majority of homes in the city in 1947 (over 80 percent) had only one or two rooms and the ownership rate was high (Munteanu and Munteanu 2002, 218). This was a rather "primitive" rental market dominated by the petty bourgeoisie and landlord-tenant relationships that ran the gamut from "exploiter-exploited" to, more often, tenants as part of the household or even charges of the landlord (Chelcea 2004, 36–38). Overall, this was less about profit and more about investing in social relationships and the kin's future (Chelcea 2004, 81–82).

Nationalized and expropriated owners contesting the taking of their houses often pointed out that the houses were "family homes," many of them originally acquired as dowry, a key nexus point between concepts of family and patrimony.[2] They talked about the extent to which the nationalized houses represented the apex of their lives and how all their savings and work were geared toward buying houses to ensure the well-being and future of their families. For example, the heir of a former owner describes in the following manner the owner of the house, whom he had inherited: "The deceased . . . was a small craftsman, a tailor, who all his life worked with the clients' fabric and no employees. After tens of years of work, he acquired through his work this house . . . because he only lived for his work and his family. . . . He invested in this house all his labor of 40 years."[3]

This understanding of houses as the nexus of family and work, of private and public, as the physical and symbolic space for the family unit emerges from many complaints filed by former owners and is reminiscent of Kantian and Hegelian, rather than Marxian theories of property and personhood (an understanding reinforced by Decree 92/1950 clustering buildings belonging to the husband, wife, or minor children). For Marx and Engels, private property structurally encourages individuals to view others as separate and antithetical, as obstacles and limitations, rather than possible aids, and thus has a negative, rather than a positive effect on the development of human personality (clear from Marx's *On the Jewish Question*). Moreover, for them the connection between the modern, monogamous family and private property is deeply troubling because it strengthens inequality within marriage and the protection and privileging of private property (*The Origin of Family, Private Property and State*).

By contrast, Kantian and Hegelian theories of property and personhood contend that property is essential for individual development and freedom by providing material support to agency.[4] Contemporary personhood theories have added yet another layer and point of emphasis, as property and the various "objects" it embodies matter not just in an instrumental sense, but also from an emotional and psychological point of view. Thus, property is seen as constitutive of people, both individuals (Radin) and collectives (the movement for cultural property). In the former sense, property signifies "an assertion of self and control of one's environment [that] provides human beings with a place of deep psychological refuge" (Underkuffler 2003, 1). Thus, peoples' lives are "dominated by an intuitive sense of property and belonging" (Gray 1994, 158) and property rights are bound up with respect for persons: "Most people possess certain objects they feel are almost part of themselves. These objects are closely bound up with personhood because they are part of the way we constitute ourselves as continuing personal entities in the world" (Radin 1982, 959).

Former owners in Timişoara similarly understood ownership of their homes as a multifaceted, multifunctional concept (von Benda-Beckmann, von Benda-Beckmann, and Wiber 2006, 1–39). Houses were the locus of labor, income, and security, family and continuity, at individual, communal and ethnic levels (e.g., for the Germans living in the city). The dual nature of houses—homes and assets—that informed the citizens' understanding of private property clashed with the regime's ideological focus on houses as means of production and site of power at the root of societal inequalities that needed to be eliminated. This is not only a clash between different understandings of property and houses, but also one between "culture" and "ideology." In this latter sense, the symbolic organization of life through the frameworks provided by pre-communist private property came under attack by a new, closed off, definitive, official state ideology invested with absolute authority. "Culture," on the other hand, is not a closed, uniform, static system, but "a set of polyvalent practices, texts, and images that may, at any time, be contested" (Comaroff and Comaroff 1991, 17).

Ideologically, the Romanian communist regime attempted to reposition private property from a pre-communist, Western-oriented discourse of property as protection, empowerment, power, and efficiency to a socialist discourse that stressed labor and social responsibility. Western theories of property were at the basis of Eastern European regimes of property prior to communism, including in Romania. Communism directly targeted them, and failed to a large degree. Countries of the region are still rife with "folk" models of property drawing from liberal, communitarian, socialist, and even older "commons" theories, as anthropologists working on Eastern Europe found out after 1989 (Hann 2000).

PREPARING FOR TAKINGS: THE 1948 CENSUS

Historically, Timişoara had always kept good track of both its population and urban real estate—as part of the Habsburg Empire, censuses had begun as early as 1784, and were on average undertaken every ten years (Munteanu and Munteanu 2002, 140). Much of the information needed for the state to gain control over the housing market and later for nationalization was collected through the 1948 buildings census, which was finalized in December of that year and involved 550 census takers, controllers, and technicians.[5] The census included all inhabitants, dwellings, kitchens, stores, and other urban real estate and agricultural tools, excluding household items. Also excluded were public institutions, hospitals, and functioning factories (but attached housing was included) (as explained in the local newspaper, *Luptătorul Bănăţean*, on December 13, 1948, which published a number of articles on the census in the days preceding it).

Each owner, tenant, or custodian of an apartment had to fill out a census form and if more than one family lived in an apartment, all "heads of the family" had to sign the form. An apartment was defined in the "usual way" to include rooms and annexes (hallway, bathrooms, kitchen, pantry, etc.), which "from the point of view of construction constitute an architectural unit." For housing in public institutions and large enterprises, temporarily each separate part of the building was considered one apartment, and each separate floor one apartment, unless there were rooms that were permanently inhabited, which were themselves counted as one apartment (*Luptătorul Bănăţean* from December 12, 1948).

All citizens had to allow in the census takers, provide all information necessary for the census form, and the census takers had the right to see all the rooms in the house. Refusing to provide information, posing any obstacles to the census or providing false information was considered sabotage (*Luptătorul Bănăţean* from December 11, 1948). Landlords had to submit a report regarding the rent due after August 15, 1947, by a specific deadline (November 30, 1947) (*Luptătorul Bănăţean* from November 17, 1947). Homeowners also had to include a sketch of the dwelling on the census sheet. Those who refused were subjected to official inquiries, singled out in newspaper articles, and potentially arrested as saboteurs (*Luptătorul Bănăţean* from December 18, 1948). Very helpfully, the local newspaper also published an

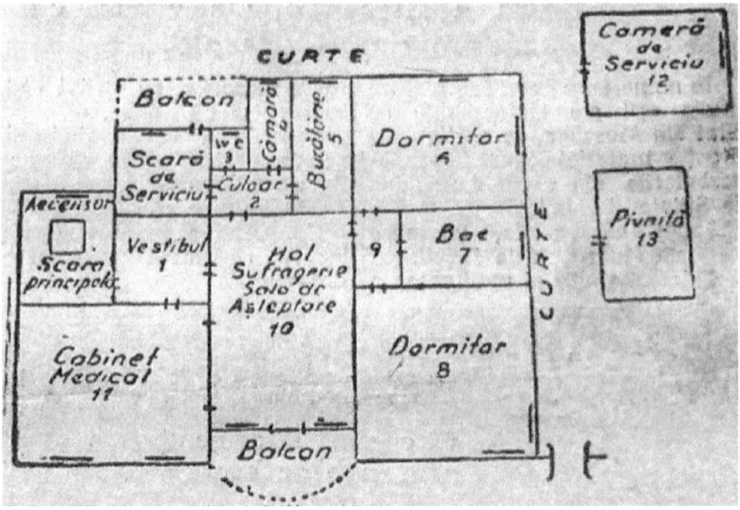

Figure 3.2. Newspaper Example of a Sketch of an Apartment. Translation: 1) Entryway, 2) Hallway, 3) Toilet, 4) Pantry, 5) Kitchen, 6) Bedroom, 7) Bathroom, 8) Bedroom, 9) Hallway, 10) Hallway/Living Room/Waiting Room, 11) Medical Office, 12) Service Entry, 13) Basement. *Source*: Published in *Luptătorul Bănățean,* December 11, 1948.

example of how apartments should be sketched, based on a home/medical office (see Figure 3.2).

Open threats to discourage disobedience were disconcertedly played off by the polite, almost pleasant tone of many of the newspaper articles, for example "the inhabitants are warmly invited to stay home during the census taking activity," or "census takers are only too happy to help with completing the forms" (*Luptătorul Bănățean* from December 13, 1948). The census process showcases the regime's governing prowess and the extent to which it acted as a characteristically modern form of power. Alternately threatening and cajoling, the communist regime, which was still at the stage of state capture, enrolled the population for its knowledge building purposes and later used the information directly provided by the owners, such as the sketches, for nationalization and other takings, in effect for their own subjugation. The ultimate goal, in Foucaldian terms, was the production of an obedient, useful communist subject, a goal to be achieved to a large extent through novel techniques of power, of obtaining, organizing, and exploiting knowledge about individuals, rather than sheer repression.

The extensive coverage of the census in the local Party paper aimed to prepare the population psychologically and establish the legitimacy of the regime's encroachment on the housing market and of the takings more generally (there had also been a population census earlier in the year, as well as a rural census). The regime had a three-pronged strategy: first, to gain updated knowledge about the housing situation in the city through the census; second, to take over the rental market by establishing rental offices to control tenancy relationships in the city; and third and last, to nationalize urban housing.

The lead article for December 11, 1948, in the main local newspaper, *Luptătorul Bănățean*, justified the need for the census precisely from the angle of the housing crisis:

> The area of rentals was one in which the control of the state could not be exercised. This resulted in real chaos with regard to rentals of apartments or furnished rooms. Owners and the so-called rental agencies engaged in shameless profiteering, unheard of exploitation of all working people. Although the law protects tenants by automatically extending leases and pegging the rent to the value of the house, owners who had available apartments, as well as some tenants rented them out according to their whims, aiming for high rents that working people could not afford. . . . Faced with this intolerable situation, the state found it necessary to establish rental offices. . . . In order to find out exactly the status of the housing market in Timişoara, and in conformity with the Instructions received from the Ministry of Interior, the City Hall organizes, starting on December 12th, a general census of all buildings and apartments in the city.

A favorite strategy to keep the housing crisis in the public's mind was the publication of short pieces and op-eds in the local newspaper about the difficulty of finding an apartment for rent. The articles blamed the shortage of rental property on the owners' deviousness and efforts to hide "empty apartments" from those with little money. The authors bemoaned the process of finding an apartment and the requirements imposed by landlords, and accused them of "specula" (profiteering, speculation), one of the newly emerging code words for enemies of the regime (*Luptătorul Bănățean* from October 4, 1947). *Luptătorul Bănățean* tracked the progress of the 1948 census, ostensibly undertaken for the benefit of the workers in order to establish the "real situation of dwellings in the city" and to strike at the "greedy house owners, middlemen and profiteers" in this field. Newspaper articles identified by name various owners (later indeed nationalized), calling them out for living in luxurious circumstances, such as three people in seven rooms, while the workers "had nowhere to go," and furthermore refusing to allow others to rent rooms (December 17, 1948).

In yet another type of articles, Timişoara was depicted as a city that had grown out of hand, with no control or planning—houses, small gardens, and sheds popped up "like mushrooms after the rain," with no canalization or paved roads. Former politicians were blasted for corruption, incompetence, and indifference, particularly regarding traffic, and the city was described as "bloated" ["supra-dimensionat"], yet lacking in fundamental areas, such as sufficient housing (Bodascher 1948). In reality, the dire state of the housing market in the city had been known long before the war, through the regular censuses, while historically the city had gone through several massive waves of reconstruction and modernization, the most recent one at the beginning of the century. Moreover, in 1939 City Hall had issued a new plan for the systematization of the city, focused precisely on zoning to encourage new industrial and commercial activities, and on redrawing internal and external traffic routes.

The propaganda leading up to the nationalization emphasized the class divide and blamed the middle and upper-middle classes for the lack of housing. Yet the ideal trumpeted was ambiguous: tenants were described as belonging to "the category of people without their own shelter/home" ["categoria oamenilor fără adăpost propriu, din categoria chiriaşilor"], thus appearing to promote private property as the solution to housing (*Luptătorul Bănăţean* from September 25, 1947). This ambiguity would never really disappear, as the regime allowed private construction of housing while simultaneously trying to dismantle private property.

URBAN HOUSING NATIONALIZATION

The term "nationalization" commonly refers to the process of governmental takeover of private industries or businesses. It is not usually employed vis-à-vis housing, but the use of the term in this context was not accidental: the early Romanian communist regime was making a point about houses (particularly multi-apartment units), namely that, similarly to business and industry, houses were a means of exploitation within the Marxist framework. The regime nationalized housing with no compensation in two ways: directly, through Decree 92/1950, and indirectly, where houses were attached to nationalized businesses, industries, or land.

Housing nationalization, like the other takings, was overwhelmingly planned and achieved legally, rather than extra-legally. The full title of the relevant legal text is Decree 92 from April 19, 1950, "for the nationalization of some houses (of former manufacturers, bankers, businessmen, and other elements of the high bourgeoisie, houses of exploiters of housing, hotels and others like them)."[6] The decree was published in the Official Bulletin no. 36 from April 20, 1950, and had 12 short articles.

All the main newspapers, including *Luptătorul Bănăţean*, the Party newspaper in the region, published the decree on Friday, April 21, 1950. Nonetheless, this was not meant to achieve transparency: while the decree was published, the more important parts, the appendixes, were not, and neither were the myriad secret local and central Instructions adopted later on (as late as 1953). Furthermore, the takings themselves took place for the most part on April 20 and 21, thus before or simultaneously with the publication. The publication of the text of the decree communicated, at a minimum, the regime's goals and commitment, but was also an expression of (class) justice and perpetuated a regime of fear and insecurity regarding targets, procedures, and timing of the takings. The publication also illustrates the emerging socialist legal formalism of the period and the effort to build regime legitimacy through legality.

Article 1 introduced the goals of the decree: "to strengthen and develop the socialist sector in Romania," "to better administer the housing stock at risk of dilapidation because of the sabotage of the high bourgeoisie and exploiters who own a large number of buildings," and "to deprive exploiters of an important means of exploitation." These goals signal the incompatibility of capitalist and socialist routes, the construction of the categories of saboteurs and exploiters in the housing field, and the extent to which the regime placed "exploitation" at the core of private property that needed to be eliminated.

The decree nationalized:

1. "Buildings that belonged to former manufacturers, great land estate owners, bankers, businessmen, and other elements of the high bourgeoisie.
2. Buildings that belong to housing exploiters.
3. Hotels and their inventory.
4. Buildings currently erected for purposes of exploitation that were abandoned, and all the building materials.
5. Buildings damaged or destroyed during the war or the earthquake, built for purposes of exploitation and whose owners did not repair or rebuild."

These categories, and in particular the second one, which turned out to be at the core of takings, would be somewhat clarified only three years after the adoption of the Decree. In the meantime, homeowners and the regime clashed precisely around the question of who qualified as a housing exploiter.

Article 2 of the Decree excluded from nationalization buildings that belonged to workers, civil servants, small craftsmen, intellectuals by profession, and retirees. Article 2 has been the bedrock of restitution cases post-1989, but abuses and its widespread disregard were clear from the very beginning. Open violations of Article 2 were so excessive that Decree 524/1955 (not published, dealing with restitution) reiterated the exemption in the following terms: "There are not subject to the decree [Decree 92] and cannot be nationalized buildings belonging to workers and retired workers, as well as clerks, small craftsmen, professional intellectuals and all other retirees whose income was based on labor ('provenite din muncă'). These dispositions are applied starting April 19, 1950. There cannot be nationalized buildings built after April 19, 1950." These exempt categories, as we will see, were never truly exempt, as their Article 2 ascription was often superseded by even the smallest tinge of "exploitation."

Nationalized buildings became state property, with no compensation and free of any debts or third-party rights over them (Article 3). Article 4 of the Decree defined "buildings" to include land, constructions, and all accessories and installations used for their maintenance. Article 5 clarified that buildings belonging to the husband, wife, or minor children were considered to belong to one owner in the application of the decree. Through Article 6, the state replaced the former owners in all their rights vis-à-vis the building; furthermore, all those living in the nationalized buildings, including former owners, became state tenants from the moment of the nationalization. Concretely, nationalized buildings were to be managed by the Temporary Committees of the municipal People's Councils—the local administrative bodies at the time (Article 7).

Articles 8 and 9 punished with five to ten years of hard labor and confiscation of all property those who damaged, destroyed, or sold nationalized property, as well as those who thwarted or attempted to thwart the nationalization. The Temporary Committees of the People's Councils had to formally register the state's rights created on the basis of the decree (Article 10), and the State Commission for the Implementation of the People's Councils Statute was charged with implementing the nationalization decree (Article 11). Finally, the last article prescribed that the decree entered into force on the date of its publication. Yet the takings themselves took place on the same day the decree was published, in large part to prevent resistance.

The appendixes to the decree listed, in alphabetical order by owner's name, by towns and cities, the nationalized buildings. For example, the Timişoara appendix, which has 1,022 names (a few repeat), starts with: "1. Ardelean Iosif, 4 apartaments, Timişoara, Emanoil Gojdu St no 10." The appendixes and the listing numbers are key for all procedures related to Decree 92, including submitting and resolving petitions, both during communism and in post-communism. Petitions were categorized and solved based on whether and where the house was listed in the appendixes, and all documentation about the house (such as subsequent petitions by heirs) was linked through the appendix number. In effect, the number under which a house was listed in the nationalization appendix became the most important part of that house's history and bureaucratic life throughout the communist and post-communist regimes. The appendix and the personal elements it contains also distinguish Decree 92 from other nationalization statutes and decrees, and mark it as a type of private bill.

Decree 92 nationalized about a quarter of privately owned urban houses in the country as a whole, approximately 120,000 apartments (Chelcea 2004, 1, 112; Dawidson 2004, 125). This number does not include secondary urban housing nationalization. In Timişoara, Decree 92 nationalized 1,022 owners for a total of 1,030 buildings and 10,400 apartments, offices, small stores, and so on (in more detail, these included 9,231 apartments, 151 sheds, 32 garages, 606 small stores and workshops, and 6 hotels [Mioc 2007, 208]). The total number of nationalized dwellings in the city, according to City Hall records, was 11,132, which represents about 35 percent of the total number of dwellings in the city at the time.[7] This total number includes *de jure* and *de facto* nationalizations—the former means that owners were listed in the appendix, the latter that they were not, but the house was taken "in the spirit" of Decree 92.

Many of these apartments and houses were among the best in the city: centrally located, spacious, relatively new, and in good to very good condition. Approximately 75 percent of the nationalized buildings were in good condition, while 25 percent were in bad shape (Mioc 2007, 208). While there is no clear pattern of nationalization, what Chelcea (2004) notes for Bucharest holds for Timişoara, as well: the farther away from the downtown, the better chances a building had for escaping nationalization (see Figure 3.3).

Timişoara had a slightly higher nationalization rate than the rest of the country's big cities—35 percent versus 25 percent (smaller cities and towns had smaller nationalization rates). Bucharest, for example, lost about 22 percent of its apartments through nationalization, most of them in the downtown areas (Chelcea 2004, 19–20). Timişoara, like other Transylvanian cities, is

Figure 3.3. Typical Nationalized House, Containing a Pharmacy and Four Apartments, Nationalized in 1950 (Postcard circa 1920). *Source*: This particular house was listed as Number 823 in the Timişoara appendix.

also distinct because a large number of the nationalized owners were German, Jewish, or Hungarian. Based on the appendix, only approximately 25 percent of them were Romanian. This has a significant impact on restitution claims post-1989, since former owners or their heirs who had left the country, as is the case for many German or Jewish owners, are pitted against tenants, many of them ethnic Romanian, who continued to live there. Like other Transylvanian big cities, but unlike Bucharest or Iaşi (the historical capital of the province of Moldavia), which experienced massive demolitions throughout communism, most of Timişoara's nationalized housing survived.

"Mrs. A, whether you sign or not, the house is taken"

Preparations for nationalizing urban housing had been taking place for some time by 1950 and the local administration had collected information at least since the 1948 census. I could not find archival data regarding the initial creation of the nationalization appendix for Timişoara prior to the 1950 nationalization, or the criteria used. There is significant data, however, about planning for the second wave of urban housing nationalization. Here, I use data from local newspapers of the time, archives, secondary sources, and interviews to reconstruct the process of the takings themselves.

The nationalization itself took place with no notice on April 20 and 21, 1950, and involved 126 Party activists (50 employed and 76 volunteers), 244 policemen, and 233 administrators (Mioc 2007, 208). Like previous takings, preparations were shrouded in secrecy—the "strictly secret" instructions to the local Party committees ordered that "the entire preparations for the nationalization must be undertaken in complete secrecy" (underlined in the original document) (CADCR Report 2006, 617).

The process was relatively low-key initially: a Party activist and a policeman showed up with the official nationalization notice, which had to be signed by the owner and the state representatives. One interviewee, who was sixteen years old at the time of the nationalization, remembers that one day in April 1950, two men came to the house and told her mother that the house was being nationalized. They did not scream or threaten her, but simply said: "Mrs. A, whether you sign or not, the house is taken." ["Doamna A, ori semnaţi, ori nu semnaţi, casa e luată."] Although most takings took place during those two days in April, some happened as late as June of 1950. The officials retro-dated the nationalization memo, despite complaints from the owners, claiming: "these are our instructions."[8]

Official nationalization notices read as follows:

> Today, April 20th, at 7 am, the undersigned . . . , living at . . . , as the representative of the Temporary Committee of the city of Timişoara, and on the

basis of permit no 120/1950, came to this address . . . , where I found . . . the owner, whom we told that

1) On the basis of Decree 92/1950 for the nationalization of some buildings, the
   Room
   Apartment
   Building   becomes state property
   Shed
   Garage
2) In the future, rent will be paid to the state.
3) Overdue rent will be paid to the state, as well.
4) The lodger is responsible for maintenance of the building.

We asked the lodger to show us the last rent receipt, which we stamped. . . .
I, the lodger, have been given notice and will conform.
This notice has been written in duplicate, one of which is given to the lodger."
(Signed by both parties.)

The nationalization notice is striking in multiple ways, not the least of which is that it exists. Why did the regime bother at all? The meaning of the nationalization notice can be construed on at least three distinct levels. First, it reaffirms the lack of absolute control of the regime at this point and its attempt to build legitimacy through legality. Second, as an example of "expressive formalism," it fulfills a juridico-political function, emphasizing the superior role of the Party to its public, the people, thus activating its power (Foucault 1975b, 49). Third, it is an expression of "consensual" legal violence that exemplifies a type of repressive law infused with a new educational-ideological role, and thus producing the new "communist solidarity." In a Durkheimian twist, this repressive law did not reflect the heart of collective consciousness, but attempted to construct it.

Internal Party and administration reports of the time noted that the general mood of the population during and immediately after the nationalization was good: the poor were happy about it, renters were indifferent, and the owners calm, signing the nationalization notices in proportion of 97 percent (Mioc 2007, 208). However, we do not know how many of these notices were actually given; by now, most of them have disappeared, and if the former owner was not listed in the Decree 92 appendix, ironically they faced greater difficulty proving the nationalization post-1989.

Occasionally, homeowners had no idea they had been nationalized, sometimes for significant amounts of time, and found out only when they attempted to sell their house and were denied the necessary permit, or when they asked local authorities for restitution, or when local officials seized construction materials and the like.[9] Some owners who thought they might be potential victims of nationalization became proactive agents and preemptively asked for either restitution or to be exempt from further nationalization. Owners' mobilization of the law points to a micro-economy of resistance through law that turned out to have a deep and lasting meaning vis-à-vis property and the role of law, as well as a cumulative impact on the regime's policies.

Sometimes, the seizing was brutal, particularly when the house was in a desirable location and a Party official wanted to move in right away: trucks and soldiers showed up and removed the furniture and the lodgers, regardless of status. At least immediately after nationalization, however, many former owners were allowed to continue to live there, although in significantly more cramped quarters. Any room that could possibly be inhabited was considered adequate, thus including kitchens, hallways and the like, sometimes for entire families (CADCR Report 2006, 616). A five-room house, for example, previously used as a two-bedroom apartment on the ground floor and a two-room medical office on the second floor, housed the former owners and three other tenants nine years after nationalization.[10] One of my more harrowing interviews with a tenant revealed that for over thirty years the family had shared the house with the former owners and never knew it. The tenants did not know the former owners had sued for restitution post-1989, and they were in shock to discover that people with whom they had shared a house for so long abhorred their presence there.

The best of the nationalized houses were reserved for public use (Party, local officials, medical offices, etc.), while the rest were subdivided and new tenants were brought in through the rental offices. Reports from the newly established housing department charged with managing the nationalized houses (ILLT) note that one of their main challenges in 1950 arose from the presence of former owners continuing to live in the houses and from their relationships with tenants and staff (such as janitors). Moreover, tenants did not take care of the houses and apartments, as expected of them.[11]

A secondary, but significant outcome of the nationalization was the labeling of owners as "former owner of a nationalized house," which in turn entailed lack of access to jobs, education, social services, and so on. They became official second-class citizens, barred from political and social participation, at best aspiring for anonymity and very low-key lives. Against this background, the former owners' petitions against nationalization, discussed in chapter 4, are even more poignant.

INDIRECT HOUSING NATIONALIZATION

Housing, urban housing in particular, was the direct target of Decree 92/1950, the flagship legal act for housing nationalization in Romania. Yet houses and apartments throughout the country became state property indirectly as well, primarily when they were secondary to other nationalizations, such as the nationalization of industry, private enterprises, and land takings. Housing was not the direct object of takings in these cases, but the indirect target, as they were taken as part of the patrimony of "exploiters," however defined. The nationalization of industrial enterprises, for example, included the nationalization of all ancillary buildings, whether owned by the enterprise or not (such as leased). Houses taken in this manner represented not an inconsequential percentage of the housing stock, and the owners affected were disproportionately ethnic minorities.

Secondary Urban Housing Nationalization

Timişoara, which by the beginning of the Second World War had become one of the most important economic centers of Romania, with a diverse economy and producing quality products, was seriously hit by the nationalization of industry and commerce. According to the local Chamber of Commerce, as of January 1, 1939, there were 721 industrial firms and small entrepreneurs active in the city, covering activities as diverse as furniture manufacturing, chemicals, printing presses, making musical instruments, and a flourishing textile industry. Although the population of Timişoara represented only 0.54 percent of the total population of Romania, it covered 4.2 percent of its industrial needs (Munteanu and Munteanu 2002, 283). Most of the city's industry and commerce were controlled by Hungarian, German, and Jewish owners, with Romanians, who lacked both the capital and the know-how, controlling only 5 percent of the small enterprises and none of the big ones. Consequently, most Romanians worked primarily in low-skill jobs and were largely absent from higher-level positions in industry and commerce (Munteanu and Munteanu 2002, 284–85). Many of them would benefit from the imposition of communism.

The Second World War had a significant impact on the city, especially when the Eastern Front line crossed the city in September 1944 and later when Soviet troops occupied it. During the war, thousands of small firms disappeared and by fall 1944, all remaining firms and manufacturers lacked fuel and prime materials, and functioned with difficulty. The bombardments of 1944 destroyed or severely damaged the transportation system, primarily the railway, and the Armistice Convention allowed massive requisitions of goods by the occupying Soviet Army. Starting in 1945, the state introduced measures to control most industry and commerce (such as fixing prices), rationalize basic goods, continue to allow requisitions for itself and the Soviet army, and limit production in some areas exclusively for the Soviet army (e.g., shoes). Moreover, direct control over more than 250 important industrial firms with German and Hungarian capital was transferred to the state, inflicting a significant wound to the private local industry. Between 1945 and 1948, over 1,500 firms and enterprises of all sizes ceased their activity (Munteanu and Munteanu 2002, 289–91).

The nationalization laws of 1948 thus delivered a final blow to the already weakened local industry and commerce. In a single year, 1948, the state nationalized industrial enterprises, banks, insurance companies, mining companies, transportation companies, private educational institutions, private railroad companies, private medical institutions, and the cinematography industry. Law 119/1948, the main legal instrument for this nationalization, directly nationalized all major industry and manufacturers in the country, listing them by name and city/town in its appendixes. In the entire country, the statute nationalized 1,050 plants, companies, and other enterprises, virtually all the major industry, such as 20 iron and steel plants, 112 metal manufacturing plants and shipyards, 25 oil and gas companies, and so on.

The preparation and carrying out of the nationalization were shrouded in secrecy, with the local officials in charge learning the procedure just a day in advance. The statute itself was announced on the radio and published in the Official Bulletin only after the end of the takeover (Mioc 2007, 202–3). Just like housing nationalization two years later, part of the information about the numbers and types of enterprises in the city was collected through an industry census, undertaken between October 15 and 20, 1947. The census aimed to catalogue all industrial, commercial, and transportation enterprises, and the directors or owners had five days to pick up, fill in, and return the census forms (*Luptătorul Bănățean* from October 13, 1947).

In the Timiş-Torontal county and the city of Timişoara, Law 119 nationalized fifty-eight plants, from iron processing plants to cotton-based manufacturers, chemical plants, perfume makers, and fruit-drying factories (most of them located in Timişoara). On the basis of Law 119 and its Implementation Instructions, according to an internal report of the Prefecture, there were further nationalized 123 mills, 61 oil presses, 8 electricity plants, 3 bakeries, 3 dairy farms, 1 ice plant, 1 printing press, 1 weaving mill, and 3 quarries.[12] A year later, Law 134/1949 nationalized eighty-seven pharmacies, labs, and medical warehouses in the county, fifty-seven of them in the city.[13] Decree 302/1948 nationalized eight hospitals from Timişoara. Decree 303/1948 for the nationalization of the movie industry transferred into state property over thirty-four movie theaters in the entire county. Finally, Decree 232/1948 nationalized three private railroad companies in the county.

Overall, the nationalization laws and decrees mentioned above seized 110 large industrial enterprises in the county, but allowed 1,547 small enterprises to remain in private hands. Many of them, such as some of the mills and oil presses, had been severely damaged during the war, however, and were not functioning. Over time, most of the remaining private firms increasingly faced significant challenges functioning in a socialist system and would either disappear or become cooperatives (Munteanu and Munteanu 2002, 291). Vestiges of private enterprises, such as some private pharmacies that survived the nationalization wave, were dispatched four years later, in 1952. Through these nationalization statutes and decrees, the state took possession of virtually all industry and commerce, effectively neutering private initiative and the capitalist market in Timişoara and the surrounding county.

Law 119 had an explicitly broad reach, as incorrect names, or changed or partial addresses, did not make any difference to the nationalization. Once nationalized, businesses and enterprises were managed by the respective government agencies, or at the local level by city halls. Like Decree 92 later, one nationalized enterprise "tainted" the entire patrimony of the owner, and all remaining property was subsequently taken. Unlike Decree 92, Law 119 included various mechanisms for resolving disputes related to either the nationalization itself, or preexisting, as well as the procedure for nationalization (Decree 92 was conspicuously silent on both). Also unlike Decree 92, Law 119 surprisingly included provisions for compensating owners, as well as a dispute resolution mechanism.

The buildings attached to nationalized companies or belonging to their owners were also seized as part of the nationalization package. This included, for example, private houses or apartments belonging to different owners, but rented by them to nationalized companies, hospitals, and so on (Article 2 of Law 119). While I could not find a definitive tally on how many houses and apartments were thus seized, I estimate this number is approximately five hundred houses (in the region studied).

An example of this type of indirect housing nationalization is the 1950 case of a seventy-three-year-old shoemaker from Timişoara, who challenged the nationalization of his house. In his written complaint, he presented himself as a "worker shoemaker" and recounted how he and his wife managed to earn enough in the prewar days from their work to buy a small house. During the war, in 1943, they had to rent it out to a leather factory because they could not make ends meet. They lost the house when all industrial enterprises were nationalized. The shoemaker argued that the nationalization of his house was done through an erroneous interpretation of the nationalization statute (119/1948), and asked for his house back.[14]

In response, the architect heading the Section of Communal Management (responsible for housing issues) of the Timişoara Popular Council undertook a fact-finding mission. He reported back to the Council that the shoemaker had in the past worked with three to four apprentices and that the small house included three apartments. One of these was in very poor shape, but the other two were newer and in good shape. Of these two, one had been rented to the factory, while the shoemaker and his family lived in the other one. The Municipal Council reported in turn to the Regional Popular Council and indicated they wanted to uphold the nationalization based on Article 2 of Law 119/1948 (which nationalized all installations that served the enterprise permanently, even if they had a different owner, as was the case here). In addition, the Council argued, the petitioner clearly did not need the apartment, otherwise he would not have rented it out. The Regional Popular Council advised the Council of Ministers to uphold the nationalization.[15] In this case, while labor was not discounted, it was trumped by the size of the house, creating a presumption of exploitation, combined with the perceived lack of need of the petitioner. Altogether, this was enough to transform a seventy-three-year-old shoemaker into a "housing exploiter."

Other cases were significantly more complex. In 1956, for example, Maria H., a worker at a hosiery mill in Timişoara, petitioned for the restitution of a third of the building where she lived. It took six months and a spate of correspondence between the Timişoara executive committee, the regional committee, and the General Direction of the Council of Ministers to find out the specifics of the situation. The house in question, it turned out based on the information provided by the Timişoara committee, was both included in the list of proposals for nationalization and had been managed by the state's housing management authority (ILLT) since 1950. The entire building included apartments and a bakery, which was nationalized based on Law 119/1948.

Based on this initial nationalization act, the housing authority took over the bakery in 1950, but unsure about the rest of the building and not convinced that they had a legal basis for taking it over, inquired whether the entire building was indeed nationalized. The Municipal Council answered affirmatively in 1952, but only issued a decision explicitly giving the entire building into ILLT management in 1955. In fact, the building had been managed by the housing authority since 1950, and had been listed in the tax authority's files as nationalized and thus property taxes had not been collected. Neither the owner (Nicolae H., the same last name as the petitioner) nor the building was listed in the Decree 92 appendix, but they were proposed for nationalization in 1953.[16]

Although arbitrariness is the feature most commonly associated with law under repressive conditions, the nationalization process in Romania reveals a fairly coherent picture, where the regime cast its net extremely widely, but not inherently irrationally. Yet as Maria's case indicates, the process of takings, petitions, and restitution was marred by deeper flaws, the most significant of which were *de facto* nationalization and the situation of houses proposed for nationalization. *De facto* nationalization includes all of the illegal takings: those not listed in the Decree 92 appendixes but treated in the same manner, houses seized with no statutory basis, houses nationalized retroactively (including back dating the takings memos), those nationalized under the wrong owner's name, or cases of extension of nationalization to the entire building with no legal basis. Some of the houses proposed for nationalization also belong to this latter category.

Maria's case, which is not unusual, is an illustration of *de facto* nationalization and its consequences: initially taken over as a package deal with the nationalization of the bakery, the house was managed by the state starting in 1950. We are in a twilight zone legal status, as the house was simultaneously nationalized and proposed for nationalization; furthermore, no property taxes were paid and yet apparently the owner was allowed to continue to live there. For five years, some municipal authorities thought the house was nationalized (the tax office), some knew it wasn't yet still managed it (the housing authority), while others added it to the list of houses proposed for nationalization (the municipal nationalization commission). The house was in legal limbo for an extended period of time, which meant that although the owner continued to live there and paid no property taxes, she also could not dispose of it in any way. Yet this held for the housing authority, too, which could not fully manage the building and make changes to it without clear ownership.[17]

Registration in the real estate registry was the crucial last step in any transfer of ownership, and caused significant headaches for the regime. While attempting to finally register all nationalized houses in 1956, the Timişoara Council had to stop and ask for guidance regarding the status of 132 buildings that were not listed in the Decree 92 appendix, yet had been seized based on the order of the Ministry of Communal Householding and Municipal Industry.[18] The consequences of *de facto* nationalization extended backward and forward in time: the unclear legal basis for the takings and consequently the legal regime of the buildings, legal limbo for many buildings over extended periods of time, and the constant shuffling and reclassification of houses. The reclassification of houses and of the legal basis for their initial taking happened relatively frequently when there was ambiguity, in part because it increased the odds for restitution in cases where the municipal authorities wanted the house off their hands.

Secondary Rural Housing Nationalization

Urban housing was overwhelmingly affected by nationalization and expropriation. Rural housing was not entirely exempt, however, as the expropriation of land also included houses and other real estate. The rural middle and upper classes suffered major losses. Landowners lost not only their land but also their houses and all other property. As late as 1945, Romania was overwhelmingly a rural economy, with over 80 percent of the population living in the countryside and only 20 percent in urban areas. However, the boundaries between city and village were rather fluid, especially for the landed class, which usually had residences both in the city and the countryside. Obtaining the compliance and cooptation of Romania's rural population was a main target of the communist regime.[19]

The transformation of agriculture and new property patterns were imposed in two stages. Initially, Law 187/1945 for agrarian reform expropriated (with no compensation) all land and related property belonging to Romanian citizens of German origin, war collaborators, post-1944 refugees, absentees, those who had not personally cultivated their land for the prior seven years, volunteer fighters against the United Nations, *mortmain* property, as well as all land over 50 ha (Articles 3 and 7). Part of the land expropriated—up to 5 ha per family—was allotted to soldiers and peasants with little or no land. The 1945 land reform statute expropriated a total of 36,842 houses from the entire Timişoara region.[20]

In the entire country, there were expropriated 1,468,000 ha, out of which 75 percent, approximately 1,109,000 ha, were allotted as private property to peasants and the rest stayed in the state's hands.[21] As a result, approximately 900,000 poor peasant families received land under the 1945 agrarian reform statute. In the Timiş-Torontal county, by the middle of February 1946, there were expropriated 173,000 ha, out of which 143,000 ha were redistributed and 30,000 ha became state property. In the entire county, 34,000 indigent peasants received 93,000 ha in property, and 7,000 internally displaced persons (IDPs) received 50,000 ha (although property titles were issued only two years later) (Mioc 2007, 210; *Luptătorul Bănăţean* from February 18, 1946). The IDPs, called "colonists" in Romanian, were for the most part ethnic Romanians who had been displaced by the territorial changes at the end of the Second World War, primarily the seizing of land from the eastern part of the country by the Soviet Union. They were relocated to other parts of Romania, also in an attempt to increase the percentage of Romanians in Transylvania and Banat.

Despite various abuses and irregularities, there was overall satisfaction with the reform, which did not last long. Only three months later (July 1945), the government blocked the harvest, fixed prices, and introduced quotas (Mioc 2007, 211–12). In less than two years, the regime would begin the collectivization of agriculture, preceded by the second phase of the land reform: the expropriation of estates of 50 ha (left over from 1945) and model farms. By the end of the collectivization process, about 9 percent of land remained in private property, in areas not suitable for collectivization. Of the collectivized land, peasants were left with 6 percent for personal use (Deletant 1999, 109).

In the second stage of the transformation of agriculture, Decree 83/1949 expropriated an estimated 17,000 landowner families that still had up to 50 ha of land. This included land, inventory, buildings, machines and tools, all titles, and credits. Former owners were evicted from their homes and assigned forced domicile in a distant city (Deletant 1999, 76; Cioroianu 2005, 76). In the early morning of March 2, 1949, landowners' families were abruptly woken up, sometimes not even allowed to get dressed or take any personal clothes with them, loaded up in trucks bound for Timişoara, triaged, and immediately sent to various cities in the country, with no money and allowed only the clothes they were wearing. Once there, they had to fend for themselves, while being specifically excluded from social services and even jobs as "enemies of the people."[22]

Throughout Romania, Decree 83 expropriated 6,258 estates and 4,456 country halls (Mioc 2007, 221). According to Securitate statistics, 2,000 families were forcibly evicted, totaling over 3,000 persons (Dobrincu 2006, 111). In the Timiş-Torontal county, out of 190 estates initially proposed by the Ministry of Agriculture, the local Prefect's office expropriated 113 (85 from the initial list, plus 28 not on the initial list). Overall, in the final phase of the rural estates expropriation of 1949, the state seized from the entire county 7,595 ha, 3,794 various animals (oxen, cows, calves, horses, sheep, etc.), and 3,413 birds (hens, ducks, geese, etc.). All owner families, which tallied 192 persons, from infants to grandparents, as well as 6 estate administrators and their families were evicted, detained, and assigned forced domicile. Twenty-two owners were not at home, as well as 7 administrators. Two persons apparently escaped during the eviction.

To execute the expropriation and eviction, the Prefect's office "mobilized" 473 workers and 539 peasants, totaling 1,012 persons, and for the effective takeover, an additional 442 peasants.[23] This amounts to a ratio of five to one—five adult men for every man, woman, or child. Unsurprisingly, and given the time and procedure employed, there wasn't a lot of immediate resistance to the takeover. Decree 83 stipulated that those who resisted the expropriation were subject to prosecution and hard labor between five and fifteen years (Article 4). Landowners lost not only their land but also their houses and all other property, thus another 100–150 houses and apartments throughout the county.

EXPROPRIATION

Also known as eminent domain, expropriation refers to governmental takeover of private property for public interest and with compensation. In this narrow sense, expropriation exists in most legal systems. The Romanian communist regime's use of expropriation differs in three significant ways: it was used both for punitive purposes and in the public interest, it was broadly interpreted, and compensation was only sometimes included, and it often had only symbolic value.

Although "expropriation for public interest" would take center stage only during the latter stages of communism in Romania, the regime began using it rather liberally from the very beginning. For the most part, this type of expropriation was not punitive in character. Expropriation aimed to enlarge various local industries, allot more land and buildings to various government ministries (such as the Ministry of Internal Affairs), or make space for new construction. In the Timiş-Torontal county, for example, substantial expropriations took place in the city of Reşiţa, where a gigantic metallurgical plant was located.

Urban real estate was commonly expropriated to make room for new apartment buildings, for which there was endless demand at a time of rapid urban growth. In 1962, the city of Timişoara lacked approximately 17,000 apartments, and did not meet even the low official standard of 8 square meters per person.[24] The regional People's Council [sfatul popular] commonly started out expropriating land (with no constructions on it) for the purpose of building new apartments. The Council sometimes offered the option of land exchanges when possible, but when not, which was often the case, the owners were compensated. Compensation was low, however. In 1962, for example, local authorities proposed for expropriation ten lots, ranging from 384 to 930 square meters (4,133 to 10,000 feet), all located in relatively central parts of the city. The compensation for all lots, regardless of location or other characteristics, was 2.25 lei per square meter, which amounted to a maximum of 2,082.50 lei for the largest lot. Most other lots received around 1,300 lei based on their size.[25] The average gross monthly salary at the time (1962) was 947 lei, according to Ministry of Labor statistics.

The process was relatively straightforward: once a particular plot was identified by the regional and city planners and officials, the evaluation commission, which included architects, engineers, and financial specialists, identified the purpose for the land, for example building apartment blocks (the explanatory memo usually specified square meters of livable space). The local and the regional executive officials had to collaborate, but they did not always agree on the land to be expropriated, or on the manner and extent of compensation. The issue here was offering land in exchange, versus monetary compensation (compensation rates were determined nationally, based on the classification of cities): the former came from the city, while the latter from the regional coffers (and was insignificant by comparison). Unsurprisingly, the city commonly refused to agree to an exchange of land and opted for monetary compensation.

The full expropriation file included the evaluation of the land and its intended use, as well as an evaluation of the owners and their socioeconomic status, similarly to the urban housing nationalization process. This, however, tracked only two items: occupation of the owner, and whether the owner's name had been included in the appendixes for Decree 187/1945 (land reform) or 92/1950 (urban housing nationalization), which would make the taking easier as there would be no question of compensation. Unlike takings intimately tied to the owner-as-exploiter paradigm, however, this type of expropriation was relatively detached from exploitation and much more oriented toward the needs of the regime. It was a tool easily and conveniently adapted from the prior ("bourgeois") property regime.

The Council of Ministers mandated that local authorities obtain the agreement of the owners to the expropriation. The local People's Council thus summoned the owners to let them know about the expropriation plans, and attempted to convince them to agree to the expropriation. If they did, owners signed an agreement, which always included language about the intended new construction, for example:

> Today, December 11, 1961,
>
> The undersigned E.I. and P.E., living at street S.B. no 5, and working at I.R.T.A., declare that we agree to the expropriation of 799 square meters from our garden for the construction of elementary school no. 5. The expropriation will be compensated based on official standards.[26]

If the owners did not agree to the expropriation, the expropriation file noted it. Some owners refused to engage with the local authorities, and refused to accept other property in exchange for the expropriated one. Ana P. from Timişoara gave the local People's Council a headache in 1958–1959, as she completely refused to even talk to them. The city wanted to use her land to expand the public transit system, and apparently reached out to her numerous times. She eventually relented, only to change her mind at the last minute and refuse the land exchange. The expropriation did eventually go forward, although it is unclear whether Ana received another property in exchange, or compensation.[27]

De facto expropriation, as in the case of nationalization, was also not uncommon, but the procedure did not essentially change. The explanatory memos and the agreement with the owners noted that the new construction had already been erected, and that the land was retroactively expropriated. In January 1962, for example, an owner agreed to this type of retroactive expropriation and in addition to the regular statutory compensation, shrewdly negotiated for compensation for 62 fruit-bearing trees, valued at 300 lei per tree (which added up to 18,600 lei, significantly more than compensation for the land itself), as well as rent covering the period between the *de facto* and *de jure* expropriation.[28] Expropriated owners did not have a choice about the ultimate outcome, but to the extent that they had any voice in the process, many nonetheless fought to minimize their loss.

There are clear similarities and differences between nationalization notices and the expropriation "agreements." In both cases, the consent of the owners did not make a difference and the takings proceeded as planned, and in both cases the notices represented an effort to build legitimacy through legality. This type of expropriation, unlike nationalization, was not punitive, however, and the regime's process of reaching out to the owners, explaining the public interest purpose of the expropriation, and seeking their agreement signal the substantive justice thrust of these expropriations, and the effort to distinguish them from punitive takings (conceptually, public interest expropriations are not specific to communism, although their scale and the lack of compensation were unique to the regime). It was an ingenious approach that put the owners in a difficult position. Their reluctance or outright refusal to sign the "agreements" could easily indicate their refusal to contribute to the public good, especially if the expropriation was partial. Micro-resistance, cooptation, and the construction of communist subjectivity were all intertwined—after all, how could one say no to furthering the public interest?

Formally, the last step in the process was the decree issued by the Council of State, signed by the president (Gheorghiu-Dej during this period). The expropriation decrees all had the same format and text and were issued "blank." The appendixes listed the names and properties taken, and were attached to the text of the decree at the local level. There are clear formal rational characteristics to this process, more so than for most other takings.

Punitive Expropriation

Punitive expropriation, by contrast, or confiscation, concerned the partial or total seizure of property of individuals found guilty of crimes, specifically war-related crimes. Article 3 of Law 312/1945 was explicit on this point, but later legislation did not stop there and expanded the concept to include all takings of property of those convicted of crimes (e.g., Decree 221/1960). Law 10/1948 gave the confiscated property, with the exception of agricultural, commercial, and industrial goods, to the local municipalities on whose territory they were located.

Even in its original understanding, however, confiscation aimed at a large group of people. Law 312 laid out seventeen categories of individuals guilty of contributing to the "national disaster," which included some very broadly defined crimes such as "attacking the country in writing, orally or through any other means." An April 3, 1947, order of the Ministry of Internal Affairs identified 657 individuals from the entire country who had been sentenced on the basis of Law 312 and specified the procedure for expropriation. The great majority were from Northern Transylvania and Bucharest, and included politicians, local officials, members of the army, journalists, and others, such as a "forest owner." There were eight individuals from Timişoara, including journalists, members of the police, and of the army.[29]

While ostensibly aiming at land reform, Law 187/1945 had in fact a dual purpose and also included punitive expropriation, which mainly targeted Romanian citizens of German origin. Those who had left the country to join the German army were similarly punished, but in a region like Timiş-Torontal, which had historically been heavily populated by ethnic Germans and Hungarians, the facts were not always clear. It was not uncommon for the parents of those who were presumed to have retreated with the German army to lose their property, as well as for all members of the German Ethnic Group (whose raison d'être was to deploy the German minority in Romania in the service of the Nazi state, as in other European countries under Nazi control). Officially, all ethnic Germans were automatically enrolled in the German Ethnic Group while Romania was allied with Germany during the Second World War,[30] but cases were sometimes more complex on the ground.

In 1948, for example, a widow from B. petitioned the Prefect's office regarding the expropriation of her house on the basis of her membership in the German Ethnic Group. At seventy-five years old, she was in charge of seven family members, including three children under five. The house had been empty since her eviction. In her petition, she included a 1942 order from the local leadership of the German Ethnic Group excluding her and her family from the German minority and the German Ethnic Group: "You have shown yourselves as enemies of the German people, and through your anti-Hitler machinations you have proven yourselves unworthy of the title 'German.'" The local administration investigated and determined that the house had been both expropriated and nationalized on the basis of two different statutes: land reform (Law 187/1945), and nationalization of industry and commerce (Law 119/1948—her husband had owned three mills), and that her family, in their opinion, was composed of only four family members.[31] They never addressed the issue of the expulsion from the German Ethnic Group.

Covert Expropriation

The communist regime deployed a variety of legal mechanisms that aimed to "catch" houses that had somehow escaped the explicit nationalization and expropriation processes. They include requisition, debt payment to the state, donations to the state, abandonment, displacement, and the statute of limitations. On their face, these legal mechanisms are not particularly predatory, but their application revealed that they functioned as alternative expropriation tools. Their arbitrariness and diversity are yet another indication that the regime was grasping to build a coherent overall policy regarding housing.

Requisitions

Requisitions were primarily intended to help wartime efforts (e.g., Law 139/1940), but were nonetheless extended after the war for a significantly longer period during the 1950s and were often used as a default measure for takings (Law 439/1945). Local administrative bodies relied upon requisition for seizing desired private property, real and mobile, but not without resistance from individuals who complained and petitioned for restitution as late as the 1960s. The Armistice Convention also allowed massive requisitions of goods by the occupying Soviet Army.

Houses and apartments under these legal provisions could only be requisitioned for use and during a specific time period. The implementation of these provisions, however, seems to have been wildly inconsistent. Some local authorities forbade it entirely, others approved it unconditionally, while yet others tried to convince those asking for a house to be requisitioned to reach an agreement with the owner. A variety of public interest purposes were at stake, such as establishing local kindergartens, schools, birthing centers, and so on.[32] In January 1949, for example, the local chapter of the Union of Democratic Women of Romania asked the Timiş-Torontal prefect to approve the requisition of an eight-room house (the Union already had space there) for housing sixty-seven poor children in its care. The building where the children lived was in fact a school, and once classes started, the children would be evicted. The Union claimed they could not find another building, and at any rate, there were only four individuals occupying the eight rooms (a dentist and his family), who could be relocated, so there was plenty of space. The requisition was approved and the dentist removed.[33]

While it is not clear how many houses were seized in this manner, archival documents include numerous cases of requisition. Margareta W., for example, was a widow who petitioned the taking of her family home in the town of B. (a well-known health resort town) in 1949. She was reassigned to work in a different town between 1949 and 1952, and she had barely moved out, when her house was seized on the basis of an order from the General Labor Union, and together with her furniture redistributed to the Ministry of Health: "Today my house is managed by the B. General Administration of Baths, with no legal basis, it is not used for those who are sick, it is not appropriate for that purpose, and it is used by private individuals. Because of these just reasons, please investigate this case and return my house to me" (December 8, 1955). An internal administrative investigation of the case admitted as much in February 1956, finding that the house was a family home, not built for exploitation, and not used for medical purposes. The house had been divided into two apartments, used by employees of the resort and by the petitioner since her return.[34]

These are relatively typical cases. Three elements seem to have determined the success of a requisition request: who made it (local administration, the Party, others), the purpose, and whether the building was underutilized or empty. The rather liberal use of requisitions continued throughout the early 1950s, despite a Ministry of Internal Affairs order from November 1948 that banned all requisitions.[35] In 1955, Decree 511 retroactively expropriated all property that had been seized under the requisition laws, including houses and apartments.

Debt Payment to the State

Debt payment to the state is not a creation of the communist regime, yet its use by the regime, and two peculiarities in particular, indicate that it was merely another takings mechanism. Decree 224/1951 allowed the local tax/financial office to initiate court proceedings regarding the sequestration and subsequent selling of real estate property when the debtor failed to pay her taxes. Two provisions stand out and reveal the predatory nature of this legal mechanism: first, the house(s) could not be sold to private buyers, only public entities (Article 17); second, if there were no buyers the first time the house was auctioned off, the state simply took it over with no pay (Article 18). It is not clear how many houses were seized in this manner.

Donations to the State

Decree 478/1954 regulated donations to the state, which may seem a benign mechanism for transferring property. Donations were clearly used as a coercive mechanism, however, primarily when one examines the identity of donors and the purposes of the donation. Donors included churches that were persecuted by the regime during this period (e.g., Catholic Church and the Baptist Church), or ethnic groups in similarly dire straits (Germans), as well as individuals (such as those who had left the country, or those who inherited and could not afford the taxes). The official motivation for making and accepting the donation is usually explicitly stated, for example, to build a new apartment building, or to help with the expansion of local schools or hospitals. In July 1959, the Roman Catholic archbishop donated 3,107 square meters of church land to the town of A., to be transformed into an open-air fruit and vegetable market.[36] Unlike expropriations or nationalization, donation decisions were a summary affair: an offer to donate, a brief check of the property, followed by a quick decision issued by the regional People's Council accepting the donation.

The identity of the donors, the "public purpose" of many donations, the pro forma nature of the donation offers and acceptances indicate that the donations, whether punitive or not, functioned in practice in a manner similar to expropriation, and were possibly preferred because they entailed much less administrative work, were ostensibly based on consent, and could easily slip under the radar. Occasionally, individual owners had been approached and "convinced" to donate for a public purpose, and sometimes the donation had a retroactive character (the state had already erected buildings on land, for example). Finally, it is worth noting here that the state did not necessarily accept all donations, for example, in the case of donations from those who had been otherwise nationalized or expropriated.[37]

Abandoned Property

Decree 111/1951 dealt with abandoned property and covered a wide array of the regime's property sins (consequently enjoying quite an infamous reputation). Decree 111 came as a package deal with instructions issued by the Ministry of Finance in August 1951, which clarified that a key goal of the decree was to create a source of income for the state budget, and included detailed procedures for the maintenance and disposition of seized goods.[38]

The regime labeled as "abandoned" and therefore seizable by the state the property of those who had fled immediately after the end of the war, or those sent to labor camps in the Soviet Union. Those who had fled were implicitly suspected to have collaborated with the German army, as was Iosefina Z. from the town of Reşiţa. In 1956, the seventy-one-year-old widow petitioned for the return of her house, which she had co-owned with her husband (who died in 1945). Iosefina and her husband fled to Czechslovakia in 1944 and returned in June 1945. Upon her return she found out that her half of the house had been expropriated, but not her husband's. The office in charge with managing enemy property eventually ordered the restitution of her half of the house in 1949, but the local administration did not comply. Iosefina claimed neither she nor her husband could have been considered landlords or exploiters, as they only owned a local bar and restaurant, and that two of her children went missing during the war. The local administration countered that she had collaborated with the Nazis, and that was the reason for the expropriation of her half of the house. Her husband's half, on the other hand, remained his property. By 1956, the house was occupied by the local Securitate headquarters.[39]

Those who had fled after the war, even when there were no suspicions of collaboration, were commonly targeted. A couple from the small town of O. on the Danube left Romania and settled in Czechoslovakia sometime after the war, renting their house. The state nonetheless considered it abandoned because the couple did not have any heirs in the country, and seized it under Decree 111 in 1955.[40]

Decree 111 and its implementation instructions explicitly included, inter alia, property that was confiscated on any legal basis (e.g., following the loss of Romanian citizenship), property that should have been confiscated following a criminal sentence, vacant successions, and property abandoned for over a year. In 1955, for example, twenty-four buildings were confiscated on the basis of criminal decisions issued by the Timişoara Tribunal.[41] Decree 111 had a wide scope, including both movables and immovables, it was relatively often contested before local administrative organs, and raised a variety of problems during its application (particularly for household objects and other movables that were easily stolen, misplaced, or the authorities simply did not know how to dispose of them, as was the case for many objects that were old and in bad shape, so could not be sold, but could also not be legally destroyed).[42]

In 1958, the Ministry of Finance issued detailed instructions for the management and sale of Decree 111 property. The goal was to keep what was valuable in state property, and sell the rest "at the most advantageous prices for the socialist sector." The Ministry ordered art objects to be donated to museums, stamps and stamp collections to the philately association, foreign cigars, cigarettes, and the like to the Bucharest cigarette factory. Pianos were either to be donated to local institutions, if they wanted them, or sold to the Doina piano factory, again in Bucharest. Jewelry and watches were to be sold, and all proceeds went to the state budget.[43]

Displacement

Loss of property through displacement was specific to the region. Council of Ministers Decision no 326/1951 created a separate category of dispossessed owners, spurred by the internal politics of the Soviet bloc, in particular Yugoslavia's split from the USSR and the ensuing anxiety over a possible war, which would have placed Romania squarely in the middle of the hostilities. In anticipation of this potential conflict, approximately 44,000 inhabitants of the border zone with Yugoslavia were detained, transported, and abandoned in a different part of the country during the night of June 18, 1951. The resettlement area was in Bărăgan, the eastern part of the country, a relatively unpopulated region with a harsh climate (CADCR Report 2006, 204). From the Timişoara region there were forcibly displaced 688 families of ethnic Serbs, 639 of whom returned by 1956 (Council of Ministers Decision no 2694/1955). Following the displacement, 661 houses were seized by the state.[44] Also forcibly displaced were 4,389 families of other nationalities (Romanian, Bulgarian, Germans, Czechs, etc.), out of which 3,830 families returned in 1955 (Council of Ministers Decisions 29/1955 and 623/1956).[45]

The displaced population was allowed to return in 1955–1956, but in the meantime their homes and assets had been taken over by the state. In a 1953 report to the Council of Ministers, the regional People's Council reported that 90 percent of the property of those displaced and missing ("absenteisti") from the Timişoara region had been disposed of. The goods had either been distributed to various state institutions, or sold off. The rest were in storage for a variety of reasons, and some were in very poor shape. The Council asked for permission to sell them under market value so they could achieve 100 percent.[46]

The state often sold these goods for a nice profit. In October 1955, I.B. requested the restitution of his property upon his return from Bărăgan. In his handwritten petition, he talked about being evicted and sent away with only his clothes on, and finding all his property gone upon his return. His entire patrimony had been taken over by various state bodies in 1951, and evaluated at 65,543 lei (approximately $438 at the time). More than half was sold, various items were taken over by the local cooperative, and only very few items were ultimately returned to him.[47]

Statutes of Limitations

Statutes of limitations are not on their face seizing mechanisms. Yet Decree 218/1960 was used in precisely this manner, in particular as a last resort in the takings dragnet. The decree stated that goods of any kind under state control or custody not reclaimed within the prescribed time limit (two years) automatically became state property, regardless of how the state had come into possession. The statute of limitations was two years from the moment the state or public organization took possession, which in effect meant the retroactive legalization of all illegal takings. Time in law—particularly extinctive prescription (statute of limitations), was especially important for socialist regimes, both as a point of delimitation between political regimes and a policy instrument.

CONCLUSION

The variety, overlapping scope, uneven implementation, diversity of justifications, and duration of these various takings mechanisms for housing highlight the key issue at the heart of the communist regime's policies regarding houses and apartments: it appears the regime had no clear, comprehensive program for eliminating the private property of houses, but rather settled for obtaining as many houses and apartments as possible, particularly the "best" ones.

This lack of clarity resulted in a relatively incoherent, piecemeal, and haphazard policy regarding housing that stands in sharp contrast to the regime's policies on industry, land, and commerce. Among the consequences are the muted persistence of private property as an institution, ideology, and practice throughout the communist period. Houses, in other words, were the Achilles' heel of the communist-making project.

Some features of these policies do stand out. First, not all takings were equal. Some, like urban housing nationalization, were clearly targeted, while others, such as the regulation of abandoned property, were more of a dragnet, while yet others, such as expropriation for public interest, are fairly standard property mechanisms across legal systems and were explicitly not punitive (which meant, among other things, that the owners had no record as enemies of the people). The takings were characterized by a blend of arbitrariness and formalism that came to characterize socialist legality throughout its lifetime. A set of 1959 instructions from the regional to the local administration captures this blend very nicely. The instructions concern the legal status of houses of those who leave the country. If they belonged to the category of "housing exploiter," their housing was to be seized under Decree 92/1950. If not, and there were no administrators left for the buildings, Decree 111 on abandoned property applied. If there were administrators, the house would not be seized (in practice, this was not necessarily observed). Finally, if the local council or another state body thought the housing should be expropriated for systematization or other public interest purposes, they could use Council of Ministers Decision 1676/1959.[48] The presumption, in other words, was the arbitrary taking of property, but once that particular hurdle was cleared, it became a matter of formalism, a buffet of taking mechanisms at the disposal of the central and local administration. Another way of understanding this is as a balance between policy and legality, and perhaps, and optimistically, of legality itself as an arena that shaped the decision-making process within the communist power structure.

The availability of this vast system of takings mechanisms also meant that there was significant overlap in takings, particularly for ethnic minorities, but not only. It was by no means unusual to have houses that were simultaneously expropriated and nationalized, which is incoherent, yet never seemed to trouble the local officials. If anything, the overlap gave them peace of mind. Finally, and most obviously, takings were an important money-making machine for the new regime, both as it kept and redistributed the most valuable housing internally, and as it made a profit by selling housing, furniture, and so on to the population.

More surprising, perhaps, is that despite widespread takings, in both urban and rural places, more than half of all houses remained in private hands and continued to be used primarily as family homes. Private urban real estate represented over half of the total number of private homes, while the numbers in the countryside varied more widely, in part because of the interplay between extensive restitutions and later expropriations. Overall, as of 1960, out of the total number of 3.4 million square meters for housing in the Banat region, only 1.2 million square meters were state property, while 2.2 million square meters were private property. In other words, houses held as private property amounted to approximately two-thirds of the total housing in the region as late as 1960.[49]

The Soviet regime was also deeply conflicted about houses as objects of personal property. The abolition of private property and taking of all houses in 1918 was followed only three years later by restitution of houses with no more than two apartments (Kucherov 1962, 376). Kucherov also describes the inconsistent efforts of the Soviet regime to deal with "speculation of personal property"—such as obtaining profit from renting. Until the 1960s, urban houses held as personal property consistently made up a third of the total number of urban housing stock in the Soviet Union (Smith 2008, 285).

The takings of houses, and in particular urban housing nationalization, uniquely shaped the symbolic space of communism and post-communism, yet it is important to emphasize its flip side: a majority of all houses remained in private hands and continued to function in much the same way as before, namely as family homes. This constitutes the bottom of the housing iceberg throughout the communist period, and while less noted, it had a significant impact, primarily as a site of continuity for ideas of private property. Within the nationalized space itself, there were enough inconsistencies and ambiguities that kept the door open to older property ideas, which former owners noticed and eagerly seized. A diffuse, hegemonic, internalized cultural system of property, encoded in legal texts and practices, was suddenly and violently struck by the new, state-supported ideology. While not underestimating the power of prior symbolic frameworks (e.g., through "consciousness raising" efforts), the communist regime nevertheless failed to impose its new hegemony and ended up reinforcing, rather than undermining the bond between houses and private property. A key reason was misunderstanding the nature and operation of its chosen instrument—law.

NOTES

1. Agricultural cooperatives were created in 1949 by Decree 319/1949, ratified by Law 22/1949. Until 1962, however, there was heavy resistance to the forced process of collectivization, resulting in a series of laws and decrees punishing peasants (e.g., Decree 131/1952, ratified by Law 10/1952, Law 16/1949).

2. National Archives of Romania Timişoara, Collection Sfatul Popular Banat, Juridic, File 22/1957.

3. National Archives of Romania Timişoara, Collection Sfatul Popular Banat, Juridic, File 22/1957, pages 85–87.

4. At the end of the nineteenth century, T.H. Green, starting from the concept of human capacities, argued that property is a necessary extension of human personality, because it is essential for the realization of man's ability to form and act upon a moral will (Green 1885–1888; Macpherson 1978, 101).

5. The central nationalization commission divided cities into two categories, depending on whether the population had indoor plumbing and electricity, according to the 1953 Instructions for the implementation of nationalization. It is not clear whether this categorization existed in 1950.

6. Although issued by the Great National Assembly, which replaced the Parliament, it was a decree, not a statute.

7. National Archives of Romania Timişoara, Collection Primăria Municipiului Timişoara [Timişoara City Hall], File No. 12/1950, page 62. There were 14,471 buildings in 1947 (Munteanu and Munteanu 2002, 218).

8. National Archives of Romania Timişoara, Collection Sfatul Popular Banat, Secretariat, File 102/1960, page 82.

9. National Archives of Romania Timişoara, Collection Sfatul Popular Banat, Secretariat, File 102/1960, page 125.

10. National Archives of Romania Timişoara, Collection Sfatul Popular Banat, Secretariat, File 74/1959, page 19.

11. National Archives of Romania Timişoara, Collection City Hall, File No. 12/1950, pages 48, 69–71.

12. National Archives of Romania Timişoara, Collection Prefectură, File No. 213/1948, pages 164–73.

13. National Archives of Romania Timişoara, Collection Prefectură, File No. 50/1949, page 2.

14. National Archives of Romania Timişoara, Collection Sfatul Popular Banat, Inventar 1630, Secţia de Gospodărie Comunală, File No. 1/1958, pages 124–25.

15. National Archives of Romania Timişoara, Collection Sfatul Popular Banat, Inventar 1630, Secţia de Gospodărie Comunală, File No. 1/1958, pages 126–28.

16. National Archives of Romania Timişoara, Collection Sfatul Popular Banat, Inventar 1630, File No. 1/1956, pages 108–9, 116–19.

17. This is also what happened in the case of a milk plant that had been seized with no legal basis and where significant improvements could not be made without full ownership title for the state.

18. National Archives of Romania Timişoara, Collection Sfatul Popular Banat, Inventar 1630, File No. 1/1956, page 326.

19. The rural expropriations of land and the collectivization process have been extensively studied. See, for example, Dobrincu and Iordachi (2005).

20. There are slight differences in numbers among versions of the report cited here. I am using what appears to be the final version of the report. National Archives of Romania Timişoara, Collection Sfatul Popular Banat, Secretariat, File No. 10/1959, page 331.

21. There were also expropriated 3,130 tractors, 1,276 tractor ploughs, 682 locomotives, 1,274 threshers, 1,032 reapers, and 1,100 simple reapers (Mioc 2007, 210).

22. National Archives of Romania Timişoara, Collection Prefectură, Files No. 92–97/1949.

23. National Archives of Romania Timişoara, Collection Prefectură, File No. 4/1949, page 123.

24. National Archives of Romania Timişoara, Collection Sfatul Popular Banat, Secretariat, File No. 38/1965, pages 1–13.

25. National Archives of Romania Timişoara, Collection Sfatul Popular Banat, Secretariat, File No. 65/1961–1962, pages 1–11.

26. National Archives of Romania Timişoara, Collection Sfatul Popular Banat, Secretariat, File No. 65/1961–1962, page 132.

27. National Archives of Romania Timişoara, Collection Sfatul Popular Banat, Inventar 1630, File No. 31/1959, pages 10–20.

28. National Archives of Romania Timişoara, Collection Sfatul Popular Banat, Secretariat, File No. 65/1961–1962, page 134.

29. National Archives of Romania Timişoara, Collection Prefectură, File No. 20/1947, pages 1–30.

30. Law 830/1940; Memo Regarding the German Population in the Popular Republic of Romania 815/April 17, 1956, prepared by the Directorate of Affairs, Central Council of the Romanian Workers' Party, http://www.sferapoliticii.ro/sfera/pdf/Sfera_83.pdf.

31. National Archives of Romania Timişoara, Collection Prefectură, File No. 3/1949, pages 1–6.

32. See, for example, National Archives of Romania Timişoara, Collection Prefectură, File No. 57/1949.

33. National Archives of Romania Timişoara, Collection Prefectură, File No. 3/1949, pages 7–11.

34. National Archives of Romania Timişoara, Collection Sfatul Popular Banat, Inventar 1517, File No. 30/1955, pages 28–34.

35. National Archives of Romania Timişoara, Collection Prefectură, File No. 3/1949, page 21.

36. National Archives of Romania Timişoara, Collection Sfatul Popular Banat, Inventar 1630, File No. 32/1959, pages 65, 69.

37. For example, National Archives of Romania Timişoara, Collection Sfatul Popular Banat, Inventar 1630, File No. 32/1959; Secretariat, Files No. 26/1962, 56/1962.

38. National Archives of Romania Timişoara, Collection Sfatul Popular Timişoara, File No. 14/1958, pages 81–89.

39. National Archives of Romania Timişoara, Collection Sfatul Popular Banat, Secretariat, File No. 28/1956, pages 5–8.

40. National Archives of Romania Timişoara, Collection Sfatul Popular Banat, Inventar 1517, File No. 11/1955, pages 7, 9.

41. National Archives of Romania Timişoara, Collection Sfatul Popular Banat, Finance, File No. 12/1955, page 43.

42. National Archives of Romania Timişoara, Collection Sfatul Popular Banat, Finance, File No. 12/1955, page 181.

43. National Archives of Romania Timişoara, Collection Sfatul Popular Banat, Finance, File No. 10/1958, pages 20–22.

44. National Archives of Romania Timişoara, Collection Sfatul Popular Banat, Secretariat, File No. 18/1956, page 429; National Archives of Romania Timişoara, Collection Sfatul Popular Banat, Secretariat, File No. 46/1956, page 326.

45. National Archives of Romania Timişoara, Collection Sfatul Popular Banat, Secretariat, File No. 46/1956, page 326.

46. National Archives of Romania Timişoara, Collection Sfatul Popular Banat, Inventar 1517, File No. 29/1953, page 2.

47. National Archives of Romania Timişoara, Collection Sfatul Popular Banat, Finance, File No. 12/1955, page 240–43.

48. National Archives of Romania Timişoara, Collection Sfatul Popular Banat, Secretariat, File No. 43/1960, pages 36–37.

49. National Archives of Romania, Timişoara, Collection Sfatul Popular Banat, Secţia de Gospodărie Comunală, File No. 6/1960, pages 40–41.

Chapter 4

Resistance to Takings and the Construction of Socialist Subjectivities

How did homeowners respond to housing nationalization and expropriations? The following excerpt from a petition contesting housing nationalization, heartbreaking and cunning at the same time, brings to light the interplay of power and resistance in the early communist takings of the 1950s:

> I am a small craftsman who started work as a simple locksmith—which is known to be one of the hardest jobs there are. After 7 years of hard work, I managed to save 1,000 crowns [approx. $5,000] to buy my own tools and open my own workshop, in 1902, so I did not have to work for others anymore. Two years later I married an orphan girl . . . who helped me in the workshop . . . and after working 14 and even 16-hour days, we managed to buy, with a mortgage, our little house. . . . Later, my daughter and her husband helped us build more rooms. . . . This is how we obtained our house, with a lot of work, savings, and total devotion. Our house serves as our home primarily, and only secondarily to rent out. . . . Please admit our petition and annul the nationalization of our house. (June 24, 1950)[1]

The petition reveals a middle-class, hard-working family caught in the ideological net of the postwar transition to communism, losing their most important asset: their home. Like most other petition writers, the authors of this petition emphasize what they think would be to their advantage in the new regime: humble origins, hard work, and use of the house as a home for the extended family, rather than as a source of income. Together with thousands of other petitioners around the country, this family fought to reclaim their home, astutely perceiving the regime's deep ambivalence toward houses as objects of private property and homes.

There were approximately 500 petitions in the city of Timişoara, Romania, contesting the nationalization of houses under Decree 92/1950 and asking for restitution. Despite the lack of a formal mechanism for contesting nationalization, every other nationalized owner contested the taking, often multiple times, and the process of petitioning and answering the petitions lasted up to at least 1965 (the last year for which I had access to archival materials at the time of the research). Hundreds of petitions from the city and the county were also filed against other types of takings, most often contesting the taking of homes as part of larger nationalization packages (secondary nationalization). Also hotly contested was the nationalization of pharmacies and drugstores, where the petitions were uniformly unsuccessful, and the takings of property considered abandoned by the state (these petitions mostly focused on movable property, such as clothing, furniture, etc.).

Numerically and symbolically, Decree 92 has been more significant than all other nationalization decrees combined, as Liviu Chelcea notes (2004, 111), so I will focus mostly on these petitions here. Often neither the petitioners nor the local administration were entirely clear on the legal basis for a specific taking, so petitions relied on multiple statutes and decrees. The most common lumping together was Decree 92/1950 (urban housing nationalization), and Law 119/1948 (the great nationalization, with housing as secondary). Mistakes abounded, wrong classifications were common, and petitioners were consequently casting a wide net. Ioan H., a bricklayer with three children from the small town of C., for example, talked in his petition about Decree 92, while the local People's Council discussed his case under Law 119. After some investigation, it turned out that the nationalization commission under Law 119 had confused him with the former owner of the local tile factory.[2]

The very existence, numbers, and persistence of petitioners are among the most surprising findings of my research. At the apex of efforts to eliminate private property in the early transition to communism, and as the Stalinist repression deepened and more middle-class people became victims of the new communist regime, those most vulnerable to it did not fade quietly into the night. Surprisingly, they chose to resist the nationalization of their homes through perhaps the least likely method: law. Why did the petitioners choose this particular medium, what did they expect, what is the meaning of the petitions, and what was their impact?

Among the easiest explanations is that until 1956 (the Hungarian uprising), it was commonly believed that the regime would not last and the "Americans would come." This could certainly explain one reason for the petitioners' audacity. However, it is important to note that the petitions continued after 1956, as well, and in fact a second major wave of petitions was filed in the late 1950s.

The contestation of housing nationalization is also distinct from resistance to other takings. There was resistance across the board, heavy and violent against land takings, thinner against others. Resistance to the nationalization of big enterprises in the Timiş-Torontal county was diffuse: in some cases, the CEOs were taken by surprise and did not put up any resistance (there is one recorded nonfatal heart attack), while in others, the directors or owners attempted to resist; in some cases, workers were happy about the nationalization, in others they cried, appeared indifferent, or were silent and reserved toward the new leadership. During a meeting with the new directors of nationalized manufacturers, an official noted that in a number of factories workers cried when the owner was nationalized, which showed that "there was no class hate," a political deficiency that needed to be remedied by the new director (Mioc 2007, 204–6). However, once it became clear that the nationalization would not bring higher salaries or benefits for the workers, there were more vocal protests, attempts to bring back the old directors, and even strikes (Mioc 2007, 207). In 1951, for example, workers at the sugar factory in Timişoara went on strike because of their very low salaries, refusing to unload incoming boxes of beets (Munteanu and Munteanu 2002, 121).

Resistance to collectivization was directly against the law (Merry 1995), often violent and protracted. Close to the end of the process, in 1961, the General Secretary of the Romanian Communist Party, Gheorghe Gheorghiu-Dej, declared that more than 80,000 peasants had been prosecuted "during the fight against chiaburi," out of which 30,000 were judged in show trials (Deletant 1995, 76; Cioroianu 2005, 76). Even before the start of collectivization, peasants protested the fixed pricing and mandatory quotas imposed in 1945. In many villages throughout the county, peasants refused to surrender the harvest to state collectors unless they were paid and received from the state other goods that they were otherwise forced to buy on the black market (Gătaia); in some villages, in response to threats of army intervention, the inhabitants responded that they would resist with their clubs (Beşenova Veche); yet in other places (Cenadul Mare), fights broke out between peasants refusing to yield their produce and the local police. There were widespread complaints against the mandatory quotas, which were further increased in order to help the drought-stricken areas of Moldova (Mioc 2007, 212–15).

As conditions worsened—mandatory quotas left many peasant families with no harvest whatsoever, while buying industrial products was affected by inflation and the black market—peasants became increasingly unhappy with the new regime. Forms of resistance also escalated: peasants burned the harvest, stopped working the land, and attempted to organize politically (Mioc 2007, 215–20). In a village near Arad (in the Timiş-Torontal county), a newly established state farm was destroyed by the local peasants on July 31, 1949. Seen as a rebellion by the chief of the Timişoara Securitate, the conflict ended with ninety-eight people arrested and fourteen shot, two of them while trying to escape from detention. Common resistance techniques to collectivization included attacking and destroying Party offices, cutting phone lines, and beating up Party activists (Deletant 1999, 107).

I have not found evidence of violent or even open resistance against urban housing nationalization in my research. I have, however, found hundreds of petitions, from the city and the entire county. Nationalized owners were persistent, persuasive, and worked within the framework of the new regime. Their efforts are a clear illustration of the intricacies of power and resistance even under conditions of intense repression. Nationalized owners mobilized law in their petitions, particularly relying upon legal formalism and law as a rhetorical weapon (Lovell 2006) in order to reclaim their houses and preserve their ideas about private property in law. The petitions were partially successful, nonviolent acts of micro-resistance through law, through which the petitioners challenged the regime's understanding of private property as exploitation, the very concept of law as an instrument of the socialist regime, and ultimately undermined the regime's attempts at building legitimacy through legality.

Resistance to urban housing nationalization through law was possible because houses have a dual nature, as both homes and assets; because of the inner contradictions of socialist legality, which opened up spaces for resistance through law for ordinary citizens, not just legal experts; because of the regime's own ambivalence regarding houses and private property, which resulted in the partial and arbitrary nationalization of houses; and because petitioners operated with ideas of property rights and law that remained embedded in the pre-communist *nomos* and its communities of meaning. It is important to recognize the ambiguous nature of oppositional acts such as petitions against housing nationalization as acts of both cooptation and resistance, bearing upon both the long-term legitimacy of the regime and the deployment of law.

PETITIONS AS MICRO-RESISTANCE

Decree 92 did not include any mechanism for challenging the nationalization. Despite this, however, every other nationalized owner contested the taking, often multiple times, both through administrative and court channels, and the process of petitioning and answering the petitions lasted for years (Şerban 2010). Former owners filed petitions in large numbers and were quite persistent. Almost half of those nationalized contested the taking, themselves or their heirs doggedly pursuing their claims over the years. I manually counted 444 petitions and an estimated 75 more petitions contesting *de facto* nationalizations (not included in the Decree 92 appendix, but similarly treated by the local administration).

The total number of petitions for this period (1950–1965), which includes multiple, non-repeat petitions filed for the same house or apartment by different petitioners, including members of the same family, was 666 (this is thus higher than the number above). It is possible that many more petitions were lost. The relatively few petition files that have survived in their entirety, as well as the correspondence regarding the petitions and the administrative responses are scattered throughout twenty-five archival files and number hundreds of pages.

The filing of petitions and responses to them were uneven throughout the period studied: almost half of the petitions were filed between 1951 and 1953, and they appear to have been discussed in 1953 and 1956 (further proposals for nationalization were also put together in 1953). More than 350 petitions were filed in a second wave, roughly between 1957 and 1960, and they were tackled mostly in bulk, in 1959–1960 and 1964–1965. This breakdown does not include refiling of petitions or appeals to reconsider a rejection, most of which took place between 1960 and 1965 (see Figure 4.1).

The initial wave of petitions (1951–1953) is not surprising, as they were filed in the period right after the nationalization, when the regime was not yet well consolidated and the owners might have reasonably thought they had chances of success. In fact, almost 20 percent of these petitions were approved for partial restitution by the local administration (106 complaints), pending final approval from the central authorities (eventually only 5 percent were admitted). This result, as well as later policy developments that seemed to indicate even more opportunities for restitution, may explain the second wave of petitions.

The government issued instructions to deal with implementation problems for Decree 92 in 1953, restitution instructions in 1955, and instructions for the restitution of other urban housing throughout the 1950s.[3] As information

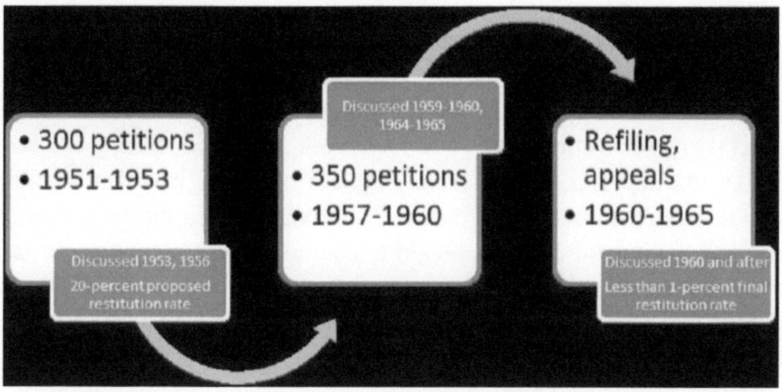

Figure 4.1. Timeline of Petitions. *Source*: Courtesy of the author.

or rumors about these secret policies trickled down to the population, those who had not received any answer from the administration about their initial petition against nationalization, as well as other nationalized owners, may have felt newly emboldened and submitted or resubmitted their petitions (1957–1960). This interpretation is backed by various internal, secret memos from the municipal People's Council to the Council of Ministers, one of them from 1956, asking them how to proceed with these new petitions in light of the fact that the Municipal Council had submitted their answers to the original petitions to the Council of Ministers for approval as early as 1953. As the Council of Ministers had never replied, the petitioners had also never heard back.[4] Possibly the Council of Ministers hoped this would all go away and that not having received any response, the petitioners would simply give up.

Most petitioners complained administratively, following a hierarchical route that started with the municipal People's Council (the lowest executive agency at the local level). The Council's nationalization commission (a three- to five-person commission) undertook the field investigation and made a recommendation. The entire file was then forwarded to the regional People's Council(s), and eventually to the Council of Ministers in Bucharest, which had the final say. If they did not hear back from the local authorities, it was not unusual for petitioners to request an audience with the local Party organs, as was the case for a retired forester who submitted petitions regarding his house in 1957, 1959, and 1964. In his case, the local nationalization commission proposed restitution, but the final confirmation never arrived from the central nationalization commission (this was one of only two cases of proposed restitution in that area).[5]

Some petitioners also sued, usually filing for a judicial declaration that the nationalization was wrongly applied, and thereby asking the court to declare the "inexistence of nationalization." However, this was not a linear process, as the petitioners pursued various administrative, political, and judicial avenues simultaneously, and the court was rarely the last resort. The nationalized locksmith introduced at the beginning of this chapter, for example, started out by filing his petition with the local People's Council, "where we were always told that our petition would be solved favorably, but we have not received any official answer to this day." The locksmith then sued, asking the court to affirm that the house could not have been nationalized, and if it was, it was wrongly nationalized because Decree 92 did not apply to the petitioner. Both the trial and the appeal courts rejected his claims, declining jurisdiction. The locksmith then wrote directly to the Presidency of the Council of Ministers, which sent the petition back to the Municipal Council, restarting the entire process.[6]

Petitioners were further thwarted in their efforts by the abolition of judicial review. On May 19, 1956, for example, the Timişoara regional tribunal in appeal rejected a former owner's challenge to the nationalization of their house, declining jurisdiction.[7] I found other cases of resistance to nationalization through the court system, all ultimately unsuccessful, all written in a language somewhat sympathetic to the petitioners.

Many petitioners went to great length in preparing and submitting their petition in terms of the documents submitted, persistence, and arguments employed. An elderly couple, for example, included a justifying memo, extracts from the land registry, the diagram of the house, an authenticated copy of the nationalization record, as well as authenticated certificates from the owners' workplaces and from the municipal housing authority.[8] At the time, collecting these documents was very difficult, time consuming, and expensive. Other petitioners included evidence of real estate registration, affidavits from former coworkers or supervisors, proofs of donation or inheritance, mortgage payments, court decisions, and so on. Many of these were authenticated by a notary public, which added significant costs to their petition effort. Many petitions were typed, relatively concise, using precise language and referring to specific laws and policies, which suggests that the petitioners had received professional help, possibly from a lawyer (the massive purging of the bar had left many lawyers adrift, and there was a flourishing black market in legal services).

Follow-up petitions were usually much briefer, for example:

> To the General Direction of Affairs of the Council of Ministers, Bucharest,
>
> The undersigned, JZ and JI, living in Timişoara, [address]
>
> We have not received any answers to our petition asking back our house, situated in Timişoara, [address], which we sent via mail on October 31, 1956, and which you received on November 6, 1956. Therefore, we respectfully inquire into how you solved our petition, or to let us know where we could inquire about its fate.
>
> Timişoara, February 2, 1957,
>
> We fight for peace![9]

This follow-up letter is somewhat unusual because it dares to hold accountable the Council of Ministers for its lack of response to the original petition. Its conciseness, language, and exact dates indicate professional help, as well as a lot of background research, possibly from a lawyer. The original petition is equally professional. It refers specifically, improbably (since they were not published) and almost correctly to the 1956 restitution Instructions;[10] it includes a plethora of supporting evidence: a justifying memo, extracts from the land registry, the diagram of the house, an authenticated copy of the nationalization record, as well as authenticated certificates from the owners' workplaces and from the municipal housing authority (ILLT).

Furthermore, the petition presents the case for restitution in formal, legalistic language, for the most part foregoing emotional appeals, common in many petitions. The petitioner pointed out that the taking was procedurally flawed, as the nationalization record of April 20, 1950, indicated a different person as the owner, which in the petitioner's opinion could not be held against him, the real owner ("opozabil"). If the house was nationalized through error, the petitioner argued, this could be rectified, especially since the local housing authority (ILLT) had not made any repairs or invested in any way in the house (ILLT refused to provide any documentation in that sense, however).

Piecing together the various petition files and the trajectories of complaints, one is struck not just by the persistence of the dispossessed owners and their families over time, but also by the responses of the administration, more fully analyzed in the next chapter, and by the extent to which their interactions over time ever so slowly eroded not just the nationalization process—there was never a second round, for example, but also official attempts to install a new property ideology. Micro-resistance through law here is not about obtaining restitution, but about the process of relentlessly engaging with the regime and subtly, subversively challenging it.

LEGAL CONSCIOUSNESS AND THE RELUCTANT MAKING OF SOCIALIST SUBJECTS

A typical petition, whether handwritten or typed, started out with a brief life history of the petitioner and the nationalized property. The petitioner would then self-categorize as an "article 2 exemption" and proceed to argue that the house had been obtained through labor, not exploitation, that its primary function was as a family home and not as rental income ("exploitation"), and furthermore that others in a similar position had not been nationalized (arbitrariness of the taking):

> The undersigned Nicolae S., retired and a war veteran, disabled from the world war from 1916–1919 . . . please order the restitution of my family's house . . . , where I live, mistakenly nationalized in 1950, despite the provisions of art. II from the nationalization decree. . . . In the spirit of this article, please see that I fit the criteria for exemption from nationalization. . . . I come from a poor peasant family, my father was an agricultural hand, as shown in the reference letter provided by the retired teacher from my native village. . . . When the Communist Party was illegal, I provided help, as shown by the attached authentic

> document. . . . Before 1944, when I worked at the prefect's office, I helped the working class . . . I was also persecuted by the Iron Guard [Romania's interwar fascist party], who suspended me and locked me up during the Iron Guard rebellion. Today I have no wealth, as shown by the attached declaration from the financial office. Since I was wounded in the kidneys during the war, I could not serve during the last one, but I worked conscientiously at my job . . . I was not a member of any political party. In light of what I have shown, it can be seen that we, the simple and anonymous people, served the Party and the working class without asking for any rewards, because we thought it was our duty and something natural to serve the working class, where we also came from. As you can see from the annexed documents, I suffered enough in the past, when still in school I had to tutor the rich children for a slice of polenta, to work in factories and the landowners' land, in order to support myself while in school. I am thus convinced that today, in the regime of liberty and legality, you will repair the mistake and return my house to me, especially since because of the nationalization I am in danger of losing my pension as well and starve, even though the house is a simple family home. (June 22, 1960)[11]

Nicolae S. was a small rags-to-riches story—he came from a poor peasant family in Moldavia and through his own efforts became a teacher, artillery officer, and afterward head accountant for the prefect's office in Timişoara. In his petition he alternately tried to shame the regime, to negotiate with it, but also to flatter it. He was proud of his hard-working life that allowed him to escape the mind-numbing poverty of early-twentieth-century Romania, but also confused as to how this same hard work so praised by the new regime landed him in this difficult position. He had bona fide credentials that he had performed his part of the social contract before the communists took power, and at the very least he expected that his home would not be taken away. His self-understanding is infused with "bourgeois" values: labor, individualism, hardship, status, wealth, and knowledge. This is a narrative where past suffering and poverty create the entitlement of a good life later on. He draws equally from bourgeois and socialist discourses while trying to reconcile them, with labor a clear, if contested site of intersection, thus revealing his own reluctant path toward becoming a socialist subject on his terms.

Like so many other petitioners, Nicolae did not openly question the nationalization *per se*, but merely its implementation in his particular case. In his understanding, it is not the law that is his enemy in this new regime of "liberty and legality." He appeals not only to "the law," but also to the compassion of those he claimed to have previously protected, and the end of his petition is a reminder that nationalization meant not just the loss of the house, but also losing access to services, social security, and so on. For many petitioners, this meant concretely the loss of retirement benefits, which could easily lead to abject poverty if one had no family to fall back on.

Nicolae's arguments illuminate how he engaged with the regime and the extent to which the process of petitioning was an act of resistance, as well as accommodating to the new power structure. The process of petitioning contributed to the creation of his socialist legal consciousness, as Nicolae and petitioners like him related to the emerging socialist legality while also falling back on older conceptions of law. In Silbey and Ewick's (2005) framework, the petitioners vacillated between "before the law" (law as an objective, majestic reality to be respected and obeyed), "with the law" (law as a game), and, more rarely, "against the law" legality. Their legal consciousness was only partially the product of communist power. Nicolae's arguments, which surface in most other petitions as well, also illuminate changes in the meaning of property and property rights during this period, and changes in how they conceived of themselves and their communities.

The secrecy, lack of transparency, arbitrariness, and ambiguity that surrounded the takings overall, not just housing nationalization, were meant to benefit the regime, but also opened up unexpected avenues for resistance and helped shape the new socialist subjects. Recall that instructions for the implementation of housing nationalization were issued three years after the nationalization, in 1953, and restitution procedures only in 1955. Both acts were unpublished and "strictly secret." Secrecy was deployed both within the state apparatus and against the population, so much so that on occasion local authorities themselves were not sure whether a house had been nationalized or not, and neither were the owners.

Secrecy, arbitrariness, and ambiguity can have unintended consequences. Petitions contesting nationalization are precisely one such consequence. The petitions matter because they forced the regime to continue a discourse over the meaning of property rights over houses, something the regime would have preferred settled, and because they constructed it as a legal discourse, shrewdly attempting to colonize legal spaces officially belonging to the regime.

The process of petitioning itself—conceptualizing the wrong and the claim ("naming, blaming, claiming," Felstiner, Abel, Sarat 1980), writing the petition, gathering supporting documents, mailing the petition, asking for an audience, waiting for a response that was often cryptic and delayed, following-up, starting all over again—pushed the former owners to articulate, perhaps for the first time, both for themselves and the local authorities, their own sense of property rights and of the injustice they thought was done to them. It thus reinforced, rather than weakened, the connections between the house, property rights, labor, history, and family for the petitioners. Yet it also required the petitioners to frame their requests in a language and ideological framework that would appeal to the new masters. It required them to look for, or construct common ground with the new regime.

The former owners were well aware of the mixed messages of the early 1950s: on the one hand, extensive takings and a prolonged nationalization process; on the other hand, some restitutions, encouragement of new private constructions, primacy of labor, and continuity of property law. For many, this could only mean that in their case nationalization was a mistake that could be repaired through persistence and patience: "we are convinced the nationalization was done through error and against the law" (May 24, 1950);[12] "my family's house . . . , where I live, mistakenly nationalized"; "as I have been told, family homes are not nationalized, so I think there must have been a mistake and therefore I ask that you investigate and annul the nationalization order" (August 28, 1950);[13] "but the house was nationalized only by mistake"; "the house is not gained from commercial business . . . and thus was mistakenly nationalized . . . with respect we ask that you order the re-examination of the situation . . . find our petition founded, order the restitution of our house and do us justice, correcting a mistake" (underlined in the original) (October 5, 1959);[14] "I believe that the . . . local organs did not and do not know in detail my and my family's situation and did not objectively understand it, because if they had, they could not have proposed my house for nationalization" (June 16, 1961).[15]

Petitioners believed that if a proper investigation were undertaken, the truth would come out and their house would be returned to them. This truth, from their perspective, was that they were not "exploiters," but mere hard-working people who did not deserve to be deprived of their home. Rarely, petitioners claimed they were victims of malice or personal hate, yet it is difficult now to know how common these cases were.

These demands for investigations indicate faith that the process will vindicate them, that the investigations will uncover the injustice of the taking and order redress, in other words, that procedural justice will lead to substantive justice as they understood it—the return of their houses. The municipal and regional nationalization commissions did in fact order the investigation of most of the petitions, but the result was not what the petitioners wanted, as substantive justice meant class justice for the communist officials. Despite vigorous complaining, only a very small percentage of houses nationalized under Decree 92 in the whole country were returned to their owners—less than 1 percent. (As of 1960, only 1,082 apartments in the whole country were returned to their former owners, which represents approximately .009 percent of the total number of nationalized apartments.)[16]

Yet the owners' complaints forced the regime to clarify both the nationalization procedure and its ideological position, for example, to determine when a house is considered "means of exploitation," as well as to reconsider further nationalizations. The regime eventually halted housing nationalization in the early 1960s, in part as a result of the petitions and requests for restitution, and of its own mishandling of the process. The open-ended nature of housing nationalization, its indeterminacy and lack of clarity showed the former owners that this was a poorly thought out and poorly implemented measure. By engaging with the petitioners, moreover, the regime admitted as much, which in turn gave them hope and reinforced their "bourgeois" concepts of private property.

Former owners turned to a legal system that was suddenly and purposely excluding them, that was not supposed to protect them. Yet they did not challenge the law or its legitimacy, but its interpretation and application in their particular cases. Petitioners attempted to capture the law for their own purposes, rather than reject it. Law itself retained attributes of "majesty," of justice and objectivity, and was a resource to be harnessed and trusted. Drawing from this pre-communist "legal consciousness capital," it was paradoxically the petitioners that turned to law even though they had the most reasons to distrust it.

DISCOURSES OF RESISTANCE

The process of petitioning, from the initial complaint to the final response (if any), is one element that helped construct the petitioners' emerging socialist legal consciousness. This process kept open channels of communication between competing property ideologies and privileged legal over nonlegal discourses. The content of the petitions and the types of discourses deployed by the petitioners are an equally important indicator of how they related to the changing political and property regimes, and how they understood their position vis-à-vis a legal system that suddenly classified them as enemies.

The locksmith petitioner introduced at the beginning of the chapter was not the only one to point out the random nature of the takings under Decree 92. He argued that his house was not listed in the appendix, and even if it were, it would still not be nationalizable because he was an Article 2 exemption.[17] Another petitioner pointed out that his house "is the smallest house on the street, which is a side street with family homes, and this is the only house that was nationalized from the entire street."[18] It was clear to the petitioners that while entire streets were targeted, particularly in the downtown area, geographically there was no overall, well-defined pattern.

Other than the randomness of the takings, petitioners commonly deployed four key discourses: labor, rights and justice, the implied social contract, and compassion. These discourses reveal both the owners' intractability regarding their homes and their simultaneous slow adaptation to the new regime.

Labor

The petitions against urban housing nationalization (which includes secondary nationalization) revealed the extent of the regime's failure to define exploitation and to make it work. The importance of the family home, the cloudiness of the nationalization criteria, and the arbitrariness of the takings—both listed and not listed in the Decree 92 appendix—were some of the key factors leading former owners to contest the nationalization of their houses and ask for restitution.

Labor was the most commonly used argument marshaled by petitioners in support of their claims, often in conjunction with an understanding of the house as their home and the embodiment of family. Former owners made extensive efforts to contextualize and historicize the nationalization and to counter the regime's own discourse that presented houses as means of exploitation. For the petitioners, the houses taken were the pinnacle of years of hard labor, rather than investment properties detached from family and belonging. Labor represented a common ground between the petitioners and the regime, as both considered it a legitimate fountain of private property rights. The following petition, excerpted at length, is an example:

> The undersigned . . . please take into consideration the reasons of a wretched creature, who has suffered since childhood, and who managed after a difficult life to build together with her husband a family home for old age, and now when I am old I end up with nothing. My father was a daily worker at the . . . woodshop, where he died in an accident in 1900, when a heap of planks fell on top of him. . . . My mother became a widow in 1900 with 5 small children and she started to provide for us by working as a laundress. But she could not even obtain enough bread to feed us hungry children, so we brothers and sisters, starting in 1900—when I was 7 years old—until 1909 sat in front of the military barracks and there the soldiers gave us some bread. Later we were also fed by the Catholic Church in . . . , and given free daily bread by the bakery . . . I started working in the tobacco factory at 11 years old, but after three years my weak body could not stand anymore the harmful atmosphere, and then I learned tailoring and I worked diligently until I got married, having put aside some money. My deceased husband was a waiter all his life, and from our honest work we built together our home in three years—from 1926 to 1929, which was three times bombarded during the war.
>
> Although my husband, who died in 1954, was retired in 1950, and I am also retired . . . , our family's home—two rooms, entryway, kitchen, pantry, bathroom—was nonetheless nationalized. Neither my husband nor I have never had employees, so there can't be talk of exploitation. Immediately after the nationalization we petitioned, but it was not definitively answered. . . . Taking into account that I am old and sick, I have no family, and that retirees were specifically exempt from nationalization under Decree 92, I beg you to order the restitution of my family home.[19]

This narrative of deep poverty and hard work, including child labor, underscores a basic Lockean understanding of labor as a legitimate basis for private property rights. Other petitions similarly stress the former owners' labor as the basis of their property claims that satisfies both bourgeois and socialist narratives. Petitioners describe themselves as mere employees, "simple people who worked to earn our existence,"[20] and stress their humble beginnings, such as the widow who asserted that "both my husband and my father are the first generation in our families to wear shoes,"[21] or the retired First World War disabled veteran who was born in a poor peasant family and built his house with a thirty-year loan from the prefect's office, which he had obtained as an employee.[22] Another petitioner, a very persistent doctor, quoted an article in the main Party newspaper, *Scânteia* (*The Spark*), where the Party had given assurances that houses obtained through labor would not be nationalized. He explained that he took out a loan from the Railroad Company Credit Company and that he paid it back over ten years, from his monthly paycheck. "If this does not mean labor," he concluded, "then nothing in this world does."[23]

The commonality of labor as a fundamental value for both the petitioners and the new regime did not mean, however, that they understood it in the same way or that the petitioners had increased chances of success. To the extent that for the regime labor competed with other values, such as equality, the petitioners were left wondering how capitalist property based on labor was different from socialist property based on labor.

Petitioners saw no contradiction between the agenda of building communism and their property rights over their home. Teodor S., "a faithful and devoted PMR member" since 1945, former Party secretary, lecturer, and propaganda official, mentioned three times in the course of his petition that he was forced by housing regulations to rent out rooms: "In my own house I have to put up with tenants." Teodor also explained that he and his wife bought their house from savings, making payments over four years, "from my honest salary and my wife's," and that his plan was to have his granddaughters, both of whom were "utemiste" (members of the Romanian Union of Working Youth), marry and live at home so that together with their parents they could support him in his old age.[24] Although many petitioners were old, this cannot be defined as a generational issue, since often the heirs took up the petitions after the owners' death.

Ultimately, the instrumental and ideological convergence around the concept and value of labor between the petitioners and the regime had two important consequences: it allowed the petitioners to engage with the regime on its own terms, and it reinforced their ideas of the legitimacy of private property rights based on labor. For the former owners, property rights encompassed ideas of labor and protection that had been prominent during the prior capitalist regime (Underkuffler 2003). Labor became the only acceptable basis of private property in communism, but property as protection was the main target for denaturalizing ideas of property through both takings and housing policies. This is thus another key area of disagreement between the communist regime and its subjects, and one that would not disappear throughout communism. The petitions reveal another aspect of how the petitioners related to law: law itself was a resource, as well as a link with the past and internalized ideas of self, property, and legality, something that was both needed but also somewhat trusted.

Rights and Justice

Most petitions against the taking of homes reveal a Lockean pre-communist "property and self" narrative: whether born poor or not, one worked hard, slowly acquired some wealth and a house or more as the ultimate value, mostly intended for the extended family and some additional income. The family home represented not just the epitome of labor, but also the nexus of family life, basic insurance against old age and other events (Chelcea 2004), a buffer between one's family and the outside world—a classic conceptualization of property as protection (Underkuffler 2003). Property rights consciousness for the former owners is more than just the basic "it is mine" because I worked for it, but also that "it is mine" in a specific way: it is legally mine, it is registered in the public property registry, it is where the family lives, it represents security and protection from the outside world for the head of the household as well as his family. It is, in this sense, a modified version of Macpherson's "possessive individualism" (1962), as family is a crucial aspect of it.

The language itself is revealing: as late as 1965, former owners routinely refer to the nationalized houses as "my house" and ask explicitly for their "rights," as the widow Margareta W. did: "Because of these just reasons, please investigate this case and return my house to me . . . return my keys and give me all my rights" (December 8, 1955).[25] An eighty-year-old blacksmith and his wife asked the Council of Ministers to investigate their case and order "restitution of possession" to them as "true legal owners" (November 12, 1956).[26] Adrian I., a construction worker, vividly recalled how in 1950 "the local authorities kicked us out of my own home. . . . We know that the right of property for workers is guaranteed by the Romanian Popular Republic State [*sic*], yet from me they took my house off my back [mi-au luat casa din spate]."[27] A university professor reassigned to Bucharest asked to be allowed to sell his house from Timişoara (proposed for nationalization), arguing that "our request is just, and we do not ask for anything else but the free exercise of a citizen's right, explicitly guaranteed by the RPR Constitution" (September 1957).[28]

Nicolae S. (quoted at the beginning of the previous section), like other petitioners, was quick to point out that Article 2 of Decree 92 regulated exemptions from nationalization and that he fit the criteria. The various arguments he brought up, as well as his supporting evidence (such as the reference letters from his childhood friend and former boss, as well as real estate registry) indicate that he was viewing law as one element in a multi-varied arsenal. Petitioners like him had their own ideas of law, justice, and rights, attempted to distinguish between "factual" and "legal" situation ["situaţia de fapt" and "situaţia de drept"], and were equally likely to deploy legal ("it is my right," I qualify as an exemption from nationalization), moral (compassion), or economic (more efficient not to nationalize) arguments.

Petitioners brought up both rights claims and justice claims—claims that they were wronged, that the taking was not right, not just. The Romanian word used by most of the petitioners was "nedreptate," which can be translated as "injustice" or "wrong," depending on the context. In Romanian, it implies both a moral and legal injustice, lack of fairness, wrongness. Elisabeta F., a sixty-seven-year-old widow "without any kind of wealth" "respectfully ask the Central Committee to please listen to my complaint regarding the injustice done to me by the local expropriation committee" (March 1, 1956).[29] A doctor from O., a nearby town, spoke this way of the nationalization of his house: "The injustice of which revolts me" (May 20, 1963).[30] Other petitioners talked about their "very righteous petition," "righteous request,"[31] "just reasons,"[32] "our request is just,"[33] "appeal . . . to your justice,"[34] "do us justice,"[35] "it is not right to take away my house,"[36] "it is our right to ask for the restitution at least of the house we live in," "just request,"[37] "screaming injustice" [nedreptatea strigătoare].[38] The petitioners' understanding of what was just, right has natural law undertones and was entirely at odds with the local authorities' understanding, for whom justice meant class justice. To the extent that the owner or anybody in his family was tainted by exploitation, broadly defined, the nationalization as class justice was justified. Furthermore, as long as legal formalities were observed, petitioners were told point blank that they were "not right."[39]

The majority of the petitioners were close to or past the retirement age, many were widows, and more than half continued to live in their house post-nationalization. From their perspective, the nationalization was not a progressive measure toward building socialism and eliminating exploitation, but an illegal taking, a punishment, an injustice. A Party member proposed for nationalization implored in his petition: "Deeply distressed by this, I beg of you to do everything in your power to exempt me from this undeserved punishment."[40] The regime's hesitancy, the adoption of implementation instructions, and the occasional restitutions merely reinforced the former owners' belief in the righteousness of their petitioning efforts.

The Implied Social Contract

A separate thread in the petitions is the claim that nationalization was wrongly applied in the petitioners' specific cases because they were not the other, the class enemy, but part of the new regime, and therefore the regime violated an unspoken social contract. Like Nicolae S., some petitioners felt they were wronged because they had been on the side of the Party, who was now abandoning them, not fulfilling their side of the bargain. Nicolae argued that he had helped the Party while the Party functioned illegally during the interwar period, as well as the working class during the Great Depression, with which he identified himself.[41] He might have thought it was natural and did not expect any rewards for his service, but he also made it clear that he was outraged by being punished through the nationalization. Mary Fulbrook makes a similar argument about the GDR and the unwritten social contract that rewarded active participants in the system, at the very least, with small privileges and opportunities (2005, 238–39).

Here is how another petitioner, a doctor, makes his case in the fourth petition he submitted:

> I want to start by declaring that what I did for the poor and destitute people in O., I swear that no other doctor did during the bourgeois period. Even for the Jews who were sick and whom the Iron Guard wanted to execute, I was the only doctor who went to them and took care of them. . . . The verification [purging] commission composed of the most trustworthy members in 1947 found me worthy of being a Party member, while a good number of Party members were excluded. The nationalization commission from 1950, by contrast, nationalized me, also contradicting the Party and the popular democratic government's communiqué in *Scânteia* [*The Spark*] from April 22, 1950, that says, I quote, "those who built their houses through labor are and will be exempt from the nationalization laws of RPR." . . . Even Decree 92 exempts me from nationalization since I am a retired doctor who worked for the Romanian Railways Company [CFR]. . . . I was ignored by the Party in O. in 1950 when I asked to see them. I was refused a right granted to me by the Party Regulations point 3, letter d, as a Party member. The same happened with the other three petitions and even after many years I did not receive any answers. I think and believe that all Party members are equal and owe each other a comradely behavior and respect and not backstabbing. When there was the verification they could have said something if they had anything against me, because that's why there were verifications. I could have been a member of a bourgeois Party and gotten a house easily in a couple of months and not borrow money from CFR, but I preferred to build the house through honest labor and effort. I have also been a lecturer with the Party cell of the O. hospital, and my daughter was for four years a UTM secretary.[42]

The doctor felt he had been wronged on multiple levels: he had built his house through honest labor, he had served the Communist Party's anti-fascist agenda during the war because he had helped O.'s Jewish population, and both he and his family were active Party members who had passed the purging. The nationalization of his house was thus both wrong per se, and from a socialist justice perspective. He was not the only one to feel he had been deeply wronged by the new regime, nor the only Party member whose pleas were ignored.

An engineer pointed out that he had been given awards for innovations improving the production process,[43] whereas Teodor S., the one-time Party secretary mentioned earlier also brought up his son-in-law, who had worked for the counterintelligence agency between 1947 and 1950, "in hard circumstances, when the reactionary forces were organized in gangs." He came as close as anybody to true bargaining: "Myself and all my family worked with devotion and showed our attachment to the Party through actions and in difficult and even dangerous conditions. . . . I am convinced that my Party activity . . . weighs more than the insinuation that I am an exploiter because I rent two rooms at the price established by law" (June 16, 1961).[44] A retired lieutenant colonel also mentioned that he had been an officer throughout the war and later had become chief of staff for the Ministry of the Interior, Securitate division. His problem was his wife, whose father had apparently owned a bank. The lieutenant general's own status was not taken into account.[45]

In a similar vein, other petitioners explicitly argued that it was wrong to nationalize their houses because they were also part of the previously downtrodden who were now on the winning side of history: "Comrade president, we are not from one of those aristocratic families that in the old days disrespected us and splashed us with their limousines as they passed us by, the same way they did to you. . . . This is our origin and our past of hard work in the middle of the working class, always with sympathy towards the fight for freedom."[46]

While neither the doctor nor the Party secretary received the positive news they were hoping for, other Party members did. The wife of a colonel and volunteer for The Romanian Voluntary Association for the Support of the Motherland Defense and mother to a twenty-two-year old enrolled in the army at the time of the petition did not receive her house back, but did receive additional housing for her family.[47] A former employer was exempt from nationalization because he had "distinguished himself in the collectivization of craftsmen,"[48] while a journalist and member of the Writers' Association decorated with the "Labor Award" [Ordinul Muncii] got to keep his very large six-room apartment.[49]

Compassion

Finally, petitioners also commonly appealed to the sense of compassion of officials. Often, they described in detail their lives of suffering and poverty and the dire circumstances of their lives in old age should the house not be returned to them. Here is how various petitioners framed their pleas: "Please . . . give me back my house and garden, as they are my only means of existence in my old age . . . when I cannot work anymore and have no other income";[50] "Mr. President, I make an appeal to your soul, I am a 65-year old man, and I am old";[51] "Cancel the nationalization order . . . so that I and my family can re-occupy the necessary space in my former house, so that we are not homeless now when winter comes";[52] "Now that I found out the truth about losing my last source of income at the age of 62 forces me to ask you for your compassion and help . . . I am alone, without the strength to work anymore, have a heart disease and my son with his own difficulties cannot help me. My only income is the rent, which is small but it's something. If this is taken from me, what am I supposed to do? In this critical situation, I appeal with these lines to your justice and compassion, please dispose that the rest of the house that I still own is exempt from nationalization, so that for the little time that I have left to live I can ensure my modest but secure living."[53]

Overall, there are two primary discourses of resistance in the petitions: the labor discourse and the legal/rights discourse. Secondary discourses include compassion and the social contract, and more rarely economic arguments (i.e., the inefficiency of nationalizing a particular house). Labor and law are not separate threads, however, as labor justified the former owners' property rights and their belief in the righteousness of these rights. The very meaning of property rights for these petitioners, therefore, did not fundamentally change. Both the process of petitioning and the discourses deployed by the former owners between 1950 and 1965 indicate that the apparently smooth transition to socialist property and the overall attempts to denaturalize private property were not accepted at face value by those caught in the crossfire. Former owners question everything in their petitions, from the regime's definition of exploitation to the implementation of nationalization procedures, appealing to moral and legal arguments and even bargaining with the regime.

The petitions against the taking of homes illustrate the myriad ways of micro-resistance against communism that are more rarely documented and can be easily dismissed as inconsequential. Yet they demonstrate the ambiguous nature of resistance under early communism, the extent to which petitioners were both conforming to and challenging the system, and the operation of the "field of force" constraining both powerful and powerless, albeit unequally (Thompson 1971; Lukes 2005). The petitions also show how resistance may contribute to domination, specifically how strategies of domination can only be understood in the context of the opposition they face (Flowerdew 1997, 318; Hollander and Einwohner 2004, 548). The regime's responses to petitions against urban housing nationalization, a form of nonviolent protest, was mild and even defensive, while in the case of violent resistance, the regime intensified its repression. The interaction between petitioners, local administration, and central bodies also reveals that neither resisters nor dominators are monolithic, and that there is variation in both groups (Hollander and Einwohner 2004, 550)—petitioners would often strive to demonstrate their commitment to socialist goals, while local authorities gave them assurances that their petitions would be positively answered because they were justified.

If counter-hegemonies start from current hegemonies, as Ewick and Silbey (2003) point out, attempts to dislodge and establish new ones in a very short period of time are bound to intensify ideological struggles, as indeed shown by the nationalization and expropriation processes. Moreover, it is not only the exercise of power that adds up in time but also that of resistance. While it may bubble under the surface, resistance based on divergent ideologies rarely entirely disappears. Throughout the regime's life, and against claims of atomization (Arendt), the most common type of resistance against communism was at the level of micro-resistance. If the communist regimes in Eastern Europe survived because everyone contributed, as Havel noted, they eventually fell because there was always ambivalence toward their claims and ultimate goals, because in the struggle of ideologies, Marxism-Leninism won some battles, but not the war. The courage and leadership of dissidents were crucial, yet the creation of a mass "oppositional state of being" eventually depended upon mundane, ordinary acts of evasion, resistance, or simply survival. The simultaneous cooperation and resistance to the regime is not exclusive to ordinary citizens, as bureaucrats were also ambivalent, and jurists, in particular civil law specialists, were similarly less than willing communist subjects and ideologues.

The remarkable fact about early communism is the extent of everyday resistance to the regime even at the height of terror, the pervasiveness of everyday, rather than extreme and extraordinary, acts of resistance, variously called secondary adjustments (Goffman 1961), tactics (De Certeau 1984) or weapons of the weak (Scott 1985). They are "the ways in which relatively powerless persons accommodate to power while simultaneously protecting their interests and identities" (Ewick and Silbey 2003, 1329). This type of "infra-politics of resistance" (Scott 1990) relies less upon the juxtaposition of public and hidden transcripts, does not necessarily challenge the regime as a whole (in the way that armed resistance did), and is not looking for a system-wide impact. Its characteristic is engagement with the regime on presumably its own terrain—law, challenging specific aspects of power—for example, who is an exploiter, what constitutes labor, how procedures should be implemented, based on similar or distinct ideologies of property and law, sometimes even speaking the language of power ("speaking Bolshevik"), and aiming toward rather modest goals—reclaiming a house, or closing a nationalization file.

NOTES

1. National Archives of Romania Timişoara, Collection Sfatul Popular Banat, Secretariat, File No. 102/1960, page 82.
2. National Archives of Romania Timişoara, Collection Sfatul Popular Banat, Secretariat, File No. 55/1960, pages 17–18.
3. Instructions 40869/1956 [40689], issued jointly by the General Director of the Council of Ministers General Affairs Department and the MCGIL Minister.
4. National Archives of Romania Timişoara, Collection Sfatul Popular Banat, Inventar 1630, File No. 1/1956, page 105.
5. National Archives of Romania Timişoara, Collection Sfatul Popular Banat, Inventar 1630, File No. 2/1964, page 169.
6. National Archives of Romania National Archives of Romania Timişoara, Collection Sfatul Popular Banat, Inventar 1630, File No. 1/1956, page 105.
7. National Archives of Romania Timişoara, Collection Sfatul Popular Banat, Secretariat, File No. 102/1960, pages 86–87.
8. National Archives of Romania Timişoara, Collection Sfatul Popular Banat, Secretariat, File 102/1960, page 139.
9. National Archives of Romania Timişoara, Collection Sfatul Popular Banat, Secretariat, File No. 102/1960, page 139.
10. Instructions 40869/1956 [40689], issued jointly by the General Director of the Council of Ministers General Affairs Department and the MCGIL Minister.
11. National Archives of Romania Timişoara, Collection Sfatul Popular Banat, Secretariat, File No. 102/1960, pages 2–3.
12. National Archives of Romania Timişoara, Collection Sfatul Popular Banat, Secretariat, File No. 102/1960, page 257.
13. National Archives of Romania Timişoara, Collection Sfatul Popular Banat, Secretariat, File No. 102/1960, page 115.
14. National Archives of Romania Timişoara, Collection Sfatul Popular Banat, Secretariat, File No. 102/1960, page 118.
15. National Archives of Romania Timişoara, Collection Sfatul Popular Banat, Secretariat, File No. 102/1960, page 287.
16. National Archives of Romania Timişoara, Collection Sfatul Popular Banat, Secretariat, File No. 102/1960, pages 82–84.
17. National Archives of Romania Timişoara, Collection Sfatul Popular Banat, Secretariat, File No. 102/1960, page 85.
18. National Archives of Romania Timişoara, Collection Sfatul Popular Banat, Secretariat, File No. 102/1960, page 141.
19. National Archives of Romania Timişoara, Collection Sfatul Popular Banat, Secretariat, File No. 102/1960, page 104.

20. National Archives of Romania Timişoara, Collection Sfatul Popular Banat, Secretariat, File No. 102/1960, page 139.
21. National Archives of Romania Timişoara, Collection Sfatul Popular Banat, Secretariat, File No. 74/1959, pages 4–5.
22. National Archives of Romania Timişoara, Collection Sfatul Popular Banat, Secretariat, File No. 102/1960, page 2.
23. National Archives of Romania Timişoara, Collection Sfatul Popular Banat, Inventar 1630, Secţia de Gospodărie Comunală, File No. 27/1962, page 68.
24. National Archives of Romania Timişoara, Collection Sfatul Popular Banat, Secretariat, File No. 102/1960, pages 280–89.
25. National Archives of Romania Timişoara, Collection Sfatul Popular Banat, Inventar 1517, File No. 30/1955, page 28.
26. National Archives of Romania Timişoara, Collection Sfatul Popular Banat, Secretariat, File No. 102/1960, page 85.
27. National Archives of Romania Timişoara, Collection Sfatul Popular Banat, Secţia de Gospodărie Comunală, File No. 1/1956, page 5.
28. National Archives of Romania Timişoara, Collection Sfatul Popular Banat, Secretariat, File No. 102/1960, pages 25–26.
29. National Archives of Romania Timişoara, Collection Sfatul Popular Banat, Secţia de Gospodărie Comunală, File No. 1/1956, pages 3–4.
30. National Archives of Romania Timişoara, Collection Sfatul Popular Banat, Secţia de Gospodărie Comunală, File No. 27/1962, pages 69–70.
31. National Archives of Romania Timişoara, Collection Sfatul Popular Banat, Inventar 1517, File No. 11/1955, page 10.
32. National Archives of Romania Timişoara, Collection Sfatul Popular Banat, Inventar 1517, File No. 30/1955, page 28.
33. National Archives of Romania Timişoara, Collection Sfatul Popular Banat, Secretariat, File No. 102/1960, pages 25–26.
34. National Archives of Romania Timişoara, Collection Sfatul Popular Banat, Secretariat, File No. 102/1960, pages 28–30.
35. National Archives of Romania Timişoara, Collection Sfatul Popular Banat, Secretariat, File No. 102/1960, page 118.
36. National Archives of Romania Timişoara, Collection Sfatul Popular Banat, Secretariat, File No. 102/1960, page 287.
37. National Archives of Romania Timişoara, Collection Sfatul Popular Banat, Juridic, File No. 22/1957, page 11.
38. National Archives of Romania Timişoara, Collection Sfatul Popular Banat, Juridic, File No. 22/1957, page 26.
39. National Archives of Romania Timişoara, Collection Sfatul Popular Banat, Secţia de Gospodărie Comunală, File No. 23/1953, page 141.
40. National Archives of Romania Timişoara, Collection Sfatul Popular Banat, Secretariat, File No. 102/1960, page 280.
41. National Archives of Romania Timişoara, Collection Sfatul Popular Banat, Secretariat, File No. 102/1960, page 8.

42. National Archives of Romania Timişoara, Collection Sfatul Popular Banat, Secţia de Gospodărie Comunală, File No. 27/1962, page 68.
43. National Archives of Romania Timişoara, Collection Sfatul Popular Banat, Secretariat, File No. 102/1960, page 266.
44. National Archives of Romania Timişoara, Collection Sfatul Popular Banat, Secretariat, File No. 102/1960, page 287.
45. National Archives of Romania Timişoara, Collection Sfatul Popular Banat, Juridic, File No. 22/1957, pages 73–76.
46. National Archives of Romania Timişoara, Collection Sfatul Popular Banat, Secretariat, File No. 74/1959, pages 4–5.
47. National Archives of Romania Timişoara, Collection Sfatul Popular Banat, Secretariat, File No. 74/1959, pages 1–3.
48. National Archives of Romania Timişoara, Collection Sfatul Popular Banat, Secretariat, File No. 85/1960, pages 11–12.
49. National Archives of Romania Timişoara, Collection Sfatul Popular Banat, Secretariat, File No. 127/1960, pages 70–73.
50. National Archives of Romania Timişoara, Collection Sfatul Popular Banat, Secţia de Gospodărie Comunală, File No. 1/1956, pages 3–4.
51. National Archives of Romania Timişoara, Collection Sfatul Popular Banat, Secţia de Gospodărie Comunală, File No. 1/1956, page 5.
52. National Archives of Romania Timişoara, Collection Sfatul Popular Banat, Inventar 1517, File No. 11/1955, page 10.
53. National Archives of Romania Timişoara, Collection Sfatul Popular Banat, Secretariat, File No. 102/1960, pages 28–30.

Chapter 5

Legality, Ideology, and the Politics of Takings

Petitions as micro-resistance pitted housing owners against Romania's communist regime and suggested early cracks in its formation. The authorities' response to the petitions and in particular their deployment of law in the aftermath of the takings are even more indicative of the fragility of the regime. Courts are largely absent from this story, as legality emerges from property practices at the administrative, municipal level. Low level bureaucrats struggled to control law, to harness its potential as an instrument of state power that was reliable, trustworthy, and malleable. Particularly in the area of takings, they wavered between treating law as a cynical instrument for takings and retroactively legalizing the de facto arbitrary seizing of houses, and deploying and understanding law in a more formal-rational manner. Their interactions with citizens and with hierarchically superior and inferior bodies, and ultimately the outcomes reveal a constant vacillation between law just pretending to respect the requirements of "normative consistency, legal hierarchy, and internal coherence" while conforming "blindly to the political requirements of the actual power" (Podgorecki 1996, 6–7), and real conflicts between law and politics.

Even in a field as contentious as the taking of housing, law did not easily give up: we see the intertwining of arbitrariness and legality in everyday administrative practices, as well as of power, cooptation, and resistance in citizens' petitions and interactions with administrative bodies. The legality that emerges from practices of nationalization, expropriation, and other takings at the municipal administrative level is primarily shaped by three distinct discourses: ideology, rationality, and skepticism that veers into arbitrariness and is steeped in secrecy. The epitome of this legality is again the 1950 nationalization process.

LAW IN ACTION: THE IMPLEMENTATION OF TAKINGS

Nationalization of urban housing was not a single moment in time, but a process that lasted for significantly longer, as homeowners contested it, the regime responded and planned more nationalizations, and because Decree 92 itself did not have a sunset provision. Over time, particularly in the early 1950s, it was used by local authorities as their default legal mechanism for urban takings, especially once the regime gave up on using requisitions in this manner. Thus many buildings not listed in the original appendix were seized by local authorities, often at the request of local state enterprises, simply on the basis of a "takings memo" (process verbal) ostensibly based on Decree 92. This was the case, for example, of a milk shop seized because the housing authority had already invested money in the building.[1] The government issued instructions to deal with implementation problems for Decree 92 in 1953, restitution instructions in 1955, and instructions for the restitution of other urban housing throughout the 1950s. None of them were published, and their implementation was rather imprecise (see Figure 5.1).

The 1950 urban housing nationalization decree was a rather brief affair, and soon enough local committees in charge with its implementation ran into significant problems. For three years, local officials functioned in somewhat of a legal-administrative void, and were left to fend for themselves during a period of repression, continuous purges, paranoia, fear, and suspicion. The major problems that arose during the housing nationalization process included the following:

- "double nationalization," that is, the taking of buildings that had already been nationalized under other nationalization laws, such as Law 119/1948;
- taking buildings that belonged to foreign states and citizens, or to expatriated Romanian citizens who had left administrators for the buildings;
- taking Article 2 buildings that had been obtained through labor (in other words, those exempt from nationalization under Article 2 of Decree 1950);
- taking buildings that were nevertheless left in possession of the former owners because they were not listed in the appendix, creating a problem of "double ownership"; and
- not nationalizing buildings that should have been nationalized.[2]

The lack of clarity in the nationalization criteria and the arbitrariness of the process did not escape the homeowners. Their complaints challenging the urban housing nationalization process was the biggest and most unexpected obstacle the regime had to face. In the first three years post-nationalization, local authorities in Timişoara received 300 petitions against

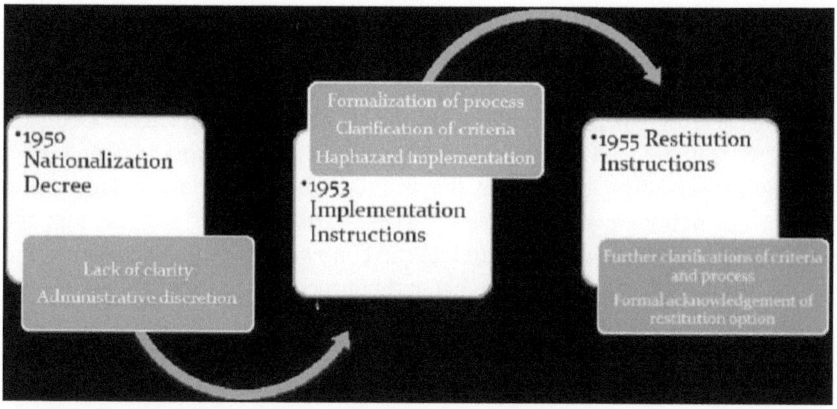

Figure 5.1. Timeline of Key Urban Housing Nationalization Acts. *Source*: Courtesy of the author.

the nationalization, approximately 30 percent of the total number of nationalized homeowners. Local authorities clearly did not expect this. They complained about having to deal with the aggrieved petitioners, as there were "countless petitions" and petitioners daily "inundate" municipal state offices, demanding restitution in a reasonable time limit.[3] With little guidance, they dealt with the petitions on an ad hoc basis and tried to guess the criteria for admitting or rejecting petitions.

This lack of clarity resulted in two apparently contradictory results: on the one hand, municipal and regional authorities had to engage with the homeowners and justify the taking, in the process arguing over what counted as "exploitation," "labor," and "property," and interpreting them, particularly "exploitation," extremely broadly (the pull of policy). On the other hand, and even under this generous ideological cover, they ended up with a high percentage of restitution proposals by 1954, as it turned out that 20 percent of the petitioners qualified as exemptions under Article 2 of Decree 92 (the push of legality). Occasionally, municipal authorities themselves openly championed some petitioners, such as a retired forester who died by the time his petition was definitively answered, and on whose behalf the local nationalization commission asked the national commission to follow their recommendation "proposing the correction of the unfair situation" and giving him back his house.[4] Initially, this wide (if lopsided) administrative discretion was condoned centrally as long as it conformed to class interests and class justice.

Urban housing nationalization was not a local matter, however, nor was it merely a problem of ironing out implementation details (which were initially sorely lacking). In an attempt to clarify implementation problems and to establish a system for further housing nationalization, the Council of Ministers issued in 1953 Decision 1390 (HCM 1390/1953) and its accompanying Instructions for the implementation of nationalization. The implementation instructions attempted to impose more formal-rational measures and regularize the nationalization process. The goals of the Decision were "to eliminate arbitrariness in the nationalization process, implement nationalization fairly, but within the framework of the class struggle, and finalize the nationalization process." These striking goals suggest that the pushback from homeowners did in fact travel upward through the system, and point toward the blending of socialist and bourgeois legality at a time of high socialist legal instrumentalism.

HCM 1390/1953 and the fourteen-page long implementation Instructions established a central nationalization commission and municipal nationalization commissions to amend the appendixes to Decree 92; clarified the criteria to be used when analyzing complaints and new proposals for nationalization; clarified categories of owners targeted; and established a points system to determine whether a building or apartment fell under the nationalization umbrella.[5] The central, regional, and municipal commissions had to establish which houses that should have been nationalized escaped the nationalization net; which houses that should have been exempted were nevertheless seized; and which petitions contesting nationalization should be approved. Nonetheless, even after this work, as the Central Nationalization Commission bemoaned in Instructions 14068/1953, serious problems remained, such as arbitrariness in rejecting or accepting petitions and further nationalization proposals.

According to the Instructions, petitions against nationalization were henceforth to be divided into two categories, based on whether the houses had been listed in the Decree 92 appendix, or had been seized extra-legally. Both types of petitions were to be analyzed in the same manner, but the final tally had to be done separately for each. Proposals for nationalization had to be justified, and for both petitions and proposals, the commission had to prepare four copies of the final lists and justificatory memos.

Post-1953, all nationalization-related matters were officially within the purview of nationalization commissions, which functioned at every level of the state administration and included only the most senior and "trusted elements" therein (in the early 1950s, members of the nationalization commissions had to be verified by the Party organs before being appointed).[6] The 1953 implementation instructions and the restitution Decree 524/1955 established the composition of the nationalization commissions at four members: the secretary of the executive committee of the regional People's Council (formally the most important position in the regional state administration), the head of the financial section, the head of the communal husbandry section (which included all housing-related matters), and the regional head of the labor union (the latest incarnation of the nationalization commission was created on March 15, 1960, and was instructed to work until they were done).[7] The entire process took place "under the supervision of the municipal Party organs,"[8] but Party members from the municipal Party bodies did not in fact participate in the meetings of the commissions, nor were there overlapping functions between the administration and the Party. Municipal administration officials were of course Party members.

Archival correspondence in the decision-making chain indicates that the opinion of the Party "was sought," although it is not apparent whether informally over the phone or in official meetings. The Party's decision was important in two types of cases: when the municipal authorities proposed restitution, and if there was conflict among the municipal and regional administrative authorities regarding restitution. I have not found any cases of stated disagreement between the Party and the municipal authorities, which suggests they were solved informally.[9] Throughout this period, the nationalization commissions did not function on a permanent basis, but were recreated every time there was a new decree or instructions or simply as needed, thus there was a fair amount of turnover.

The chain of command for the nationalization commissions was subject for a while to the principle of double subordination. The nationalization commission at the municipal level answered before the regional commission, which in turn was responsible to the central nationalization commission. Yet the nationalization commissions were also accountable to the executive committees of the people's councils at their respective levels, and ultimately to the Council of Ministers. The formal decision-making chain always passed through the executive committees of the people's councils to the Council of Ministers, which in turn had different sections dealing with nationalization over the years: General Direction of Affairs of the Council of Ministers, General Secretariat of the Council of Ministers (from 1957 on), the Direction for Problems of Municipal Bodies of State Administration, and the State Committee for the Guidance and Control of Municipal Organs of State Administration (see Figure 5.2).

The 1953 Instructions clarified both the decision-making chain and criteria for nationalization and restitution. More perhaps than in other areas, the decision-making process in the nationalization field was centralized and hierarchical, while allowing some room for discretion at the local levels, even outside of the bounds of class struggle. Ultimate decision-making power was at the central level, but the bulk of the process was the duty of the municipal committees. This included obsessive and exhaustive collection of information, as well as making recommendations to the Council of Ministers on restitutions and nationalizations. This encouraged some level of ownership and initiative municipally, including passive resistance from the municipal committees.

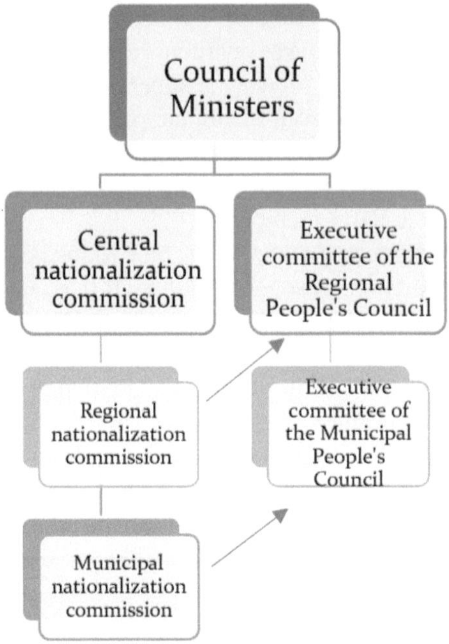

Figure 5.2. The Chain of Command for the Nationalization Commissions. *Source*: Courtesy of the author.

The relevant Soviet theory at the time was that the regional and the municipal people's councils were nothing more than "transmission belts," "levers" in the decision-making process, with the ultimate say belonging to the Council of Ministers (Stalin's view, see Boim et al. 1966, 14). The Council, however, relied both upon the information the Municipal Council chose to transmit and upon the opinion of the regional and municipal councils. The Council of Ministers expected both the municipal and the regional councils to undertake their own investigations and analysis. In a secret memo from June 24, 1958, to the regional People's Council executive committee, the Council of Ministers urged them: "You should not just communicate to us the opinion of the municipal People's Council, but form your own opinion . . . and relay it to us, relying upon your own technical bodies."[10] The Council of Ministers is often insistent that regional committees communicate their "real opinion" regarding various petitions,[11] particularly in the case of petitions proposed to be admitted.

Local authorities' power in the entire process was significant in other ways, as well. The process leading up to the exploiter label involved significant data collection efforts and was not trivial. Members of the nationalization commissions were instructed to rely upon their "personal knowledge" and collect detailed information about the houses and their owners, starting from the financial administration, specifically examining the tax records for the buildings for 1952. If this data was not sufficient, "trusted elements" confirmed by the municipal Party branches had to undertake a field investigation, which meant examining houses' internal records ("cartea de imobil"), talking to the superintendents, street captains, and the *miliția* (police).[12] In a case where the house had been sold just prior to nationalization, for example, the regional executive committee wanted to know whether the buyer had been an employer, whether the buyers recouped the money post-nationalization, and whether they had paid the entire purchase price.[13]

The decision-making process overall thus included meetings and document collection, field investigations, and sometimes meetings with the petitioners and the opportunity for them to present their cases orally. I have found only one case where the petitioner mentioned he had been threatened by the Party representatives during a meeting to discuss his petition, but I assume this was a more common occurrence. The entire process illustrates the distribution of power within the state structure, as well as the panopticism of the regime, the scope and extent of the state's intrusion in its citizens' lives, its endless rounds of classification of people and things, of gathering information at some point for its own sake.

The 1953 implementation Instructions attempted to rationalize the urban housing nationalization process, making it less arbitrary and fairer. The Instructions thus mandated a cumbersome and extremely time-consuming process for responding to complaints against nationalization and assembling new proposals for nationalization, while providing few incentives for the municipal councils to follow them. Consequently, municipal councils passively resisted full implementation. Unless and until they were directly summoned by the Council of Ministers, they simply preferred to ignore the 1953 Instructions. Time and again throughout the 1950s, and as the Council of Ministers grew hot or cold on this particular issue, the municipal executive committees procrastinated and haphazardly followed the Instructions. While they answered Council of Ministers questions on a case-by-case basis, the municipal committees rarely bothered to put together entire response files for the Council as directed by the 1953 Instructions. This did not go unnoticed: in 1953, the Central Commission complained that municipal nationalization commissions did not undertake any field research to verify the status of buildings and did not observe the instructions issued by the Council of Ministers.

Other parts of the Instructions were also not observed. As late as 1957, the municipal executive committee explicitly discussed how houses that were taken despite not being listed in the appendix, as well as exempt houses that were nevertheless nationalized, had not been returned to their owners yet. The committee argued that since these houses clearly did not fall within the scope of Decree 92, they were seized erroneously and from a legal point of view they could not be considered nationalized.[14] Notably, the Municipal Council adopted a legal formalist analysis that was also pushed by nationalized homeowners in their petitions. While it cannot be argued that the local authorities resisted urban housing nationalization, it seems they found it somewhat of a drain on their time and resources, particularly as it dragged on, and thus shortchanged it.

The Municipal Council was slightly more conscientious when proposing new buildings for nationalization than when they dealt with complaints against nationalization. Throughout the 1950s and as late as 1960, city and regional officials compiled hundreds of files with more buildings proposed for nationalization. These totaled over 1,200 for the county, more than half of which were from Timişoara (an estimated 700 more buildings). Only a handful of these were in fact nationalized, and not in a single batch, but over time. The second big wave of real estate nationalization never happened. There was a quiet end to urban housing nationalization, as revealed by the following extraordinary memo sent by the Banat Regional People's Council to the Council of Ministers on August 16, 1962:

> This is in response to your order . . . from 1962, returning to us all of our nationalization proposals, and instructing us that if some of these houses are necessary for state or economic interests, we should make further proposals regarding their taking. We think that your order regarding "state or economic interests" is open to various interpretations, which creates difficulties in the implementation of your order. Your order also indicates that we need to use laws currently in force, but Decree 92 is one of them. . . . At the meeting with the secretaries of the executive committees of regional popular councils, which took place in June this year at . . . , comrade L. interpreted this to mean that only in very exceptional situations we can use Decree 92, but he did not give us concrete examples, or examples of cases when we can use expropriation instead. Furthermore, we were not given the criteria for allowing houses proposed for nationalization to re-enter the economic circuit and be bought and sold. The interpretation given to us by comrade L. we have in turn verbally communicated to the secretaries of the raions, cities and towns, who are nevertheless asking for written clarification. Therefore, please order that we receive in writing comrade L.'s interpretation . . . , specifically the criteria for releasing buildings proposed for nationalization . . . , as well as the criteria to be used for nationalization under Decree 92 or for expropriation.[15]

For fifteen years, nationalization commissions throughout the Banat region worked intensively on putting together over 1,200 nationalization proposals, including extensive data on the social-economic status of the owners and their families, as well as the property histories and descriptions of houses proposed for nationalization. After all this work, the Party leadership changed their minds and decided to abandon urban housing nationalization as an en masse operation. Instead, the takings were to proceed piecemeal henceforth, as needed, and the regional people's councils were to rely upon a different legal basis, primarily expropriation in the public interest, with compensation and justification. The news was clearly not received well by the regional authorities, who were frustrated by this significant policy shift that discounted all their work and plans for these houses, and left them in legal and policy limbo.

Ultimately, local-central power dynamics reveal that the official hierarchical and centralized decision-making chain was constantly undermined by rapid changes in local administrative structures and staffing, the confusing nature of the principle of double subordination and of Party control, regulatory gaps, practical expediency and the very un-tenability of excessive centralization (a finding confirmed, among others, by Nelson in 1980, who also determined that practical expediency was a key element in the practice of democratic centralism in Romania). While breaking the chain was not acceptable, municipal administration did take the initiative on occasion and attempted to control more aspects of the nationalization process. In 1957, for example, the Timişoara Municipal Council asked the Council of Ministers to amend Decree 92, specifically to allow the municipal administration to decide on restitution, since it would be "faster and more efficient."[16] This combination of pragmatism/actuality and ideology, in turn, increased uncertainty, decreased internal uniformity, complicated efforts to create legitimacy inside the class of reality constructors, and contributed to the extended skepticism of law inside the power structure.

LAW AND POLITICS IN THE NATIONALIZATION PROCESS

Even with widespread acceptance of ideology in the decision-making process, however, "hard cases" occasionally arose that brought forward the clash between legality and policy. They reveal the routinization of substantive rationality in the decision-making process and the ultimate win of policy, as well as legal instrumentalism and its consequences. Perhaps the best exemplification of the law/politics distinction in this area, of the ultimate but reluctant win of policy, arises from one of the complications of the restitution process, namely if the petitioner died and the petition was successful, were the heirs automatically entitled to restitution?

A case from the Lugoj town in the region (approximately 50 km from Timişoara) raised this issue and ultimately changed the legal regime of inheritance in the country. Alexandra L. filed the original petition against the nationalization of her house on April 25, 1950, five days after the nationalization. The short (less than a page) typed petition explains that the house had belonged to her parents, and when they (the father) died it was registered in the land registry (CF) under her brother's name, who in turn donated it to her on March 25, 1949, "because it was my right and I had not received anything from my parents. . . . Now this very old house is nationalized, and I, without occupation because of a 15-year illness, find myself in an ever-greater predicament. I have never had any occupation or possibility to exploit anybody, on the contrary, when I was healthy I worked as a factory worker."[17]

Alexandra died in 1953, while the petition was still being processed, and after that the situation became rather convoluted. The municipal, regional, and central nationalization commissions all agreed relatively early on—in 1951 and 1953—that the house did not fulfill the criteria for nationalization and that it was wrongly nationalized (mistakenly counted to belong to her brother). A 1961 memorandum by the Lugoj executive committee found that the house was old, made of wood and unprocessed brick, with two rooms, a kitchen and a pantry, and the entire family was merely "all poor peasants." The original note by the financial inspector from Lugoj in charge of examining the donation contract, from April 2, 1949, noted that the house had two rooms, a hallway and a kitchen, that it was made of brick and wood/stone, was 48 square meters (approximately 520 square feet), and also included an open hay shed of 60 square meters. The house was about one hundred years old, and although it was small and had no bathroom, it had a very large garden of almost 30,000 square feet, as was customary for urban houses not situated in the downtown.[18] Alexandra's brother, the registered owner of the house, also petitioned repeatedly, although it is not clear whether in his own name, as heir, or on behalf of his mother. Although the brother died at some point before 1960, his petitions raised some red flags because he had owned twelve other apartments that had been nationalized and was listed in the Lugoj appendix.

On January 1, 1957, the Lugoj executive committee acknowledged Alexandra's death and asked the regional Council whether the house could be given back to the mother as the heir, "who has no other house."[19] They posed the same question directly to the Council of Ministers, later in 1957. The response, unexpectedly, was not a "yes" or "no" based on policy considerations, but a detailed legal opinion issued by the legal department of the Council of Ministers: "The civil law rule in the matter of inheritance is that the heirs represent the person of the deceased, therefore the deceased's property is given to the heirs. This is a special matter, however, so the common-law rules cannot be automatically applied. . . . Aside from the general criteria established by the provisions of Decree 92, the nationalization of buildings was also *intuitu personae* [because of the person], which is at the basis of the appendix to Decree 92. The restitution of houses furthermore was not left for the courts, but given to the Council of Ministers . . . in order to individualize each restitution."

The Council of Ministers' legal expert further notes that the situation of the heirs was not explicitly covered, but could be deduced based on the principles established by the nationalization and restitution legal provisions, as well as civil law more generally. However, he cautions that if the general rules applied directly, the principle of the individualization of nationalization disappeared: "Restitution to the former owner presupposes that he/she fulfills the legal criteria for restitution and that they were applied to his/her individual case." But if the former owner died, "how could we give back the house to someone who does not fulfill them, such as a former housing exploiter or former nationalized industrialist?" In these cases, argued the legal expert, obviously there could be no restitution. He further made a class justice argument, namely, that applying the "normal rules" (civil law) could lead to situations that violated the intent of the nationalization lawmaker, for example, if the heir was a distant relative or no relative at all (in case of a will), which would be "not just." His recommendation was that until formal amendments to the restitution Decree 2586/1956 were adopted, municipal authorities suspended restitution proceedings and referred the matter to the Council of Ministers.[20] Similarly to other property cases and doctrine (discussed in chapter 6), this is clearly not an effort to displace civil law, but to achieve some sort of accommodation between civil law and socialism.

The Council of Ministers adopted the recommendations of the expert: in particular, the principle of individualization of restitution. On April 14, 1958, the Council of Ministers ordered the regional people's councils to suspend restitution in all cases where the former owner died and to undertake a new investigation regarding the heirs, in particular, to find out the past and present social and economic status of the heirs. The Council of Ministers order laying out the general rules for restitution to heirs specifically singled out the Lugoj case as the cause of this policy change in the field of inheritance, and clarified that parents and children could benefit from restitution as heirs, but more distant relatives could not. The draft amendment for the restitution decree consequently established that apartments and houses could be returned to heirs—parents, spouses, and children, if they were not themselves exploiters.[21]

In Alexandra's case, the house was returned to her mother in 1957, "in her quality as both legal heir of the deceased and former owner of the house with the right of lifetime usufruct and widowhood."[22] Clearly, the municipal council did not wait for the final decisions to be taken from the top, and returned the house before the end of the investigation. The language used here is striking in other ways, as it indicates the hold of bourgeois ideas of property and family, in particular the reference to widowhood: their understanding of class justice was "tainted" by compassion and her situation as a poor, old widow.

The heirs' case illustrates two points: first, the entrenchment of policy goals and the predominance of ideological values such as eliminating exploitation; second, attempts to please two masters at the same time, to satisfy both the political and the legal logic. This explains the effort to translate policy into legal logic through the principle of the individualization of nationalization and restitution. This principle is at odds with the two major policy goals at play in the urban housing nationalization process: eliminating entire social and economic classes, and acquiring the best houses in the country for free (yet the costs of nationalization were not minor, of course, as the collection of information and the labor involved in both nationalization and restitution were significant). There was no principle of individualization of nationalization, and it is not a little ironic that a lawyer for the regime used a fundamentally "bourgeois" value to achieve these goals. The heirs' case and in particular the legal opinion issued by the Council of Ministers expert also highlight the tension between law's internal coherence and the regime's understanding of law as merely a pragmatic tool.

These tensions play out in other nationalization cases. The depth of the Council of Ministers' involvement in particular, and its attempts to balance law and policy can be seen in the following 1958 dispute concerning a nationalization proposal, which received special attention because it reached the courts. The story is captured in a single spaced three-page memorandum written by the Timişoara executive committee for the regional executive committee and the Council of Ministers (July 27, 1958). Carol and Ida P., a small merchant and his wife, owned two houses in Timişoara, one of them built by him in 1933–1934 and at the time "in exceptional condition," the other one received by him as a donation from his sister-in-law before 1930. He donated the second house to his wife in 1939, "in order to avoid tax and credit complications" (speculated the executive committee of the Timişoara People's Council). The dispute concerns this latter house and involves multiple parties.

Liviu I., a real estate broker, convinced Ida, who was old and sick, to name him executor of her will on November 19, 1957. Ida died a day later. After Ida's death, Liviu sold half of the house to Vasile B. and the other half to his wife, but the buyer was never put in possession of his share of the property, and the contract was furthermore not properly taxed (was taxed at a lower price). The Municipal Council, meanwhile, thought the house should be nationalized. The heirs and/or Vasile sued the Council (!), contesting the nationalization proposal, while Liviu petitioned the municipal council for the same reason. The Municipal Council, meanwhile, complained that being a real estate broker "is illegal in this popular democratic regime," and that even so Liviu "has never paid any taxes." To the local officials and Ida's heirs, it was also clear that Liviu "clearly wanted to defraud the legal heirs," since he sold the house to his wife while retaining a quarter of it for himself: "This is the only case in legal history when a seller is also a buyer, regarding the same object, in the same contract," fulminated the municipal executive committee.

In the municipal committee's opinion, since Carol had been a businessman, and both he and his wife were still alive and married when Decree 92 was adopted, he must be considered as having been nationalized, and thus all his buildings nationalized, even if they were not listed in the Decree 92 appendix. Yet Carol P. is listed in the Decree 92 appendix, with a similar enough address (the name of the street was misspelled). It would appear that somehow the Timişoara executive committee did not know about this, so it is possible that Carol and Ida were in fact nationalized in 1950 and nobody knew. This is not an unusual situation, as already mentioned. In 1957, apparently unaware of the nationalization, the municipal executive committee asked the regional executive committee and the Council of Ministers for instructions on how to annul the contract between the executor and the buyer in court, and for money to pay the corresponding taxes.[23]

Only part of this story was preserved in the archives, so neither the court decision nor the final outcome is known. We do know that in order to issue its final decision, the General Secretariat of the Council of Ministers wanted to see the complete nationalization proposal files, maps of both buildings (even though only one was under discussion), full descriptions of the social and economic status of the owners, heirs, and all other parties in the dispute, and the opinion of the regional People's Council of how the case should be decided. The regional Council, in turn, asked for exactly the same information from the municipal People's Council.[24]

Ida's case reveals a rational, centralized decision-making process that required significant involvement at regional and municipal levels. Like the heirs' case, it underscores the tension between legality and ideology/policy, and the efforts of the local authorities to please simultaneously two masters. The pull of formal rationality versus the push of ideology and arbitrariness are nowhere clearer than in the paradoxical effort of the regime to create clear nationalization criteria.

ARBITRARINESS, FORMALISM, AND SUBSTANTIVE JUSTICE IN THE NATIONALIZATION CRITERIA

The creation of the initial list of home owners subject to urban housing nationalization in Timişoara is not documented in the archival materials available at this point. However, the 1953 implementation Instructions and the process of dealing with the homeowners' petitions offer significant information about the nationalization criteria used for deciding on restitution claims, as well as for creating additional lists of homeowners to be nationalized. At its core, the tension between arbitrariness and formalism, law and ideology, centered on the concept of exploitation and defining exploitation for nationalization purposes.

Decree 92/1950 specifically intended "to deprive exploiters of an important means of exploitation," while implementation Instructions 14068/1953 clearly stated that "nationalization has to bring into state property houses of value [imobile clădite de valoare]." The Decree targeted both houses and their owners, yet the meaning of "housing exploiter" and "exploitation" in the context of housing was unclear. Romanian ideologues defined exploitation in general within traditional Marxist parameters as the appropriation of someone else's labor. The capitalist and bourgeois classes thus exploited the workers, whose labor was alienated as a result of this capitalist exploitation (e.g., Ministry of Education 1962, 83–99). Decree 92 mentioned two groups: former manufacturers, great land estate owners, bankers, great merchants, and other elements of the high bourgeoisie; and housing exploiters. The former category employs class categorization and type of employment as criteria, while the latter category, "housing exploiters," was left open for interpretation. It was important to determine who was a housing exploiter in order to clarify, at least in theory, those exempt from nationalization as listed in Article 2 of Decree 92 (workers, small craftsmen, intellectuals, retirees).

The urban housing nationalization process reveals that the construction of "exploitation" and "exploiter" in this context was a haphazard process. It was not limited to the obvious criterion of obtaining profit from rent, nor was it strictly about eliminating exploitation in the housing market. Urban housing nationalization had three major policy goals: to paralyze the well-to-do, to enrich the state's real estate domain, and to help deal with the housing crisis. Consequently, the criteria for defining "exploitation" in the housing field were overbroad and vague. There were four such criteria, related to the house itself, the owner, the level of state investment, and need. These criteria were applied both in the examination of petitions and for generating new nationalization proposals. Usually, fulfilling one of these four criteria was sufficient for nationalization or rejection of restitution claims. Furthermore, a presumption of "nationalizability" existed for those who had already had another building seized.

The owner. In the "technical criteria" section of the 1953 implementation Instructions, the central nationalization commission lays out the criteria used but apparently not previously communicated to the municipal authorities. Each category listed in Decree 92 is now fully laid out. Thus, the targeted categories include former owners, administrators, and directors of industrial and commercial enterprises nationalized through Law 119/1948; former landowners and estate administrators expropriated through the two land reform laws (1945 and 1949); and former owners, administrators, and directors of nationalized banks.

More interestingly, according to the Instructions, the "grand bourgeoisie" was simply defined as "large shareholders" in banks and other enterprises, regardless of leadership function (this did not help, as the content of "large shareholder" was never specified). This category also included former state ministers and other high officials and civil servants. To find out who belonged to these categories, the municipal commissions had to use their personal relationships, as well as information provided by the Party. All those listed above were subject to nationalization, even if they only had one apartment (this was also applicable to owners who had left the country).

The 1955 restitution Instructions expanded the meaning of "exploiter" to include the following criteria: the location of the estate or enterprise, the number of apartments owned and their location (those on the outskirts were of less interest), and the number of employees.[25] The regional People's Council neatly summed up in 1967 the revised criteria: "The criteria at the basis of exemptions from nationalization are the material and social status of the petitioners in the past and present, the number of apartments owned and the manner of acquisition."[26] The municipal bureaucrats in charge with examining petitions and new nationalization proposals had to undertake a thorough investigation of the social and economic status of the petitioner and his family, both past and present, as well as a detailed history and description of the property in question. They looked for three key elements: evidence of exploitation, need, and the level of state investment in the property (both potential and already done).

In the overwhelming majority of cases (both petitions for restitution and new proposals), by far the most important factor in the decision-making process was the social and economic status of the owners as evidence of exploitation, both overall and specifically in the housing market. Members of the nationalization commissions combed with a fine tooth the life histories of owners, their spouses, and respective immediate families, and interpreted them in the context of the class struggle. If the owner or anyone in his immediate family had at any point in the past or present owned or managed anything beyond the bare necessities of the family, the nationalization commissions labeled it "exploitation" and either refused restitution, or proposed nationalization. Moreover, from their perspective "exploitation" tainted not only the formal owner but all his family. One was labeled "exploiter" in general, for example, if he or she had had employees in the workspace, such as "employed 3–5 hired hands in auto shop," or at home, such as a maid. To determine the quality of exploiter as it pertained to the housing market, the nationalization commissions looked at the number of apartments and their location, and whether the owner had made a profit from rent, since renting apartments meant "unearned/not labored for income" ("câştig nemuncit").[27]

A dyer, the son of a housewife and locksmith, for example, was characterized by the local nationalization commission in the following manner: Although apolitical, he always wanted to work on his own to accumulate more and more money, had a dying workshop since 1926, did not observe the Party directions to join workers' cooperatives, still worked on his own, and had other nationalized buildings. Furthermore, "he was and still is a 'patron'" (employer) (yet there is no note in this file about the dyer having had apprentices at any time).[28] A butcher who used to have his own shop and employees had also had his petition rejected,[29] as well as a petitioner who used to have a small tailor shop with employees.[30] "Classic" exploiters include a doctor with four apartments whose parents had been merchants, his wife who was a lawyer, and a daughter a medical technician (the doctor died at some point after filing the petition, and his daughter took over the petitioning).[31] Their petition was also rejected.

Death was no impediment to takings and classification as exploiter, either, as the label once affixed was hard to shake off and hovered over the entire family's life, as children of exploiters could not go to college or get good jobs. For example, a widow who was a housewife for most of her life petitioned unsuccessfully for the return of a house she had built with her first husband. A daughter of workers and a nurse, she was twice married, both times to doctors. The house in question belonged to her and her first husband, while the second husband, deceased, had had a six-apartment house that was also nationalized.[32]

The house. The size, number, level of upgrading, manner of acquisition, and purpose of houses and apartments were also key to the exploitation discourse put forward by the regime. The "exploitation presumption" covered both the means of acquisition of the house, such as commerce, and the presumed purpose. If the house was bigger than the needs of the family, officially defined as 8 square meters per person, it automatically qualified as exploitative, that is, meant to be rent out (regardless of whether that happened at any point). Of the 1,022 names listed in the Timişoara appendix, 65 percent had ten or less apartments, 26 percent between eleven and twenty apartments, and only 9 percent more than twenty apartments. Since one- and two-room apartments were prevalent in the city at the time (around 80 percent), and the primary uses of the houses and apartments was as homes for the extended family, it becomes clear that there was little left over for exploitation in the housing market. At most, only the 9 percent with more than twenty apartments had clearly relied on houses as a primary means of production, while for the rest renting out a studio or one bedroom represented merely supplemental income. This 9 percent category also includes banks and other commercial enterprises, thus leaving a truly small number of individuals who might have been qualified as exploiters in the housing market.

The nationalization proposals in particular illustrate the paucity of housing suitable for takings. For example, nationalization proposals from 1951 include a house with two apartments, six total rooms, and eleven annexes, already inhabited by four tenants and thirteen lodgers; a house with one apartment, composed of one room, one kitchen, one bathroom, one pantry, built of brick, with indoor plumbing and electricity, and one tenant; a house with two apartments, five total rooms, six annexes and a garden, inhabited by four tenants and six lodgers. It is not clear whether the local officials' distinction between lodgers and tenants was meant to separate owners from tenants, and whether the tenants were included in the total number of lodgers. Either way, tenants and owners lived in crowded conditions in modest middle-class abodes.[33]

Moreover, even the definition of a house or apartment was not necessarily clear. For example, a house listed in the Decree 92 appendix as having five apartments had been built as a three-apartment house, while the other two apartments were in fact a basement converted into two studio apartments with no kitchen or bathroom. In another case, a house listed in the appendix as having five apartments and eleven rooms was built as a one family residence (one apartment), and was later divided into five apartments (the size of the house was 207 square meters/2,228 square feet).[34]

For the most part, these were not single ownership houses, rather many houses were co-owned, usually by members of the same family (through marriage, inheritance, donation, dowry, etc.). Many of the owners listed in the appendix were either not owners anymore by the time of the nationalization, for example, if they had sold the property but the new owners had not registered the property rights yet, or were only one of multiple co-owners. Yet Decree 92 froze ownership in time, ironically individualizing it and preserving the connection between owner and house.

The 1953 Instructions somewhat clarified the nationalization criteria regarding homeowners and more importantly shifted the focus of nationalization from the owner to the house, attempting yet again to formalize the house-related criteria. The Instructions explicitly mentioned hotels and inns, garages built for renting out spaces for cars, and sheds and storage areas over 150 square meters (regardless of the purpose of the construction) as a basis of exploitation. Owners of these types of buildings were automatically and fully nationalized, regardless of the location, size, or any other characteristics of their housing. Also nationalized were houses built for exploitation purposes and whose owners had abandoned them, which meant all such houses with a ground floor surface over 120 square meters; houses that had been damaged or destroyed during the war, and whose owners had not repaired them, if the ground floor surface was over 120 square meters; villas in resorts; and apartments belonging to a single owner in category I cities, where the building material had to be at least cement, stone, bricks, or wood, and the apartments had to have minimum utilities (indoor plumbing and electricity).

To make the job of the municipal nationalization commissions easier, the Instructions established a grading system. Each "nationalizable" apartment received points based on the following criteria: surface (a minimum of one point for apartments smaller than 40 square meters, and a maximum of six points for apartments over 190 square meters), and one point each for plumbing, electricity, heating, and separate bathroom. If an apartment did not have water and electricity, it was not nationalizable, regardless of surface or any other feature. Attics did not receive any points. The maximum an apartment could receive was ten points (surface received the most points). In category II cities (those without indoor plumbing and electricity), the only criterion was surface, and only apartments bigger than 70 square meters were nationalizable.

The Instructions give plenty of examples of calculating the points for various situations, for both categories of cities, and further introduce some minor changes. An apartment was defined similarly to the 1948 census, with one difference: rooms that had been rented out, with common access to kitchen, and so on, were not defined as separate apartments anymore. For co-owners, the points needed to be calculated for each co-owner. All outbuildings were nationalized together with the building (e.g., fire hose and water hose). Apartments belonging to the great bourgeoisie that had been donated or otherwise transferred into the family's property after 1945, totaling over thirteen points, were also to be nationalized.

The key paragraph in the Instructions, however, is the following: "In order for the building to be classified as built for purposes of exploitation, the apartments owned by a single owner must total 13 points" (nine points in category II cities). This meant that even if one apartment on its own would not be nationalizable, if it was part of a building totaling over thirteen points, it could be nationalized. If homeowners otherwise exempt under Article 2 fulfilled the points system, the nationalization commissions still needed to prepare memos justifying the exemption, to include information about the social origin of the owners, past and current occupation, and the way in which they became owners. In other words, despite the specific provision in the decree itself, exempt categories still had to jump through the technocratic hoop of the points system.

After laying out in exhaustive detail the points system, however, the Instructions shift gears and basically give carte blanche to nationalize and reject petitions for buildings based on other criteria, as well, for example, in category I cities, solid buildings even without indoor plumbing and electricity, and in category II cities, smaller houses but with all "amenities" (i.e., indoor plumbing and electricity). The same applied to apartments belonging to "well known enemies of the people," even though the commissions needed to justify their act. On the other hand, apartments that fulfilled the points criteria could still be exempt from nationalization if the owners were "useful" to the regime.

This same set of Instructions also applied to proposals to nationalize. The municipal nationalization commissions had to describe whether the targeted building had been previously proposed for nationalization, its intended use (e.g., dwelling, office, and storage), its general condition ("grad de uzură"), whether the state had already invested in it and how much, whether it was administered by the housing authority and on what basis, how many apartments and outbuildings it had, how many square feet, amenities, number of points, history of the building, current ownership, whether the owners had other houses and whether those had been nationalized, and the social category of owners. The latter, in particular, was often a stretch, for example, the proposal to seize the house of an owner who was a homemaker, but whose parents had owned a wood processing factory and bought the house from someone who emigrated to England and had gained the house through exploitation. Finally, the commission had to summarily justify whether to nationalize the house or not, and if yes, whether it would be total or partial nationalization (e.g., if there were many co-owners but only one fulfilled the conditions).[35] An example is the proposal to nationalize a house with thirteen apartments and ten rooms that did not fulfill the points requirement. However, because the owners had left for the United States and were housing exploiters, the house was nationalized according to the 1953 Instructions.[36]

For each petition and proposal to nationalize, the municipal commission had to put together a chart covering specific criteria, from the owner's social origin to whether the house had heating and indoor plumbing (see Table 5.1).

The points system and the 1953 Instructions suggest that the newly installed communist regime heard the complaining homeowners and consequently tried to achieve its rapacious ideological goals by, paradoxically, attempting to de-ideologize the process. If de-ideologization in the USSR represented a 180-degree shift, in Romania these efforts are more consistent with the thesis of inertia and continuity with the past. That this happened through law underscores its duality even at the height of the repression, as the regime mobilized law's semi-autonomy and formalism in an attempt to gain legitimacy for its takings. The regime translated "exploitation" into a technocratic points system in order to sidestep the problem of defining "exploitation" and to resolve issues of arbitrariness and fairness. It thus attempted to make the entire process seem more transparent, objective, and beyond critique.

Table 5.1. Example of Nationalization Criteria and Proposal

Name	*Mr. A.*
Occupation	Civil servant
Social origin	Small craftsman
City	Timişoara
Address of nationalized apartment	A. St.
Position in the annex (Decree 92)	
Destination	Dwelling
Number of rooms	3
Building material	Brick
Surface (in sq. m)	80
Points	3
Water/indoor plumbing	1
Electricity	1
Bathroom	1
Heating	–
Total	6
Proposal	House should not be nationalized

The continuous stream of petitions after 1953 shows this was not a successful effort, in large part because the authorities themselves did not observe the points system and the 1953 Instructions. Since it involved significant more work than the previously improvised decision-making process, the points system was not enthusiastically embraced by the municipal nationalization commissions. Expediency and inertia remained the name of the game: if the commission used the official form provided by the Council of Ministers, they applied the points system because it was already incorporated in the form, but if the form was not used, the points system was simply ignored.[37]

The level of state investment in the house was a separate criterion. If the state had made any repairs or renovations to a house that was nationalized, requisitioned, or otherwise managed by the state, the owner was unlikely to receive it back, regardless of any other criteria. This was particularly the case for buildings that the state renovated and used for various manufacturing or commercial purposes, such as butter manufacturing.[38] From a property rights perspective, the state's reliance on labor echoes Lockean ideas of property and reinforces the connection between labor and ownership.

Finally, need was the most problematic of all the criteria that construed the meaning of exploitation. The regime's analysis was that if one had more space than one needed, it was automatically exploitative, regardless of whether the extra space was rented, used for storage, or not used at all.[39] Need itself, of course, was defined by the regime. Interpreting "need" this way, however, stripped the concept of exploitation of ideological sharpness, made the Article 2 exemptions irrelevant and ultimately undermined the goals of the regime. An example is a retired railway headmaster ("şef de tren") who had four nationalized apartments in a house. His parents had been peasants, he was never involved in politics and had two children who had their own homes, not nationalized. The local nationalization commission argued that because the houses of the children had not been nationalized, and the petitioner lived with his children, he did not really need his apartments, so the nationalization was justified.[40] This line of reasoning ignored not only the specific exemption in the nationalization decree but also the professed respect for labor in the new regime.

These four criteria—owner, house, state investment, and need—are overlapping and not exclusive. A 1952 document, for example, lists former owners initially proposed to be exempt from nationalization, a decision that was later reexamined and reversed. The four criteria are partially present, if not explicit, but so are others that have nothing to do with "exploitation." The document lists owners by their number in the Decree 92 appendix, and explains why they should remain nationalized: a homemaker with a new villa in the downtown district, with "every amenity"; a doctor who owned a two-story villa in the downtown that had "all amenities"; a villa again with "all amenities," occupied by the Soviet army; the daughter of a merchant, with three apartments in a building otherwise fully nationalized (this is an example of how the presumption of nationalizability operated); an owner who could not justify how she obtained the property; the owner of a house bought in 1946 with money from commerce; owner left for Israel; house built especially for exploitation; house bought in 1947 during the inflation (thus presumably very cheaply and for exploitation purposes); a lawyer, former legal counsel for City Hall, with significant disposable income; a farmer who had worked in the United States, came back to buy the house and worked in agriculture, raised pigs for commercial purposes, and had land as well; a milliner whose husband used to be technical engineer and co-owner of the nationalized hat factory, whose house in the downtown district was in very good state and had "all amenities"; owner with no occupation, but "good house" in the downtown area; a civil servant whose father still owned a fur shop and whose husband had retreated with the German troops.[41]

To illustrate how the nationalization commissions deployed the ideological trope of exploitation and how these various criteria entered into the regime's calculus, I summarize in Table 5.2 the first nine rejection memos, out of over one hundred, analyzing petitions against nationalization in 1960.[42]

A complete response to a petition contesting nationalization had four sections. I use here the example of Victor V., from Arad, who petitioned for the restitution of the house where he continued to live post-nationalization, listed in the Decree 92 appendix for Arad. The first section of the memorandum described the house—surface, number of apartments, amenities, mode of acquisition, whether the house had land attached to it, the type of street,

Table 5.2. Rejections to Nationalization Petitions

Name of Petitioner	*Sq. m*	*Socioeconomic Status*	*Resolution*
Ecaterina A. (widow) and Ghita I.	338 and 891 (land)	Husband was patron tinsmith, Ghita also patron, both were exploiters	No, house was obtained from exploitation
Arso	233?	Husband was baker with employees, and part of the house was rented	No
Albert	248	He was a technical drawer, now retired, war invalid, the house was inherited from parents	No, house is bigger than his needs so it is used for exploitation, plus he was a member of the German Ethnic Group
Albert F.	?	Bricklayer, retired	No, had two houses, both nationalized, so they must have used for exploitation because they were more than needed, plus he worked privately. (NB: the fact that he did not have any employees seems not to have mattered here.)
Susana	346	Cook	No, she cannot prove title for the two apartments she says she bought from the former owner, who was nationalized, and she could not have afforded them from her income as cook
Serena	1,000	Patron merchant	No, had another house, also nationalized, houses were both used for exploitation, plus she lives in Israel
Persida	120	Teacher, retired	No, house was built for exploitation since it is bigger than the family's needs
Aurora	181?	Musical store owners	No, because the house was bought from exploitation
Ludovic	201 200 land	Mill worker, retired	No, "taking into account that the house is much larger than what is needed, it means it was built for exploitation purposes"

the destination of the house, how much the state invested in it since the nationalization, if the house had been donated to or had been inherited by the former owners, occupation of original owners (in this case the original owners were small merchants, but the house was bought, not inherited or donated), how the property was divided and used, and what kind of material it was built from. In Victor's case, there was a handwritten map of the building attached to the memo. The second part was an analysis of the social and economic status of the petitioner—Victor had been a tailor with one apprentice, but at the time of the petition he was a customs official. This part also included information about the parents and children of the petitioner. The third part included other data regarding the petitioners. In Victor's case, this included information about another apartment that had been added in the basement, with one room and one kitchen, and the fact that the petitioner had requested permission and was "registered to leave" (the country). The fourth part was the resolution to the petition: "The house fulfills the criteria of Decree 92, so it remains nationalized" was the standard language. Often, there was another pro forma sentence to the effect that "the house comes from exploitation and/or is intended for exploitation," but in this example there was no other explanation (the petitioner's plan to leave the country is the clear reason for the rejection of the petition, albeit it is not spelled out).[43]

THE RESTITUTION PROCESS

Once the investigation was finished and administrative authorities at all levels agreed to return a house—a process that took years—the Council of Ministers issued a nationalization exemption decree. A complete nationalization exemption file prepared by the regional People's Council for the Council of Ministers in 1967, for example, included a cover letter, an explanatory memo, a draft for the Council of Ministers Decree, and biographies of the owners. The explanation was that the owners "do not match the criteria of the nationalization statute 92/1950." Of the twenty-six cases listed, fifteen were mistakenly taken under the name of different title holders, and eleven belonged to owners who were not "elements of the former exploiting classes." The former owners proposed for restitution included ten workers and sixteen peasants.[44] The only thing left for the Council of Ministers to do was sign on the dotted line. The names of many of the petitioners included here come up repeatedly throughout the archival files, and over the years their petitions had been variously proposed for rejection or admission by the municipal and regional councils.

The Council of Ministers nationalization exemption decrees were secret and had two components: the text of the decree with two articles, and its appendix (symmetrical to the nationalization decree itself). The text of the decree stated in Article 1 that "there are exempt from nationalization and to be returned to the owners the apartments and houses from," while Article 2 specified that the restitution was done by the executive committees of the municipal people's councils. The decrees were signed by the president of the Council of Ministers. The second part of the decrees, the appendixes, listed by town/city each property to be returned: the name of the petitioner, the name listed in the Decree 92 appendix, appendix number, and address.

Detailed provisions for restitution were adopted only in 1955 (Decree 524/1955, amending Decree 92/1950). Decree 524/1955 established that the Council of Ministers could decide to exempt from nationalization any houses or apartments ("scoaterea de sub naţionalizare"), and added provisions regarding the restitution procedure for both houses and apartments listed and not listed (thus seized illegally) in Decree 92 appendixes. The 1955 provisions also forced the municipal nationalization commissions to reopen files they had already closed. (Some petitions filed prior to 1955 had not even been considered because "the nationalization process is finished." The 1955 Decree and Instructions forced the municipal authorities to reopen them.)[45]

Restitution had to be effectively done within forty-five days from the official notice of exemption from nationalization, and the house or apartment was returned "as is," with no claims for compensation admissible. Investments and reparations to the building that were less than 20 percent of the value of the dwelling benefitted the owner, but if improvements surpassed 20 percent, the owner had to pay the difference (between 20 percent and the higher percentage), or could be given another house/apartment instead (if this was not possible, the owner was entitled to land and construction materials to build a home of equal value to the nationalized one). If the owner could not pay at once, monthly payments were allowed, but for no more than two years. If the owner refused to pay the over 20 percent value, the municipal council had to give him another apartment, but of less value than the nationalized property.

The same compensation rules applied if the building was demolished between nationalization and restitution, or if the building had become the property of a cooperative. There were not entitled to compensation owners whose buildings had been demolished because they were not inhabitable, or were destroyed during a natural disaster (earthquake, fire, flood, etc.). The restitution itself had to be done based on an official restitution memo (process verbal), for each building/apartment, even if more than one was given back. Owners who had owned more than one apartment or house could, theoretically, get back all, part or just one house/apartment (in this latter case, they could choose which one, unless otherwise specified in the restitution decree, however, I am not aware of more than one apartment ever having been returned).

Lest one thinks the regime was too generous, there was a one-year statute of limitations for former owners to reclaim their houses. However, former owners who regained even one apartment benefited in another way from restitution: they were not considered anymore "former owner of a nationalized house," which in effect meant the lifting of restrictions in other areas of life that had been tainted by the "enemy of the regime" label, such as access to education, social services, jobs, housing, and so on. Another bonus was that all restitution formalities, such as transcribing the title, were tax-exempt. The restitution Instructions directed the municipal councils to issue certificates to the owners to that effect (that they were not considered anymore as "nationalized owners"). The regime's clemency indicates its growing pragmatism: their punishment was over, and now they were ready for cooptation and mobilization as socialist subjects.

Instructions for restitution (No 40869/1956) followed the 1955 Decree.[46] Once again, this is an extremely detailed, sixteen-page long document, reiterating the basic rules for restitution and adding clarifications. For example, in order for former owners to get back their house, they had to present the original title, and the legal office of the municipal People's Council had to verify it. If the legal office was not satisfied, the Instructions directed the owner to file suit to establish title! According to the Instructions, the executive committee of the municipal People's Council made restitution decisions based on the opinions of the legal office and of the "technical commission" established according to the Instructions. The legal office had to verify the title and whether the restitutions conditions were fulfilled, while the technical commissions (made up of engineers and architects) had to evaluate renovations, determine the value of buildings, and establish the baseline value for all buildings to be returned to the owners, regardless of improvements. The value of the building in 1950 was considered to be equal to the value of the building at the time of the restitution. Similar standards and procedures were applied to restitution of expropriated buildings. The Instructions gave detailed examples of how the value of the buildings was to be calculated (the bulk of the Instructions).

In light of this fairly detailed process, it may come as a surprise that for the most part the results were predetermined, as the regime was not quick to return property already taken, even in the face of legitimate reasons according to its own criteria. As already, mentioned, only a very small percentage of houses nationalized under Decree 92 in the whole country were returned to their owners—less than 1 percent.[47] In Timişoara, the municipal People's Council proposed for admission 106 petitions, or 20 percent of all petitions, mostly partially (for one apartment), and most of them in 1953, the year the Instructions for restitution were adopted. This was not the final number of admitted petitions, however—by 1960, most of the petitions proposed to be solved favorably had in fact been ultimately rejected, and restitution happened in only 5 percent of the cases.

The very forms used by the nationalization commissions shows that the deck was stacked against the petitioners: they were one-page blank forms, pre-typed with the text "the city commission proposes to reject the petition"—in other words, the official presumption was against admission of petitions. Members of the nationalization commissions filled in only the details relevant for particular cases. As already mentioned, the main criteria for being considered for restitution were the social and economic status of the petitioners (past and present), the number of apartments, and the manner of acquisition. The restitution Instructions themselves were meant only to lay out the process once the restitution decision was taken, yet in practice the nationalization commissions used them as substantive criteria in the decision-making process.

In particular, despite the provisions of the restitution Instructions, petitioners whose houses had been damaged and renovated by the state, or simply significantly improved, were not likely to have their petition accepted, or to receive any compensation. For example, a retired clerk whose house had been bombarded and significantly damaged during the war was considered but eventually rejected for restitution, because the state had repaired and renovated the house after nationalization, and the owner had another house in Bucharest.[48] Similarly, an eighty-one-year old widow whose children had left the country received nothing, because the state had made major repairs to the house.[49]

In other cases, rejection is the result of combining multiple factors, as in the case of a petitioner who had asked for the return of a two-room apartment with kitchen, bathroom, pantry, and maid's room. The exterior of the house had been repaired by the state after nationalization, and the petitioner used to be a merchant with his own store; his wife worked from home, and they had a maid ("I saw they have a maid," wrote the field investigator). In this case, the maid seems to have been the tipping point.[50] In cases where the house was destroyed, petitioners most commonly did not receive compensation, despite the Instructions. A widow whose house had been demolished because it was in very bad shape and considered dangerous did not receive compensation because the land was in the downtown area and was only suitable for large constructions, such as tower blocks for workers' apartments, not individual family homes.[51]

The questionable relevance of the Instructions is also indicated by the reasoning behind restitutions that did happen. A homemaker's petitions were admitted because the two houses had been obtained through inheritance from her parents, her father had been a small craftsman, and her husband was employed and a member of the Romanian Workers' Party (the predecessor to the Romanian Communist Party). The house was ninety years old, it had six rooms, and overall measured approximately 1,200 square feet.[52] In this case, the reason for restitution is clear—the husband's Party membership, but others are a cipher, especially when the petitioners lacked obvious status or power. An older woman and her daughter, both employed, received back a house centrally located,[53] bought in 1949 with money obtained from selling a house and some land in the suburbs, and savings. The house had been bought for the family's needs, and was inhabited by the petitioners and their parents, respectively grandparents. The house had three apartments, five rooms, and overall measured about 1,400 square feet.[54] A rare case of an admitted Article 2 exemption concerns a retiree who had built the house from savings and loans, and "not for exploitation." The petitioner had two children, one of them a daughter with three children of her own. The house was inhabited by the petitioner and his sister-in-law, was thirty-five years old, had four apartments, and each apartment had two rooms and annexes.[55] In another proposal for restitution, the local commission found out that the house in question was nationalized by mistake, as the nationalization commission confused it with the house of the former owner of the local tile factory. Interestingly here, the owner and his family, a bricklayer with three children, all working class, had never been evicted from the house, and had wired the house for electricity as late as 1956 (which may have prompted his petition to reconcile the de facto and de jure ownership situation).[56]

Former co-ownership was no guarantee for restitution, either, if one of the co-owners received their share back. For example, a petitioner who had bought a house together with his sister-in-law (with three apartments, two one-bedrooms and one studio) did not receive back his share, but the sister-in-law did. No reason is stated for rejecting his petition, although possibly this happened because even though his parents were peasants and he was a clerk and accountant for most of his life, he had also owned at some point in time a bookstore (with no other employees).[57]

Even when the exploitation test was passed, owners seeking restitution had to pass the "needs" test—do they need the space requested. The 1955 Instructions requested municipal officials to list separately admitted petitions, rejected petitions, Article 2 petitions where the number of apartments significantly surpassed the needs of the family, and houses belonging to VIPs that significantly surpassed the needs of the family.[58] Based on the "needs" test (8 square meters per person), in the overwhelming majority of cases petitioners failed to obtain restitution. In rare cases when a convincing argument was made, former owners could request more space, but this was dealt with as a separate administrative matter. For example, a former owner from Arad contested the nationalization of her house and declared that as a result she and her family (husband and a twenty-two-year-old son) had been limited to living in the kitchen of their former house, which totaled 13 square meters. The Arad People's Council investigated the case, and while it rejected the petition, it advised her to ask for additional space and solved that separate petition favorably.[59]

The restitution Decree and Instructions are an example of how the regime, ostensibly fighting "bourgeois formalism,"[60] was in fact employing legal formalism as a weapon against former owners, begrudgingly returning their property and bringing forward the slightest reason to deny their petitions. Yet in light of the small number of apartments and houses ultimately returned, why did the regime bother to set up such detailed restitution procedures that were neither published ("strictly secret") nor observed, as former owners were rather unlikely to obtain them and even learn restitution was an option? In other words, why not simply ignore the petitions altogether?

The combination of regularizing the nationalization and restitution processes while simultaneously reaching predetermined solutions does not have self-evident answers. One answer is that the internal contradictions of the nationalization process present insights for the legitimacy-building efforts of the regime both vis-à-vis its subjects and within its power structure. The timeline—five years between the nationalization and restitution decrees—as well as the deluge of petitions suggest that the communist regime did not expect resistance to urban housing nationalization, and certainly not this type of "weak," legalistic resistance. The petitioners were relentless, however, and their push back and contestation of the meaning of "exploitation" highlighted the municipal authorities' own acknowledgment of the deep flaws of the nationalization process (also revealed by the high initial rate of admitted petitions before 1953). The restitution was thus an afterthought that exposed the extent to which alternative ideologies of property continued to struggle as late as ten years into the construction of socialism, and the extent to which the regime was still struggling for legitimacy and control.

Those caught in the urban housing nationalization net were not outliers whose resistance did not matter, but workers, peasants, clerks, teachers, and so on whose cooptation was important. There is a parallel here between petitions against nationalization and petitions that peasants wrote to be taken out of chiabur (kulak) status. As Verdery (2009) explains in her study of making and unmaking classes, in the case of chiaburi the Party was deeply involved in encouraging petitions, primarily for legitimacy reasons. In the case of nationalized owners, I have not found any evidence that this was the case (occasionally, petitioners would be reassured, orally, that their petitions were under consideration). Despite this distinction, there is a similarity between the cases: the regime needed to co-opt both groups, but it used different strategies toward this end. For chiaburi, it was local, case-by-case reclassification; for owners of nationalized houses, there were attempts to regularize and legalize the nationalization and petition process. In both cases, however, albeit to different degrees, petitions can be considered both acts of cooptation and resistance.

In this context, even the appearance of procedural fairness was a helpful legitimacy-building exercise, as the petitioners were perhaps more likely to accept the rejection if they thought their case was given a fair investigation (Tyler 2002). Building legitimacy through legality could be equally valuable inside the power structure, as it reinforced familiar habits of formalism, certainty, and predictability so important for the well-functioning of any bureaucracy. In addition, the formalist restitution system could show municipal bureaucrats that substantive and formal justice need not be polar opposites.

The restitution process, albeit insignificant numerically, is hugely important from a symbolic perspective. As a legitimacy-building exercise, it created a space for the continued circulation of pre-communist property rights discourses and consciousness. It was also a space of communication and negotiation between the regime and its subjects regarding the meaning of private property, labor, exploitation, as well as identities—workers, professionals, clerks, housewives, and ultimate goals—building socialism, eliminating exploitation, achieving equality. The contradictions of nationalization, however, also constructed a type of legality that sent mixed ideological messages about the values inscribed in law and the regime's commitment to legality, property, and even its own ideological goals.

THE AMBIVALENCE OF COURTS

The implementation of takings was a complex, prolonged process. It destroyed the lives of millions of people, and created endless problems for administrators in charge. One might expect courts to be heavily involved, but for the most part courts were conspicuously absent from this story (and not just because judicial review of administrative action had been abolished in 1948). So were legal scholars. There are no law review articles on either housing nationalization or other types of takings. The nationalization of industry and commerce is barely covered in 1948 and 1949 (one overview article per year), while expropriation for public interest similarly is addressed once in 1948. There was official silence regarding one of the most consequential changes in the country. Property overall received a fair amount of coverage, in particular as the contours of state property became clearer, and so did landlord-tenant relations once most takings were settled.

There are some court decisions from around the country that were considered significant enough to be published by law reviews. Overwhelmingly, lower courts supported former owners, and were eventually quashed by the Supreme

Tribunal. It is unclear to what extent they were the exception, rather than the rule, and the decisions published were selected precisely to send a message to all courts and promote the construction of socialist legal consciousness in the area of property. There is only one decision where legality wins and policy loses.

In February 1952, the financial section of the city of Botoşani (in the province of Moldavia) asked the local court to declare the house belonging to E.V. and I.C.V. abandoned and therefore state property, on the basis of Decree 111/1951 (abandoned property). The court initially obliged, but the owners appealed. The appeal court found that the trial court did not summon the owners and as they were not missing or absent, the property could not be considered abandoned. The appeal court ruled in favor of the owners and against the state. The author of the lengthy comment discussing the decision noted that the appeal court's decision was correct, since Decree 111 required the cumulative fulfillment of two conditions: the building was abandoned for more than a year, and the owners were absent or unknown. Neither one of these conditions was fulfilled in this case, as the owners were known and lived in the city, and the one-year statute of limitations was not met.[61]

Dispossessed owners were fairly creative, and indirectly fought nationalization or expropriation by challenging the titling process. Six years after nationalization, for example, the city of Baia Mare (northern Transylvania) filed a non-adversarial motion for the inscription in the real estate registry of a house on the basis of Decree 92/1950, in effect a request to formalize the nationalization. Both the local court and the appeal court rejected the request because the real owner was a different person than the one listed in the registry, a common error during the nationalization process. The owners argued that they were exempt from nationalization, and asked the court to reject the motion of the city on this substantive basis, rather than procedural (wrong name listed). The regional tribunal, however, declined to address the issue of ownership, sidestepping that debate, and simply found that the consent of the owners was irrelevant for this type of ownership transfer and the court had to implement the law.[62]

Lower courts again ruled in favor of the former owners in an expropriation case where the claimant indirectly challenged expropriation on the basis of Law 187/1945 (agrarian reform). The petitioner wanted the local cooperative (GAC) to pay her rent for the house and garden in its possession, and restore the house to its previous condition. Both lower courts (first instance and appeal) found in her favor and decided that the house had been wrongly expropriated (it had been mistakenly considered to be her son's house, who was missing, therefore subject to expropriation). The Supreme Tribunal disagreed and reminded lower courts that they did not have the power of judicial review over administrative acts, including over acts of expropriation. The only option for the petitioner was administrative complaint.[63]

By far the roughest treatment was reserved for former owners of nationalized companies. In 1949, for example, the Fălticeni court (a small town in north-eastern Romania) issued an emergency injunction in response to an urgent request to evict the former owners of a nationalized forestry and logging company, who continued to live in a three-room apartment on the premises of the nationalized company. The state company claimed that it needed the apartment for offices, and that the continued presence of the former owner jeopardized the safety and security of the company "in light of the intensified class struggle." The court fully agreed with this rationale, and did not even notify the former owners.[64] Former owners of nationalized companies were also responsible for the debts of the companies, such as any fines or civil penalties, which were subtracted from whatever meager compensation they might have received.[65]

Courts and court decisions are even less mentioned in the archival material from Timişoara. To the extent that any pattern can be discerned, it would be again that lower courts tended to rule in favor of petitioners. In 1952, for example, Vasin J. from the village of Cernăteaz was illegally evicted from his house by the local council to make room for the newly created cooperative. He sued, and the court agreed with him and compelled the cooperative to pay him rent until 1955, when the council requisitioned the house and stopped paying rent. Vasin petitioned the regional council, which rejected his petition, as in the meantime Decree 511/1955 had nationalized all requisitioned property.[66]

Local bureaucrats were also frustrated by courts' formalistic approach in other types of takings. Romanian citizens who wanted to emigrate to Israel, for example, gave up their property in exchange for a passport, as handwritten on a proposal to nationalize a house in Timişoara. Courts, however, ignored this arrangement and allowed trustees to administer the property left behind, slowing down the takings.[67] The most common types of cases involved owners whose homes had been nationalized under Decree 92/1950, and who asked courts, in non-adversarial filings, to find and declare that their house had not been listed in the appendix, and therefore that they had been mistakenly nationalized. This was often after the former owners had petitioned the local council multiple times to no avail.

Finally, the state often resorted to prosecuting custodians of expropriated goods who stole or could not justify what happened with goods seized on the basis of Decree 83/1949 (agrarian reforms and expropriations). This involved more expensive items, such as silverware, but also clothing, shoes, household items, and more, which often was stored in poor conditions and simply decayed. Local officials, not uncommonly, lied and claimed the goods had been distributed to the poor, which could be difficult to check since formal reports for expropriations could take as long as one or two years to be filed, to the chagrin of the central authorities but also of the financial officials, who could not keep track. Punishments (fines) were imposed on officials who sold expropriated goods to the public for very small sums, or if local officials distributed expropriated goods to any state bodies or local authorities who simply asked. This included items as minor as bicycle parts. Prosecution was primarily reserved for cases of missing goods, which were considered stolen from the state property.[68]

ARBITRARINESS AND ITS DISCONTENTS

The implementation of the takings and the process of limited restitutions illustrate the advantages and pitfalls of the regime's decision-making process and of deploying law instrumentally. On the one hand, there was the intoxicating freedom of unbridled power—takings dictated by state and economic interests, by municipal political arbitrariness and by the need to eliminate exploitation on the road to communism, assisted by goal-oriented legal interpretation and anti-formalism. On the other hand, there were the costs of revolutionary fervor—the stress of uncertainty, the waste of human resources, the craving for stable expectations and structured direction. It may have seemed like a good idea at the time to seize a milk plant or a private home with little regard for "legal formalities," but as it turned out, dealing with the consequences of these acts invariably summoned the ghosts of formalism and proceduralism of older days. The points system and the exhaustive data collection process and justificatory exercises illustrate well this unique blend of arbitrariness, formalism, and substantive justice.

Legality as formal-rational law encompasses the concept of a rule-governed system, where the government follows its own rules and there is relatively little scope for administrative discretion. Law is systematic, impersonal (general), equally applied, predictable, and transparent. Legal decisions are not obviously political or influenced by other factors such as religion or morality, and are consistent with legal rules.[69] By no stretch of the imagination can communist legality be understood as formal rational, yet it would be equally a mistake to discount its formal-rational dimensions, in particular because they explain everyday dynamics of power and resistance within the administration and vis-à-vis citizens. Communist jurists critiqued bourgeois formalism as ideological, excessively procedural, abstract, decontextualized, and severely lacking in terms of providing substantive justice. Yet the communist regime's own practices were relatively rule-bound, hierarchical, centralized, and procedural while being openly ideological and relatively indifferent to substantive justice (however defined). Moreover, legal certainty, stability, and predictability were deeply attractive for local-level bureaucrats. The unholy combination of formalism and ideology had consequences for the decision-making process vis-à-vis nationalization petitions and proposals, the most curious of which was the imposition of some procedural fairness leading to predetermined ideological outcomes (the points system).

Examining the fifteen-year span between 1950 and 1965 shows that there is no clear progression from a substantive rational type of legality dominated by Marxist-Leninist ideology to a more formal-rational system, rather these two dimensions of legality coexist at all times. Yet this is not the reason communist legal systems are simultaneously characterized as arbitrary and lacking in legality (e.g., Krygier 1990), as well as pervasive, with "an inherent, 'octopuslike,' all-embracing potential" that "almost hysterically abhors situations and behaviors which are not covered by its substantial and formal pre-arrangements" (Podgorecki and Olgiati 1996, viii).

It is the third facet of the communist legality pyramid that is the most visible and controversial, the penumbras of legality stretching from outright arbitrariness such as the de facto takings to areas of ambiguity and legal limbo. These penumbras indicate the limits of communist legality, as well as the love-hate relationship between the regime and its purportedly trustworthy instrument. The penumbras of communist legality in Romania in particular encompass obsessive secrecy and lack of transparency, as well as arbitrariness and ambiguity.

Secrecy and openness anchor the ideal-type democratic versus totalitarian states model. Hannah Arendt argued that there exists an inverse relationship between secrecy and power: "The more visible government agencies are, the less power they carry, and the less is known of the existence of an institution, the more powerful it will ultimately turn out to be" (1948, 101). Adam Podgorecki in his discussion of totalitarian law dubbed the secret instructions, decrees, orders, etc. "shadow law," and argued that a defining feature of law in totalitarian systems is that "a given norm is valid only as long as it is not in conflict with its shadow counter-part" (1996, 13).[70] Romania was no exception, as its regime was a serious user of secrecy. The last sentence of the oath taken by judges when they took office, for example, was "I swear to protect the laws of the RPR and to maintain the secrecy of the job" (Ionescu-Gură 2005, 294). The regime used secrecy as a means to control information, such as the targets and criteria for property takings, and to control the lives of those nationalized.

The regime deployed secrecy both against its citizens and within its own apparatus. Decree 92 itself was published, but its appendixes were not, and neither were the subsequent decrees amending Decree 92. Similarly, decrees that regulated other sensitive areas, such as the status of internally dislocated persons, were not published. Their status ranged from "secret" to "strictly secret." Instructions no 14068/1953, for example, aiming to remedy the mistakes and abuses that happened with the initial implementation of Decree 92, were strictly secret. The Instructions provide a unique insight into the calculus of the regime in this area. Signed by the president of the Central Commission for Urban Nationalization, they combine a slightly informal style, suspicion, pedagogy, and the need for complete control. More than once throughout the Instructions the need for complete secrecy is underscored, "so as not to create opportunities for enemy elements to launch biased rumors and thus create unease among the population," and elsewhere "so as not to create a state of anxiety among the population."[71] Six years later, another set of Instructions for the implementation of Decrees 92/1950 and 524/1955 (restitution), also strictly secret, urges the nationalization commissions to undertake their investigations while "keeping the greatest secrecy."[72]

Inside the administrative apparatus, secrecy was the universal currency of the takings. All of the correspondence regarding the petitions, restitutions, and takings was classified as either secret or strictly secret. Municipally, nationalization files—including the petitions—were kept in special registries and locked up either in a special office or in the safe of the president of the nationalization commission.[73] Once a file was closed, the entire documentation was sent to the Council of Ministers. The need for control from the center extended to withholding crucial information from the municipal people's councils. On June 27, 1956, for example, the Reşiţa People's Council asked the regional People's Council to send them an "authentic copy" (notarized) of the Decree 92 appendix for the city of Reşiţa, so they could proceed with registering the nationalized houses in the real estate registry.[74] Incidentally, this raises interesting questions—how did they nationalize if they did not have the list, and perhaps answers some—if the municipal authorities did not know who was nationalized, it's not a surprise the owners themselves did not know, either.

The secrecy practice breaks down and has both intended and unintended consequences. As some of the petitions themselves reveal, the secret decrees and instructions did trickle down—after all, these were all relatively small towns and cities, with still functioning social networks. While all of the correspondence to and from the Council of Ministers was invariably secretive, municipal communication and documentation (between regional and municipal levels) was not necessarily secret, despite the official edict to that effect. There was continuous back and forth between them, a slow accretion of paper and data, some of it secret, some of it following normal communication channels. During periods of high activity in the nationalization field, and when admonished from above, the regional council would occasionally become more stringent: "You will take measures that the documents and files you send us are complete, in order not to create superfluous correspondence and taking into account the conspiratorial nature of this process" (May 17, 1956, letter from regional to Timişoara nationalization commission).[75]

At a basic level, secrecy in the nationalization field achieved its primary purpose of control through selective communication of the regime's goals and lack of certainty and transparency regarding the targets, procedures, timing, and means of redress. The process of dealing with the petitions itself was secretive, although there were limits regarding how secret it was given that the petitioners had started it. Yet secrecy has unforeseen consequences, too, since there is an element of shame in it, "the concealment of something which is negatively valued by the excluded audience and, in some instances, by the perpetrators as well" (Warren and Laslett 1977, 44). The extensive interpretation of the meaning of "exploitation" and "exploiter" and the secrecy of the entire process together underscore the failure of creating the "other," the limits of class justice, and the difficulty of cooptation in repression. It ultimately decreased trust, negatively impacted legitimacy-building efforts, as well as the ultimate goal of reality reconstruction. As forms of power, secrecy and silence are themselves suspicious and open up possibilities of resistance that can be as simple and unconscious as diffusion of information.

NOTES

1. National Archives of Romania Timişoara, Collection Sfatul Popular Banat, Secretariat, File No. 102/1960, page 15.
2. National Archives of Romania Timişoara, Collection Sfatul Popular Banat, Secretariat, File No. 43/1960, pages 7–11.
3. National Archives of Romania Timişoara, Collection Sfatul Popular Banat, Secţia Gospodărie Comunală, File No. 23/1953, page 83.
4. National Archives of Romania Timişoara, Collection Sfatul Popular Banat, Secţia de Gospodărie Comunală, File No. 2/1964, pages 169–71.
5. National Archives of Romania Timişoara, Collection Sfatul Popular Banat, Secretariat, File No. 95/1953, pages 1–14.
6. National Archives of Romania Timişoara, Collection Sfatul Popular Banat, File No. 95/1953 [double], pages 22–28.
7. National Archives of Romania Timişoara, Collection Sfatul Popular Banat, Secretariat, File No. 64/1960, page 1. National Archives of Romania Timişoara, Collection Sfatul Popular Banat, Secretariat, File No. 43/1960, pages 7–10.
8. National Archives of Romania Timişoara, Collection Sfatul Popular Banat, Secretariat, File No. 43/1960, pages 7–10.
9. National Archives of Romania Timişoara, Collection Sfatul Popular Banat, Secţia de Gospodărie Comunală, Files No. 2/1964, 20/1963, pages 1–4.
10. National Archives of Romania Timişoara, Collection Sfatul Popular Banat, Secţia de Gospodărie Comunală, File No. 20/1958, [page no. not assigned].

11. National Archives of Romania Timişoara, Collection Sfatul Popular Banat, Secretariat, File No. 84/1960, pages 130–36.

12. National Archives of Romania Timişoara, Collection Sfatul Popular Banat, Secretariat, File No. 95/1953*.

13. National Archives of Romania Timişoara, Collection Sfatul Popular Banat, Secretariat, File No. 84/1960, pages 130–36.

14. National Archives of Romania Timişoara, Collection Sfatul Popular Banat, Secţia Gospodărie Comunală, File No. 23/1953, page 83.

15. National Archives of Romania Timişoara, Collection Sfatul Popular Banat, Secţia de Gospodărie Comunală, File No. 27/1962, page 43.

16. National Archives of Romania Timişoara, Collection Sfatul Popular Banat, Secţia Gospodărie Comunală, File No. 23/1953, page 83.

17. National Archives of Romania Timişoara, Collection Sfatul Popular Banat, Secretariat, File No. 102/1960, page 53.

18. National Archives of Romania Timişoara, Collection Sfatul Popular Banat, Secretariat, File No. 102/1960, pages 43–52. National Archives of Romania Timişoara, Collection Sfatul Popular Banat, Secretariat, File No. 102/1960, page 64.

19. National Archives of Romania Timişoara, Collection Sfatul Popular Banat, Secţia de Gospodărie Comunală, File No. 1/1956, page 120.

20. National Archives of Romania Timişoara, Collection Sfatul Popular Banat, Secretariat, File No. 102/1960, pages 57–60.

21. National Archives of Romania Timişoara, Collection Sfatul Popular Banat, Secretariat, File No. 102/1960, pages 61–62, 65.

22. National Archives of Romania Timişoara, Collection Sfatul Popular Banat, Secretariat, File No. 102/1960, pages 43–52. But if her mother died before 1949, as Alexandra's petition seemed to indicate, who got the house back? This never became clear from the archival documents.

23. National Archives of Romania Timişoara, Collection Sfatul Popular Banat, Secţia de Gospodărie Comunală, File No. 20/1958, pages 47–50.

24. National Archives of Romania Timişoara, Collection Sfatul Popular Banat, Secţia de Gospodărie Comunală, File No. 20/1958, pages 42–43.

25. National Archives of Romania Timişoara, Collection Sfatul Popular Banat, Secretariat, File No. 43/1960, page 30.

26. Excerpt from a justificatory memo prepared by the regional People's Council Banat as part of a package of proposals of exemption from nationalization. National Archives of Romania Timişoara, Collection Sfatul Popular Banat, Secretariat, File No. 79/1967, page 62.

27. National Archives of Romania Timişoara, Collection Sfatul Popular Banat, Secretariat, File No. 102/1960, page 27.

28. National Archives of Romania Timişoara, Collection Sfatul Popular Banat, Secretariat, File No. 74/1959, page 14.

29. National Archives of Romania Timişoara, Collection Sfatul Popular Banat, Secretariat, File No. 74/1959, page 25.

30. National Archives of Romania Timişoara, Collection Sfatul Popular Banat, Secretariat, File No. 74/1959, page 34.

31. National Archives of Romania Timişoara, Collection Sfatul Popular Banat, Secretariat, File No. 74/1959, page 18.
32. National Archives of Romania Timişoara, Collection Sfatul Popular Banat, Secretariat, File No. 74/1959, page 19.
33. National Archives of Romania Timişoara, Collection Sfatul Popular Banat, Inventar 1517, File No. 14/1951, pages 17–18.
34. National Archives of Romania Timişoara, Collection Sfatul Popular Banat, Inventar 1517, File No. 14/1951, pages 17–18.
35. National Archives of Romania Timişoara, Collection Sfatul Popular Banat, Secretariat, File No. 124/1960, pages 339–40.
36. National Archives of Romania Timişoara, Collection Sfatul Popular Banat, Secretariat, File No. 102/1960, pages 88–92.
37. E.g. National Archives of Romania Timişoara, Collection Sfatul Popular Banat, Secretariat, File No. 74/1959; Secţia de Gospodărie Comunală, File No. 1/1956, page 115.
38. National Archives of Romania Timişoara, Collection Sfatul Popular Banat, Inventar 1517, File No. 11/1955, page 5.
39. National Archives of Romania Timişoara, Collection Sfatul Popular Banat, Secretariat, File No. 124/1960, pages 398–99.
40. National Archives of Romania Timişoara, Collection Sfatul Popular Banat, Secretariat, File No. 74/1959, page 13.
41. National Archives of Romania Timişoara, Collection Sfatul Popular Banat, Inventar 1517, File No. 11/1955, pages 3–4.
42. National Archives of Romania Timişoara, Collection Sfatul Popular Banat, Secretariat, File No. 75/1960, pages 186–288.
43. National Archives of Romania Timişoara, Collection Sfatul Popular Banat, Secretariat, File No. 75/1960, pages 159–61, front and back.
44. National Archives of Romania Timişoara, Collection Sfatul Popular Banat, Secretariat, File No. 79/1967, pages 59–61.
45. E.g. National Archives of Romania Timişoara, Collection Sfatul Popular Banat, Inventar 1517, File No. 11/1955.
46. National Archives of Romania Timişoara, Collection Sfatul Popular Banat, Secretariat, File No. 84/1960, pages 9–24. The full title is "Instructions 40869 for the application of HCM 2586/1955 regarding the manner and conditions for the restitution of houses or apartments exempted from nationalization under Decree 92/1950."
47. National Archives of Romania Timişoara, Collection Sfatul Popular Banat, Secretariat, File No. 102/1960, pages 82–84.
48. National Archives of Romania Timişoara, Collection Sfatul Popular Banat, Secretariat, File No. 74/1959, page 26.
49. National Archives of Romania Timişoara, Collection Sfatul Popular Banat, Secretariat, File No. 74/1959, page 30.
50. National Archives of Romania Timişoara, Collection Sfatul Popular Banat, Secretariat, File No. 74/1959, page 37.
51. National Archives of Romania Timişoara, Collection Sfatul Popular Banat, Secretariat, File No. 74/1959, page 38.

52. National Archives of Romania Timişoara, Collection Sfatul Popular Banat, Inventar 1630, File No. 2/1964, page 60.

53. The memo does not say the house is centrally located, this is my conclusion based on its address. For all other petitioners, the central location of the house was definitive for nationalization, regardless of any other factors.

54. National Archives of Romania Timişoara, Collection Sfatul Popular Banat, Inventar 1630, File No. 2/1964, page 60.

55. National Archives of Romania Timişoara, Collection Sfatul Popular Banat, Inventar 1630, File No. 2/1964, page 60.

56. National Archives of Romania Timişoara, Collection Sfatul Popular Banat, Secretariat, File No. 55/1960, pages 17–18.

57. National Archives of Romania Timişoara, Collection Sfatul Popular Banat, Secretariat, File No. 74/1959, page 21.

58. National Archives of Romania Timişoara, Collection Sfatul Popular Banat, Secretariat, File No. 43/1960, page 29.

59. National Archives of Romania Timişoara, Collection Sfatul Popular Banat, Secretariat, File No. 74/1959–1960, pages 1–7.

60. For example, Bunaciu (1949, 175). The author was the Minister of Justice at the time, and this article was also published in the main national Party newspaper, *Scânteia* [*The Spark*].

61. Decision and comment published in *Justiţia Nouă [New Justice]* 7/1956, pages 1195–96.

62. Decision published in *Justiţia Nouă [New Justice]* 5/1957, pages 883–84.

63. Supreme Tribunal decision 457/March 29, 1957, published in *Legalitatea Populară [Popular Legality]* 12/1957, p. 1507.

64. Decision published in *Justiţia Nouă [New Justice]* 10/1949, pages 1211–12.

65. Supreme Court decision 3638/December 15, 1948, published in *Justiţia Nouă [New Justice]* 1–2/1949, p. 192.

66. National Archives of Romania Timişoara, Collection Sfatul Popular Banat, Secretariat, File No. 46/1956, pages 75–78.

67. National Archives of Romania Timişoara, Collection Sfatul Popular Banat, Secretariat, File No. 79/1967, pages 177–80.

68. National Archives of Romania Timişoara, Collection Sfatul Popular Banat, Financiar, File No. 12/1955, pages 10–13.

69. Fuller's *The Morality of Law* lists eight criteria: laws must exist and those laws should be obeyed by all, laws must be published, must be prospective, should be clear and enforced fairly, should avoid contradictions, not command the impossible, remain constant yet open to changes, and official action should be consistent with the official rule.

70. He further discusses the parallel legal realities brought on by this system and its impact (Podgorecki 1996, 20).

71. National Archives of Romania Timişoara, Collection Sfatul Popular Banat, Secretariat, File No. 95/1953*, page 1–15.

72. National Archives of Romania Timişoara, Collection Sfatul Popular Banat, Secretariat, File No. 43/1960, pages 7–10.

73. For example, the strictly secret memo 866/January 29, 1958, from the Executive Committee of the People's Council of the Timişoara Region to the subordinate Lugoj Committee, attached to a copy of the restitution decree 524/1955, advising the recipient to keep it locked in the safe since the Decree is an "especially secret document" ["caracterul deosebit de secret al acestui document"]. National Archives of Romania Timişoara, Collection Sfatul Popular Banat, Secretariat, File No. 65/1958, page 86.

74. National Archives of Romania Timişoara, Collection Sfatul Popular Banat, Inventar 1630, File No. 1/1956, page 322.

75. National Archives of Romania Timişoara, Collection Sfatul Popular Banat, Inventar 1630, File No. 1/1956, page 91.

Chapter 6

Surviving Property

Private Property in Early Communism

By late 1945 to early 1946, Lucreţiu Pătrăşcanu had been paid a substantial amount of money for his multivolume books *Under Three Dictatorships* and *Currents and Tendencies in Romanian Philosophy* (a Marxist analysis of Romanian society), and had been considering his options for spending it. He eventually settled on building a summer house in the posh resort area of Snagov (Betea 2001, 62–63). Lucreţiu Pătrăşcanu is perhaps the most famous Romanian communist aside from Nicolae Ceauşescu, sharing a mystique not unlike Trotsky's, in part because their fates were somewhat similar: Pătrăşcanu was imprisoned in 1948 and executed in 1954. The Snagov villa, initially seized, was eventually repaired by the Party and given back to his wife in 1968. She had also been imprisoned for eight years (Betea 2001, 364).

There is nothing unusual about this episode, other than the fact that Lucreţiu Pătrăşcanu was, at the time that he was considering investing his money, the first communist Minister of Justice. His decision to increase his private property—on the basis of his labor—was made in the midst of purges and takings, planning the nationalization of the country's economic life, and imposing drastic changes in housing laws and policies, such as the "sanitary" housing norm of 8 square meters per person. The "great nationalization" of 1948–1949 wiped out most of the country's private industry and commerce. Petre Groza, the prime minister of Romania at the moment of the 1948 "great nationalization," confessed later that as he was reading the list of nationalized companies in front of the Great National Assembly, some of which had been his own, he could not help sadly musing: "I am losing this one . . . and this one . . . and this one" (Lăcustă 2005, 32–33). Urban housing nationalization would come only two years later.

Locally, the temporary committee of Timişoara (the local administrative body of the transition period) complained to the central administration about the extent to which internally displaced persons (IDPs) (post–Second World War), who had been given title to land and houses expropriated from local ethnic Germans, showed no respect for property. The undated, unsigned memo noted that houses and their inventory were being systematically destroyed and that some IDPs had received two to three rounds of houses and inventory, which they ruined (wood houses had been dismantled and the wood used for fire). The local authorities' inability to handle the situation, arguably at a time of high totalitarianism, is also shown by complaints that the new settlers displayed an attitude of indifference toward authorities, that they had a "recalcitrant attitude toward legal dispositions," and if the state authorities tried to force them to observe the law, the IDPs just liquidated their households and left. They also destroyed public goods, such as bridges, wells, and so on, and did not pay any taxes.[1] Similar internal reports noted that as a result, entire villages were in ruins and urgent measures were required to remedy the situation.

These vignettes are emblematic of the ambivalence and turmoil of the period in general and for property, in particular. Private property seemed to be in free fall as a result of massive takings and destruction, new housing policies, as well as significant redistribution of property. Yet at the same time, the new regime aggressively continued pre-communist policies of encouraging constructions of private housing, made few changes to the 1864 civil code and the regulation of property, and was concerned about the efficient use of the property it now owned—for example, nationalized companies kept their legal and economic structure for a while after the nationalization, in order to avoid panic, smooth the transition, and sustain the economy. The Prime Legal Counsel in the Ministry of Justice explained that at the heart of nationalization was "not destruction, not the seizing and dismemberment of machines, tools and companies, but the seizing of active, productive economic units for the benefit of the people" (Volanschi 1948, 413).

The centrality of property for the communist project would suggest that at least in this area, if not others, the communist regimes would be coherent, consistent, and ultimately successful. Nonetheless, the story here is not about the disappearance of private property, or about socialism creating truly new forms of ordering property relations. Rather, this is a story of mutual adaptation: property adapting to socialism and socialism adapting to private property—ideologically, structurally, institutionally, and in its materiality—and about the conflicting property messages, ideologies, and practices embedded and constituted in law. The result was a hybrid concept of private property, drawing from both capitalist and socialist sources.[2]

Deep continuities between the pre-communist and communist legal structure of property and more generally civil law have of course not been ignored by scholars of socialist law, both Western and Eastern (e.g., Markovits

1968, 2007; Feldbrugge and Simmons 1982; Ioffe 1982). The *longue durée*, however, allows us to understand how these continuities mattered in the broader legal culture of property in early communism—ideology and consciousness—and in terms of unsettling the hegemony of private property. The doctrinal and jurisprudential narratives explored here clearly delineate not only technical continuities in the legal discourse of property, but also the interpretive commitments embodied in these narratives (Cover 1983, 7), and consequently the meaning of law caught in this peculiar normative transition from capitalism to communism.

AN UNEASY MARRIAGE: CAPITALIST PROPERTY AND SOCIALISM

The birth of socialist property (state and collective), and the massive takings of early communism were without a doubt momentous. But they were not truly revolutionary because they did not reconceptualize property, as they took part within the legal structure of property created by the 1864 civil code. This was a half-hearted project, and vis-à-vis houses at best ambiguous. There are significant continuities in the legal and mental map of property, property attributes, and the legal language of property between pre-communism and early communism. The property universe throughout socialism continued to be defined by capitalist legal concepts: the normal rules were those inscribed in the pre-communist civil code, while the exceptional ones were fashioned by socialist lawmakers.

This matters from three perspectives. First, it pinpoints a fundamental continuity in the legal regime of property, despite changes imposed during communism. Second, it reinforces the centrality of property as capitalist private property—bourgeois rule, socialist exception. If the goal was to denaturalize bourgeois private property, this goal became almost impossible to achieve with the preservation of the pre-communist property regime as the normal one, while the communist amendments were *ab initio* defined as exceptional. Third, maintaining the basic structure of property also preserved the legal ideologies of property embedded therein.

This "business as usual" model is apparent, for example, in the tone and direction of civil law scholarship. Of forty-nine law review articles published between 1945 and 1965, only four had a "pure" ideological content—discussing the need to "staunchly defend socialist property." The rest were devoted to discussions of controversial or difficult legal issues in the following areas: housing and constructions (sixteen articles), various issues pertaining to socialist property (e.g., leasing of buildings, other real rights) (nine articles), personal property (five pieces, two of them written by a Supreme Tribunal

Justice), two articles each on *rei vindicatio*, acquisitive prescription, superficies, transfer of ownership, real estate registration system, and one each on expropriation for public utility, nationalization, immovable accession, inheritance, the Soviet civil code, and possessory actions.

Between 1864 and 2011 (when a new civil code entered into force), the core elements of private property and the legal regime governing property were the same, and while at least one socialist civil code was drafted, it was never adopted. Despite significant amendments to the 1864 civil code during the communist period, the sections on movables, immovables, and property rights remained largely intact. The legal provisions governing property did not change (Article 480), which also means that the legal map and main attributes of property did not fundamentally change from its pre-communist days. The property hierarchy was different: state, collective and lastly personal property, but ownership was still the pinnacle right among all other property rights.

The basic definition of property continued to include use, possession, and disposition. While most authors further stated that these elements did not exhaust the concept and right of property and that the social content of ownership must be taken into account, no indication was given as to how this fundamentally challenged the property paradigm inherited from Justinian (e.g., Venediktov, Ministry of Justice). On the contrary, these authors seemed to bolster the centrality of property by arguing that the total—ownership, is bigger than the parts—use, possession, and disposition.

Within the communist property universe, firmly ensconced within the Roman/Napoleonic Code model, the fundamental building blocks of ownership were thus still possession, understood as effective power [stăpânire] over the good, physical or economic, directly or indirectly; use—the right to use economically the good and its fruits; and disposition, or the right to decide over the legal fate of the good (Ministry of Justice 1959, 207; Popescu 1952, 107). All other rights in the property universe were combinations of these three key elements, for example, usufruct as the right to use and possess property that belongs to someone else. Even when all three elements were lacking, such as in the case of judicial sequestration, ownership could still be present as there remained a "real residuum of property," so if the creditor's claim disappeared, the property right was fully restored. This legal model of property held for all property rights, including the state's, so the rights of administrative state bodies also included use, possession, and limited disposition, which were opposable to all except for the state (Ministry of Justice 1959, 207–12).

Ownership, according to Article 480 and next of the civil code and the explanations of the Ministry of Justice, was acquired through the "usual methods" (i.e., capitalist), divided into primary (original) and derivative. The former included occupancy, acquisitive prescription, accession, and acquisition of fruits by the good-faith possessor, while the latter included contract, conveyance, inheritance, and judicial decision (Ministry of Justice 1959, 247). State property was "born" through nationalization—an "original, revolutionary method"; socialist reproduction; loss of property by the previous owner (abandoned, or through the effects of special laws such as exempting gold from private property); expropriation (with compensation) and confiscation (forced, no compensation, as punishment, administratively); mandatory quotas; taxes; civil fines and penalties; contracts; inheritance (goods with no heir); and acts regulated by civil law—accession, acquisitive prescription, and good-faith possession (Ministry of Justice 1959, 209–10). Most of these methods represent new species of the old genus—the bourgeois property model.

Property was lost through sale, destruction, accession, loss, usurpation, as well as confiscation, nationalization, and expropriation (Ministry of Justice 1959, 260). The most important legal means of defending private property was still *rei vindicatio*. *Rei vindicatio* is the primary legal remedy for the protection of ownership in civil law systems, specifically a legal action through which the owner demands that the defendant return the plaintiff's *res* [thing]. There is nothing new here in terms of the property model. The most significant change is the extent to which nationalization and expropriation were used, but these are not specifically socialist legal tools, either. No Romanian socialist legal authors discussed the ideological effects of the structure of property or the theoretical assumptions and implications of these elements.

Fundamentally, capitalist property and socialism adapted to each other. Socialism was parasitic upon property: it imagined itself in the language and structure of capitalist property, while it allowed private property to survive. Thus, socialist state property embodied the most absolutist version of ownership, was "absolute to the extreme," for example, opposable even to those who possessed in good faith; exclusive (could not be "dismembered"); imprescriptible (could not be lost through adverse possession); inalienable; and could not be seized by creditors (Ministry of Justice 1959, 212). It was unitary, indivisible, and permanent (Hilsenrad 1950, 513; Diaconescu and Oprişan 1955, 714). Its mere exercise enjoyed the broadest means of defense under civil law (Paşalega 1959, 43–45). The entire bourgeois property package was simply transferred onto newly labeled categories, such as "socialist state property," thus belying any attempts to transcend the capitalist concept of property.

The price for the survival of private property was steep, however: its domain was severely diminished, its status vis-à-vis state property was downgraded, and it needed to adapt. There were four major categories of private property restrictions. First, the communist regime undertook extensive takings, primarily nationalization and expropriation. Second, the scope of private property was very narrow, as it included only the home and household objects, objects of personal use, some land, income, and savings. Moreover, Romania had even more drastic rules than other communist regimes—no dachas or multiple cars were allowed later in the regime's life, as a result of Ceauşescu's infatuation with Chinese and North Korean communism.

Third, there were numerous regulatory restrictions on the circulation of property, as well as building and demolishing houses. These included requirements to notarize contracts and administrative approval for property transfers (Decrees 151/1950, 221/1950). Decree 144/1958 replaced Decree 221/1950 and regulated permits for construction, repair, demolishing of constructions, as well as selling or dividing land with or without constructions. Inheritance was protected in principle, however.

Fourth, housing regulations established as part of a policy of gaining control over the housing market represented perhaps the most significant conceptual restriction. Owners could not decide anymore on the destination or use of their houses without the approval of the rental offices. Separately from property issues, this was also intended to be a move away from "bourgeois contractual individualism" (Dima 1948, 449). Most of these restrictions continued throughout communism, and their severity cannot be underestimated.

Housing Law

The regime had begun working on gaining control of the housing market immediately after the war. The 1947 tenancy law froze rentals to current tenants, stopped "arbitrary evictions" and set the rent at 1938 levels (progressive rent system) in the following manner: workers, civil servants, retirees, and students paid the 28th part of the 1938 rent, the others the 50th part of the 1938 rent; for contracts sealed after October 26, 1940, employees paid 45 percent of the 1938 rent, civil servants not part of a collective contract, small craftsmen, and the liberal professions the entire 1938 rent, and merchants and industrialists three times the 1938 rent.[3]

The all-powerful rental offices were established and started work in 1948, at the end of the census. Rental offices were regulated by Law 359/1948, Decision of the Council of Ministers 29/1949, and an order of the Ministry of Internal Affairs from March 1, 1949 (published in *Luptătorul Bănăţean* from December 6, 1948). Once rental offices began to function, rental contracts and all relationships between landlords and tenants became subject to the jurisdiction of the rental offices—apartments could only be rented on the basis of rental orders from the rental office, and only to those indicated by the office (further limited by the legally imposed individual "space allowance" of 8 square meters per person). For almost twenty years, rental offices wielded huge power over the population and arguably they were even more feared than the repressive state apparatus.[4]

The purported beneficiaries of the new rental regulations and of the rental offices were "outstanding workers," "workers, technicians and clerks with large families who live in unhealthy circumstances," "party activists and employees who moved to the city for work," and especially "political and mass organizations, public institutions and the military," also canteens, nurseries, and newly created kindergartens. Requests for space were solved based on a database of rooms and apartments put together by city hall and rental offices (CADCR Report 2006, 617).

The rental offices' power was continuously resisted by the population, who invented ever more creative ways to subvert it. The most widespread form was "filodorma"—money abusively requested by someone for a privilege or ceding of a benefit. Basically, private parties entered into private rental agreements, outside of the control of the rental offices, with the help of an intermediary. It was criminalized in 1957 and announced in the main local Party newspaper, *Drapelul Roşu*, on October 19, 1957. Regularly, the City Hall's housing department and rental offices undertook field investigations to discover "space," that is, rooms and apartments not registered with these offices, and thus not officially distributed. A quarterly report from December 1949 notes that during one such inspection, housing officials discovered 666 cases of "hidden spaces."[5]

There was no freedom of contract in the rental market, as tenants were assigned by the rental offices. Oral contracts for renting and sub-renting were invalid, and landlords and tenants had to finalize a written contract within thirty days, or could be indicted for sabotage. As a lawyer noted in 1948, "for the first time in Romanian law there is punishment for those who avoid entering into a contract" (Dima 1948, 449). Civil law experts tried to fit these forced contracts within the traditional civil law framework (e.g., Anghel 1958).

Owners did not enjoy any preferential treatment in the rental market, and cases involving owners fully illuminate the difficulties of adapting socialist changes to a capitalist property framework. There was no uniformity in how courts decided, for example, cases of administrative eviction of owners who occupied rooms that had become available in their building without an assignment order from the state. Some courts, including the Supreme Tribunal (guiding decision of the plenum no 24/September 5, 1957; decision no. 195/Feb 18, 1958), ruled that owners also needed assignment orders to occupy the rooms, and they did not enjoy any preference in terms of being assigned the newly freed space. Other courts argued that if there was no preferential right of the owner, the right of use as part of ownership was in fact annulled. Various prosecutors' offices (who were automatically involved) also gave different solutions, with some, for example, in Iaşi and Timişoara, arguing that owners had ownership rights protected by law, which could not be separated from the use of the property, so owners could not be evicted. These prosecutors thought that ownership "inherently" meant that the owner did not occupy the rooms abusively. Others, in Hunedoara and Deva, approved the eviction. Two prosecutors from the Central Prosecutors' Office, Drăgoescu and Oprescu, discuss this at length in a 1958 article (pages 25–27).

Space designated as "additional" had to be rented out by law and there was a special category of sanctions for housing law violations, for example, "abuse of use," for which even an owner could be evicted (Groza 1958, 54). It is key to note that these rules applied to nationalized housing and non-nationalized housing built before the 1948 and 1952 housing decrees came into force, thus exempting most housing built afterward, whether private or not. In all exempt cases, however, the space had to be occupied by owners and their families. If the owners of the new building rented, they lost the exemption and came under state regulation by rental offices (Anghel and Pătulea 1962, 14). Paradoxically, ownership was somewhat protected in other areas, for example, interior renovations to a building could not be done without the owner's consent, and the owner's consent could not be replaced by the state's consent or a court decision (Drăgoescu and Oprescu 1958, 32).

While housing and tenancy regulations are not the primary focus of this book, understanding their severity, scope, and reach is important for two reasons: first, like the takings, they represent one extreme in the process of dismantling private property; second, the local legal and political struggles to implement them, as well as the regime's compromises, reveal yet again the difficulty of the process and one of the many reasons for the ultimate accommodation of capitalist property and socialist ideology.

CAPITALIST AND SOCIALIST PROPERTY DISCOURSES

The legal regime of property was only one of the battlegrounds for recreating property. Ideology was a close second, and at stake here was cutting off ties between private property and individual freedom, well established in the legal and philosophical treatment of property. The association of property with concepts of autonomy, protection, individualism, privacy, and identity can be traced to all major philosophers, from Locke to Kant and Hegel. Labor, which became crucial for socialist theories of property, plays a key role in Locke's justification of property. Together with natural law, labor gives private property a moral grounding, increases the amount of goods available in society for others, and connects private property, self and liberty, as ownership of labor is connected substantially to the primal ownership of self (Waldron 2004).[6] The Lockean ideal, later embedded in Blackstone's *Commentaries on the*

Laws of England, is one of property as autonomy, control and self-control, and creating a clear separation between the individual and the society, a critique developed by Marx.

Marx thought private property and freedom were antithetical because he disagreed with Locke's concept of freedom, and associated freedom not with privacy, but with rationality and community—the conscious planning of one's life, and freedom from external, irrational, uncontrollable forces. On a societal plan, rationality implied a harmony of interests and rational planning, which also meant the destruction of private property, which separates and divides people (Brenkert 1979). Marx would have likely agreed with Macpherson's theory of possessive individualism, and in particular with his insight that all classical political theories embody an assumption about the nature of the individual that is conceived in terms of property. The individual is defined by property relations and functions as property to be bought and sold, which universalizes the so-called bourgeois individual (Carter 2005, 832–35; Alexander 1991, 276–77; Macpherson 1962, 1978). Freedom as property (and property as freedom) was the primary ideological target of the Romanian communist regime, partially following the Soviets, partially carving its own way.

Other property ideologies were somewhat less of a concern for communist thinkers, but there are interesting overlaps. Private property in capitalism is instrumental in the development of human personality, both individually as self-mastery, and collectively, as it leads to increasing participation and ultimately democratic self-governance (Weinrib 2003; Waldron 2004; Radin 1982). Property is also tied with personhood and agency. Margaret Radin, for example, argues that respect for existing property rights is bound up with respect for persons (1982, 959). Hume had made a similar argument regarding the importance of the connection between possession and personal identity (expectations and ourselves extended in time) (Waldron 2004, 27). Both property and individual development are merely instrumental, however: stages in the growth of social responsibility leading to *positive* freedom—the freedom to choose rationally and responsibly for the wider social good (Waldron 2004). Interestingly, socialist ideologies of private property, as discussed below, also justify it based on "development of human personality," but in its Marxist version, thus not for purposes of full participation in society but more narrowly based on needs.

Property as power is a more contested concept between the pre-communist and communist ideas of property. Property understood as a power relationship over persons and things (Macpherson 1978, 4; Gray and Gray 1999, 13; Alexander 1991, 276–77) is both a means of distributing power and of resistance against power, at all levels of society and vis-à-vis the state. As a power relationship, property embodies the coercion or exercise of power by the propertied against the property-less, the state as a non-neutral party (that specifies and enforces property rights), the self as a non-individualistic entity that arises from social relations, and the idea that property rights grow out of social relations that are highly contextualized (Munzer 2001, 4, 40–44; Singer 1987–1988, 655).[7] From this perspective, there is thus no single concept of property, or private property, rather all property systems are inherently complex and plural, they all have specific ideological effects (as Marx pointed out regarding "commodity fetishism"), and property as a social relationship of power is deeply interconnected with other types of power in society (Coombe and Herman 2005; Hann 1994, 1998; Verdery 2004).[8]

Echoing critiques of capitalist law and following in the footsteps of Soviet jurists, Romanian legal scholars and practitioners criticized bourgeois definitions of property as uniform, abstract, and formal, with no preoccupation for its subject or object. They particularly zoomed in on the class character of private property, as expected, and distinguished between the social and economic content of the right to private property over means of production versus property rights of small producers or craftsmen. Moreover, they critiqued definitions of property and the right to property as external, as an independent report, as only a metaphysical, legal illusion (Oprişan 1959, 203–4). Some scholars also attempted to distinguish between capitalist and socialist state property in the early 1950s, but that line of scholarship was abandoned by the 1960s (e.g., Hilsenrad 1950, 511–12; Beligrădeanu 1967, 77–82). Debates over differences between socialist and capitalist property never quite went away in Yugoslav revisionism. Revisionists claimed that socialist property resembled capitalist property, and that only if the means of production were in the property of a collective of producers was social property truly realized (Editor 1958, 391).

Ironically, the Marxist juggernaut attempted to dislodge the rather abstract, decontextualized, ahistorical assemblage of capitalist property with another abstract concept. There are fundamental ideological continuities between the two concepts, primarily the centrality of property, property as power, and labor as a legitimating value. The major differences are the extensive takings and the exceptionality of state property, which unintentionally, however, also bolstered the centrality of the property model.

Property as Power

In the Romanian socialist discourse, property was primarily a social relationship of power and only secondarily a right. Property, argued socialist doctrinaires, echoing the contemporary social relations school, was never about an object, but about the social relationships among people regarding objects—means of production and products (Oprişan 1959, 203–5). Property was power over the means of production—objects,[9] and a social relationship of production. The language itself is suggestive: in Romanian, one way of describing ownership is literally as mastery over something: "a deveni stăpân peste" [becoming master of].

Overall, Romanian authors reproduced the Soviet definitions of property (e.g., Venediktov, translated in Popescu 1952, 109; Oprişan 1959, 205). The Ministry of Justice textbook from 1959 explained that property in a broad sense was the totality of relations of production of society at a given point in time, while in a narrow understanding, property was an act an appropriation, a condition of production, a special relation between the individual/collectivity and the means of production (1959, 204).

As a relationship of power, property in the Marxist universe was the appropriation of someone's labor and thus fundamentally exploitative, promoting and sustaining inequality and egoism (Brenkert 1979, 127). Marx himself worked with a dual concept of property, drawing from Locke, Rousseau, Roman law (via Carl von Savigny) and Germanic law and history. This dual concept included an "economic" type of property (akin to Locke's or Rousseau's idea of appropriation), as well as a legal form of property—exclusive title to something, with "economic property" always historically preceding "legal property" (Cahan Axelrad 1994).

Defining property as the appropriation of someone's labor is key for identifying legal and ideological continuities, because it is possible to purge property of its associations with private exploitation and domination, while not challenging the essence of property as power, as control over things and relationships. This allows the property paradigm to stand and moreover bolsters the connected political project of gaining legitimacy for state property. Socialist legal scholars easily transferred capitalist attributes of private property onto socialist property, which they endowed with features such as permanence, indivisibility, exclusivity, inalienability, uniqueness, and absolute protection (Hilsenrad 1950, 513; Paşalega 1959, 45–47). Socialist property, whose owner was the "entire people," thus represented a "qualitative leap in the age-old notion of property" (Volanschi 1948, 412) and was "in the dominant position that is its due" (Diaconescu and Oprişan 1955, 714).

This understanding of socialist property sounds suspiciously like the abstract concept of bourgeois property critiqued by socialist writers—an abstract, eternal, almost mystical notion, with even the language acquiring metaphysical overtones: "socialist property is the holy, untouchable basis of our popular-democratic regime" (Rîpeanu 1955, 99). Even fundamental critiques had been turned on their head. Socialist writers had also targeted the origin of private property, and claimed that to the extent that the origin of private property, the act of first appropriation, was even partially due to force, the whole system was illegitimate. Violence on a societal scale was at the origin of socialist property, yet this violence was exalted as an outcome of historical and class justice.

Just like in capitalism, property as a concept, and not just (and more obviously) state property, was central in socialism: “property is key to any society, law and civil law are built on solving this issue” (Hilsenrad 1950, 509); “[o]f all real principal rights, the most important one is the right to property” (Oprişan 1959, 203); “defending property is key for all regimes” (Diaconescu and Oprişan 1955, 707). Moreover, the legal model of property was not challenged even in the case of personal property, as the content of the right was theoretically “absolute” (Nedelschi 1953, 347).

The centrality of property in socialism and its conflation with power are both key commonalities with the pre-communist property system. The values at the heart of capitalist ideas of property—freedom, labor, power, efficiency, development of human personality, justice—have also not disappeared in the socialist retelling. The right to personal property, for example, was “the material basis for the development of human personality for every working person, as well as at the basis of formation and development of new moral features, development and perfectibility of personal features of every person” (Lupulescu 1967, 21). With the exception of freedom, of property as protection, which suffered the biggest blow and was largely absent from the public transcript of property, all other property discourses are still part of the newly rearranged socialist property universe.

Property, Labor, and Exploitation

In the quest for ultimate modernity and justice, aiming to supersede all that bourgeois societies had achieved, socialist property was supposed to have solved ab initio, by its very existence, both questions of efficiency and social justice. It was meant to eliminate private exploitation—in Romanian known under the slogan “exploatarea omului de către om” [exploitation of man by man], position labor as the only legitimate base of acquiring private property, foster equality through limiting private property, and ultimately contribute to the development of human personality, distantly echoing Marx. It is therefore not surprising that the values most frequently discussed in the new ideological discourse of property were labor, exploitation, and social responsibility. Labor and exploitation were also at the heart of urban housing nationalization and of resistance to it because they held different meanings for the citizens and the regime.

In Romania as in the Soviet Union, labor was the essence of the socialist narrative of property, where it appeared in three distinct capacities. First, labor was the flip side of exploitation: the right over someone else's product and labor (per Venediktov, Voitinovici 1958, 3). Second, labor rewarded: workers, civil servants, small craftsmen, retirees, and intellectuals, for example, were officially not deprived of their property through nationalization because it had been obtained through labor (Solomon 1955, 320). Inheritance was also justified based on labor (e.g., Bratus 1949; Eliescu 1967; Stătescu and Stoenescu 1967). Third, labor not only rewarded, but was also an iron cage: "he who doesn't work doesn't eat," the effective guarantee for claiming rights such as housing and social security. Those who did not want to work simply had no place in society, they were free riders, "discomposed elements," parasites (Lenin) (Editor 1958, 393) to be punished accordingly (what mattered was not effective labor, but officially registered work).

Housing construction illustrates well the entanglement of property, labor, domination, and ultimately subjectivity. The regime allowed personal property over houses in order to ensure a permanent workforce in industry and the economy, and linked the acquisition of housing to workplace performance. Housing ownership obtained in this manner became "complete" and acquired its "autonomy" only after a certain period of time, however, and only if the employee continued to work for the state company that facilitated the acquisition of housing (Georgescu 1956, 396–97). Workers could buy housing built by the company on the basis of long-term credit contracts, but the ownership right was conditional: the owner had to continue to work with the company until at least half of the money was repaid, otherwise the apartment was lost and the money returned.

Enthusiastic lawyers came up with three different property rights in this common situation: a potential ownership right over the construction before the construction was finished, a conditional right of ownership while less than half of the apartment was paid off, and an autonomous (final, absolute) ownership right after half was paid off. In all three phases, the land underneath was allocated for use in perpetuity, a right considered to be "a novel creation of socialist law and society" (Georgescu 1956, 402–3). This is different from mortgages in bourgeois law, argued Georgescu, because of the deep link between the two aspects: work and property, and credit and property.

The three communist constitutions of Romania provide a chronological snapshot of the growing ideological centrality of labor and its complicated relationship with its doppelganger—"exploitation." The constitutional language signals the transition from private property based on exploitation—to be eliminated, to personal property based on labor—to be protected, with labor as a bulwark against exploitation. This ideological shift was met with mixed results, as housing nationalization shows, in part because the underlining model of property did not change, and in part because both "labor" and "exploitation" were differently interpreted by the regime and citizens.

The 1948 constitution still recognized and guaranteed private property and the right to inherit in general and promised "special protection" to private property earned through labor and savings (Article 8). Land belonged to "those who work it" (Article 9), a provision at the basis of the future socialist collectivization. Labor was at the basis of the economic structure and a duty of every citizen. The state supported all those who worked, defended them against exploitation, and raised their standard of living (article 12). The latter provision is the only place in the 1948 constitution where exploitation was directly mentioned. Takings were not justified directly in terms of exploitation, but as a means to advance the economic development of the country. At this point in time, when the new regime had just gained power, the state still protected "private initiative," but only when it served the general interest (Article 13).

The 1952 constitution, adopted only four years later after the bulk of nationalization and expropriation, was more extreme in both language and content. "Exploitation" was mentioned twice in the preamble: first, "the workers led by the Communist Party . . . are destroying the exploiting classes," and second, "the policy of the popular democratic state is to eliminate exploitation and build socialism." The language of "eliminating exploitation" or "destroying the power of the landowners and capitalists" showed up five times within the first fifteen articles. For example, the state protected small craftsmen's workshops, but only if they were not based on exploiting labor (Article 10). Article 15 was devoted to labor: "Labor is a duty and matter of honor for every citizen capable of work, based on the principle 'he who does not work, does not eat.' The Popular Republic of Romania widely implements the socialist principle 'from each based on his capacities, to each based on his work.'"

The 1952 constitution also introduced the concept of "personal property." Article 12 stated that "the right to personal property of the citizens of the Popular Republic of Romania over income and savings that originate from labor, over the family house and ancillary household, personal objects, as well as the right to inheritance, are defended by law." The right to personal property was based on socialist property and the constitution promised to limit the private-capitalist mode of production of chiaburi [kulak] households, private commercial enterprises, and small, not nationalized industrial enterprises based on the exploitation of salaried labor (Article 11). The second paragraph of this article included the unmitigated threat that the "popular-democrat state consistently pursues a policy of limiting and eliminating capitalist elements."

The 1965 constitution, the latest and most enduring of Romania's communist constitutions, signaled the end of the transition: Romania had a socialist economy, based on socialist property over means of production, where exploitation was forever abolished (the only place the word is mentioned), and labor was a duty of honor for every citizen of the country, to be rewarded based on quality and quantity (Article 5). Some private property was protected: that of peasants who could not form collectives and worked their own land, small craftsmen's workshops (Article 11), as well as personal property over income and savings, home and household objects, land and personal objects (Article 36). The 1965 constitution also guaranteed the right to inherit (Article 37), and established that expropriations of land and constructions had to be based on public interest and just compensation (Article 12).

The doctrinal niceties discussed here matter to the extent that they reflect the political significance of the underlying project (Markovits 1968, 2–3). Early communist jurists, ideologues, and constitutional drafters were engaged in a conscious process of building communism. In this process, the goal was not to destroy property as such, but to reconceptualize it, to denaturalize ideas of property as private property and ensconce instead a new normal—state and collective property. Extensive takings, in particular the nationalization of economy, were a necessary, but not sufficient step. Equally important was to change the meaning of ownership itself, yet this particular shift was constrained from the very beginning by the Marxist definition of private property as inherently exploitative.

Using a somewhat different framework of analysis, that of "translation" (Merry and Levitt 2009), the question was one of translating the concept of private property from a capitalist to a socialist locale. Like any good translation, its success depended on drawing from some familiar sources, perhaps reframing them, as well as bringing in new elements that would nonetheless still resonate with the intended audience. From this perspective, the communist project makes perfect sense: it aimed to maintain the meaning of property as power (control over things and relationships), as well as its centrality to economy and society, since they were indispensable factors in the naturalization of "socialist property" (state and collective property). Simultaneously, situating exploitation and labor as the two sides of the same coin ensured both a fundamental change of meaning and some continuity. The legal and institutional embodiment of this ideological repositioning was the introduction of the concept of personal property and the discarding of private property.

PRIVATE VERSUS PERSONAL PROPERTY

Labor and exploitation are central to the most important ideological move attempted by socialist jurists, namely distinguishing private-capitalist property from socialist personal property. This was not a specifically Romanian endeavor. In the Soviet Union, the outright abolition of private property and inheritance in 1918 was partially reversed in 1921 and 1922, but the 1936

Soviet constitution talked about personal, not private property. Article 10 of the 1936 Soviet constitution established that Soviet citizens had the right to personal property, which was distinguished from private property yet fulfilled a similar function, namely, as incentive for the workers. "Personal property" in the USSR was property that was used by its owner for his person and family only, without employing hired labor—it had strictly a consumption character (Malfliet 1986, 85–86). The objects of personal property were income from work and savings, dwelling houses and subsidiary household economy, household furniture and utensils, and articles of personal use and convenience (Kucherov 1962, 385).

Two major developments took place in 1948. First, Soviet citizens gained permission to buy or build residential houses as their personal property, to help deal with the postwar housing crisis. These houses were limited to one or two stories with one or two apartments of not more than five rooms. Houses could be built within or outside the cities, and plots of land were allocated for use in perpetuity. Based on this statute, about 30 percent of the entire dwelling space of 781,000,000 square meters was the personal property of Soviet citizens as of January 1, 1959 (Kucherov 1962, 385). Second, Soviet jurists began to theorize personal property, an explicit admission of its official status. Venediktov's theory of the deduced character of personal property stated that personal property developed from socialist property, more specifically the income at the basis of personal property was a reward for labor performed in socialist state enterprises. Personal property had a clear function: as a material incentive for workers and peasants to work harder, more efficiently, and increase productivity (Malfliet 1986, 82–83). It was also tightly connected with the socialist principle "to everyone according to his work." It lost its personal character and became private property, thus forbidden, if used as a source of unearned income (Kucherov 1962, 389).

Romanian jurists adopted most of this basic understanding. According to them, there were four key differences between personal and private property. First, private property was exploitative, while personal property was consumptive. The right to private property encapsulated the "exploitative essence of bourgeois property," a single concept that bundled under the same umbrella property over means of production, property of peasants and small craftsmen/traders, and individual property over objects of consumption: "The universal, abstract character of bourgeois property hides its class character, its exploitative character" (Fekete 1954, 199). Capitalist property, which was still acknowledged by the 1952 constitution of Romania, included chiaburi [well off peasants, kulaks], small companies, and non-nationalized industrial ones based on exploiting salaried labor. By contrast, personal property concerned only objects of consumption and could not be exploitative in character, thus could not include means of production.

Second, private property originated in exploitation, whereas personal property originated in labor. Third, the right to personal property derived from and was based on the right to socialist property. Labor was at the basis of both socialist and personal property and was the guarantee for the achievement of all rights and freedoms. The economic liquidation of the bourgeoisie and landowners through various takings meant that workers and peasants became owners [stăpâni] over the products of their work and over the means of production, which formed socialist property. As the editors of *New Justice* eagerly explained, freeing the masses from exploitation was the main freedom brought by the socialist revolution and constituted the basis of all constitutional rights and freedoms. The growth of socialist property—based on everyone's labor, it is understood—was thus essential, since it ensured the achievement of all these rights and freedoms (1958, 389–91).

Labor was the one and only legitimate basis for the acquisition of personal property. Personal property was first and foremost property over the results/products of one's own work and was connected to the principle "from each according to his capacity, to each according to his work" (Bratus 1949, 141). Personal property could not be opposed to socialist property, to which it was indissolubly linked (Nedelschi 1954, 182–84).

Fourth, the right to private property was not a relationship between owner and thing, as described by bourgeois authors, but one between people with regard to things, an exploitative relationship. By contrast, the right to personal property truly represented a relationship between owner and object (Nedelschi 1953, 342–43; Ministry of Justice 1959, 222–26). This is yet another way in which the basic conceptualization of ownership as power over a thing was preserved in the communist discourse of property.

In sum, the core of the right to personal property was power over objects obtained through labor and whose destination was exclusively consumption. Accordingly, the right to personal property in the Popular Republic of Romania was defined as that "property right that belongs to workers, derives from socialist property and is inseparably linked to it, whose objects are only goods of individual consumption and which cannot become a source for appropriating others' labor" (Nedelschi 1954, 185). Personal property could not be used to exploit other people, according to the basic principles of socialism (Lupulescu 1967, 23–24). This is the main sticking point here, namely, the exploitative potential of objects of consumption—whether and how they can become means of production. This turned out to be a special problem for houses, which are simultaneously homes—means of consumption, and assets—means of production.

Romanian jurists were at pains to stress that labor could never become exploitation, for example, landlords could not make a profit, but could only use rental income to maintain and repair their property (Solomon 1955,

320–21). Houses could never be used for anything else but living, and only one house per nuclear family was allowed, even if others were obtained through donation or similar means (following decisions of the Soviet Supreme Tribunal). This did not mean that any income not obtained through personal labor was forbidden, only if it was obtained directly or indirectly from exploiting others. There was a fine line here: for example, it was permissible to rent a room in a personal house, but not to build a whole house just as rental property (Nedelschi 1953, 349).

It was not entirely clear whether personal and private property could coexist except during the transition from capitalism to socialism, or whether one could simply morph into the other. Lawyers who directly used the term "private property," used it interchangeably with "personal property" or just renamed private property, personal property, were criticized for having misunderstood it all. Private and personal property, they were told, could not logically coexist once communism is achieved: once exploitation and thus commodification are eliminated, objects of consumption cannot become means of production (Fekete 1954, 200–3). For houses, of course, this was questionable, since the partial etatization of the housing stock allowed for the continued existence, albeit limited, of a housing market. Houses and apartments, the most important objects of personal property in socialism, never lost their dual character (homes and assets), and consequently the legal ideology of personal property was also internally contradictory.

The transformation of private into personal property had practical and ideological goals. In Romania as in the Soviet Union, it was a way to alleviate the housing crisis in the post–Second War World context, as well as a reward and incentive for labor. There were also two legal ideological goals: first, to preserve the utility of capitalist legal concepts for socialist purposes; and second, to bolster the legitimacy of the regime and the sweeping transformations it brought by delegitimizing property based on exploitation, while simultaneously protecting property based on labor. The result, unsurprisingly, was mixed: personal property continued to be regulated by the same civil code provisions as private property in all its aspects (Article 480 of the civil code, in force since 1864), while limitations on its object elevated houses to a special place, as houses were the most important piece of property one could own. Moreover, by defining personal property as the link between owner and object, primarily houses, socialist law inadvertently reinforced the link between property and personhood.

Labor as the key ideological and moral value at the core of personal property in socialism provided continuity with bourgeois ideas of property, particularly Lockean theories—property as an incentive for labor (exemplified by the socialist principle of repartition according to work). As a concrete example, each company had a part of its profits set aside through the "director/

CEO's fund" for various employee-oriented expenses (a concept copied from the USSR). Part of the justification was that "knowing that part of the profit will be used for their benefit, employees will work better, too" (Hilsenrad 1949, 778–80). Labor also provided ideological continuity with personality theories—the end result of ownership was the socialist person who fully participated in civic life (in Stalin's words, the goal was to make all "learned and cult people," quoted in Nedelschi 1953, 340). Property in early communism was thus based on ideas of social responsibility, it was the nexus between needs—labor—socialist consciousness and personhood. As such, the narrow scope of personal property dovetailed with a rather puritanical concept of socialist personhood that revolved around needs, avoiding exploitation, and being a responsible owner. Surprisingly, although equality hovers large over the socialist ideological landscape, it is rarely mentioned explicitly in connection with private property. Since private property is defined as exploitation and inequality, its elimination, it is assumed, will lead to equality. Equality, rather than equity, played a huge role in housing policies.

Personal property was thus meant to satisfy the individual needs of the people, specifically "citizens' material and cultural needs," again following the Soviet lead (Nedelschi 1953, 344, 347). "Needs" remained a wide-open category and as urban housing nationalization shows, one that was narrowly interpreted by the authorities. Needs and exploitation, one narrowly, the other expansively interpreted, squeezed personal property significantly. For example, the rights to dispose of and use one's property were restricted if an owner exploited his property not in order to satisfy his material and cultural needs, but to become "rich without work" (Nedelschi 1953, 142).

As a social institution, the right to personal property was part of the superstructure, expressing the "harmonious union of personal and social interests" ["îmbinarea armonioasă a intereselor personale cu cele obştești"] (Lupulescu 1967, 21; Nedelschi 1954, 197), and imposed duties on the owner, such as maintaining the house (Nedelschi 1953, 350). This is not unusual, of course. Germany is often noted as a model in this regard, as its constitutional right to property includes the "social obligation of ownership" (Article 14). The right to property is not viewed as a matter of protecting subjective preferences, or from the perspective of the night-watchman state, but from a moral dimension, which implicates the values of human dignity and self-governance (close to Radin's conceptions) (Kommers 1997; Alexander 1999, 103). The social responsibility basis of property in socialism pervaded areas as diverse as housing policies or installment purchases, as well as the socialist property field, for example, the social use of socialist companies' profits.

Attempting to change the meaning of private property and replace it with "personal property" was an important step in reconceptualizing the very concept of property. Yet significant continuities with bourgeois understandings of property remain: first, the continued conflation of property and power; second, the persistent centrality of property; third, establishing labor as the key legitimating factor for both private and state property. Takings and elevating state property to the top of the property hierarchy, while by no means negligible, were also achieved based on the careful translation of bourgeois concepts into socialist terms. Ultimately, personal property can be considered simply a subtype of private property, much narrower, but nonetheless not significantly different, because of the ideological significance of labor and the continuity in the legal regime of personal property (Article 480 civil code). Uncritically adopting the categories created by the object of study—the communist regime—is also a factor.

SURVIVING PROPERTY: RESISTANCE AND CONTINUITIES IN THE INSTITUTION OF PROPERTY

Major restrictions on private property, the steep climb of state property, and the introduction of personal property are great successes in the quest to reconceptualize property. They are not, however, the end of the property story in communism. The legal and mental map of property inscribed in the 1864 civil code and continuously applied post-1945 reveals significant continuities between the pre-communist and communist concepts of property, as does the preservation of the real estate registration system.

Ownership is one element in the institution of property. Others, such as acquisitive prescription, possession, *rei vindicatio,* and superficies, raised difficulties for Romanian legal practitioners and theoreticians during early communism. Their jurisprudential and case law struggles showcase the mutual adaptation of socialism and property and the continued hold of pre-communist concepts of property. The more technical a legal issue was, the more likely it was that it would escape the communist storm relatively untouched. Although the focus throughout the book is on private property in connection with housing, not land or commercial enterprises, property ideologies and the legal structure of private property are not inherently limited to houses.

Acquisitive Prescription

Acquisitive prescription (*usucapio*), the civil law cousin of adverse possession, is a primary mode of acquiring ownership or other real rights over immovables through the passage of time. All things can be thus acquired, except those that are not in the civil circuit (movables are subject to immediate acquisition through possession, based on Article 1909 civil code). At the core of acquisitive prescription (Article 1890 and following of the civil code) is "useful possession" within the prescribed time period. Useful possession means continuous, undisturbed, public, and exercised for himself/herself (the possessor) (Article 1847 civil code). Title and just cause determine time to ownership. If the possessor believes in good faith that the title was issued by the owner, and good faith is presumed (sufficient to have existed at the moment of acquiring possession), time to ownership is ten to twenty years (short acquisitive prescription). If possession was based on no title, regardless of good or bad faith, the time limit to ownership is thirty years. The effect of acquisitive prescription is retroactive ownership for the possessor (Brădeanu 1956; Bărbieru 1961; Ministry of Justice 1959, 250–27).

This outline of acquisitive prescription is based only on the provisions of the 1864 civil code and their exegesis by communist legal scholars and practitioners. It is virtually indistinguishable from pre-communist (Hamangiu et al. Vol. II, 148–85), or for that matter postcommunist descriptions of *usucapio*. This is important both in itself, as it shows significant continuity in the area of property, and for the ideology that it embodies and transmits, namely, that ownership is the ultimate goal, the supreme right in the property pantheon. The continuities are not really surprising given the authors and their legal training. Salvator Brădeanu, for example, was a civil law star in Romania. Like almost all other top legal scholars and lawyers in Romania, he went to law school in Paris, obtained his doctorate in law in 1932 with a dissertation on inheritance, and as a policy-maker in the Ministry of Justice reorganized the land registry and geodesy systems. He also wrote landmark treatises on the real estate registry system and civil law, was a law school professor, and a researcher at the Institute for Legal Studies (the only institution dedicated exclusively to legal research in the country). Bărbieru was a judge at the Cluj Tribunal.

What type of difficulties related to acquisitive prescription occurred in court? One issue, not resolved uniformly by courts, was whether an heir could acquire based on short acquisitive prescription. Most courts said yes for good-faith heirs, because the heir title was considered title for purposes of acquisitive prescription. Another question was whether two or more possessions could be joined to achieve acquisitive prescription, and again courts answered mostly positively. Possession had to be useful, and there were different ways of counting, depending on whether both possessions were of the same or different type (good faith vs. bad faith) (Brădeanu 1956, 1445–46).

An example of acquisitive prescription in practice is a case from Baia Mare (Northern Transylvania). The plaintiffs and the Barbu family each bought half of one plot of land in 1937. When the land was divided, however, the Barbus got more than half of the land. The defendants bought this plot of land from Barbu in 1945 and used it since. The unequal size of the parcels was discovered when a cadastral engineer measured the properties in 1958. Consequently, the plaintiffs—initial buyers of the smaller plot, brought suit.

The Baia Mare regional tribunal (civil decision no 35/January 14, 1959) reasoned that the defendants bought the larger plot of land from a non-*dominus* in good faith and used it for thirteen years in plain sight of the plaintiffs. The possession was thus continuous, not interrupted, not disturbed, public and as owners, none of which was contested. The defendants thus became owners through acquisitive prescription.

Published in *Popular Legality* in 1960, with a dissenting opinion and an explanatory note, this case is technically uncomplicated, but it is notable for three reasons: the very ordinariness of the dispute; the existence of a separate opinion in the case—not an ordinary occurrence; and the existence of the explanatory note, by one of the judges, in the published version. The judge who dissented argued there was no just title, while the explanatory note, authored by one of the Baia Mare regional tribunal judges, reaffirmed the decision and discussed how the real issue in the case was the conflict of laws in time (specifically, whether the civil code or the real estate registration law was applicable).[10] No word or sentence indicate that the larger social and political context was fundamentally different or revolutionary. On the contrary, this case reads as if property law is a closed system that exists in an ahistorical, acontextual bubble, where judges are adept practitioners of mechanical jurisprudence. As other cases in the civil law field discussed throughout this chapter suggest, however, this can also be interpreted as a very passive, unintentional form of judicial resistance—judicial inertia, often in tandem with doctrinal resistance.

State property could not be acquired through acquisitive prescription, based on the principle that there could be no change from a higher to a lower form of property, that is, from state to private or cooperative (Georgescu 1956, 792; Brădeanu 1956, 1453; Paşalega 1959, 46; Ministry of Justice 1959, 256). This rule is also not unusual, adverse possession, for example, usually does not operate against state property, either. The state, however, could acquire property through acquisitive prescription. Both cooperatives and individuals were prohibited from using acquisitive prescription against the state. In principle, cooperatives could use it against another cooperative, although there were too many legal and practical obstacles against that in a planned economy (Brădeanu 1956, 1453–35).

Romanian courts protected ownership in principle even when acquisitive prescription operated. In a decision signaling doctrinal resistance to any deep changes in property law, the Supreme Tribunal held in 1953 that regardless of how long the owner was passive, he was not degraded from pursuing his ownership claim in court, and the property right did not simply lapse through the passage of time. However, that did not mean that acquisitive prescription was not possible (Civil Division decision no 539/July 4, 1953, in Paşalega 1959, 40–41).

How did communist jurists justify the existence and utility of acquisitive prescription, and was it any different from capitalist discussions of the issue? The Ministry of Justice textbook on the principles of socialist law stated that the utility and function of *usucapio* were "to inscribe stability, security and trust to *de facto* situations." Acquisitive prescription was meant to impede situations that could endanger legal and economic security, and to confirm the presumption of indifference on the part of the owner (1959, 256). The effect of acquisitive prescription was thus to endorse a title that was not valid (Bărbieru 1961, 123). Stability, security, trust, reconciling *de facto* and *de jure* situations, and punishing the neglectful owner have been the main justifications for the institution of *usucapio* since Roman law and still are in both civil and common-law systems. Not surprisingly, the underlining value system is also familiar: reinforcing the connection between labor and property, rewarding the productive use of land/immovable, and even protecting personhood interests (e.g., Dwyer and Menell 1999). Like adverse possession, acquisitive prescription diminishes legal and economic insecurity through reducing the risk of litigation, which generally aims to protect the market. Presumably, this was not one of the issues considered by the communist legal scholars writing about acquisitive prescription but is rather an example of the hold of unquestioned assumptions about property in law. Since the authors are highly skilled legal experts in the matter, it is difficult to believe they did not understand the implications of their position, specifically its potential to undermine the communist project.

Legal certainty was at the heart of the importance of acquisitive prescription in the personal real estate transcription system, since it was the only absolute proof of ownership. In the Transylvanian system of real estate registration, its utility was more restricted because the registry has evidentiary as well as substantive value for the acquisition and transfer of property. However, even in the latter system, there were some situations when acquisitive prescription was possible, for example, when the title holder possessed in good faith for ten years on the basis of a bad title: "this is called the convalescence of the title, meaning that the passage of time cleanses the title of its vices and the appearance of property becomes real" (Brădeanu 1956, 1447–48). The language in this paragraph is striking: the property title is compared with a sick body that is getting cured through the passage of time, and consequently becomes real. If, as Conley and O'Barr argue, much of the work of language is done in the nonreferential realm, including constructing, reflecting, and resisting social structure (2005, 147), the paragraph above suggests that communist legal scholars remained deeply entrenched in ways of imagining and discussing property that still placed ownership on a legal pedestal, romanticized it, and was overly formalist.

Acquisitive prescription could appear to weaken ownership, as the security and exclusivity of ownership are sacrificed for other policy goals, such as legal certainty and economic efficiency (Van der Walt 2009, 187). Surprisingly, communist scholars and practitioners did not attempt to appropriate it for purposes of subverting property and building socialism, but in fact discussed its uses and justifications squarely within the bourgeois property paradigm, indicating the importance attached to ownership and to *usucapio* itself as a deeply pragmatic and utilitarian institution.[11]

Possession

Possession is a distinct legal category from ownership in civil law systems, including the Romanian one during socialism. Even more striking perhaps than acquisitive prescription, Romanian jurists from the 1950s drew clear lines of continuity with the past and the French legal system and were at pains to point out distinctions from the Soviet system. The Soviets rejected possession as a bourgeois concept, while Romanian authors staunchly defended its utility (e.g., Georgescu 1956, 772, 777–78). Some Soviet scholars criticized possession for implying a relationship between person and thing. Nothing more is said on this topic in Romanian law reviews, and it is clear from the writing that Romanian scholars saw nothing of interest on this topic in Soviet scholarship.

The notion of possession in the civil law of Romania, explained attorney Georgescu in a landmark 1956 article, is based on the French civil code model, which created a subjectivist conception of possession. Possession had two elements: the material act of power over a thing and *animus domini*—the subjective element, the intention to possess. The Romanian civil code, Georgescu further explained, included in some cases the objective conception of possession, the corpus only, for example, Article 676 code of civil procedure, which gave the option of possessory action to custodians. This included both corporeal and non-corporeal things, as well as possession of a right. Scholarly debates zoomed in on whether possession and ownership were exercised over a thing or over the right to it, thus openly contradicting the official definitions of property as social relationships of production, and lapsing into more familiar property theory.[12] The Romanian Supreme Tribunal held that possession must be understood in the "normal and general way" as "effective power over a thing or of using a right, exercised by the owner directly or indirectly based on consent" (civil decision 2430/December 10, 1955).

Possession, Georgescu further explained, had a double nature: on its own and as a constitutive element of other rights, such as ownership, landlord-tenant relations, and so on. Possession as a legal institution and a right produced its own legal effects and had its own defense mechanisms—the possessory action, which could be raised by the possessor against all those who disturbed her possession. Possessory actions were a simplified, "fast," and "energetic" defense of possession, particularly in areas where there was no real estate registry system and there was a need for the "diabolical proof" of ownership title, that is, proof of continuity of valid title during the period of acquisitive prescription (Georgescu 1956, 779).

Even more interesting from a legal continuity perspective is the genealogy of possessory action terminology: the term "possessory action" was used in the 1907 legislation, then replaced in 1948 by "request concerning possession" (article 674 code of civil procedure) and "possessory claim" (Article 676). Regardless of name, possessory actions were divided according to type of disturbance: simple versus violent. Simple disturbance also included new construction, which in the French system is a separate action. The legal concepts as of 1956 were "action for disturbance of possession" and "action for reinstatement in possession" (Georgescu 1956, 780).

Possessory actions are real immovable actions (e.g., Georgescu 1956, 780–81; Hamangiu 1928, 2002, Vol. I, 595–600) that could be initiated by the possessor (Article 674 code of civil procedure), which in pre-communism included the owner and all other right holders (e.g., use, abitation, etc.). Standing was expanded after 1948 to include easement holders (if the easement was continuous and obvious), and the keeper of a thing for his own interest (Georgescu 1956, 780–81). The extent to which possession continued to be a cherished right even under socialism is further revealed by the discussion on standing: scholars and practitioners wrangled with the question whether the possessor with non-exclusive or precarious possession had standing to sue. The practicing attorney cited here argued for extensive standing rules, even for vitiated possession or common possession, which would allow each co-possessor separate cause of action. The "nude" owner also had cause of action, independently of the user or usufructus owner, as did the tenants, although not against owners (Georgescu 1956, 782–86).

The statute of limitations for possessory actions was a year from the date of disturbance or dispossession. The plaintiff had to prove possession for one year before the disturbance happened, and if the disturbance was violent, for one day.[13] Disturbance of possession was defined as intentional, *de facto* or *de jure*, and had to be distinguished from simple disturbance of material use, the latter giving rise only to damages. Finally, the violence could be physical or moral, although in practice courts asked for some kind of material violence. Possessory actions did not have res judicata for petitory actions (actions that involve title), but the opposite was true. Another question was whether possessory and petitory actions cumulated. French law forbade it, but the Romanian system had no specific legal provision, and socialist law "did not want to insist on a formalist distinction between possession and ownership," so this could be an option, argued Georgescu (1956, 788–89). Again, we see a very pragmatic approach that took advantage of ideological openings to preserve the past.

Delving into doctrinal discussions of possession during early communism reveals that this was not about recreating property or even about positioning socialism at the core of possession, but about adaptation and continuity: possessory actions, similarly to pre-communist times, were considered useful because they offered a quick resolution and did not involve title.[14] Most possessory actions originated from disputes over private rural property, collectives, and private and personal property, and overall there were significant differences from Soviet theory and practice (Georgescu 1956, 793–96).

Courts protected both possession and ownership. An example is a 1955 decision of the Supreme Tribunal that held that the success of a possessory action over land did not automatically lead to the demolition of constructions erected by the losing defendant on the land: "The possessory action aims to end cases of dispossession or disturbance of possession and to protect possession as a *de facto* state that expresses real rights." The plaintiff did not have the obligation to prove ownership or other property right, which could be difficult. Buildings erected on the land (a small wooden house here) belonged to a different property category and their ownership was itself protected (decision no 400/March 25, 1955).[15]

Overall, socialist jurists valued possession because it bestowed "legitimate appearance to ownership and other property rights," it played "the role of appearance, exterior coverage or presumption for all rights" (Georgescu 1956, 772), and generally it created a presumption of ownership, especially for movables (Brădeanu 1956, 1143 fn). The defense of possession through possessory actions eliminated any illegal disturbance or deprivation of possession and forced the dispossessed to use the law, rather than personal justice. However, the right to possess could never protect a right based on the "real title" [ownership]. By comparison, possession was "nothing more than a mere manifestation, façade," yet at the same time, possession was stronger than other property rights (Georgescu 1956, 775–79).

I presented possession in such detail here because it showcases very well the centrality of property, the hierarchical structure of property in the civil law system, and because socialism seemed to come into the picture only somewhat incidentally. Possession was described in very strong terms and the lengthy discussion of possessory actions suggests images of possession as a castle that needed to be defended and protected (structurally through the all-embracing standing rules). Possession could also be "disturbed"—the opposite, of course, was a pure concept of possession that was continuous, public, transparent, secure, and so on. Possession was also clearly placed between full, titled ownership and all other rights in the property hierarchy, where it played double duty: on the one hand, it acted like ownership, building the legal fiction of ownership, embodying ownership, and as such enjoying significant protection, arguably even more than ownership itself—as the Supreme Tribunal decision presented above shows, the relaxed procedural requirements for possessory actions made it the first line of defense of ownership itself; on the other hand, it reinforced the division between ownership and other property rights—at the end of the day, it is title that separates true ownership from everything else, confirming ownership's place at the pinnacle of property rights. In addition, title and title registration play key roles in reinforcing the centrality of property.

Rei Vindicatio

One of the most important ways of gauging the place of property in any legal system is to examine its legal defense mechanisms. In the Romanian civil law system—pre- and postcommunist, as well as communist, this is the *rei vindicatio* action [acţiunea în revendicare] for regaining lost ownership: the claim of the non-possessive owner against the possessive nonowner (Paşalega 1959, 40), a "typical civil law tool, developed through doctrine and case law" (Diaconescu and Oprişan 1955, 709). At stake was the ownership title (it is a petitory real action), as well as stopping all those who hindered the owner in his exercise of property (also a negatory action) (Nedelschi 1954, 188). Only the title holder has standing against illegal possessors who "state they will not abide by the general obligation to abstain from any violation of the property right of the owner" (Diaconescu and Oprişan 1955, 709).

The focus on title indicates the victory of the absolutist language of the property paradigm, with titled ownership at the top of the property hierarchy. It is virtually indistinguishable from pre-communist as well as other civil law descriptions of *rei vindicatio* (e.g., Hamangiu et al. 1929 Vol. II, 61–71), acontextual, and ahistorical.[16] It sets the general rules, which socialism tried to adapt to. Although *rei vindicatio* is the key legal action for the defense of ownership rights, it is not specifically regulated by the civil code, but was developed by judges and jurists over time. Romanian socialist jurists never even considered disposing of it.

The key questions in cases of *rei vindicatio* are the statute of limitations, proof of ownership, and the good faith of the possessor as a defense. According to the civil code, there is no statute of limitations for the owner to start the action (ownership does not lapse through the passage of time);[17] the owner/plaintiff must prove title; and the nonowner possessor/defendant can defend herself is she possessed in good faith. Socialist jurists explained all these elements in great detail in their writings, yet they made no connection between the ideological assumptions at the core of *rei vindicatio* and socialist goals and principles. For example, the statute of limitations rule encompasses the ideology of permanence and universality of bourgeois private property, as time does not erase ownership. In socialism, only state property is considered permanent in the same way, yet *rei vindicatio* applied across the board for private and state owners, reinforcing these ideas for property as a general concept, and hence the hegemony of property as capitalist property.

Diaconescu and Oprişan, the latter also an author for the property law sections of the 1959 Ministry of Justice textbook, set out to explain in 1955 how *rei vindicatio* was not just a legal remedy for private citizens, but also a tool for defending socialist state property. The goal itself—applying a fundamental institution of bourgeois property law to socialist property—determined the tone for the rest of the discussion and more broadly for debates among Romanian property law experts at the time. The goal, in brief, was to bring state property and collective property under the *rei vindicatio* umbrella. Socialist jurists determined the adapted rules for defending socialist property through *rei vindicatio*: there was no statute of limitations (no different from the general rule), there was a presumption of title for the state (contrary to the general rule, where the plaintiff had to prove title), and there was no good faith and acquisitive prescription defense for the respondent (Paşalega 1959, 51; Diaconescu and Oprişan 1955, 710–19).

The presumption of title for the state was borrowed from Soviet law, where this presumption covered everything except personal property and household objects. The goal of reversing the burden of proof was to avoid putting the state in a position of having to prove its ownership, "which is difficult in our civil law." Diaconescu and Oprişan found legal support for this position in art. 1169 civil code (ironically, freedom of contract!) combined with the socialist principle of the active role of the judge (1955, 715–17). Lawsuits initiated by cooperatives or collectives fell more closely within the normal rules for *rei vindicatio*, as there was no presumption of ownership working in their favor and acquisitive prescription was a defense unless the respondent was a private person (Paşalega 1959, 54).

The interesting part, however, concerned standing rules. Some scholars argued that socialist organizations could use *rei vindicatio* against each other, even though they were not title holders but merely had the right to manage state property (Diaconescu and Oprişan 1955, 712–14). This raises an obvious question: why use *rei vindicatio* at all in these cases as opposed to arbitration or other rules? In other words, why use a civil law procedure that reinforces the sanctity of property for a dispute over possession within the state? It is discussions such as these, over apparently minor and technical points, that clarify just how hegemonic the civil law concept of property remained.

To the extent that socialist organizations used *rei vindicatio*, how did they prove their factual "ownership"? In other words, how useful was the presumption of ownership for the state? As it turns out, not very useful, even for the authors of the official Ministry of Justice textbook, who argued that a state institution had to prove that the good was listed in its inventory, that it was no longer in its possession, and that the item claimed was identical to the one listed (1959, 245). Sensibly, the company lawyer Paşalega noticed that this amounted in reality to proof of ownership and suggested instead that all the plaintiff should have to do was prove that the item was listed in its inventory, while the respondent needed to prove title (1959, 50).

In practice, courts dealt with *rei vindicatio* cases as they always had, within the confines of the civil code. In a 1950 decision from the Suceava general trial court, for example, a panel composed of one judge and two lay judges held that a good-faith buyer from a fictitious heir was protected from a *rei vindicatio* action started by the real heir, whose only recourse was to sue the false heir for unjust enrichment. The case itself was rather colorful: Mrs. Adam died with no legitimate heirs, leaving behind a house. Mrs. Barbu faked her will and took possession of the house. She, in turn, was murdered, and her heirs (the false heirs) consequently sold the house to Constantin and David (valid contract). The real heir of Mrs. Adam eventually showed up and sued all of them, claiming the house. His *rei vindicatio* suit was rejected by the court for three reasons: first, he had seemed to abandon the inheritance; second, fairness—Constantin and David did not know the real situation and were in complete good faith; and third, the need to preserve the security of social relationships formed through the contract.[18] This is a standard property versus contract dispute, once again reasoned and resolved strictly within the confines of bourgeois civil law.

The structure, uses, debates, and language surrounding *rei vindicatio* during early communism in Romania tell the same story as possession and acquisitive prescription: the legal universe was rooted in the civil code and socialism adapted. While this may appear to benefit the socialist state above all else, for example, through the absolute protection of state property, there were also unintended consequences: the realm of property, its internal structure, its rhetoric and daily operation carried on, without much fuss or attention. *Rei vindicatio*, for example, continued to be seen as a fortification in the battle to protect ownership against all invasions.

Superficies and "Use in Perpetuity"

The basic map of property discussed so far has not changed since the civil code was adopted in Romania more than a century and a half ago. Yet during communism, some property rights gained more prominence than others. One of them was superficies—the protection of ownership over a construction or plantation on someone else's land. The very existence of superficies was mired in legal clashes. Although a Roman law institution, it is not specifically mentioned by the 1864 Romanian civil code. The Hamangiu treatise (pp. 311–13) mentions pre-Second World War scholarly debates over the existence of superficies in Romanian law, which continued unabated during communism. Superficies was expressly mentioned by the 1939 real estate registry statute, as well as by Decree 167/1958 on statute of limitations. Although rarely used before communism, both pre-communist and communist courts recognized superficies as a property right (Brădeanu 1957, 39).

The construction owner (superficiary) had the right to use the land, while the land owner had the right to compensation or payment for the use of the land, unless otherwise specified. In another small instance of property ideology at work, if the superficies was created *ex legem*, money had to be paid for using the land, otherwise it was considered unjust enrichment for the user (Brădeanu 1957, 45–46). The superficiary had to observe the conditions in the act establishing the superficies as well as the destination of the land, while the owner of the land had to allow and guarantee the peaceful use of the land during the superficies. The owner of the land could not unilaterally end the superficies—as a real right, it did not disappear through lack of use (Ministry of Justice 1959, 261–63; Brădeanu 1957, 38; Vurdea 1960, 1076–80).

Superficies is a wonderful example of thrusting communism in the civil law straitjacket. Despite rhetorical noise to the contrary, the property paradigm deployed by communist legal scholars and practitioners working on superficies was rooted in bourgeois universality and abstractness. The main question they wrestled with was whether superficies was the appropriate legal status for private housing on land that belonged to the state—for example, housing built with credit given by the state, with the land underneath to be used in perpetuity (established by Council of Ministers Decrees 4015/1953, 493/1954, 1099/1955). Other common cases of superficies during communism included members of cooperatives building on cooperative land, and spouses building together on land that belonged to just one of them. The state could also become superficiary in cases where it erroneously took over abandoned property under Decree 111/1951. When the land was returned by courts, the owner of the land could not ask for the construction erected in the meantime to be demolished, but had only the right to ask for compensation for the use of the land (Vurdea 1960, 1080). It is unclear how common such cases were. Brădeanu cynically suggested expropriating the land in such cases, to avoid legal complications (1957, 43–44).

Superficies was the most commonly seen property right in socialism, after ownership, certainly as late as 1960 (e.g., Vurdea 1960, 1079). By the 1970s and 1980s, other prominent civilians, such as Stătescu, came to consider superficies too weak, and instead argued that there was full ownership over the construction combined with eternal use of land.[19] Yet other property scholars argued that the constitutional protection of personal property and the various decrees encouraging personal housing construction created a property right over housing, "indissolubly and eternally linked to the accessory right for eternal use of the land underneath." This was extended to housing built without credit from the state. The justification was that even though the Roman law rule was accession—land is the principal, house is accessory, accessory follows the legal regime of the principal—in this case there was a reversal, "otherwise the personal right over housing could not exist, it would be swallowed by the state's property right over land" (Georgescu 1956, 396).

The reasons for this doctrinal shift are unclear, but the result is not: while superficies was a real immovable right, it could be eternal or temporary; by contrast, guaranteed use in perpetuity of the land as an accessory to house/apartment ownership came as close to full ownership over house and land as possible in a communist system, at least formally. This was not lost on communist policy-makers. In July 1957, the regional administration of Timişoara proposed to the Council of Ministers to amend Decree 4015/1953 (regarding construction of housing on the basis of cooperation among dwellers and construction of individual housing with state credits) to allow registration in the land registry of the right to use land in perpetuity "in order to eliminate any hesitation people might have regarding how long the right of use in perpetuity might last and encourage constructions."[20] Whether an act of scholarly defiance or mere legalistic nitpicking, this is yet another piece in the larger puzzle of the mutual adaptation of socialism and property that simultaneously showcases the difficulty of unmaking the hegemony of private property.

The Real Estate Registration System

Nothing quite captures the subtle ways channeling the survival of the institution of private property like the real estate registration system. *Cartea Funciară* (the land book), commonly known as CF, beautifully reveals how inscribing the materiality of houses preserved pre-communist ideas of property in law and society because it created an individualized, highly specific record of houses and their legal lives that emphasized ownership, the nexus of property and personhood, and the importance of security and stability of property rights. The CF system shows that thinking about property only as rights, rather than in material terms as well, means that we "lose sight of the ways in which propertied practices and representations are often caught up in some very practical, embodied activities" (Blomley 1998, 573).

We need to embrace a property conception that has both spatial and temporal dimensions, as struggles over property are both representational and material (Blomley 1998, 568; Verdery 2003; Underkuffler 2003; Clark 1982). The study of both histories and geographies of property seems particularly important for societies in transition not only because "socially produced space is saturated with power relations" (Blomley 1998, 569), but also because such histories and geographies make it more difficult to build ideological narratives of property that silence or overemphasize specific aspects, or that lapse into static conceptualizations of property and societies.

Throughout communism, there were two types of real estate registration systems in Romania: the CF for Banat and Transylvania, and the civil code system of real estate publicity for the rest (Wallachia and Moldavia). The CF system has been used in Banat and Transylvania for over two hundred years, and has been expanded to the entire country post-1989. The system has a long history, having been known to exist in Austria, for example, since the fifteenth century. Banat and Transylvania acquired it when they were part of the Austro-Hungarian system (Gheorghian 1933, 5–6). However, versions of the system exist in other countries as well, for example, Switzerland. The CF is a public registry that includes every piece of information about land and buildings, from their physical description to ownership rights and liabilities. For each piece of land and house, the registry is composed of three parts: the first part describes the property—land or house, address, size, individual elements (e.g., house and yard), sometimes more details, such as building material. The second part concerns property title and its history: date, type of property transfer (private contract, inheritance, public auction, nationalization, etc.), and former owner. The third part concerns liabilities on the property, such as easements.

There were three corresponding types of CF transcription: registration, temporary inscription, and notation. The first two refer to real immovable rights, while the last one refers to personal rights, legal facts, and so on, such as legal capacity issues, patrimonial rights enforced against third parties, displacements or burdens on real rights under suspensive condition, various actions, legal regime of immovables based on various statutes of expropriation or appropriation [împroprietărire] (Brădeanu 1958, 437).

The CF is not just a mere record, however. Property rights and the very (physical) existence of the land and houses depend upon their inscription in the registry. The "rule of the CF," as it is commonly known, equally valid throughout pre-communism, communism, and postcommunism, is that everything that is noted in the registry exists, while everything that is not, does not exist (in other words, a house or piece of land without a CF record is not considered to exist). Article 32 of the original 1938 CF statute (Law no 115/1938) thus established a double presumption: the existence of the right that was transcribed, and correspondingly the inexistence of the right that was not mentioned in the CF. This double presumption was at the basis of the principle of the evidentiary force of the CF (Brădeanu 1957, 48–49). The protection of third parties through the CF did not extend to those who acquired the property for free (such as donation or will).

CF registration was thus key to the very existence of property rights, it was not a mere issue of publicity or opposability. It was also not just an issue of recording the deeds, as the registration phase involved controlling the legality of contracts or other acts at the basis of the creation, transfer, or extinction of property rights (art. 17 of the 1938 CF statute). The basis for CF registration was the consent of the parties (although the statute did allow, exceptionally, for a court decision or administrative order to replace it). As the registry is coupled with the land survey system, the physical boundaries and characteristics of a piece of land or house form an integral part of the registry system and its corresponding property status.

Figure 6.1 shows a blank CF page. The translation reads as follows:

Village/town/city of . . .
Part I Immovable
Cadastral number, Description of immovable, Surface, Observations
[For example, a house with a courtyard and a garden]
Part II Property [For example, the Romanian state bought it at auction in 1950]

This is an example of the first two parts of a CF record. Each of the three parts includes further details, for example, for acts of transfer of property, such as donation, the CF record notes the donor, the recipient, whether the donation was authenticated/notarized, when, and so forth.

The CF was meant to create complete publicity for immovables, including the alienation, constitution, change, or extinction of real rights, as well as legal facts, personal rights, or other legal relationships that impact the legal status of an immovable (explained the CF guru Salvator Brădeanu 1958, 436). The consequences are important, as third parties were protected if the CF was not complete, for example, a buyer who acquired a house in good faith was protected from eviction. The goals of the CF system were to avoid disputes, maintain a complete record of all immovables and immovable rights, and uphold public trust attached to the CF system (Brădeanu 1956, 1448). In other words, the CF system was meant to achieve transparency, the clear demarcation of property rights, and the overall security and stability of the property system—a perfect encapsulation of capitalist property.

The important exception was state property rights, which could be enforced even if they were not transcribed in the CF: "Real rights will be acquired without transcription in the CF if based on death, accession, forced selling, and expropriation, but the title holder cannot dispose of them until the transcription" (art. 26 of the 1938 statute). However, this did not mean transcription did not have to happen eventually, so local authorities regularly took steps to "legalize" the state's CF situation in cases of illegal takings.

Anexa la actul autentic
Nr............./............
Notar Public,

ANCPI

Nr. cerere..................
Ziua.......................
Luna........................
Anul........................

OFICIUL DE CADASTRU SI PUBLICITATE IMOBILIARA ....

EXTRAS DE CARTE FUNCIARĂ
pentru
AUTENTIFICARE

Cartea funciară cu nr. .... Comuna/ Oraş/ Municipiu ....

A. Partea I-a

Nr.crt.	Nr. cadastral	Descrierea imobilului	Suprafaţa în mp.	Observaţii

B. Partea a II-a

Nr.crt.	Înscrieri privitoare la proprietate	Observaţii

C. Partea a III- a

Nr.crt.	Înscrieri privitoare la sarcini	Observaţii

Certific că prezentul extras corespunde întru totul cu poziţiile în vigoare din cartea funciară originală, păstrată de acest birou
Prezentul extras de carte funciară poate fi folosit exclusiv la autentificarea actelor notariale, conform art.56 din Legea nr.7/1996 modificată şi completată, la notarul public ....
Termenul de valabilitate al extrasului de carte funciară, eliberat în scopul autentificării actelor notariale, este de 5 zile lucrătoare, calculate începând cu ziua şi ora înregistrării cererii în registrul special de intrare şi terminând cu sfârşitul celei de-a cincea zi

S-a achitat tariful de .... lei, prin chitanţa nr. .... /20..., pentru serviciul de publicitate imobiliară cu codul nr. P.I.0[illegible]

Asistent - registrator,

Figure 6.1. ***Carte Funciară* Record.** *Source*: Courtesy of the National Agency of Cadastre and Real Estate Publicity.

(Until 1960, special courts dealt with transcription and publicity issues. Decrees 377/1960 and 378/1960 changed this, primarily by establishing the monopoly of state notaries over the authentication of titles, deeds, etc., as well as over publicity and transcription of deeds for immovables. The effect was to centralize the control of registration and publicity.)

A 1959 secret memorandum from the municipal council to the Council of Ministers (commenting on proposed amendments to the 1938 CF statute) slyly noted that up to that point, on the territory of the Timişoara region there had been very few registrations in the CF of the takings carried out under various nationalization and expropriation acts, which the municipal council only began to register in 1958.[21] CF registration was not a simple matter and it was not inexpensive. Council of Ministers Decree 911/1955 established the registration fee at 7 lei (annual net salary at the time was 499 lei),[22] so the retroactive registration cost a significant amount of money.

The lack of CF registration displeased both individuals and the local and central authorities, since property was literally in limbo, frozen in a legal no man's land (noted, for example, in the letter admonishing the Timişoara council to register all nationalized houses in Arad).[23] Occasionally, this resulted in somewhat absurd situations when no one wanted to take charge, including the state. Illustrative is the story of Felicia and her husband Emil, a forestry engineer, whose house was on the nationalization proposal list. They built the house with money from her dowry between 1934 and 1936, and both of them had been political detainees between 1948 and 1953, working to build the Danube-Black Sea Channel (notoriously deadly). The house was requisitioned between 1949 and 1952 and used for a midwives' school, then occupied by the Soviet army until 1958. Tenants had lived there since 1958, but they did not pay rent, since neither the owner nor the local housing authority wanted to receive the rent because its ownership status was not clear. The house badly needed repairs but none had been undertaken. The nationalization proposal indicated that the house had in fact been seized under Law 119/1948, not requisitioned, and the CF also noted an appeal by Felicia against the nationalization, apparently unresolved.[24]

The lack of registration or clarity of CF registration was also dangerous because it offered possibilities of resistance to takings, as shown by a 1956 court case from Baia Mare (Northern Transylvania). The popular tribunal there rejected the request of the municipal council to register a house that had been nationalized on the basis of Decree 92/1950 because it was not clear who the nationalized owner was (in effect rejecting the nationalization). In appeal, the regional tribunal agreed. The municipal council appealed again, arguing that nationalization operated regardless of who was registered as owner in the CF. The owner's counterargument was that Decree 92 nationalized the property of certain kinds of people, rather than houses per se, and since this particular house had only one floor and belonged to a person who was exempt from nationalization, the court should reject the registration claim. Eventually, the appeal court dismissed the latter arguments and held that the registration of the taking in the CF did not need the consent of the owner, since the transfer of property operated on the basis of the law, not consent of the parties. A different solution would amount to judicial review of legislation (which was not admissible anymore at the time). If nationalization was wrong, held the court, it should be corrected through statute.[25]

Although ultimately unsuccessful, this case exemplifies both the instrumentalism of law in early communism and the extent to which the courts resisted it: the initial decisions of the trial and appeal courts rejected registration claims, and thus indirectly the nationalization itself, ex officio and not at the request of the nationalized owner. This is even more interesting in light of the existence in the CF statute itself of explicit provisions regarding cases where the consent of the parties was not required. Once various presumed owners were summoned before the court, the court accepted their arguments as well. The regional appeal court ultimately clamped down on this, but this does not obscure the turmoil that urban housing nationalization caused and various strategies for resistance. A final interesting note here is that the legal journal *New Justice* chose to publish this decision, given that the case was not difficult doctrinally and it showed explicit court resistance to nationalization on a formalist basis.[26]

The transparency, completeness, and binding-ness of the real estate registration system were meant to achieve certainty and security of private property as crucial components of a capitalist system. Yet when the communist regime took over, it was rather enthusiastic about the system—communist lawyers and scholars consistently praised it and held it in higher regard than the personal publicity system prevalent in Wallachia and Moldavia (Ministry of Justice 1959, 258–60). The CF system proved to be a double-edged sword, however; while initially it provided complete information for purposes of nationalization, expropriation, and generally knowledge about land and houses throughout Transylvania, in the long run it cast a legal net over all property transactions, as it was originally meant to do. Therefore, all takings, sooner or later, had to be transcribed, for each piece of property in turn, thus preserving a concept of property tied to its pre-communist physical and legal attributes. Expropriation files throughout communism, for example, became increasingly formalistic: they included not only CF extracts, but also justificatory memos for the expropriation, technical memos, evaluation memos, as well as pictures of the property and information about the owners' class and personal history.

Because the registry system was the heart and soul of property in the region, the communist regime ended up playing by the rules instituted by the bourgeois regime of property, which had the unintended consequence of preserving ideas and practices of property that had been integral to the pre-communist system. The CF system placed individual houses and plots of land literally at the center of the universe and represented them in the language and with the concepts developed by capitalist law. The values underlining it, such as consent of the parties, also spoke of bourgeois individualism and formalism, and helped preserve the centrality of property and its values.

There were other unintended consequences of relying on the CF system. Post-1989, Katherine Verdery (2003) had a wonderful discussion of the vagaries of using the CF for land restitution claims, particularly when they were incomplete or for various reasons did not correspond to other types of ownership records. This was not a new problem, however. In the early 1960s, the Lugoj council (a small town close to Timişoara) struggled to legalize the situation of buildings and land seized illegally between 1950 and 1960. This involved about 15,000 plots of land, and the Lugoj authorities were trying to explain to the county authorities the depth of the problem: the CF owners were not the same as the *de facto* owners in many cases, the *de facto* owners donated, sold, etc. the land, inheritance was not often pursued legally, but rather informally, some of the plots had been subject to *comasare* (forced adjoining of land), it was expensive to do the CF work, and the council lacked manpower, experts, and money.[27]

RESTITUTIONS AND THE CIRCULATION OF HOUSING

The first serious dent in the newly installed communist regime's policy of dismantling private property over the means of production was the partial and haphazard policy of nationalization and expropriation. House owners lost their homes for no clear reason, saw their houses used for various purposes—bringing in tenants to alleviate the housing crisis, using the space for a public purpose (such as kindergartens, factories, etc.), or more often becoming the seat of a state institution, and, more confusingly, saw that not everybody had their house nationalized or expropriated. Overall, a majority of all houses and apartments remained in private hands during the period studied and continued to function in much the same way as before, namely as family homes.

Yet the most unexpected aspect of the regime's policies regarding housing was restitutions. Communist restitutions—which some might call an oxymoron—are nonetheless the clearest example of how the regime's overall goal of eliminating private property clashed with immediate policy goals that subverted it and in the long term significantly impaired its achievement.

Housing restitutions happened primarily in conjunction with the ethnic politics of the period. Postwar transitional justice measures targeted all those who in any way could be considered to have collaborated with the Nazi regime, which for the most part meant ethnic Germans. The majority lost both their property and their freedom (deported to the USSR), while others fled with the retreating German army and returned only years later. At the beginning of 1945, the communist regime sent 6,545 men (between the ages of 18 and 45) and 7,330 women (between the ages of 16 and 35) to forced labor in the USSR from the Timişoara region. From the entire Banat region, there were deported over 30,000 persons, out of which approximately a quarter died. By 1950, approximately 11,000 ethnic Germans had returned from the USSR. Of the 15,644 individuals from the Timiş-Torontal region who had retreated with the German army in 1944, almost 75 percent (11,566) had returned by 1947 (almost 70 percent from the entire Banat region returned) (Mioc 2010, 107–13).

Stalin's death prompted a change of direction within the Soviet Union, which was followed by the Romanian Workers' Party as well (the predecessor of the Communist Party). These new policies included restitution measures (Mioc 2010, 113). Restitution to Romanian citizens of German ethnicity began in 1954 and continued through 1957. The year 1956 reinforced this trend, particularly as the Romanian government become increasingly interested in reestablishing economic exchanges with Western European countries, including the Federal Republic of Germany (Tismăneanu 2003, 82–83).

The return of the German population posed significant problems for the communist regime: "We point out that the problem of repatriated persons is an extremely important issue of international politics for our country and you bear significant responsibility for fulfilling your duties in this regard" (May 1956 memo from regional to local administrative branches of the state apparatus).[28] The duties mentioned here include restitution of property taken under Law 187/1945 (punishing Romanian citizens of German origin, war collaborators, post-1944 refugees, absentees, etc.). As a result of this statute, more than 50,000 German families in the Timiş-Torontal county were deprived of all their property (Mioc 2010, 108). Approximately 75 percent of the assets seized in this manner were initially redistributed to poor peasants and internally displaced persons—for example, up to 5 ha per family was allotted to soldiers and peasants with little or no land.

It should be noted here that despite the portrayals of the communist regime, the redistribution process was unequal, specifically regarding the Roma population. A memorandum from the General Association of Roma from Romania, to the Minister of Internal Affairs from February 7, 1948, reports the results of an inspection in Banat and Crişana (including Timiş Torontal). The report found that the Roma in these regions lived in "deep misery," in huts built on swamp land, a very unsanitary and dangerous environment. Almost all the Roma had fought during the war, and they were entitled, based on the law for agrarian reform, to receive land, houses, and so on. The Roma had been farmers "for a very long time, having worked on the lands of the landowners and in German households," and they had hoped that the democratic reforms would help them, too, as they did other citizens. As it turned out, they were wrong, as local authorities ignored their claims and excluded them from the reforms. The report mentioned that the Roma were forced to beg or continue to work as servants. The Association had been in contact and petitioned the local authorities, but for the most part received no response, nor resolution. In the city of Arad, the commission for the implementation of land reform claimed that there had been no discrimination in the redistribution of land and houses, and that everyone received some, as long as there was availability. In response, the Association showed that no Roma had received any land or houses. In Lipova, another town, the city hall promised them land and houses, but eventually received none because the city hall did not communicate to the local representative of the Roma Association when and where the proceedings took place.

Land wasn't the only asset seized from ethnic minorities and redistributed. Their houses were too. As mentioned in an earlier chapter, the 1945 land reform statute expropriated a total of 36,842 houses from the entire Timişoara region.[29] With the return of those repatriated ten years later, the state undertook an obligation to return their assets, at least in part. The result was that 32,462 of the houses initially seized in the county, or almost 90 percent, were approved for restitution. Of these, 9,452 houses were given back under Decree 81/1954, while 27,390 were proposed for restitution under Decrees 268/1956 and 461/1957. Decree 81/1954 regarding the gain and loss of rights over some goods was signed by the Presidium of the Great National Assembly on March 18, 1954. It was subsequently amended in 1956, and applied through Council of Ministers Decision 370 from March 19, 1954, and its Instructions. Decree 81 initially stipulated that peasants who agreed to become part of collectives were entitled to get their houses back (CADCR Report 2006, 155), clearly a buy-in to ensure the success of collectivization. The 1956 amendments, however, specifically returned houses to ethnic Germans and Hungarians.

Local authorities in villages and towns issued property titles for 23,010 of these houses, while 4,374 houses (11 percent) could not be returned for various reasons, including the following: 489 houses were demolished or destroyed after the expropriation, 166 houses had belonged to landowners, 716 houses had belonged to those with multiple houses, 47 houses would have been nationalized under Decree 92 had they not been expropriated, 314 houses belonged to owners who had died without heirs, 1,731 houses belonged to those who had left the country and had no close relatives, and 629 houses were used by various state institutions and collective organizations.[30]

Leaving out houses that were destroyed and those used by state organizations, a total of 2,974 houses (1 percent) remained in state property, to be sold back to the population (cf. Instructions of the Ministry of Finance no. 2003/1958). Selling the houses back to the population had its own problems, however, such as the fact that the prices mandated by the Ministry of Finance were higher than the "real price of circulation" (i.e., the market value), therefore the local administration had no buyers for them.[31] There was no significant difference between urban and rural areas in terms of restitutions under Decree 81, but overall the urban-rural divide in terms of takings was significantly skewed toward the urban areas (primarily because of Decree 92/1950).

Restitution was hardly justice here, however, since many of these houses were given after the 1945 expropriation to IDPs. As of 1950, 15,230 families of IDPs who came to the Timişoara region were given land, houses, inventory, and whatever else they needed, and were encouraged by local administrative officials to strengthen and improve their new property. The families resettled in the region after the war came from Dobrogea (3,179 families), Ardeal (3,883 families), Basarabia (2,571 families), Macedonia (1,116 families), Moldova (713 families), Bucovina (911 families), Oltenia (559 families), Muntenia (367 families), and 1,931 families from other parts. They were given land, on average 5 ha per family, for a total of 76,150 ha, which represented 14 percent of the total tillable land of the region. This was also the best land, as apparently they had turned down anything else.[32]

The restitution of these houses to the owners expropriated in 1945 raised new problems for those who had afterward received title or possession to them and who had effectively owned them for ten years. The policy solution was to extend special credit lines to this most recent group of expropriated owners to either buy themselves new houses or build them. A 1959 report mentions that 1,660 new houses were built this way, 843 houses were in construction, and 853 houses had already been bought. Local authorities also distributed 3,945 lots for building new homes and 666 more were needed.[33] These are still low numbers compared to the number of houses given back, so in effect the 1954 restitution decree created a new class of expropriated, disappointed owners, who in turn pursued their own restitution claims even after 1989. It may also have strengthened the deep disappointment of the ethnic German population with the socialist regime, prompting the first of the many waves of emigration from the Banat region: between 1957 and 1961, 1,631 Romanian citizens of German origin emigrated to the Federal Republic of Germany (Mioc 2010, 116).

The ramifications of these policies stretch until today. Sonia's case is illustrative. In 2003, the Supreme Court of Romania rejected the claim of Sonia A. for restitution of a house that had been owned by her father between 1946 and 1954 in a Saxon village of Transylvania.[34] Sonia's father,

George A., had received title to the house and some land in 1946 (had been "împroprietărit"—became an owner). In 1954, the house was returned to its pre-1946 owner, Karol I. George died in 1960, the re-instated owner Karol left Romania in 1976, and consequently the house became state property. Sonia began the restitution process in 1990, shortly after the fall of the communist regime, but her claim was rejected at every level of the administrative and judicial system. In summary, the house in question had been expropriated from its (ethnic German) owner as a punitive measure of transitional justice following the Second World War, given in property to a new owner, who in turn was expropriated when the house was returned to the original owner eight years later. The case is one of more than 120,000 restitution cases in postcommunist Romania.[35]

Not rarely, the newly expropriated owners refused to leave the house, so the new and original owners lived together until the deadline specified by the restitution decree (to give the newly expropriated time to find new housing). When time ran out, the original owners wanted to evict the new owners and often the courts agreed. Courts sometimes admitted the eviction actions even if the new owners had nowhere to go.[36] These types of struggles did nothing to dispel ideas about the importance of ownership.

The original owners who could not get their house back in the early 1950s because it had been demolished or for any other reason were entitled to compensation of 50 percent of the value of the houses and similar special credit lines for the rest of 50 percent to build or buy new homes. By 1959, 118 former owners were approved for credit and compensation, but of these, only 27 in fact pursued their rights. The others refused because the compensation was too small and because they were obliged to open the credit line simultaneously in order to receive the compensation, which they found unacceptable. Finally, some refused the compensation in hopes that the socialist organizations using their houses would give them up, in which case the former owners were indeed entitled to restitution in kind.[37]

In a similar situation were homeowners who lived in border towns and who were forcibly displaced in 1951 because of fears of a potential war with Tito's Yugoslavia. They were also entitled to restitution of their house and some other property upon their return. Thus, from the Timişoara region there were forcibly displaced 688 families of ethnic Serbs, 639 of whom returned by 1956 (Council of Ministers Decision no. 2694/1955). According to a memo to the Council of Ministers, 629 of these homeowners got their houses back.[38] Out of 661 houses seized, 588 were fully returned and 25 were partially returned (the owners were obliged to rent rooms to socialist organizations who occupied them pre-restitution). Some of the houses could not be given back because they were occupied by collectives, the army, and so on, or had been demolished or destroyed. For these cases—forty-four for the Timişoara region, similarly with German property, there was compensation and special credit lines.[39]

Also forcibly displaced were 4,389 families of other nationalities (Romanian, Bulgarian, Germans, Czechs, etc.), out of which 3,830 families returned in 1955 (Council of Ministers Decisions no. 29/1955 and 623/1956). A total of 1,691 families got their houses back entirely (although not necessarily the house they had lost), 271 partially, 56 houses were occupied by socialist organizations so were exempt from restitution, and the rest had been destroyed or demolished. In these cases, the returnees were entitled to some compensation (but only if the houses had been completely destroyed) and credit to build or buy new homes. Interestingly, the official report containing this data criticized those village officials who proposed compensation instead of restitution of houses themselves, even though there were houses available to be given back, and urged them "to do this properly," that is, to return the houses, as opposed to compensation.[40]

Housing restitutions complicate the larger communist picture of displacing private property. On the one hand, massive restitutions took place along ethnic lines, and when restitutions were not possible, the state offered some help so that individuals and their families could acquire or build houses as private property. On the other hand, many of these restitutions happened in the countryside, not in urban areas, and were restricted in scope (as discussed in a previous chapter, there was minimal restitution of houses seized under Decree 92). Their very existence, however, particularly when seen in the larger context of communist takings and housing needs, signaled that houses as objects of private property held a special place even during times of building socialism. This, in turn, gave the institution of private property more time to breathe.

THE STATE AS LANDLORD

The partial and random nationalization and expropriation of houses and apartments, the limited restitution policies, the ideological ambivalence, and the preservation of the bourgeois architecture of the legal institution of property significantly limited the overall attempt to eliminate private property over houses as means of production and sustained the institution and concept of private property during a period of intense property transformation. Pragmatic issues played a part, too. The never-ending housing crisis pushed the regime toward encouraging new constructions of private housing, while playing the role of landlord for so much housing stock ironically prompted attempts to privatize the management of houses in state property.

Timişoara ceased to be primarily a military city guarding the edges of the Austro-Hungarian Empire toward the end of the nineteenth century.

Subsequently, local architects and city officials developed urban plans for the city or parts thereof in 1895, 1911–1913, 1929–1930, 1939, 1942–1946, 1950 (preliminary study), 1955, 1959, and 1965 (Munteanu 2002, 189–223).[41] Massive constructions started in the early 1960s and continued through the 1970s and 1980s. While the country as a whole moved through different stages of urban planning at different political moments, one post–Second World War imperative remained constant: there was never enough housing for the ever-increasing population of Banat and Timişoara in particular. The housing need, moreover, had to be fulfilled within a particular vision of what a modern socialist city should look like.

Housing construction haltingly started as early as 1948 and in this first phase continued until 1962, when the master vision began to shift.[42] During this period, local officials were caught between conflicting goals: on the one hand, they had to fulfill the key ideological goal of denaturalizing private property, including private property in housing, which practically meant becoming the landlord of the city, a mission they were unprepared for (as evidenced, for example, by initial reports of the state management company for nationalized houses, ILLT, from 1950).[43] On the other hand, they had to deal with the housing needs of the cities, which led to encouraging state as well as private constructions of houses and apartments. One unintended consequence of these distinct pressures was yet another blurring of key ideological messages about private property.

Newspaper articles from the period reflect this struggle: they cover the housing crisis and exalt private property. For example, in the late 1940s and early 1950s, at the height of the class struggle, there were relatively few and short articles on nationalization in the local paper (*Luptătorul Bănăţean*), such as the one on the necessity of nationalizing the National Bank (June 29, 1946), the nationalization of hospitals and entertainment industry (November 4, 1948), the big nationalization (June 14, 1948), or expropriations of ethnic Germans (January 12, 1946). Almost daily, however, there were published articles related to the housing crisis, its causes and ways to fix it, including new constructions, distributing land titles and plots for individual construction, and encouraging private housing construction through state credits (e.g., "We built ourselves new houses with the state's assistance," May 6, 1954). Examples of these include a factory that wanted to build free housing for its workers but had trouble getting plots from city hall (May 10, 1946); an article in a series entitled "Encouraging Private Initiative" talking about city hall efforts to increase its income by selling plots at public auction (June 20, 1946); giving away land titles (May 15, 1946); housing lots for workers and new housing constructions (March 8, 30 1947); IDPs and their property (January 18, 1947); housing, rental offices and the housing census, but also building new housing for the workers (July 16, 1948); protection of tenants (April

28, 1948); urban planning needs (lead article September 9, 1948); "railway workers are building new houses for themselves" (October 25, 1953).

Ownership was explicitly not shunned, for example, a 1947 article regarding land titles for IDPs reassured them that changes in the titling process were meant precisely to safeguard "the sanctity of your property" (January 18, 1947). While the reality was somewhat different (many IDPs did not work their land, so were at risk of losing it through this process), the property rhetoric was reassuringly familiar.

Later changes in rhetoric, on the other hand, could not eschew the fact that the state had trouble managing its property and was willing to cede effective ownership to the tenants. An article in *Luptătorul Bănățean* from May 10, 1952, mentioned that 370 houses from Timişoara were "taken for socialist safekeeping" on a contract basis by citizens: the local council did not have the money to maintain these houses, many of them probably nationalized only two years earlier, and convinced the tenants to take effective ownership and pay for maintenance and repairs themselves. Occasionally, local authorities even tolerated "housing exploiters," as in 1962 in the town of Oravița, where two buildings with ten apartments each had been continuously managed by an administrator since 1939. When the heirs of the owner, who lived in Hungary, asked for compensation or an equivalent property in Hungary, the local commission claimed the houses had not been nationalized by mistake, which is hard to believe given the otherwise efficient dragnet of the regime.[44]

It appears that the communist regime was unintentionally sabotaging its own efforts to destabilize private property, at least insofar as houses were concerned, because of the ongoing housing crisis. In the Timiş region, local authorities were overwhelmed by the amount and diversity of property they were expected to manage; hence, the "socialist safekeeping" solution may have been intended to solve a short-term problem, yet it also inadvertently reinforced the bourgeois connection between private ownership and efficient property.

The urban housing nationalization and other takings were intended to solve at least partially the housing crisis. Yet this was clearly not the case and housing nationalization was nothing more than a temporary band aid, since only about 400 new apartments were created through the vaunted "more efficient use" of bigger nationalized apartments.[45] Throughout the 1950s and 1960s, local planners were obsessed with the growing needs of the region. They were concerned that Timişoara was too spread out, therefore hard to modernize and manage, and that it did not have sufficient housing space: the actual median was 7 square meters per person, which was even less than the officially mandated housing norm of 8 square meters per person.[46] This is one reason the regime decided to give up some of the houses it had originally seized, for example, some of the houses that were in bad shape to begin with and too expensive to maintain. This was the case with 228 urban houses and 547 rural houses from the Timişoara county that were evaluated and proposed to be sold to the population (tenants) based on the argument that private owners would take good care of them (!): "We are sure that once the tenant becomes the owner of the house, he/she will show an interest in repairing and maintaining it."[47]

Discussing the expansion of personal property in socialism, secretary general of the Party Gheorghe Gheorghiu-Dej explained in a speech on August 22, 1953, that as the economy improved, the Party would introduce new forms of salary payment, build dwellings for over 50,000 families, and allow individuals to build houses on the basis of cooperation among lodgers, as well as individual dwellings with state support (in Nedelschi 1954, 180–81). New constructions proceeded indeed at an accelerated pace throughout the 1960s, 1970s, and 1980s, and entirely new neighborhoods were built from scratch. The housing needs of the region never truly abated, and the regime continued its policies of simultaneous state and private housing construction. By 1960, as noted in an earlier chapter, the balance was still in favor of private property: out of the total number of 3.4 million square meters for housing in the Banat region, only 1.2 million square meters were state property, while 2.2 million square meters were private property. In other words, houses held as private property amounted to approximately two-thirds of the total housing in the region as late as 1960.[48] The regime allowed the formation of private associations for building private houses (OCLPP—Office for the Construction of Personal Ownership Homes) quite early on (e.g., Decision of the Council of Ministers/HCM 4015/1953), and citizens took advantage of it. In 1971, for example, 860 housing units allotted were state property, while citizens had built 2,068 units as private housing (Munteanu and Munteanu 2002, 224–25).

From the very beginning of the communist regime, deprivation of property happened in parallel with new constructions and giving private property titles for houses and/or land. Starting in the late 1950s to early 1960s, even as it was still wrapping up urban nationalization of housing, the socialist state undertook massive constructions of new housing, a significant portion of it as personal property. The regime had little choice in the matter, as it had to cope with a housing crisis that harked back to the interwar period, had gotten worse during the war, and was expanding as the country's rapid industrialization produced major demographic shifts. The regime needed private initiative in the housing area, and consequently adapted its policies to encourage "personal property" while proclaiming the end of private property. For citizens, this reinforced both the fragility and the importance of private property, and most importantly it signaled that perhaps the death of private property might yet be long in coming.

CONCLUSION

Property was central to the communist project politically, legally, ideologically, and pragmatically. Understanding how and why the communist project failed entails understanding the extent to which its key efforts to hollow out private property and replace it with new forms of ordering property relations faltered. Continuities abound at the level of values, ideology, and institution of property. In the legal geometry of property, the most significant changes happened at the top, at the most visible yet superficial level—namely, change of ownership title from private owners to the state. This change of title was definitive for land, industry, commerce, and other areas of the economy, but for houses there was significant movement between state and private property domains, consequently blurring the ideological messages regarding the role of private property in a socialist system. The circulation of houses between the state and the private domain—takings, redistribution, and restitution in the Timişoara region—shows the flux in property rights during the period studied, the regime's own ambivalence, and the extent to which this sent contradictory messages about the place of private property in communism. Private property restrictions merely reinforced this confusion.

Restrictions in the housing field signaled a movement of private property from the civil law realm to state law, as the main issues came to include construction and credit, as well as housing policies that infinitesimally focused on the management of people and things, and positioned the state administration as a major actor in setting the concrete boundaries and content of personal property. There is little doubt that these restrictions seriously chipped away from private property. Yet focusing only on them can obscure deeper continuities in the legal concept of property, which become apparent when examining more technical aspects of property law, such as acquisitive prescription, possession, *rei vindicatio*, and superficies.

More significant changes happened at the "bundle of rights" level, where the communist regime attempted to create new rights, such as the right to use in perpetuity the land under constructions that were private property, or the rights of administrative bodies to use, dispose of, and possess state property in perpetuity (without formally amounting to a "full" property right, which remained vested in the state). This is a hybrid property buffet that includes both bourgeois and socialist concepts, and is premised on a tri-partite "bourgeois" concept of property—possession, disposition, and use, both as a legal and ideological matter. These continuities also embodied older property values, expressed through legal language and perhaps unintentional and unconscious doctrinal resistance. These continuities are best exemplified in the materiality of property and the unquestioned hegemony of the real estate registration system (*Cartea Funciară*).

Ideologically, the reliance on labor as justification for private property is simply a variation on Lockean property theory, while elevating state property also falls back on classic theories of property as power. Pragmatically, the housing crisis led the regime to tolerate and even encourage private property in housing, and even the return of some housing. The counterpoint to new constructions and tolerating *de facto* or *de jure* private ownership of housing was the oppressive tenancy and housing policy, but this policy did not pose an existential threat to private property either.

NOTES

1. National Archives of Romania Timişoara, Collection Prefectură, File No. 28/1950, page 6.

2. This is also not a comprehensive description of the property regime of socialism. Katherine Verdery has talked at length about socialist property in Romania as a legal, cultural, and power system in *The Vanishing Hectare* (2003).

3. "Milioane de cetăţeni îşi văd adăpostul asigurat" [Millions of Citizens Obtain Shelter], *Luptătorul Bănăţean*, September 25, 1947.

4. "Oficiile de închirieri vor începe să funcţioneze după efectuarea recensământului apartamentelor şi clădirilor" [Rental Offices Will Begin to Function After the End of the Buildings Census], *Luptătorul Bănăţean,* December 10, 1948. The frontpage article in *Luptătorul Bănăţean* from December 9, 1948, was titled "Apartments of Exploiters Will Be Rented to Workers," and explained how year after year the latter were forced to live in miserable and unsanitary huts on the outskirts of the city, while exploiters built for themselves villas and palaces like in fairytales in the downtown, on the backs of the workers.

5. National Archives of Romania Timişoara, Collection City Hall, File No. 10/1950, page 54.

6. There are two qualifications to Locke's theory of acquisition of property: no wasting and no hoarding.

7. The conception of property as power in social relations is represented by the social relations school in the United States, and scholars such as Morris Cohen (1927), Felix Cohen (1954), Hale (a lawyer and economist), Kennedy (1991), Singer (1987–1988), MacPherson (1978), and Nedelsky (1990, 1993).

8. Highlights of property studies in anthropology have included Malinowski (1935), Gluckman (1965), Caroline Humphrey (1983), and Jack Goody (1962, 1976).

9. Ioffe (1982) extensively discusses parallels and fundamental continuities between Soviet law and Roman law, particularly in the area of property/ownership, which are even more pronounced in the case of Romanian law.

10. *Popular Legality* No 5/1960, pages 129–32.

11. Soviet civilians had long argued for the introduction of acquisitive prescription in Soviet law, for similar reasons, for example, a 1949 article discussing the proposed new Soviet civil code by Bratus. The structure Bratus envisioned was very similar to the classic *usucapio* model.

12. This echoes Anglo-American debates about eliminating any necessary connection between property rights and things, which renders unclear the way in which property rights differ from rights generally (Grey 1980, 69–71).

13. Possession must have been continuous (for one year), uninterrupted, peaceful, and public (same as for acquisitive prescription). The plaintiff could unite his possession with that of his author, for example, seller, nude owner from user, and so on (Georgescu 1956, 787–88).

14. Most of the disputes relating to state and collective land were however filed as administrative, rather than civil law, disputes, thus following a different set of rules.

15. Published in *Popular Legality* No. 2/1955, page 168.

16. Hamangiu et al. (Vol II, 61) describe *rei vindicatio* as the legal action through which the plaintiff asks a court of law to recognize their ownership right over a thing not in their possession. It is a real, petitory action (concerns title).

17. The specific rules were as follows: the statute of limitations for adjudicated immovables was five years (Article 561 code of civil procedure) [executare silită imobiliară], and three years for movables lost, stolen, or possessed in bad faith (Article 1909 civil code). Against the bad faith possessor, the statute of limitations was thirty years.

18. Suceava general trial court, civil decision 194/October 6, 1950, published in *New Justice* No. 1/1951, pages 80–81.

19. Constantin Stătescu, together with Corneliu Bârsan, who served as the Romanian judge at the European Court of Human Rights between 1998 and 2013, wrote the most widely used civil law treatise throughout late communism, particularly the obligations and torts parts.

20. National Archives of Romania Timişoara, Collection Sfatul Popular Banat, Secţia de Gospodărie Comunală, File No. 23/1953, page 88.

21. National Archives of Romania Timişoara, Collection Sfatul Popular Banat, Secretariat, File No. 64/1959, pages 136–38.

22. National Institute of Statistics, http://www.insse.ro/cms/rw/pages/castiguri1938.ro.do.

23. National Archives of Romania Timişoara, Collection Sfatul Popular Banat, Inventar 1630, File No. 1/1956, page 318.

24. National Archives of Romania, Collection Sfatul Popular Banat, Secretariat, File No. 127/1960, pages 25–29. The nationalization proposal was from April 20, 1960.

25. Regional tribunal Baia Mare, civil decision no. 1322/July 12, 1956, published in *Justiţia Nouă* No. 5/1957, pages 883–84.

26. The timing of the publication indicates that there may have been many cases of this nature.

27. National Archives of Romania Timişoara, Collection Sfatul Popular Banat, Inventar 1630, File No. 27/1962, page 10. The document is from January 30, 1962.

28. National Archives of Romania Timişoara, Collection Sfatul Popular Banat, Secretariat, File No. 63/1956, page 68. Instructions 11/752/1958 issued by the Ministry of Health and Social Protection to further the implementation of Decree 462/1957 established in some detail the rights of returning citizens of German or Hungarian ethnicity. For example, time spent in the USSR was considered for pension purposes,

and those who returned were entitled to disability benefits as a result of injuries suffered while deported (Secretariat, File No. 65/1958, pages 148–51).

29. There are slight differences in numbers among versions of the report cited here. I am using here what appears to be the final version of the report. Whether all of this happened in fact is unclear.

30. National Archives of Romania Timişoara, Collection Sfatul Popular Banat, Secretariat, File No. 10/1959, page 331.

31. National Archives of Romania Timişoara, Collection Sfatul Popular Banat, Secretariat, File No. 10/1959, page 339.

32. National Archives of Romania Timişoara, Collection Prefectură, File No. 28/1950, page 6.

33. National Archives of Romania Timişoara, Collection Sfatul Popular Banat, Secretariat, File No. 10/1959, pages 351–52.

34. Civil section decision 2686/June 19, 2003. These are not the real names of the parties involved.

35. "The Second Nationalization," *FrontNews*, June 9, 2008.

36. National Archives of Romania Timişoara, Collection Sfatul Popular Banat, Secretariat, File No. 10/1959, page 359.

37. National Archives of Romania Timişoara, Collection Sfatul Popular Banat, Secretariat, File No. 10/1959, page 333.

38. National Archives of Romania Timişoara, Collection Sfatul Popular Banat, Secretariat, File No. 18/1956, page 429.

39. National Archives of Romania Timişoara, Collection Sfatul Popular Banat, Secretariat, File No. 46/1956, page 326.

40. National Archives of Romania Timişoara, Collection Sfatul Popular Banat, Secretariat, File No. 46/1956, page 326–27.

41. See, for example, an extensive memo and a historical overview on urban planning in the city from 1965, also documenting specific needs. National Archives of Romania Timişoara, Collection Sfatul Popular Banat, Secretariat, File No. 38/1965, pages 4–13, 77–121.

42. National Archives of Romania Timişoara, Collection Sfatul Popular Banat, Secretariat, File No. 38/1965, pages 77–121.

43. For example, National Archives of Romania Timişoara, Collection City Hall, File No. 12/1950.

44. National Archives of Romania Timişoara, Collection Sfatul Popular Banat Inventar 1630, Secţia de Gospodărie Comunală, File No. 23/1962, pages 25–66.

45. Munteanu and Muntean2002, 223; National Archives of Romania Timişoara, City Hall, File No. 12/1950, pages 48–49.

46. To manage and control the urban spaces better, the plan was to build in and up. National Archives of Romania Timişoara, Collection Sfatul Popular Banat, Secretariat, Files No 36, 38/1965.

47. National Archives of Romania Timişoara, Collection Sfatul Popular Banat, Secţia Gospodărie Comunală, File No. 1/1966, pages 51–52.

48. National Archives of Romania, Timişoara, Collection Sfatul Popular Banat, Secţia de Gospodărie Comunală, File No. 6/1960, pages 40–41.

Conclusion

This book set out to explore how the newly installed communist regime of Romania attempted to use law to unsettle the hegemony of "bourgeois" private property and naturalize new meanings of property. It contends with questions of power and resistance in times of repression, meanings and practices of private property, socialist legality as the anchor of hegemony, and the legal and property rights consciousness of both citizens and regime officials. Each of these issues represents a piece of the larger puzzle of understanding changes in the "taken for grantedness" of private property and the role of law under authoritarian conditions.

The nature of communism as a counter-project of modernity meant that neither power nor legitimacy and resistance were monolithic concepts, even during early, highly repressive communism. As a quintessentially modern form of power, communism was a voluntaristic, teleological project of destruction and reconstruction of reality, defined by the non-hegemonic ideological monopoly of Marxism-Leninism, the uneven concentration of state power, and the construction of willing socialist subjects. It was precisely the excessive ambition of this type of power, combined with the inexperience, insufficient means and ambivalence of its agents that provided openings for resistance. Resistance is understood here in a broad sense, encompassing overt resistance against the communist regime (such as armed resistance), covert resistance (James C. Scott's "weapons of the weak"), and acts of micro-resistance that straddle cooptation and resistance, such as the dispossessed homeowners' petitions.

Neither attempts to unmake the hegemony of private property, nor resistance to it can be understood without answering two key questions: first, how did law—pre-communist and communist, understand property? Second, how stable and reliable of an instrument for remaking property was law itself?

Chapter 1 thus focused on the travails of constructing socialist legality and traced continuities with pre-communist ideas of law, attempts to reimagine law for a brave new world and the results of these efforts. I argue, not unlike other scholars of socialist legality (e.g., Inga Markovits), that socialist legality in Romania was in fact a hybrid legality rather than a whole new type of law, still deeply rooted in its continental civil law tradition, "bourgeois" theories of law and a pre-communist *nomos*, yet also an instrument of social engineering for the communist regime.

The incomplete and unenthusiastic efforts to remake law, particularly civil law (which encompasses property), had two consequences: first, it meant that efforts to unravel the hegemony of pre-communist private property were from the very beginning stymied by continuities in the legal regime of property (described in chapter 6); second, this hybrid legality was defined by the simultaneity of arbitrariness and legality, instrumentalism and autonomy, formalism and anti-formalism. Consequently, law was not only an instrument of state power but also a site for resistance to unmaking the hegemony of private property, especially because of its limited autonomy. It is important to note that there was no evolution from arbitrariness in early communism to legality in later years, but that legality and arbitrariness, instrumentalism and autonomy, formalism and anti-formalism were intertwined at every stage. Similarly, it would be a mistake to associate autonomy with continuities with pre-communist law—the limited autonomy of law, as pointed out in chapter 1, was a stepchild of the mythology of scientificity of Marxism-Leninism and communism more broadly and thus grudgingly acknowledged as early as 1950s in Romania and elsewhere in the Eastern Block.

The evolution of property mirrors somewhat changes in law. Similarly to legality, I found a hybrid concept of private property, structurally still strongly rooted in the Napoleonic model. Even more perhaps than in the case of legality, however, where socialist jurists made some efforts to harness law entirely for the purposes of building communism, in the case of property it was socialism that attempted to adapt to property. The centrality of property was therefore not fundamentally contested, and neither were discourses of property as power, labor or social responsibility. Socialist jurists' efforts to naturalize "personal property" instead of "private property" were not convincing: their legal regimes were almost identical, and so was a key common justification—labor.

Property regime transformations during the transition to communism entailed ideological, structural, and institutional continuities and changes. Court decisions and law review articles reveal the extent of jurisprudential and doctrinal inertia in the property field, often expressed through doctrinal, legal language. Property in socialism was from the very beginning in legal and ideological disarray, in part because of the regime's own uneasiness with private property, particularly in the area of housing, in part because of unquestioned continuities with the past, and in part because of doctrinal and judicial resistance. This does not mean open and defiant resistance, rather it points to a failure of imagination, a failure to challenge the way of imagining property that had been captured in bourgeois law and its model of property—its features, attributes, and structure. These continuities complement the ideological repositioning of property, the continued centrality of property, the conflation of property and power, and labor as the only legitimating value for private property.

Private property thus survived, as key formal and structural elements of bourgeois private property were universalized, essentialized, and appropriated for communist uses. Private property survived due to continuities in form and structure, the limited autonomy and entrenched formalism of civil law, which in turn also preserved ideas of property embedded in law. Taking into account significant restrictions of private property, however, the prominence of socialist state property, and the extent of legal instrumentalism in the property field, a key question remains: did the changes brought by the communist regime amount to a property paradigm change? Significant ideological and structural continuities suggest that there was no major paradigm change, as the mutual adaptation of capitalist property and communist ideology and practices resulted in a hybrid property model ensconced in the Roman/Napoleonic tradition.

Houses are at the center of this book, however, and the middle chapters directly focus on them: the taking of houses under various guises, the former owners' efforts to regain their houses and their discourses of resistance in the petitions, the state responses to the petitions, and the intertwining of legality, ideology, and politics in this process. Statistically, two-thirds of houses remained in private hands after the 1950 nationalization, and other than personal effects, household items and cars, they were the only type of personal property allowed throughout communism. Precisely because not all houses were seized, state bodies at all levels were forced to engage in a calculus of how many houses are to be taken over, and based on what criteria. This, in turn, opened up a debate over the very meaning of private property in a communist system—does it have a place in it, how much, and on what basis. By itself, this debate questioned the communist utopia and opened up a rift between "actuality" and "ideology" that nurtured the survival of private property (Unger 1976).

The core of the takings was the nationalization of urban housing, which started out in force, with legal and extra-legal takings (1950–1952) and plans for more takings in subsequent years. Yet despite the fact that this was an era of deep repression that targeted precisely those nationalized, a surprisingly high percentage of nationalized owners in Timişoara (45 percent) fought back and petitioned, sometimes multiple times, to regain their home. Former owners noted the partial and arbitrary nature of the takings, and mobilized the law—the nationalization decree itself—to contest the regime's understanding of private property, labor, and exploitation, and to argue that their houses had been gained through labor, not exploitation.

The backlash from the petitioners, the formalities of the nationalization process and the need for regime legitimacy prompted the adoption of the 1953 Instructions for the implementation of nationalization, which attempted to eliminate arbitrariness in the nationalization process and soon bogged it down to such an extent that no second wave of takings ever happened. The push back from petitioners also helped reveal the extent to which state practices themselves were riddled with inconsistencies that sent mixed messages about the value and meanings of private property in communism. In the process of dealing with the petitions and in light of other priorities, the state readjusted its position and withdrew from further nationalizations of urban housing, despite evidence of preparations for a second nationalization wave that would have targeted 1,200 more owners throughout the county and about 700 in the city. In short, resistance through law—particularly the legal-bureaucratic construction of the category of "housing exploiter" and the procedural aspects of dealing with the petitions (the double-edged sword of the formality of law)—contributed to halting the nationalization of urban housing.

Former owners' mobilization of law in defense of what they perceived to be their violated property rights, as well as the officials' tentative responses—initially a very high rate of proposed restitutions (20 percent of all petitions), detailed investigation of petitions, attempts to regularize the process (1953, 1955), yet also the secrecy, illegality, and arbitrariness of the takings reveal three phenomena. First, the regime did not expect this kind of legalistic resistance to the takings, or to such an extent. Second, former owners continued to operate largely within the pre-communist *nomos*, despite their radically changed circumstances, thus both trusted law somewhat and deployed it for their own purposes—defending their property rights. The ownership of their homes, even for those petitioners who had formally embraced the communist agenda, was clearly off limits, and dispossessed owners did not hesitate to fight within their limited possibilities. Third, local bureaucrats were caught between their own understanding of homes as private property, and the communist project of denaturalizing private property in general. They interpreted exploitation expansively, yet also quietly acknowledged that they went overboard when they proposed to return a fifth of the houses taken. They craved certainty and clarity during this process, yet did not trust an instrument—the law—that also offered "the other side" (i.e., former owners) possibilities of engagement and resistance. Perhaps surprisingly, they were warier of legality than former owners themselves, who were nonetheless officially excluded from the protection of the law.

As an instance of hegemony and counter-hegemony, the takings reveal the ambiguous nature of power and resistance and the extent to which legality can be a duplicitous ally for both. Attempts to redefine the meaning and concept of private property were caught between an actually existing past and a barely imagined future, and law, only partially redefined and ever cautious, was a reluctant instrument of the state, and yet not fully amenable to former owners, either. These efforts to reconceptualize private property were only partially successful, and only to the extent that the regime incorporated ("translated") preexisting ideas about labor and property.

The legal ideology of property rights under the communist regime in Romania thus embodied mixed messages about the value and meanings of private property and the kind of social relationships it constructs. While the communist regime attempted to deploy the legal system instrumentally, indifference to its history, internal integrity and cultural significance meant that ideas about the centrality of property did not fundamentally change and property law remained a field of ideological struggle. Although values such as labor and equality in connection with private property were reinforced, the mixed messages send through the legal system, as well as its limited autonomy, created possibilities for resistance and constrained the impact of the communist regime on identities and subjectivities.

The failure to collapse preferences into objective interests through ideology left the door open for alternative conceptualizations of life and for continuities with prior systems of value. The partial overlap of ideological grids, such as Marxism and liberalism, meant that acts such as petitions against nationalization could be simultaneously acts of cooptation and of resistance, for example, as labor is accepted as a valid basis for property in both systems. The failure to institute a new system of values also meant that mechanisms of impersonal power were only superficially successful: while they ensured outward conformity with the regime, they also tolerated ideological divergence and never constructed socialist subjects that were totally distinct from bourgeois subjects. The materiality of surveillance, normalization, and regimentation mechanisms, in other words, failed to achieve the domination from within which Hannah Arendt had predicted.

These weaknesses were eagerly exploited not just by dissidents, but also by ordinary citizens in their everyday dealings with the regime and clearly posed difficulties for the bureaucrats as well. For a system of power that attempted to colonize and collectivize life in all its manifestations, it is ironic that its ultimate demise was rooted in individual acts of resistance, silence, or even partial cooptation. These were later crystallized by dissident leaders who advanced "human rights" and "anti-politics." Together with other "subaltern" ideologies of modernity—capitalism, democracy, and nationalism most prominently, they eventually prepared the way for the existential-political revolutions of 1989.

This book raises a number of questions that I did not directly tackle and that have broader implications for the study of communism, property, and legality. First, even though every revolution is predicated on the actual possibility of radical social change, no revolutionary regime has so far been so monolithic that it succeeded entirely in achieving this type of fundamental change. Alternative ideologies are always present, resistance is always present. It may not be open or even that distinct from cooptation or simply inertia, but its mere existence and particularly accretion over time can indicate the holdout of prior hegemonic regimes within the revolutionary regime itself. I believe this was the case of private property in communism, as the separation between the base and superstructure and the focus on the material base distracted the reality constructors from fully engaging with dismantling the superstructure.

I do not intend to suggest that had the communist regime been more deliberate, more monolithic, ideas of private property would have disappeared and the new societies would have broken completely with capitalist property. It is possible, but unlikely as long as there remain fundamental, deep legal continuities in how law conceptualizes and regulates ownership, possession, and property more broadly. The more realistic project, which the communist regime indeed undertook, was to purge "bourgeois" property of its associations with "exploitation" and consequently naturalize a much narrower idea of private property, while keeping the legal institution of property. This, in turn, hinged on the distinction between means of consumption and means of production, one that is simply too complex, fluid, and context-bound to be easily encapsulated and controlled. In the case of houses, as we saw, which are both homes and assets, maintaining a rigid distinction, over-extending the reach of "exploitation" and adding "need" into the mix fatally undermined the project of unsettling the hegemony of private property over houses.

Had the regime restricted itself to taking a minimum of houses and instituting strict, but not excessive housing policies, could "private property" have become "personal property," houses only consumption goods, and communism achievable? Or would it still have been the Trojan horse in the communist refashioning of property? In answer to the first question, probably not, to the extent that completely eliminating the potential of houses as "means of production" would depend upon full knowledge and control over the housing market and the movement of population, neither one of which is realistic (other changes would have to include eliminating inheritance rights, for example, as the original communist agenda envisioned). Moreover, as long as the key justification for personal property was still labor, connections between property, personhood, and power would have been equally difficult to unmake.

Insofar as generalizing to other types of private property and the extent to which allowing one type of private property might cause a "domino effect," it is worth noting that post-1989 there have been two explosive property issues: the restitution of houses and of land. In other words, these are the two areas where there is a fine line between exploitation and labor, and where property is deeply connected to personhood, family, identity, history, and so on (an argument that was not pursued here is the extent to which private property ideas survived in connection with small plots of land around the house, allowed in the countryside). This is much less the case for industrial enterprises, commercial companies, and so on, which are easily classified as means of production. Their legal status during communism was also different, since they were exclusively state property.

Finally, I am not making an argument for the universality and permanence of bourgeois (capitalist) private property, even though I focus much more on continuities than ruptures. Rather, my interest lies in understanding the making and unmaking of hegemonic discourses around law and property, and their potential to construct or subvert the communist project. One can imagine a system that still retains some form of private property of housing that does not have the features described in this book, although it is hard to imagine it based on the current continental civil law model.

It is precisely the embeddedness of property in this specific legal paradigm that makes it difficult to reimagine it. Law's system features (from a systems' theory perspective) ensured that once the core elements of private property remained in place, so did to a large extent the ideologies and meanings they encompassed. Yet socialist legality resists easy characterizations: it cannot be normatively defined as "good" or "bad" (particularly by comparison with the "rule of law"—good), and it is not exclusively captured by the state, which meant that it could be mobilized to resist social change.

Post-1965, the changes brought by the first two decades of communism in Romania were not overturned. The Ceauşescu regime restricted the scope of private property even more, particularly through limiting the number of homes per person or family, and through systematization: a nationwide policy of expropriation, demolition, and reconstruction of villages, towns, and cities, aiming toward building a "multilaterally developed socialist society." These changes and their impact on postcommunist property developments require their own study. I will only note here that similarly to urban housing nationalization, they did not undermine in any significant measure the import or meaning of private property ideas.

Concretely, private property's survival is captured in high homeownership rates throughout communism: by 1989, 63 percent of homes in urban areas were privately owned, while home ownership in rural areas was almost entirely private (97 percent) (Dawidson 2004, 124).[1] Officially, private property returned with a vengeance in post-communism, as a main goal of the postcommunist transition has been the breakup of state ownership ("expropriating the state"), and the shift from socialist legality—law with an explicit class character, to Western legality—the rule of law (Şerban 2018). The extent and impact of Eastern European property changes have been widely studied (Verdery 2003; Hann 2000; Przeworski 1991; Frydman and Rapaczynski 1994).

Restitutions, and housing restitutions in particular, have been a central item on the de-communization agenda. Restitutions in general can have multiple, contradictory goals, including restoration, reparation, de-communization, (re) establishing the sanctity of capitalist private property, and reinforcing a new rule of law regime (Ciobanu 2013, 46–47; Elster 2004; Csongor 2009; Teitel 2000; Karadjova 2004). They also have symbolic, moral, and cultural importance, as they promote reconciliation and trust in the new democratic governments, acknowledge victims' dignity and suffering, and clarify group rights (Barkan 2000; Kritz 1995). Restitution policies in Romania have embraced a relatively fluid concept of property, grounded in historical change, the need to arbitrate between different societal interests, and reasonably attentive to the embeddedness of property in communities (Underkuffler 2003, 48, 59).

Despite its centrality, however, housing restitution remains unfinished business. The Romanian state has not, for example, prioritized the restitution of Jewish property seized during the Holocaust or by the communist regime, and has only recently passed a statute specifically addressing this issue (Law 103/May 2016). Like nationalization, the property question in postcommunist Romania turned out to be a lengthy and complex process, characterized by ambiguity and arbitrariness, if not secrecy. Restitution pitted former owners against socialist tenants/new owners, the state, and various vested interests throughout the bureaucracy and the new economy. Crucially, former owners mobilized supranational agents, primarily the European Court of Human Rights (ECHR), in support of their property claims. Claims of historical justice were countered by claims of efficiency, the needs of the market economy, and ensuring the stability of the housing market. The legislative framework of housing restitution and the implementation of restitution measures are awash in political indecision, confusion, overlapping rights, abuse at central and local levels, multiple judicial practices and inconsistency (SAR 2008).

A basic overview of the restitution landscape post-1989 includes Law 18/1991 regulating land and restitution of land, Law 112/1995 on nationalized houses, Law 54/1998 regulating the circulation of land, Emergency Ordinance 83/1999 regulating the restitution of buildings that belonged to ethnic minorities, Law 1/2000 on the reconstitution of property rights over agricultural land and forests, Emergency Ordinance 94/2000 on the restitution of religious buildings, Law 10/2001 on restitution of buildings, Law 247/2005 on reforming property and justice, and Law 165/2013 finalizing housing restitution. All these pieces of legislation have been amended a number of times, and are implemented through a plethora of governmental decrees and local ordinances.[2]

The first step in the housing restitution debate came early on in 1990, with Law 61/1990 that allowed 3 million state tenants to buy the state-owned and state-built apartments they occupied at very good prices (Stan 2006). The number sold in Timişoara was over 50,000 housing units (Mayor's Report 2008, 11) (a massive corruption scandal surrounding the illegal sale of this type of housing engulfed former top officials in the city in 2017). This included tenants who occupied nationalized buildings. Among them were members of the new elites across the political and economic spectrum, who had either lived there before 1989 or moved in right after (under five-year rental contracts, with the possibility of renewal, see Stan 2006, 188–90).

Many owners of nationalized buildings began restitution claims in court as early as 1990, with the number of court decisions throughout the country estimated in the thousands (see also Stan 2006, 191). Courts responded, for the most part, in favor of former owners and ordered the eviction of tenants. Former owners made two types of separate claims: asking courts to acknowledge the illegality of confiscation and the validity of the original title, and separately, against the tenants, to obtain de facto ownership (Baias et al. 2001). The government, meanwhile, wanted a statutory solution, while major political figures such as the president of the country at the time (Ion Iliescu) publicly criticized restitutions and the courts for resolving these types of cases, and asked for the non-implementation of court decisions in favor of former owners.[3]

It was only in 1995, after five years of bitter debates, that Parliament managed to reach some consensus over housing restitution and compensation. The result, Law 112/1995, limited natural restitution (the house/apartment itself) to cases where the houses or apartments were either vacant or occupied by the original owners, and allowed the tenants to buy their housing, again at good prices. The 1995 statute also allowed tenants to stay for five years in the building they occupied. A buying frenzy followed, while efforts to amend the law in favor of the original owners overall failed. Critics of the 1995 statute argued that favoring tenants meant, in fact, favoring the former communist nomenklatura that occupied and bought these houses.

The Constitutional Court overall confirmed the protection afforded tenants (e.g., Decision 62/June 13, 1995; Decision 126/November 16, 1994; Decision 73/July 19, 1995; Decision 2/February 3, 1998), while former owners interpreted the post-1989 restitution efforts as another nationalization. Spurred in part by the country's desire to join the European Union and eager to overturn perceptions of failing in transitional justice, modernization, and capitalism, Parliament reversed course and adopted Law 10/2001, which established the principle of natural restitution as primary, and compensation as secondary (only when physical restitution was not possible).

Law 10 expanded the scope of claimants, allowed for restitution on the basis of court decisions, protected tenants' leases and the property rights of tenants who had bought on the basis of Law 112, imposed short statutes of limitations for owners to file restitution claims, and restricted physical restitution for buildings used for institutional purposes (see Stan 2006, 195–96; SAR 2008). The implementation of Law 10 (amended multiple times) has also been problematic, plagued locally by wide discretion at the local level, extensive litigation, difficulties determining compensation, contradictions between Law 10 and its implementation instructions (which were issued two years after Law 10 itself!), and the lack of centralized coordination and unified implementation (Stan 2006; SAR 2008).

Finally, a key element distinguishing restitution post-1989 from nationalization is the mobilization of supranational power structures, and in particular the European Court of Human Rights. If nationalized owners in the 1950s and 1960s had as final recourse the Council of Ministers and the top level of the Communist Party, by the late 1990s they had the option of leveraging Romania's desire to become "European" and appeal to the ECHR. Former owners challenged in particular the practice of annulment appeals, the sale of nationalized property to tenants, and the mandatory extension of rental contracts (SAR 2008). The ECHR has responded positively and found Romania responsible for failing to provide effective mechanisms for restitution and compensation (*Străin and Others v. Romania*, ECHR 2005), failing to decide promptly on claims (*Atanasiu v. Romania*, ECHR 2010), conflicting interpretations of restitution laws, and perpetuating legal uncertainty for former and new owners (*Tudor v. Romania*, ECHR 2009) (Council of Europe 2011; DGIP 2010, 96–115).

Following the Court's judgment in *Atanasiu*, the government recognized that the statutory framework for restitution was too complex, incoherent, that the high number of unresolved claims—approximately 200,000—was unacceptable, and that the system overall was inefficient (see the statement of purpose for Law 165/2013). Three years post-*Atanasiu*, Romania adopted yet another restitution statute, Law 165/2013 (amended by Law 168/2015), which established four principles at the heart of the process: favoring restitution over compensation, equity (fairness), transparency of the process, and finally maintaining a fair balance between the interests of former owners and the general interest of society. Eerily reminiscent of the nationalization process, Law 165 established a points-based compensation procedure when restitution was not possible, and created the National Commission for Compensating Building Owners (Stan 2013).

By April 2013, based on statistics offered by then Prime Minister Victor Ponta, approximately 10,000 buildings had been physically returned to the former owners (unclear how many residential units this includes), and only 13,000 compensation claims had been solved, out of a total number of over 200,000. By November 5, 2015, the National Authority for the Restitution of Property had solved 16,373 claims initiated under Law 10/2001, and was working on approximately 700 claims per month (ANRP 2015). As of February 2019, it still had to resolve about 34,000 claims on the basis of Law 10/2001 (ANRP 2019). This government agency is also responsible for resolving approximately 4,500 claims related to the seizing of Jewish property during the Holocaust or by the communist regime, filed on the basis of Law 103/2016. So far, it has responded to almost 2,600 claims (ANRP 2019).

In Timişoara, by 2013 the vast majority of housing seized by the communist regime had been either returned or compensated (only 5 percent of the housing remained in state property), yet the restitution process has been protracted and litigious. The majority of claimants received compensation, not physical restitution of the building—for example, in 2006, only 393 housing units were given back, while for 1,732 the city hall offered compensation (Mayor's Report 2008, 11). Housing restitution claims have been the second-largest category of civil lawsuits in the city, an average of over three hundred every year (Mayor's Report 2013), with that number tapering off only recently (there were about eighty-six lawsuits related to housing restitution in 2017, according to the 2017 report of the Mayor).

Specific to Banat and Timişoara is the intertwining of property, restitution, and identity, as well as the distinction between former owners and their heirs, particularly in the case of former owners who left the country during or after communism. The number of Germans from the region, for example, has dropped from 310,000 in 1941 to 159,000 in 1977, and even further to 90,000 in 1989. Emigration continued after 1989, so by the end of 1991 there were only 30,000 Germans living in Banat (Gräf 2018, 34). Their place was taken primarily by ethnic Romanians from other regions of the country, as well as occasionally ethnic Hungarians. Similarly, the Jewish community in Timişoara dropped over time from about 12,000 at the beginning of the Second World War (which rose to 14,000 after the Ribbentrop-Molotov Pact of 1940) to less than 600 today (Laszlo 2006). The loss of these communities' homes and their struggle for restitution or compensation is thus intimately tied to larger policies of Romanian nation-state building, as they were disproportionately impacted by the vagaries of the restitution process post-1989.

Former owners, if alive, have been more invested in restitution of the housing itself, while heirs, particularly those from abroad, have been significantly less interested in fully throwing themselves into the restitution battle and often decided to pursue compensation, rather than physical restitution (Şerban 2018). Some heirs became resigned faced with the enormity of the restitution process, as was the case with the nephew of an interwar rabbi, who was living abroad and decided to pursue compensation, instead of physical restitution, for his uncle's nationalized house.

Others resented their parents' attachment to the nationalized property. Former owners had witnessed, as children or teenagers, the loss of housing and saw the impact this had on their families. I interviewed one of them, who remembered her father just passing by their former street every week to check on the nationalized house throughout communism. Still alive in 1989, he immediately began efforts to reclaim the house, looking for documents and writing petitions to authorities. My interviewee's mother, who was not alive anymore, had collected ownership documents going back to 1943 in a bundle tied with a pink ribbon. My interviewee's daughter, on the other hand, who emigrated to Israel with her family after 1989, had no emotional attachment to the house, and reproached her mother for being more attached to the house, than to her.

The value of the housing at stake in the restitution process was significant enough that an entire cottage industry of both lawyers chasing restitutions (a Romanian version of ambulance chasers) and buyers of claims emerged. The distinction between former owners with a stake in the restitution process, and peddlers of history courting heirs was recognized both by Law 165/2013 and the Constitutional Court, which upheld the provision that compensated differently former owners from those who had merely bought the claim to restitution, precisely because of the personal connection and the abusive nature of the taking vis-à-vis the former owners (Decision 197/April 3, 2014).

Early 1990s statutes that enabled tenants to buy the apartments and houses they occupied further complicated restitution, as tenants accused the former owners who asked for restitution of greediness. They thought owners had already received compensation from the communist regime (or Germany or Israel, if they emigrated), so asking for restitution or compensation after 1989 was unfair. (In fact, nationalized owners received no compensation, while those who were expropriated received a nominal sum, and certainly not always.) Owners overall, as a category, were perceived as "having no soul" if they evicted tenants after winning back their houses, if they gloated, and if they sold the houses or apartments (Şerban 2018).

The state, meanwhile, has been less interested in claims of historical justice and more concerned with the difficulty of full restitution, costs of compensation, protection of vested interests, and ensuring everyone's right to housing. The government believed that former owners had rights to their property, but that restitution needed to reflect the "juridical, social, temporal and material changes these properties suffered" under communism (Stan 2006, 191–92). The ruling coalition within the government, the social democrats, clearly privileged the tenants/new owners' property rights, with use more important than old title. Finally, and aside from the issue of corruption, for the government this was fundamentally a housing problem, and only secondarily a historical property rights problem (Stan 2006, 191).

Looking back at almost seventy years of property turmoil, we ultimately see a legal culture of property that centers the state, although its role is by no means exclusive even during communism. More importantly, this property field is rich with property discourses and ideologies traversing both communism and post-communism, shaped by time and identity, and ultimately somewhat autonomous of the state, even when the state makes massive, targeted efforts to change it. During communism, housing nationalization and other takings resulted in a type of legal culture of property that was still infused by multiple conceptions of legality and justice and did not fundamentally reject private property, while the postcommunist legal culture of property remains tethered to the past and its contradictions. Restitution thus becomes a proxy war for history and validating certain histories over others, as different historical narratives are embedded in distinctive understandings of property and property rights.

NOTES

1. This part of the chapter draws significantly from Şerban (2018).
2. A full list and the text of all relevant legislation (in Romanian) can be found on the site of the National Authority for the Restitution of Property, http://www.anrp.gov.ro/legislatie.html.
3. The Supreme Court obliged in 1995, when it banned lower courts from hearing cases before the adoption of the restitution statute. Moreover, the Prosecutor General began to use the "recurs in anulare" (annulment appeal) to overturn final court decisions (Stan 2006). This practice was intensely criticized locally and internationally and was finally abandoned in 2008 under EU and ECHR pressure (SAR 2008).

Bibliography

Ajani, Gianmaria. 2002. "Formalism and Anti-formalism under Socialist Law: The Case of General Clauses within the Codification of Civil Law." *Global Jurist Advances* 2(2):1535–1661.

Albu, Ioan. 1960. "Problema prescripţiei dreptului la acţiune privind drepturile reale principale determinate de proprietatea socialistă" [The Problem of Statute of Limitations Regarding Property Rights Connected with Socialist Property]. *Legalitatea Populară* 6:19–30.

Alexander, Gregory S. 1991. "Time and Property in the American Republican Legal Culture." *New York University Law Review* 66(2):273–352.

Alexander, Gregory S. 1999. "Constitutionalizing Property: Two Experiences, Two Dilemmas." In *Property and the Constitution*, edited by Janet McLean, 88–108. Portland, OR: Hart Publishing.

Alexandrov, A. 1949. "Cu privire la critica rămăşiţelor ideologiei burgheze în definiţia dreptului" [A Criticism of the Remains of Bourgeois Ideology in the Definition of Law]. *Justiţia Nouă* 1–2:155–159.

Althusser, Louis. 2001 (1969). "Ideology and Ideological State Apparatuses: Some Notes toward an Investigation." In *Lenin and Philosophy and Other Essays*, edited by Louis Althusser, 127–186. New York: Monthly Review Press.

Anca, Petre. 1958. "Dreptul de închiriere al organizaţiilor socialiste cu privire la clădirile aflate în folosinţa lor" [The Right of Socialist Organizations to Lease Buildings in Their Use]. *Legalitatea Populară* 12:17–23.

Anghel, Ioan. 1958. "Probleme în legătură cu încheierea contractului de închiriere a locuinţelor în dreptul RPR" [Problems Regarding Housing Rental Contracts]. *Legalitatea Populară* 3:21–33.

Anghel, Ioan and Vasile Pătulea. 1962. "Întinderea atribuţiilor organelor administraţiei de stat în materie locativă" [The Scope of Power of the State Administration in the Field of Housing]. *Justiţia Nouă* 6:14–16.

Antonescu, Nicolae and Mihai Constantinescu. 1960. "Câteva consideraţii asupra formalismului în practica de casare" [Thoughts on Formalism at the Appeal Level]. *Legalitatea Populară* 5:52–55.

Arendt, Hannah. 1948. *The Origins of Totalitarianism*. New York: Harvest Books.

Arendt, Hannah. 1970. *On Violence*. New York: Harvest Books.

Arjanov, A. 1949. "Despre problemele curente în domeniul teoriei statului şi dreptului" [Current Problems in the Field of Theory of State and Law]. *Justiţia Nouă* 1–2:147–154.

Association of Owners Forcibly Dispossessed by the State. 2005. *Gardianul*, July 27, 2005.

Association of Owners Forcibly Dispossessed by the State. 2008. "The Second Nationalization." *FrontNews*, June 9, 2008.

Auslander, Maximilian. 1951. "Lucrarea tovarăşului Stalin cu privire la Marxism în lingvistică şi unele probleme de teorie şi practică judiciară" [Comrade Stalin's Paper Regarding Marxism and Linguistics and Some Issues of Legal Theory and Practice]. *Justiţia Nouă* 4:386–389.

Autoritatea Naţională pentru Restituirea Proprietăţilor (ANRP) (National Authority for the Property Restitution). 2015–2019. Accessed February 20, 2019. http://www.anrp.gov.ro.

Baias, Flavius, B. Dumitrache, and M. Nicolae. 2001. *Regimul juridic al imobilelor preluate abuziv. Vol. I: Legea Nr. 10/2001 comentată şi adnotată [The Legal Situation of Nationalized Property. 1st Volume: Law 1/2001 Discussed and Annotated]*. Bucharest: Rosetti.

Banciu, Angela. 1996. *Istoria vieţii constituţionale în România (1866–1991) [The Constitutional History of Romania]*. Bucharest: Casa de editură şi presă ŞANSA – S.R.L.

Barkan, Elazar. 2000. *The Guilt of Nations: Restitution and Negotiating Historical Injustices*. New York: W. W. Norton.

Bărbieriu, Dumitru. 1958. "Pe marginea practicii judiciare a Tribunalului judeţean Cluj în legătura cu efectuarea schimbului de locuinţe" [A Comment on the Practice of the Cluj Tribunal Regarding the Exchange of Apartments]. *Legalitatea Populară* 5:47–49.

Bărbieru, Dumitru. 1961. "În legătură cu prescripţia scurtă de 10–20 ani" [About the Short Usucapio of 10–20 Years]. *Justiţia Nouă* 6:123–127.

Bârsan, Nicolae. 1955. "Ridicarea calificării ideologice şi profesionale, sarcina de bază a lucrătorilor din justiţie" [Raising the Professional and Ideological Level of Workers in the Justice System]. *Legalitatea Populară* 3:209–223.

Berman, Harold J. 1974. *Justice in the USSR: An Interpretation of the Soviet Law*. Cambridge, MA: Harvard University Press.

Betea, Lavinia. 2001. *Lucreţiu Pătrăşcanu. Moartea Unui Lider Comunist [The Death of a Communist Leader]*. Bucharest: Humanitas.

Blomley, Nicholas. 1998. "Landscapes of Property." *Law & Society Review* 32(3):567–612.

Bockman, Johanna and Gil Eyal. 2002. "Eastern Europe as a Laboratory for Economic Knowledge: The Transnational Roots of Neoliberalism." *American Journal of Sociology* 108(2):310–352.

Bodascher, Otto. 1948. "Timişoara—un oraş supradimensionat" [Timişoara—A Sprawling City]. *Luptătorul Bănăţean*, July 21, 1948.

Boia, Lucian. 2005. *Mitologia Ştiinţifică a Comunismului [The Scientific Mythology of Communism]*. Bucharest: Humanitas.

Boiu, Octavian. 1955. "Doi preşedinţi de tribunal – două activităţi cu două rezultate diferite" [Two Tribunal Presidents—Two Activities with Different Results]. *Legalitatea Populară* 2:110–117.

Borkenau, Franz. 1940. *The Totalitarian Enemy*. London: Faber & Faber.

Bourdieu, Pierre. 1977. *Outline of a Theory of Practice*. Cambridge: Cambridge University Press.

Bowring, Bill. 2013. *Law, Rights and Ideology in Russia: Landmarks in the Destiny of a Great Power*. London: Routledge.

Brădeanu, Salvator. 1956. "Problema Dobândirii Dreptului de Proprietate şi a Altor Drepturi Reale prin Uzucapiune în Lumina Dreptului Socialist" [The Problem of Acquiring Ownership and other Property Rights through Usucapio in Light of Romanian Socialist Law]. *Legalitatea Populară* 12:1443–1459.

Brădeanu, Salvator. 1957. "Probleme de Drept cu Privire Speciala asupra Dreptului de Superficie" [Legal Issues Concerning the Right of Superficies]. *Justiţia Nouă* 1:38–52.

Brădeanu, Salvator. 1958. "Se poate oare încuviinţa notarea în cartea funciară, pe baza unei cereri unilaterale a soţului, caracterul de bun comun al unui imobil dobândit în timpul căsătoriei?" [Is It Acceptable to Register in the CF, on the Basis of the Unilateral Request of One of the Spouses, the Common Goods of the Spouses?]. *Justiţia Nouă* 3:436–441.

Bratu, A. 1949. "Caracterul de clasă al justiţiei" [The Class Character of Justice]. *Justiţia Nouă* 7–8:807–808.

Bratus, C. 1949. Review of *Socialist State Property*, by V. Venedictov. *Justiţia Nouă* 9:10.

Bratus, S. N. 1949. "Engels despre dreptul civil" [Engels on Civil Law]. *Justiţia Nouă* 3–4:359–366.

Bratus, S. N. 1949. "Unele Probleme ale Proiectului Codului Civil al URSS" [Some Problems Concerning the Draft Civil Code of the USSR]. *Justiţia Nouă* 1–2:113–143.

Brenkert, George G. 1979. "Freedom and Private Property in Marx." *Philosophy and Public Affairs* 8(2):122–147.

Broşteanu, Traian. 1948. "Liniile mari ale Constituţiei RPR" [The Broad Outlines of the Constitution]. *Justiţia Nouă* 3–4:65–70.

Brunner, Georg. 1982. "Legitimacy Doctrines and Legitimation Procedures in East European Systems." In *Political Legitimation in Communist States*, edited by T. H. Rigby and Ferenc Fehér, 27–44. New York: St. Martin's Press.

Buia, V. 1959. "Despre consiliile de judecată din întreprinderi şi instituţii" [About Lay Courts in Enterprises and Institutions]. *Justiţia Nouă* 1:45–55.

Bumiller, Kristen. 1988. *The Civil Rights Society: The Social Construction of Victims*. Baltimore, MD: Johns Hopkins University Press.

Bunaciu, Avram. 1949. "Procesul de creare a justiţiei populare" [The Process of Creating a Popular Justice System]. *Justiţia Nouă* 1–2:175–177.

Butler, William Elliott. 1988. *Soviet Law* (2nd ed). London: Butterworths Law.

Cahan, Jean Axelrad. 1994. "The Concept of Property in Marx's Theory of History: A Defense of the Autonomy of the Socioeconomic Base." *Science & Society* 58(4):392–414.

Cain, Maureen and Alan Hunt. 1979. *Marx and Engels on Law*. London: Academic Press.

Calancea, V. 1960. "Regimul legal al autorizării lucrărilor din sectorul construcţiilor şi al circulaţiei unor terenuri" [The Legal Regime of Authorizing Constructions and Land Transmission]. *Justiţia Nouă* 3:488–494.

Căpăţână, Octavian. 1962. "Modificările aduse regimului transcrierii şi inscripţiei imobiliare ca urmare a reorganizării notariatului de stat" [Changes to the Legal Regime of Real Estate Registration as a Result of the Reorganization of the State Notary Public System]. *Justiţia Nouă* 5:63–68.

Carter, Adam. 2005. "Of Property and the Human; or, C. B. Macpherson, Samuel Hearne, and Contemporary Theory." *University of Toronto Quarterly* 74(3):829–844.

Casals, Felipe Garcia (Pavel Câmpeanu). 1980 (2002 ed). *Societatea Sincretică 1980 [The Syncretic Society]*. Translated by Nadia Badrus. Bucharest: Polirom.

Ceterchi, Ioan. 1958. "Caracterul reacţionar şi anti-ştiinţific al conceptiilor revizioniste cu privire la funcţiile statului socialist în perioada de trecere de la capitalism la socialism" [The Reactionary and Anti-Scientific Character of Revisionist Concepts of the State's Functions during the Transition to Socialism]. *Justiţia Nouă* 6:971–979.

Ceterchi, Ioan. 1959. "Necesitatea dictaturii proletariatului şi revizionismul contemporan" [The Necessity of the Dictatorship of the Proletariat and Contemporary Revisionism]. *Legalitatea Populară* 1:3–17.

Chelcea, Liviu. 2004. *State, Kinship and Urban Transformations During and After Housing Nationalization*. Ph.D. Dissertation. University of Michigan.

Chiribucă, Dan. 2004. *Tranziţia post-comunistă şi reconstrucţia modernităţii în România [The Post-Communist Transition and the Reconstruction of Modernity in Romania]*. Cluj-Napoca: Dacia, Eikon.

Chkhikvadze, V. M. 1969. *The Soviet State and Law*. Moscow: Progress Publishers.

Ciobanu, Monica. 2013. "Recent Restorative Justice Measures in Romania (2006–2010)." *Problems of Post-Communism* 60(5):45–57.

Cioroianu, Adrian. 2005. *Pe Umerii lui Marx. O Introducere în Istoria Comunismului Românesc [On Marx's Shoulders. An Introduction to the History of Romanian Communism]*. Bucharest: Curtea Veche.

Clark, Gordon L. 1982. "Rights, Property, and Community." *Economic Geography* 58(2):120–138.

Clark, Roland. 2015. *Holy Legionary Youth. Fascist Activism in Interwar Romania*. Ithaca, NY: Cornell University Press.

Cohen, Morris. 1927 (1933). "Property and Sovereignty." *Cornell Law Review* 13(1):8–30.

Comaroff, Jean and John Comaroff. 1991. *Of Revelation and Revolution: Christianity, Colonialism, and Consciousness in South Africa*. Chicago: University of Chicago Press.

Comaroff, Jean and John Comaroff. 1992. *Ethnography and the Historical Imagination*. Boulder, CO: Westview Press.

Comisia Prezidenţială pentru Analiza Dictaturii Comuniste din România [The Presidential Commission for the Analysis of the Communist Dictatorship in Romania] [CADCR]. 2006. *Raport Final [Final Report]*. Bucharest, Romania.

Constantiniu, Florin. 2002. *O istorie sinceră a poporului român [An Honest History of Romanians]*. Bucharest: Univers Enciclopedic.

Coombe, Rosemary and Andrew Herman. 2005. "Rhetorical Virtues: Property, Speech, and the Commons on the World-Wide Web." *Anthropological Quarterly* 77(3):559–574.

Cotterrell, Roger. 1992. *The Sociology of Law*. London: Butterworth.

Cotterrell, Roger. 1997. *Law's Community. Legal Theory in Sociological Perspective*. New York: Oxford University Press.

Cotterrell, Roger. 1999. *Emile Durkheim: Law in a Moral Domain*. London: Stanford University Press.

Council of Europe. 2011. "Case-law of the European Court of Human Rights: Summary of Selected Judgments and Decisions on Property Restitution/Compensation." http://www.coe.int.

Courtois, Stéphane, Nicolas Werth, Jean-Louis Panné, Andrzej Paczowski, Karel Bartošek, and Jean-Louis Margolin. 1999. *The Black Book of Communism: Crimes, Terror, Repression*. Cambridge, MA: Harvard University Press.

Cover, Robert. 1983. "Nomos and Narrative." *Harvard Law Review* 97(4):4–68.

Cowan, Dave. 2004. "Legal Consciousness: Some Observations." *Modern Law Review* 67(6):928–958.

Creţulescu, N. 1958. "Activitatea judecătorilor în şedinţa de judecată" [The Activity of Judges in the Courtroom]. *Legalitatea Populară* 3:3–6.

Csongor, Kuti. 2009. *Post-Communist Restitution and the Rule of Law*. Budapest: Central European University Press.

David, René and John E. C. Brierley. 1985. *Major Legal Systems in the World Today: An Introduction to the Comparative Study of Law*. London: Stevens.

Dawidson, Karin E. K. 2004. "Conflicts of Interest in the Restitution and Privatization of Housing since the Fall of Socialism: The Case of Central Timişoara City—A Problem of Democracy?" *Europe-Asia Studies* 56(1):119–141.

Deletant, Dennis. 1999 (2001 ed). *Teroarea Comunistă în România. Gheorghiu-Dej şi Statul Poliţienesc 1948–1965 [The Communist Terror in Romania. Gheorghiu-Dej and the Police State]*. Translated by Lucian Leuştean. Bucharest: Polirom.

Deletant, Dennis. 1995 (2006). *Ceausescu and the Securitate. Coercion and Dissent in Romania, 1965–1989*. London: Hurst & Company.

Denize, Eugen and Cezar Mâţă. 2005. *România Comunistă. Statul şi Propaganda 1948–1953 [Communist Romania: State and Propaganda 1948–1953]*. Târgovşte: Editura Cetatea de Scaun.

Diaconescu, Alexandru and Constantin Oprişan. 1955. "Acţiunea în Revendicare ca Mijloc de Apărare a Proprietăţii Socialiste de Stat" [Rei Vindicatio as Means of Defending Socialist State Property]. *Legalitatea Populară* 7:707–719.

Diaconescu, Gheorghe. 1955. "Introduction." *Legalitatea Populară* 1:3–7.

Dima, Marin. 1948. "Oficiile de închiriere" [Rental Offices]. *Justiţia Nouă* 9–10:448–455.

Dimitriu, A. 1955. "Sarcinile avocaturii în RPR şi condiţiile create pentru îndeplinirea lor" [The Tasks of Lawyers in the RPR and the Conditions Created for Their Achievement]. *Legalitatea Populară* 3:232–244.

Drăgoescu, Vasile and Gheorghe Oprescu. 1958. "Unele probleme de legislaţie locativă în practica Tribunalului Suprem şi a organelor de procuratură" [Housing Issues in the Case Law of the Supreme Tribunal and Procuracy]. *Legalitatea Populară* 11:25–32.

Drăgoescu, Vasile and Constantin Paţac. 1957. "O verificare competentă a respectării legislaţiei locative" [A Competent Verification of the How Housing Laws Are Being Observed]. *Legalitatea Populară* 12:1447–1451.

Editor. 1948. "Legea prelungirii închirierilor" [The Statute for Extending Leases]. *Justiţia Nouă* 5–6:130.

Editor. 1948. "Naţionalizarea" [Nationalization]. *Justiţia Nouă* 5–6:121–122.

Editor. 1948. "O nouă procedură civilă" [A New Civil Procedure]. *Justiţia Nouă* 2:46–47.

Editor. 1949. "Constitutirea Societăţii de Ştiinţe Juridice 'Justiţia Nouă'" [The Creation of the Society for Juridical Sciences "New Justice"]. *Justiţia Nouă* 7–8:709.

Editor. 1949. "În legătură cu şcolile juridice" [About Law Schools]. *Justiţia Nouă* 7–8:814.

Editor. 1951. "Şcolile de calificare profesională" [Schools of Professional Training]. *Justiţia Nouă* 3:328.

Editor. 1952. "Constituţia Marilor Realizari ale Democraţiei Populare în Republica Populară Română" [The Constitution of the Great Achievements of the Popular Democracy in the Popular Republic of Romania]. *Justiţia Nouă* 4:449–454.

Editor. 1955. "Comemorarea lui Montesquieu la Academia RPR" [The Commemoration of Montesquieu at the Romanian Academy]. *Justiţia Nouă* 6:895.

Editor. 1955. "Sesiunea ştiinţifică a universităţii Babeş Bolyai, secţia ştiinţe juridice" [The Scientific Session of Babes-Bolyai University, Legal Science Department]. *Justiţia Nouă* 3:383–385.

Editor. 1956. "Câteva aspecte ale activităţii asociaţiei juriştilor din RPR" [Some Features of the Activity of the Jurists' Association]. *Justiţia Nouă* 7:1167.

Editor. 1956. "Cea de a doua sesiune ştiinţifică a Institutului de Cercetări Juridice" [The Second Scientific Session of the Institute for Juridical Research]. *Justiţia Nouă* 5:869.

Editor. 1956. "Răspunsuri la întrebările cititorilor" [Answers to Readers' Questions]. *Legalitatea Populară* 4:502–503.

Editor. 1958. "Apărarea Proprietăţii Socialiste—Sarcina de Bază a Tuturor Juriştilor din Republica Populară Română]. *Justiţia Nouă* 3:389–405.

Editor. 1959. "Din activitatea Asociaţiei Juriştilor din RPR–Timişoara" [From the Activity of the National Association of Jurists, Timişoara Branch]. *Justiţia Nouă* 1:82–84.

Editor. 1960. "Cu privire la unele accesorii ale suprafeţei locative" [Regarding Some Accessories of the Living Quarters]. *Justiţia Nouă* 6:1084–1086.

Efremovici, E. 1951. "Executarea hotărârilor judecătoreşti civile" [The Execution of Civil Decisions]. *Justiţia Nouă* 1:67.

Ehrlich, Eugene. 1922. "The Sociology of Law." *Harvard Law Review* 36:130–145.

Ehrlich, Eugene. 1936. (2001 ed). *Fundamental Principles of the Sociology of Law.* New Brunswick, NJ: Transaction Publishers.

Elian, Gheorghe. 1965. "Legalitatea socialistă, mijloc important de realizare a politicii PMR" [Socialist Legality, an Important Means for Achieving the Policies of the Party]. *Justiţia Nouă* 1:13–17.

Elster, Jon. 2004. *Closing the Books: Transitional Justice in Historical Perspective.* Cambridge: Cambridge University Press.

Engel, David M. 1984. "The Oven Bird's Song: Insiders, Outsiders, and Personal Injuries in an American Community." *Law & Society Review* 18(4):551–582.

Engel, David M. 1987. "Law, Time, and Community." *Law & Society Review* 21(4):605–638.

Engel, David M. 1998. "How Does Law Matter in the Constitution of Legal Consciousness?" In *How Does Law Matter?* edited by Brian Garth and Austin Sarat, 109–144. Evanston, IL: Northwestern University Press.

Engel, David and Frank Munger. 2003. *Rights of Inclusion: Law and Identity in the Life Stories of Americans with Disabilities.* Chicago: University of Chicago Press.

Engels, Frederick. 1882. "Engels to Marx. In Ventnor." Accessed February 15, 2019. www.marxists.org/archive/marx/works/1882/letters/82_12_15.htm.

Engels, Frederick. 1884 (2004 ed). *The Origin of the Family, Private Property and the State.* Chippendale, Australia: Resistance Books.

Engels, Frederick. 1893. "Letter to Franz Mehring." Accessed November 20, 2018. http://www.marxists.org/archive/marx/works/1893/letters/93_07_14.htm.

European Court of Human Rights. 2013. "The European Court of Human Rights in Facts and Figures." Accessed February 12, 2016. www.echr.coe.int.

European Court of Human Rights. 2018. "Violations by Article and by State." Accessed November 20, 2018. https://www.echr.coe.int/Documents/Stats_violation_1959_2017_ENG.pdf.

European Parliament, Directorate General for Internal Policies (DGIP), Policy Department: Citizens' Rights and Constitutional Affairs. 2010. *Private Properties Issues Following the Change of Political Regime in Former Socialist or Communist Countries.* Albania, Bosnia and Herzegovina, Bulgaria, Croatia, Romania, and Serbia. Accessed February 12, 2016. www.europarl.europa.eu.

Ewick, Patricia and Susan S. Silbey. 1998. *The Commonplace of Law.* Chicago: University of Chicago Press.

Ewick, Patricia and Susan S. Silbey. 1999. "Common Knowledge and Ideological Critique: The Significance of Knowing the Haves Come Out Ahead." *Law and Society Review* 33:1025–1041.

Ewick, Patricia and Susan S. Silbey. 2003. "Narrating Social Structure: Stories of Resistance to Legal Authority." *American Journal of Sociology* 108(6):1328–1372.

Fehér, Ferenc. 1982. "Paternalism as a Mode of Legitimation in Soviet-type Societies." In *Political Legitimation in Communist States*, edited by T. H. Rigby and Ferenc Fehér, 64–81. New York: St. Martin's Press.

Fekete, Gheorghe. 1954. "Cu Privire la Problema Proprietăţii Personale" [Regarding the Problem of Personal Property]. *Justiţia Nouă* 2:198–203.

Feldbrugge, F. J. M. 1993. *Russian Law: The End of the Soviet System and the Role of Law*. Dordrecht: Martinus Nijhoff.

Feller, S. 1952. "Poate fi substituită revizuirea prin îndreptare? Natura juridică a îndreptării" [The Legal Nature of Îndreptare]. *Justiţia Nouă* 1:60.

Feller, S. 1953. "Noua constituţie a RPR" [The New Constitution of the Popular Republic of Romania]. *Justiţia Nouă* 1:43–73.

Feller, S. 1955. "Încă odată despre folosirea literaturii juridice burgheze în munca noastră practică de înfăptuire a legalităţii populare" [Once Again about Using Bourgeois Legal Doctrine in Our Practical Work of Popular Legality]. *Legalitatea Populară* 6:585–592.

Felstiner, William, Richard L. Abel, and Austin Sarat. 1980–1981. "The Emergence and Transformation of Disputes: Naming, Blaming, Claiming. . . ." *Law & Society Review* 15(3/4):631–654.

Feraru, Emil. 1951. "Constituţia RPR-arma legislativă de bază a democraţiei noastre populare în construirea socialismului" [The Constitution—the Fundamental Legislative Basis of Our Popular Democracy in the Construction of Socialism]. *Justiţia Nouă* 3:264.

Fleişiţ, Alexandru. 1949. "Dreptul civil burghez în slujba capitalului monopolist" [Bourgeois Civil Law in the Service of Monopoly Capital]. *Justiţia Nouă* 10:1157.

Flowerdew, John. 1997. "Reproduction, Resistance and Joint Production of Language Power: A Hong Kong Case Study." *Journal of Pragmatics* 27(3):315–337.

Foucault, Michel. 1975a. ''Film and Popular Memory: An Interview with Michel Foucault.'' *Radical Philosophy* 11:24–25.

Foucault, Michel. 1975b, 1995 ed. *Discipline & Punish. The Birth of the Prison*. New York: Vintage Books.

Foucault, Michel. 2000. *Power.* Vol. 3. Edited by James D. Faubion. New York: The New Press.

Frankowski, Stanislaw. 1987. "Eason-Weinmann Center for Comparative Law Eighth Annual Symposium: An Examination of the Unity and Diversity within the Socialist Legal Family: The Procuracy and the Regular Courts as the Palladium of Individual Rights and Liberties – The Case of Poland." *Tulane Law Review* 61:1307–1338.

Friedman, Jack R. 2003. *Ambiguous Transitions and Abjected Selves: Betrayal, Entitlement and Globalization in Romania's Jiu Valley*. Ph.D. Dissertation. Duke University.

Friedrich, Carl J. and Zbigniew K. Brzezinski. 1956. *Totalitarian Dictatorship and Autocracy*. Cambridge, MA: Harvard University Press.

Friling, Tuvia, Radu Ioanid, and Mihail Ionescu. 2004. *Final Report of the International Commission of the Holocaust in Romania*. Iasi: POLIROM.

Frydman, Roman and Andrzej Rapaczynski. 1994. *Privatization in Eastern Europe: Is the State Withering Away?* Budapest: Central European University Press.

Fuller, Lon L. 1948–1949. "Pashukanis and Vyshynski: A Study in the Development of Marxian Legal Theory." *Michigan Law Review* 47:1157–1166.

Gallagher, Mary E. 2006. "Mobilizing the Law in China: 'Informed Disenchantment' and the Development of Legal Consciousness." *Law and Society Review* 40(4):783–816.

García-Villegas, Mauricio. 2003. "Symbolic Power without Symbolic Violence? Critical Comments on Legal Consciousness Studies in USA." *Droit et Société* 53(1):137–163.

Garlicki, Leszek. 1987. "Eason-Weinmann Center for Comparative Law Eighth Annual Symposium: An Examination of the Unity and Diversity within the Socialist Legal Family: Constitutional and Administrative Courts as Custodians of the State Constitutions – The Experience of East European Countries." *Tulane Law Review* 61:1285–1306.

Geertz, Clifford. 1983. *Local Knowledge: Further Essays in Interpretive Anthropology*. New York: Basic Books.

Geertz, Clifford. 2000. *The Interpretation of Cultures*. New York: Basic Books.

Georgescu, Vlad. 1956. "Acţiunile Posesorii" [Possessory Actions]. *Legalitatea Populară* 7:771–796.

Georgescu, V. 1956. "Proprietatea Personală asupra Locuinţelor Construite sau Cumpărate cu Credite Acordate de Stat" [Personal Property of Homes Bought or Built with State Credit]. *Legalitatea Populară* 4:395–404.

Gergely, Eugen. 1955. "Metoda dialectică în munca justiţiei populare" [The Dialectical Method in the System of Popular Justice]. *Justiţia Nouă* 3:307–319.

Gergely, Eugen. 1957. "Dialectica formei şi conţinutului dreptului în activitatea judiciară" [The Dialectics of Form and Content of Law in Judicial Activity]. *Legalitatea Populară* 5:515–529.

Gliga, Iona. 1957. "Unele probleme ale organizării, perfecţionării şi simplificării aparatului de stat în RPR" [Some Problems Regarding the Organization, Development and Simplification of the State Apparatus in the RPR]. *Justiţia Nouă* 4:606–622.

Gluckman, Max. 1965. *The Ideas in Barotse Jurisprudence*. New Haven, CT: Yale University Press.

Goody, Jack. 1962. *Death, Property and the Ancestors*. Stanford, CA: Stanford University Press.

Goody, Jack. 1976. *Production and Reproduction. A Comparative Study of the Domestic Domain*. Cambridge: Cambridge University Press.

Gough, Tim. 2008. "Resistance: Under What Grace." *Resistance Studies Magazine* 1:17–23. Accessed November 3, 2009. www.rsmag.org.

Gräf, Rudolf. 2018. "Germanii din Banat sau istoria între două emigrări. Cercul care s-a închis" ["The Germans from Banat or a History Between Two Migrations. The Closing Circle"]. In *Germanii din Banat prin povestirile lor [The Germans from Banat and Their Stories]*, edited by Smaranda Vultur. Bucharest: POLIROM.

Gramsci, Antonio. 1971 ed. *Selections from the Prison Notebooks*. New York: International Publishers.

Gray, Kevin. 1991. "Property in Thin Air." *Cambridge Law Journal* 50:252–307.

Gray, Kevin. 1994. "Equitable Property." *Current Legal Problems* 47(2):157–214.

Gray, Kevin and Susan Francis Gray. 1999. "Private Property and Public Propriety." In *Property and the Constitution*, edited by Janet McLean. Portland, OR: Hart Publishing.

Grey, Thomas. 1980. "The Disintegration of Property." In *Nomos XXII: Property*, edited by Roland Pennock and John Chapman. New York: New York University Press.

Groza, Ioan. 1958. "Asupra abuzului de folosinţă în materie de locaţiune" [Abuse of Use in Housing]. *Legalitatea Populară* 12:47–55.

Hamangiu, Constantin, I. Rosetti-Bălănescu, and Alexandru Băicoianu. 1928 (2002 ed). *Tratat de drept civil român [Treatise of Romanian Civil Law]*. Bucharest: ALL BECK Publishing.

Hann, Chris. 1993. "From Production to Property: Decollectivization and the Family-Land Relationship in Contemporary Hungary." *Man* 28(3):299–320.

Hann, Chris. 1994. "After Communism. Reflections on East European Anthropology and the Transition." *Social Anthropology* 2(3):229–249.

Hann, Chris. 1998. *Property Relations: Renewing the Anthropological Tradition*. Cambridge: Cambridge University Press.

Hann, Chris. 2000. "The Tragedy of the Privates? Postsocialist Property Relations in Anthropological Perspective." Working Paper 2. Max Planck Institute for Social Anthropology.

Haugaard, Mark. 2003. "Reflections on Seven Ways of Creating Power." *European Journal of Social Theory* 6(1):87–113.

Hazard, John. 1970. *Communists and Their Law*. Chicago: University of Chicago Press.

Heller, Agnes. 1982. "Phases of Legitimation in Soviet-Type Societies." In *Political Legitimation in Communist States*, edited by T. H. Rigby and Ferenc Fehér. New York: St. Martin's Press.

Heller, Agnes. 2002. "Is Marxism Still Relevant?" Presented at The International Conference on Constitutionalism in Transition: Africa and Eastern Europe, Kampala, January 14–17, 2002.

Hertogh, Marc. 2004. "A 'European' Conception of Legal Consciousness: Rediscovering Eugen Ehrlich." *Journal of Law and Society* 31(4):457–481.

Hilsenrad, Artur. 1949. "Despre Fondul Directorului" [About the Director's Fund]. *Justiţia Nouă* 7–8:778–781.

Hilsenrad, Artur. 1950. "Despre Obiectele Proprietăţii Socialiste de Stat" [About the Objects of Socialist State Property]. *Justiţia Nouă* 4:509–524.

Hollander, Jocelyn A. and Rachel L. Einwohner. 2004. "Conceptualizing Resistance." *Sociological Forum* 19(4):533–554.

Hull, Kathleen. 2003. "The Cultural Power of Law and the Cultural Enactment of Legality: The Case of Same-Sex Marriage." *Law & Social Inquiry* 28(3):629–657.

Humphrey, Caroline. 1999 (1983). *Marx Went Away, but Karl Stayed Behind*. Ann Arbor: University of Michigan Press.

Ioffe, Olympiad S. 1982. "Soviet Law and Roman Law." *Boston University Law Review Online* 62:701.

Ionescu-Gură, Nicoleta. 2005. *Stalinizarea României. Republica Populară Română 1948–1950: Transformări Instituţionale [The Stalinization of Romania. The*

Popular Republic of Romania 1948–1950: Institutional Transformations]. Bucharest: Editura BIC ALL.

Isaac, Jeffrey C. 1987. *Power and Marxist Theory: A Realist View*. Ithaca, NY: Cornell University Press.

Karadjova, Marianna. 2004. "Property Restitution in Eastern Europe: Domestic and International Human Rights Responses." *Review of Central and Eastern Europe Law* 3:325–363.

Kaugia, Silvia. 1996. "Structure of Legal Consciousness." *Juridica International* 1:16–20.

Kelsen, Hans. 1955. *The Communist Theory of Law*. New York: Frederick A. Praeger, Inc.

Kelsen, Hans. 1982. "The Concept of the Legal Order." *American Journal of Jurisprudence* 27:64–84.

Kennedy, Duncan. 1991. "The Stakes of Law, or Hale and Foucault." *Legal Studies Forum* 15(4):327–367.

Kritz, Neil J., ed. 1995. *Transitional Justice: How Emerging Democracies Reckon with Former Regimes*. Washington, DC: U.S. Institute of Peace.

Kommers, Donald. 1997. *The Constitutional Jurisprudence of the Federal Republic of Germany*. Durham, NC: Duke University Press.

Kronman, Anthony T. 1983. *Max Weber*. London: Edward Arnold.

Krygier, Martin. 1990. "Marxism and the Rule of Law: Reflections after the Collapse of Communism." *Law & Social Inquiry* 15(4):633–663.

Laszlo, Tomi. 2006. "Câteva cuvinte despre istoria comunității evreilor din Timişoara" [A Brief Overview of the History of the Jewish Community of Timişoara]. Accessed February 20, 2019. http://www.bjt2006.org/Discurs_TL_2311.pdf.

Lavrov, Gheorghe and A. Tătaru. 1959. "Despre partinitatea judecătorilor socialişti în legătură cu principiul independenţei judecătorului şi supunerii lui numai legii" [About the Partiality of Socialist Judges and the Principle of Judicial Independence]. *Legalitatea Populară* 4:3–14.

Leblanc, Lauraine. 1999. *Pretty in Punk: Girls' Gender Resistance in a Boys' Subculture*. New Brunswick, NJ: Rutgers University Press.

Lefort, Claude. 2002. "Thinking with and Against Hannah Arendt." *Social Research* 69(2):447–459.

Lenin, V. I. 1934. *The Proletarian Revolution and the Renegade Kautsky*. New York: International Publishers.

Lenin, V. I. 1907. "The Agrarian Programme of Social-Democracy in the First Russian Revolution, 1905–1907." Accessed February 15, 2019. https://www.marxists.org/archive/lenin/works/1907/agrprogr/ch01s5.htm.

Leonard, Sarah. 2017. "Why Are So Many Young Voters Falling for Old Socialists?" *New York Times*. Accessed June 16, 2017. https://www.nytimes.com/2017/06/16/opinion/sunday/sanders-corbyn-socialsts.html.

Linz, Juan J. 1975. "Totalitarian and Authoritarian Regimes." In *Handbook of Political Science*, edited by Fred I. Greenstein and Nelson Polsby. Cambridge: Addison Wesley.

Linz, Juan J. 2000. *Totalitarian and Authoritarian Regimes*. Boulder, CO: Lynne Rienner Publishers.

Linz, Juan J. and Alfred Stepan. 1996. *Problems of Democratic Transition and Consolidation: Southern Europe, South America, and Post-Communist Europe.* Baltimore, MD: Johns Hopkins University Press.

Linzmayer, C. 1958. "Probleme de drept în legătura cu supraetajarea clădirilor" [Legal Issues Concerning Adding Floors to the Buildings]. *Legalitatea Populară* 5:37–41.

Locke, John. 1988. *Two Treatises of Government.* Cambridge: Cambridge University Press.

Lovell, George I. 2006. "Justice Excused: The Deployment of Law in Everyday Political Encounters." *Law & Society Review* 40(2):283–325.

Lubonja, Fatos. 2001. "Privacy in a Totalitarian Regime." *Social Research* 68(1):237–255.

Lukes, Steven. 2005. *Power: A Radical View* (2nd ed). New York: Palgrave MacMillan.

Lupulescu, Dumitru. 1967. "Dreptul de proprietate personală în lumina constituţiei Republicii Socialiste România" [The Right to Personal Property in Light of the Constitution of the Socialist Republic of Romania]. *Revista Română de Drept* 7.

Luptătorul Bănăţean. 1947. "Depunerea declaraţiilor de impunere pentru clădirile închiriate" [Submitting Tax Information for Rentals]. November 17, 1947.

Luptătorul Bănăţean. 1947. "Milioane de cetăţeni îşi văd adăpostul asigurat" [Millions of Citizens Obtain Shelter]. September 25, 1947.

Luptătorul Bănăţean. 1947. "Proprietarii Invizibili" [The Invisible Owners]. October 4, 1947.

Luptătorul Bănăţean. 1947. "Recensământul întreprinderilor timişorene" [The Census of Timişoara's Enterprises]. Monday, October 13, 1947.

Luptătorul Bănăţean. 1948. "Azi începe recensământul locuinţelor la Timişoara" [Today Begins the Census of Dwellings in Timişoara]. December 13, 1948.

Luptătorul Bănăţean. 1948. "180 Avocaţi în Colegiul din Timişoara" ["180 Lawyers in the Timişoara Collective"]. April 28, 1948.

Luptătorul Bănăţean. 1948. "Recensământul populaţiei şi a gospodăriilor din Timişoara şi Fratelia se va face la 13, 14 şi 15 noiembrie" [Census of Population and Homes in Timişoara and Fratelia will be undertaken on the 13th, 14th and 15th of November]. December 13, 1948.

Luptătorul Bănăţean. 1948. "Câteva sfaturi în legătură cu recensământul clădirilor şi al apartamentelor din Timişoara" [Some Advice Regarding the Census of Buildings and Apartments in Timişoara]. December 12, 1948, 7.

Luptătorul Bănăţean. 1948. "Duminică începe recensământul clădirilor şi apartamentelor din Timişoara" [Sunday Begins the Census of Buildings and Apartments in Timişoara]. December 11, 1948.

Luptătorul Bănăţean. 1948. "Mersul recensământului locuinţelor la Timişoara—Foşti directori de fabrici care se lăfăesc în apartamente spaţioase şi luxoase" [The Progress of the Buildings Census—Former Factory Owners Living Large in Luxury Apartments]. December 17, 1948.

Luptătorul Bănăţean. 1948. "Azi se încheie lucrările pe teren ale recensământului clădirilor şi locuinţelor" [Today Ends the Field Work for the Census]. December 18, 1948.

MacPherson, C. B. 1962. *The Political Theory of Possessive Individualism: Hobbes to Locke*. Oxford: Clarendon.

MacPherson, C. B. 1978, 1999 ed. *Property: Mainstream and Critical Positions*. Toronto: University of Toronto Press.

Malinowski, Bronislaw. 1935. *Coral Gardens and Their Magic*. Vol. 1. London: Routledge.

Mancovschi, A. 1949. "Legalitatea socialistă sovietică şi principiile ei" [Soviet Socialist Legality and Its Principles]. *Justiţia Nouă* 10:1139–1156.

Mănescu, C. 1959. "Apărarea proprietăţii socialiste în RPR prin mijloace de drept" [Defending Socialist Property through Legal Means]. *Justiţia Nouă* 4:595–610.

Mańko, Rafał, Cosmin Cercel, and Adam Sulikowski. 2016. "Law and Critique in Central Europe: Laying the Cornerstone." In *Law and Critique in Central Europe: Questioning the Past, Resisting the Present*, edited by Rafał Mańko, Cosmin Cercel, and Adam Sulikowski. Oxford: Counterpress.

Manoliu, Ion. 1955. "Instanţele judecătoreşti şi procuratura apără şi consolidează legalitatea populară în Republica Populară Română [Courts and Prosecutors Defend and Consolidate Popular Legality in the Popular Republic of Romania]. *Legalitatea Populară* 1:12–23.

Markovits, Inga S. 1968. "Civil Law in East Germany. Its Development and Relation to Soviet Legal History and Ideology." *The Yale Law Journal* 78(1):1–51.

Markovits, Inga S. 1989. "Law and Glasnost: Some Thoughts about the Future of Judicial Review under Socialism." *Law & Society Review* 23(3):399–447.

Markovits, Inga S. 2007. "The Death of Socialist Law?" *The Annual Review of Law and Social Science* 3:233–253.

Markus, Maria. 1982. "Overt and Covert Modes of Legitimation in East European Societies." In *Political Legitimation in Communist States*, edited by T. H. Rigby and Ferenc Fehér. New York: St. Martin's Press.

Marshall, Anna-Maria. 2003. "Injustice Frames, Legality, and the Everyday Construction of Sexual Harassment." *Law & Social Inquiry* 28(3):659–690.

Marshall, Anna-Maria. 2005. "Idle Rights: Employees' Rights Consciousness and the Construction of Sexual Harassment Policies." *Law & Society Review* 39(1):83–124.

Marx, Karl. 1970. *A Contribution to the Critique of Political Economy*. Translated by S. W. Ryazanskaya. Edited by Maurice Dobb. New York: International Publishers.

Marx, Karl. 1978. "The German Ideology." In *The Marx-Engels Reader*, edited by Robert C. Tucker (2nd ed). New York: W. W. Norton.

Marx, Karl. 1992. *Capital*. London: Penguin Books.

Marx, Karl. *Manifesto of the Communist Party*. www.marxists.org.

Marx, Karl. *On the Jewish Question*. www.marxists.org.

Mayo, Mihail. 1948. "Consiliile populare locale" [Local Popular Councils]. *Justiţia Nouă* 3–4.

Mayo, Mihail. 1950. "Noua organizare a profesiunii de avocat" [The New Organization of the Legal Profession]. *Justiţia Nouă* 9–10:950–967.

McCann, Michael. 1994. *Rights at Work: Pay Equity Reform and the Politics of Legal Mobilization*. Chicago: University of Chicago Press.

Merry, Sally Engle. 1990. *Getting Justice and Getting Even: Legal Consciousness Among Working-Class Americans*. Chicago: University of Chicago Press.
Merry, Sally Engle. 2006. *Human Rights and Gender Violence: Translating International Law into Social Justice*. Chicago: University of Chicago Press.
Merry, Sally. 1985. "Concepts of Law and Justice among Working-Class Americans: Ideology as Culture." *Legal Studies Forum* 9(1):59–71.
Merry, Sally and Peggy Levitt. 2009. "Vernacularization on the Ground: Local Uses of Global Women's Rights in Peru, China, India and the United States." *Global Networks* 9(4):441–461.
Merryman, John. 1989. "The Public Interest in Cultural Property." *California Law Review* 77:339–364.
Mihalca, Adrian. 1949. "Justiţia populară, factor important al statului de democraţie popular" [Popular Justice, an Important Element in a State of Popular Democracy]. *Justiţia Nouă* 3–4:299–300.
Ministerul Muncii [Ministry of Labor]. n.d. "Salariul mediu annual 1938–1990" [Average Annual Salary 1938–1990]. Accessed November 25, 2018. http://www.mmuncii.ro/pub/imagemanager/images/file/Statistica/Statistici%20lunare/s38-90.pdf.
Mioc, Eugen. 2007. *Comunismul în Banat [Communism in Banat]*. Timişoara: Editura Excelsior Art.
Mittelman, James H. and Christine B. N. Chin. 2005. "Conceptualizing Resistance to Globalization." In *The Global Resistance Reader*, edited by Louise Amoore. London: Routledge.
Moldovan, Sabin. 1949. "Procesul civil în concepţia socialistă" [The Civil Process in the Socialist System]. *Justiţia Nouă* 9:973–978.
Montesquieu, Baron de. 1752. *The Spirit of the Laws*. Accessed November 25, 2018. http://www.constitution.org/cm/sol.htm.
Munteanu, Ioan and Rodica Munteanu. 2002. *Timişoara. Monografie [Timişoara. A Monography]*. Timişoara: Mirton.
Munteanu, Vasile. 1957. "Natura şi Consecinţele Juridice ale Actului de Înstrăinare Neperfectat Formal din Vina unei Părti în condiţiile Decretelor 151 şi 221/1950" [The Nature and Consequences of Conveyance Acts Not Formally Perfected because of One Side's Fault, under Decrees 151 and 221 from 1950]. *Legalitatea Populară* 4:409–415.
Munzer, Stephen R., ed. 2001. *New Essays in the Legal and Political Theory of Property*. Cambridge: Cambridge University Press.
Muraru, Ioan and Gheorghe Iancu. 1995. *Constituţiile Române [Romanian Constitutions]*. Bucharest: Monitorul Oficial.
Nedelschi, Gheorghe. 1949. "Împotriva cosmopolitismului în ştiinţa juridică" [Against Cosmopolitism in Legal Science]. *Justiţia Nouă* 7–8:725–738.
Nedelschi, Gheorghe. 1953. "Dreptul de Proprietate Personală în Societatea Socialistă" [The Right to Personal Property in the Socialist Society]. *Justiţia Nouă* 3:340–358.
Nedelschi, Gheorghe. 1954. "Dreptul de Proprietate Personală în Republica Populară Română" [The Right to Personal Property in the Popular Republic of Romania]. *Justiţia Nouă* 2:179–192.

Nedelsky, Jennifer. 1990. "Law, Boundaries, and the Bounded Self." *Representations* 30:162–189.

Nedelsky, Jennifer. 1993. "Property in Potential Life? A Relational Approach to Choosing Legal Categories." *Canadian Journal of Law and Jurisprudence* 6(2):343–365.

Nelson, Daniel E. 1980. *Democratic Centralism in Romania: A Study of Local Communist Politics*. Boulder, CO: East European Monographs.

Neumann, Victor, ed. 2015. *Istoria Banatului. Studii privind particularitățile unei regiuni transfrontaliere [The History of Banat. Studies on the Characteristics of a Transborder Region]*. Bucharest: Editura Academiei Române.

Niţulescu, Stelian. 1948. "Structura social-economică a RPR" [The Social and Economic Structure of the Popular Republic of Romania]. *Justiţia Nouă* 3–4.

Niţulescu, Stelian. 1960. "Munca juriştilor în etapa actuală" [The Work of Jurists in the Current Period]. *Justiţia Nouă* 4:601–607.

Niţulescu, Stelian. 1952. "Noua lege de organizare judecătorească" [The New Law of Judicial Organization]. *Justiţia Nouă* 4:457–459.

Nolte, Ernst. 1998. "The Three Versions of the Theory of Totalitarianism and the Significance of the Historical-Genetic Version." In *The Totalitarian Paradigm after the End of Communism*, edited by Achim Siegel. Amsterdam: Rodopi.

Nonet, Philippe and Philip Selznick. 1978. *Law and Society in Transition: Toward Responsive Law*. New York: Octagon Books.

Oancea, Paraschiva. 1949. "Cum am aplicat lupta de clasă în justiţie" [How I Applied Class Struggle in Law]. *Justiţia Nouă* 9:1011–1012.

Onescu, Marcu. 1958. "Unitatea de conţinut dintre norma juridică, izvorul de drept şi raportul juridic socialist" [Unity of Content between the Legal Norm, the Source of Law and the Socialist Legal Relation]. *Justiţia Nouă* 6:1000–1014.

Oprea, Marius. 2002. *Banalitatea Răului. O Istorie a Securităţii în Documente 1949–1989 [The Banality of Evil. A History of Securitate in Documents]*. Bucharest: Polirom.

Opriş, Petre. 2005. "Despre Numărul Membrilor Partidului Comunist din România la 23 August 1944" [About the Number of Members of the Communist Party of Romania on August 23, 1944]. July 7, 2010. www.stindard.ro.

Panu, Gheorghe. 1951. "Lenin despre stat şi drept" [Lenin about State and Law]. *Justiţia Nouă* 1:3–10.

Paşalega, D. 1959. "Acţiunea în revendicare—mijloc de drept civil pentru apărarea proprietăţii socialiste" [Rei Vindicatio—Civil Law Means for Defending Socialist Property]. *Legalitatea Populară* 8:39–55.

Pashukanis, E. B. 1979. *Law and Marxism. A General Theory*. Translated by Barbara Einhorn. Edited by Christ Arthur. London: Pluto Press.

Patulea, V. and I. Anghel. 1960. "Probleme în legătura cu restructurarea arhitectonică a spaţiilor locative" [Problems Concerning the Architectonic Restructuring of Housing]. *Justiţia Nouă* 4:683–693.

Patzelt, Werner J. 1998. "Reality Construction under Totalitarianism: An Ethnomethodological Elaboration of Martin Drath's Concept of Totalitarianism."

In *The Totalitarian Paradigm after the End of Communism*, edited by Achim Siegel. Amsterdam: Rodopi.
Paul, Andrei. 1949. "Statul de drept în democraţia populară" [The Rule of Law State in Popular Democracy]. *Justiţia Nouă* 5–6:569–570.
Petcu, Ioan. 1959. "Unele aspecte teoretice şi practice ale controlului jurisdicţional asupra legalităţii actelor administraţiei de stat" [Some Theoretical and Practical Aspects of Judicial Review of Administrative Acts]. *Legalitatea Populară* 4:19–27.
Pierson, Paul. 2000. "Not Just What, but *When*: Timing and Sequence in Political Processes." *Studies in American Political Development* 14:72–92.
Pile, Steve. 1997. "Opposition, Political Identities and Spaces of Resistance." In *Geographies of Resistance*, edited by Steve Pile and Michael Keith. London: Routledge.
Podgorecki, Adam and Vittorio Olgiati (eds.). 1996. *Totalitarian and Post-Totalitarian Law*. Brookfield, USA: Dartmouth.
Pohlmann, Friedrich. 1998. "The "Seeds of Destruction" in Totalitarian Systems. An Interpretation of the Unity in Hannah Arendt's Political Philosophy." In *The Totalitarian Paradigm after the End of Communism*, edited by Achim Siegel. Amsterdam: Rodopi.
Ponta, Victor. 2013. "Prime Minister Speech before Parliament." April 17, 2013. Accessed February 12, 2016. http://www.gov.ro.
Popescu, Ioan. 1948. "Organele supreme ale puterii de stat în constituţia RPR" [The Supreme Organs of State Power in the Constitution]. *Justiţia Nouă* 3–4.
Popescu, Vera. 1952. Review of *Socialist State Property*, by V. Venedictov. *Justiţia Nouă* 1:106–114.
Popovici, Mihai. 1948. "Organele judiciare şi parchetul în Constituţia RPR" [Courts and the Prosecution in the Constitution]. *Justiţia Nouă* 3–4.
Popovici, Mihai. 1948. "Scopul în drept" [The Aims of Law]. *Justiţia Nouă* 2.
Priban, Jiri. 1999. "Legitimacy and Legality after the Velver Revolution." In *The Rule of Law in Central Europe*, edited by Jiri Priban and James Young. Aldshot, UK: Ashgate/Dartmouth.
Primăria Timişoara [City Hall]. 2004–2017. "Raportul Primarului" ["Mayor's Report"]. Accessed February 20, 2019. https://www.primariatm.ro.
Protopopescu, G. 1948. "Organele administraţiei de stat în noua constituţie" [The Organs of State Administration in the New Constitution]. *Justiţia Nouă* 3–4.
Proudhon, Pierre Joseph. 1840. *What Is Property?* http://dhm.best.vwh.net/archives/proudhon-property-is-theft.html.
Przeworski, Adam. 1991. *Democracy and the Market. Political and Economic Reforms in Eastern Europe and Latin America*. Cambridge: Cambridge University Press.
Radin, Margaret Jane. 1982. "Property and Personhood." *Stanford Law Review* 34:957–1015.
Radin, Margaret Jane. 1996. *Reinterpreting Property*. Chicago: University of Chicago Press.
Râpeanu, Gheorghe. 1955. "Să Apărăm cu Hotărâre Avutul Nostru Obştesc" [Decisively Defending our Common Property]. *Legalitatea Populară* 2:99–109.

Râpeanu, Grigore. 1951. "Legalitatea socialistă" [Socialist Legality]. *Justiţia Nouă* 2:141–149.

Raţiu, Ciprian. 1948. "Noua politică legislativă" [The New Legislative Politics]. *Justiţia Nouă* 1.

Reeve, Andrew. 1986. *Property*. Herndon, VA: Humanities Press.

Reynolds, Sarah J. 1994. "The Role of Law in the Soviet System: Looking Back and Moving Forward." Review of *Russian Law: The End of the Soviet System and the Role of Law*, by F. J. M. Feldbrugge. *Michigan Journal of International Law* 15:797–815.

Rigby, T. H. 1982. "Political Legitimacy, Weber and Comunist Mono-organizational Systems." In *Political Legitimation in Communist States*, edited by T. H. Rigby and Ferenc Fehér. New York: St. Martin's Press.

Rofel, Lisa. 1999. *Other Modernities. Gendered Yearnings in China after Socialism.* Berkeley: University of California Press.

Romanian Academic Society (SAR). 2008. "Property Restitution: What Went Wrong in Romania?" *Policy Brief* 34:9–12. www.sar.org.

Rotman, Liviu. 2004. *Evreii din România în perioada comunistă [The Jews in Romania during Communism].* Iasi: POLIROM.

Rousseau, Jean Jacques. 1754. *A Discourse on Inequality.* www.constitution.org/jjr/ineq.htm.

Rousseau, Jean Jacques. 1762. *The Social Contract.* www.constitution.org/jjr/socon.htm.

Rousseau, Jean Jacques. 1997. *The Social Contract and Other Later Political Writings.* Edited and translated by Victor Gourevitch. Cambridge: Cambridge University Press.

Rucăreanu, D. and I. Luchian. 1965. Review of *Conştiinţa juridică socialistă [Socialist Legal Consciousness]*, by Anita Naschitz. *Justiţia Nouă* 1.

Rusan, Romulus. 2007. *Cronologia şi Geografia Represiunii Comuniste în România. Recensământul Populaţiei Concentraţionare (1945–1989) [The Chronology and Geography of Communist Repression in Romania. The Census of the Prison Population].* Bucharest: Fundaţia Academia Civică.

Sadurski, Wojciech. 1984. "Marxism and Legal Positivism." In *Essays in Legal Theory*, edited by Dennis Galligan. London: Carlton.

Sajó, András. 1994. "Law and Legal Scholarship in the Happiest Barrack and Among the Hungry Liberated: Personal Recollections." In *Marxism and Communism: Posthumous Reflections on Politics, Society, and Law*, edited by Martin Krygier. Amsterdam: Rodopi.

Samuel, Geoffrey. 1999. "The Many Dimensions of Property." In *Property and the Constitution*, edited by Janet McLean. Oxford, Portland, OR: Hart.

Sârbulescu, Petre. 1948. "Magistratul şi asesorii populari" [The Magistrate and the Lay Judges]. *Justiţia Nouă* 7.

Schreiber, Albert. 1948. "Legea de organizare judecătorească" [The Law for Judicial Organization]. *Justiţia Nouă* 1.

Schreiber, Albert. 1948. "Noua structură a justiţiei" [The New Structure of Justice]. *Justiţia Nouă* 5–6.

Schwarzschild, Maimon. 1986. “Variations on an Enigma: Law in Practice and Law on the Books in the USSR.” Review of *Soviet Law in Theory and Practice*, by Olympiad S. Ioffe and Peter B. Maggs, and Soviet Law, by W. E. Butler. *Harvard Law Review* 99(3):685–702.

Scott, James C. 1985. *Weapons of the Weak: Everyday Forms of Peasant Resistance*. New Haven, CT: Yale University Press.

Scott, James C. 1990. *Domination and the Arts of Resistance: Hidden Transcripts*. New Haven, CT: Yale University Press.

Scott, James C. 1998. *Seeing Like a State. How Certain Schemes to Improve the Human Condition Have Failed*. New Haven, CT: Yale University Press.

Şerban, Mihaela. 2010. “Surviving Property: Resistance against Urban Housing Nationalization during the Transition to Communism (Romania, 1950–1965).” *Special Issue: Interdisciplinary Legal Studies: The Next Generation, Studies in Law, Politics, and Society* 51:29–66.

Şerban, Mihaela. 2014. “The Loss of Property Rights and the Construction of Legal Consciousness in Early Socialist Romania (1950–1965).” *Law & Society Review* 48(4):773–805.

Şerban, Mihaela. 2015. “The Exceptionalism of Housing: Ideology and Politics in Early Communism in Romania (1945–1965).” *Europe-Asia Studies* 67(3):443–467.

Şerban, Mihaela. 2018. “Regime Change and Property Rights Consciousness in Post-Communist Romania.” *Law & Social Inquiry* 43(3):732–763.

Siegel, Achim. 1998. “Carl Joachim Friedrich’s Concept of Totalitarian Dictatorship: A Reinterpretation.” In *The Totalitarian Paradigm after the End of Communism*, edited by Achim Siegel. Amsterdam: Rodopi.

Siegel, Achim. 1998. “Introduction: The Changing Fortunes of the Totalitarian Paradigm in Communist Studies.” In *The Totalitarian Paradigm after the End of Communism*, edited by Achim Siegel. Amsterdam: Rodopi.

Silbey, Susan. 1998. “Ideology, Power and Justice.” In *Justice and Power in Socio-legal Studies*, edited by Bryan Garth and Austin Sarat. Evanston, IL: Northwest University Press.

Silbey, Susan S. 2005. “After Legal Consciousness.” *Annual Review of Law and Social Science* 1:323–368.

Singer, Joseph William. 1987–8. “The Reliance Interest in Property.” *Stanford Law Review* 40(3):611–751.

Solomon, Barbu. 1955. “Din practica de casare a Tribunalului Capitalei RPR în materie locativă” [The Housing Case Law of the Bucharest Tribunal]. *Justiţia Nouă* 3:320–343.

Stan, Lavinia. 2006. “The Roof over Our Heads: Property Restitution in Romania.” *Journal of Communist Studies and Transition Politics* 22(2):180–205.

Stan, Lavinia. 2013. “Denying Justice by Delaying It? The ECHR and Property Restitution in Romania.” *Journal of Property Rights in Transition*. Accessed January 13, 2015. http://propertyrightsintransition.com/denying-justice-by-delaying-it.

Stănescu-Bellu, Panait. 2006. *Memorii pentru Viitor [Memoires for the Future]*. Timişoara: Brumar.

Stângu, Aurel. 1962. "Soluţionarea unor probleme juridice privind înstrăinarile cu titlu oneros ale unor imobile" [Legal Problems Regarding Selling and Buying Immovables]. *Justiţia Nouă* 8.

Stere, Gheorghe. 1952. "Organele puterii de stat în lumina proiectului de constituţie" [State Bodies in Light of the Constitution Draft]. *Justiţia Nouă* 4:464–467.

Stone, Alec. 1992. *The Birth of Judicial Politics in France: The Constitutional Council in Comparative Perspective*. New York: Oxford University Press.

Sypnowich, Christine. 1990. *The Concept of Socialist Law*. Oxford: Clarendon Press.

Takacs, Ludovic. 1960. "Hotărârile de importanţă istorică ale Congresului al III-lea al PMR şi unele probleme ale invăţământului juridic universitar" [The Historic Decisions of the Third Congress of the Workers' Party and Some Problems of Legal Education]. *Justiţia Nouă* 4:594–600.

Teitel, Ruti G. 2000. *Transitional Justice*. New York: Oxford University Press.

Thompson, E. P. 1975. *Whigs and Hunters*. New York: Pantheon Books.

Thompson, Mark R. 1998. "Neither Totalitarian nor Authoritarian: Post-Totalitarianism in Eastern Europe." In *The Totalitarian Paradigm after the End of Communism*, edited by Achim Siegel. Amsterdam: Rodopi.

Tismăneanu, Vladimir. 2003. *Stalinism for All Seasons. A Political History of Romanian Communism*. Berkeley: University of California Press.

Tyler, Tom. 1990. *Why Do People Obey the Law*. New Haven, CT: Yale University Press.

Tyler, Tom and Huo YJ. 2002. *Trust in the Law*. New York: Russell Sage Found.

Underkuffler, Laura. 2003. *The Idea of Property: Its Meaning and Power*. Oxford: Oxford University Press.

Unger, Roberto M. 1976. *Law in Modern Society*. New York: The Free Press.

Văleanu, S. 1955. "Despre unele probleme ridicate de soluţionarea litigiilor izvorâte din dispoziţiile de repartizare a unei suprafeţe de locuit" [Solving Disputes Regarding the Allocation of Housing]. *Legalitatea Populară* 2:118–125.

Vasilescu, Albu. 1948. "Probleme actuale în ştiinţa dreptului" [Current Issues in the Science of Law]. *Justiţia Nouă* 9–10.

Verdery, Katherine. 1994. "The Elasticity of Land: Problems of Property Restitution in Transylvania." *Slavic Review* 53(4):1071–1109.

Verdery, Katherine. 1996. *What Was Socialism and What Comes Next?* Princeton, NJ: Princeton University Press.

Verdery, Katherine. 1998. "Fuzzy Property: Rights, Power, and Identity in Transylvania's Decollectivization." In *Transforming Post-Communist Political Economies*, edited by Joan M. Nelson, Charles Tilley, and Lee Walker. Task Force on Economies in Transition Commission on Behavioral and Social Sciences and Education National Research Council.

Verdery, Katherine. 2003. *The Vanishing Hectare. Property and Value in Postsocialist Transylvania*. Ithaca, NY: Cornell University Press.

Verdery, Katherine and Gail Kligman. 2011. *Peasants under Siege: The Collectivization of Romanian Agriculture, 1949–1962*. Princeton, NJ: Princeton University Press.

Verdery, Katherine and Michael Burawoy, eds. 1999. *Uncertain Transition: Ethnographies of Change in the Postsocialist World.* Lanham, MD: Rowman & Littlefield Publishers.

Viorel, R. 1961. "Termenul în care se poate valorifica un ordin de repartiţie" [The Statute of Limitations for Enforcing a Housing Order]. *Justiţia Nouă* 6.

Voitinovici, Alexandru. 1958. "Apărarea avutului obştesc, principiu de aplicaţie permanentă în construirea socialismului" [Defending Public Property, a Permanent Principle during the Construction of Socialism]. *Legalitatea Populară* 12:3–16.

Voitinovici, Alexandru. 1958. "Tribunalul Suprem al RPR în apărarea legalităţii populare" [The Supreme Tribunal of RPR Defending Popular Legality]. *Justiţia Nouă* 6:965–970.

Voitinovici, Alexandru. 1959. "Dreptul în slujba construcţiei socialiste" [Law in the Service of the Construction of Socialism]. *Legalitatea Populară* 8:3–38.

Volanschi, Alexandru. 1948. "Întreprinderile Industriale Naţionalizate, Bunuri Comune ale Întregului Popor" [The Nationalized Enterprises, Common Goods of the People]. *Justiţia Nouă* 9–10.

Von Benda-Beckmann, Franz and Keebet Von Benda-Beckmann. 1994. "Property, Politics, and Conflict: Ambon and Minangkabau Compared." *Law and Society Review* 28(3):589–608.

Von Benda-Beckmann, Franz and Keebet Von Benda-Beckmann. 1999. "A Functional Analysis of Property Rights, with Special Reference to Indonesia." In *Property Rights and Economic Development. Land and Natural Resources in Southeast Asia and Oceania*, edited by T. van Meijl and F. von Benda-Beckmann. London: Kegan Paul International.

Von Benda-Beckmann, Franz, Keebet Von Benda-Beckmann and Melanie Wiber. 2006. *Changing Properties of Property.* New York: Berghahn Books.

Vurdea, I.C. 1960. "Aspecte teoretice şi practice ale dreptului de superficie" [Theoretical and Practical Issues Regarding the Right of Superficies]. *Justiţia Nouă* 6:1076–1083.

Vyshinsky, A. 1948. "Despre unele chestiuni în legătura cu teoria statului şi dreptului" [Some Issues Regarding the Theory of Law and State]. *Justiţia Nouă* 8:303–314.

Walder, Andrew G. 1994. "The Decline of Communist Power: Elements of a Theory of Institutional Change." *Theory and Society* 23(2):297–323.

Waldron, Jeremy. 2004. "Property." In *The Stanford Encyclopedia of Philosophy (Fall 2004 Edition)*, edited by Edward N. Zalta. http://plato.stanford.edu/archives/fall2004/entries/property.

Weber, Max. 1947. "The Types of Legitimate Domination." In *The Theory of Social and Economic Organization*, translated by A. M. Henderson and Talcott Parsons. New York: The Free Press.

Weinrib, Ernest J. 2003. "Propter Honoris Respectum: Poverty and Property in Kant's System of Rights." *Notre Dame Law Review* 78:795–828.

White, Stephen. 1986. "Economic Performance and Communist Legitimacy." *World Politics* 38(3):462–482.

Woodward, E. L. 1920. *The Congress of Berlin 1878*. London: HM Stationery Office. https://dl.wdl.org/11911/service/11911.pdf.

Wrong, Dennis H. 1988. *Power. Its Forms, Bases, and Uses*. Chicago: University of Chicago Press.

Index

Note: Page numbers in 'italics' refers to figures and tables.

About the Author

Mihaela Şerban is associate professor of law and society at Ramapo College of New Jersey. Her research and writing focus on law and society in Eastern Europe, human rights, constitutional law, and transitional justice. Her most recent publications include "Stemming the Tide of Illiberalism? Legal Mobilization and Adversarial Legalism in Central and Eastern Europe," in *Communist and Post-Communist Studies* (2018), and "Regime Change and Property Rights Consciousness in Post-Communist Romania," *Law & Social Inquiry* (2017). Dr. Şerban is a cofounder of the Collaborative Research Network on Law and Society in Central and Eastern Europe, Balkans, Russia, and Eurasia within the Law and Society Association, and a member of the advisory board for the *Law & Society Review.*

www.ingramcontent.com/pod-product-compliance
Ingram Content Group UK Ltd.
Pitfield, Milton Keynes, MK11 3LW, UK
UKHW041633031026
15587UKWH00001B/252

9 781498 595674